D0164313

THE SUN
DANCE
RELIGION

THE SUN DANCE RELIGION

Power for the Powerless

Joseph G. Jorgensen

The University of Chicago Press
Chicago and London

The University of Chicago Press, Chicago 60637
The University of Chicago Press, Ltd., London
© 1972 by The University of Chicago
All rights reserved. Published 1972
Printed in the United States of America
International Standard Book Number: 0–226–41085–4
Library of Congress Catalog Card Number: 70–182089

Contents

Illustrations

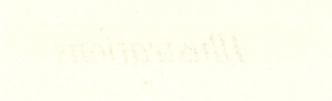

Acknowledgments

Many people must be acknowledged for their contributions to this book, but none, save me, is to be held responsible for the errors of omission and commission within. First, I owe my greatest debt to the Ute and Shoshone people who have served variously as my hosts, friends, and employer since 1958. I wrote this book for them with the intention of helping rather than hurting; telling the truth rather than promulgating falsehoods; and conveying an understanding of how their lives are today and the forces that made them such, rather than passing along more of the errant nonsense embedded in so many "acculturation" studies of American Indians, nonsense that has so bothered American Indian scholars and other American Indian people (see especially Deloria [1969] and Costo and Henry [1970]).

Over the years I have learned vast amounts from my Ute friends in particular. I especially want to thank Harriett, Rita, Jimmy, Wally, Francis, Jason, Henry, Ouray, Floyd, Alvin, Homey, Dale, Darrell, Edmund, Eddie, Rodney, Virgil, Rodell, Francesco, Franklin, Harry, Fernando, Bobby, Maggie, John, Ethel, Wes, Duane, Tony, Roland, John, George, Leo, Lee, Chris, Guy, Harold, and Juanita. I should like to list another fifteen hundred names, but shall not. Suffice it to say that I have been the student and friend of all of the people listed here, as well as of many hundreds more Utes and Shoshones. I hope this book meets with their approval.

Upon completion of the first draft of this manuscript in late 1969, I sent copies to fifteen Shoshone and Ute friends, Sun dance leaders, and tribal leaders. Seven responded with comments that helped me to correct many errors and erroneous impressions. Two kind souls told me to publish it as it was. Wherever possible I have followed the wishes of my friends, and I have tried to maintain the confidentiality and preserve the anonymity of all Shoshones and Utes throughout. In some places, however, simply because the five tribes studied here are small and because leaders are easy to recognize, some people will be recognized.

I wish to thank all of the Bureau of Indian Affairs personnel who have cooperated with this study. This includes people such as ex-Commissioner of Indian Affairs Robert Bennett, several area officials, and many employees located on the five Shoshone and Ute reservations. There are too many people to list all of them here.

I owe a debt to my many friends and relatives who reside close to the Ute and Shoshone reservations. I hope, in turn, they recognize the debt they owe to the Indians in whose midst they reside. My white friends and relatives may not be completely happy with the analysis here.

The Northern Ute Tribe employed me in 1960 and 1962, and my associations at these times have left indelible impressions. I suppose no experience could have been better for sensitizing me to the neocolonial niche in which tribal governments operate, the good intentions of tribal employees, and the horrible odds these governments must cope with in order to survive successfully. The conflicting pulls from the federal government and the white world on the one hand and the Indian community on the other, causes constant and massive strains on those who would lead.

Indiana University supported my field research among Utah and Colorado Utes in 1963 and 1964, as well as my library research on Shoshone-Ute ethnohistory in the Bancroft Collection, University of California, Berkeley. The National Institutes of Health supported my field research among the Shoshones and Utes during 1966 (Public Health Service Research Grant MH 12347–01). The American Philosophical Society supported my field work among Shoshones and Utes in 1967 and 1969 (Penrose Fund Grants 4462 and 5119). I am very grateful to these three institutions.

In various ways several other people have contributed to this book. Mr. Tom Johnson and Dr. Don Fowler provided information about the Wind River Shoshones. Mr. Johnson also read the first draft of this manuscript and made many helpful comments. Dr. Sven Liljeblad provided some information about the Fort Hall Shoshones. Dr. Lynn A. Robbins, Dr. Edwin L. Kozlowski, and Dr. Deward Walker, Jr., read the first draft and influenced me to emphasize some points that were buried in the original. Dr. Harold Driver also read parts of the first draft. Again I thank all of these people for their help and advice.

Dr. Mischa Titiev not only read the first draft but spent several hours in conversation with me about it. We particularly discussed the Sun dance ideology, and he encouraged me to develop my analysis further than I had originally intended. His interest and insights are greatly appreciated.

Dr. Omer C. Stewart, a student of the Utes, has always been extremely helpful to me. Since 1964 he has provided me with intelligent counsel and with information from his vast Tri-Ethnic Research Project resources. Dr. Stewart read the first draft and corrected several errors—factual and interpretive. I am, as ever, humbly indebted to him.

Finally, three people made such enormous contributions to this study that I don't know how to thank them exactly. Indeed, something like the Utes and Shoshones, these people contributed more than I can account for properly. First, my wife Katherine helped me in the field in 1966 and 1969, read every draft of this book, and provided much, much help. Second, Dr. LeRoy Johnson, Jr., not only read every word in the first draft but he challenged me to rethink (and reword) the entire analysis. I have done so. God and LeRoy only know whether the final version meets LeRoy's approval, but I want him (LeRoy) to know that his help certainly meets my approval. Third, Dr. David F. Aberle has caused me to understand my data and my analyses in ways I had not understood them before. He has that rare ability to see the forest and the trees. After reading and making extensive comments on the first draft, he got me to see the forest too. For those readers who are acquainted with Dave Aberle's own work, it will be evident that we may still quibble about the perimeter, but not the parameter.

Abbreviations

BIA	Bureau of Indian Affairs
CAP	Community Action Projects
CCDB	*County and City Data Book*
CHCIIA	Chairman, House Committee on Interior and Insular Affairs
EAP	Employment Assistance Program
GAA	General Allotment Act
HCIIA	House Committee on Interior and Insular Affairs
IIM	Individual Indian Money
IRA	Indian Reorganization Act
OEO	Office of Economic Opportunity
RCIA	Report of the Commissioner of Indian Affairs
SAUS	*Statistical Abstract of the United States*
USPNACRP	United States President's National Advisory Commission on Rural Poverty

1 Introduction

The Sun dance religion of the Shoshones and Utes of the central Rocky Mountains and Great Basin of North America was born of misery and oppression in the early reservation period (circa 1890–1900). It persisted in a context of misery and oppression, and in the late 1960s it flourished as the major religious movement on the Wind River Shoshone reservation in Wyoming, the Fort Hall Shoshone-Bannock reservation in Idaho, the Uintah and Ouray reservation (Northern Ute) in Utah, the Ute Mountain Ute reservation in Colorado, and the Southern Ute reservation in Colorado. The Sun dance on each of these reserves claims more adherents than the peyote religion, and claims many peyote adherents as well.

This book is a comparative political and economic analysis of why possibly, and how possibly, the Sun dance came to be what it was for the Wind River Shoshones in 1890, and why possibly it was diffused to their Ute and Shoshone congeners. And it is a comparative analysis of the contexts in which the Sun dance has persisted for over seventy years.

But this book is also a comparative analysis of the modern Sun dance religion, including the ritual, the religious experience, the role of chiefs, the recruitment of novices and their initiation into the religion, the participation of dancers at their home reservations and away, and the participation of nondancers. Finally, it is a comparative analysis of the Sun dance community, an interreservation phenomenon.

HOW THE STUDY DEVELOPED

The modern Sun dance captured my interest as a youth in the late 1940s. I was raised around Utes, Southern Paiutes, and Shoshones in Utah, was interested in Indian life, and had been regaled with stories by my maternal grandmother and grandfather about the "Black Hawk War" of the 1860s (stories from the lives of their parents in Sanpete County, Utah), and, from their own experiences in the 1890s, about how Utes came to my grandparents' homes and requested food. My paternal grandmother contributed stories about teaching school during the early 1930s in the Uintah and Ouray Ute agency town, Fort Duchesne. I also heard stories from some of my kin who occupied erstwhile reservation lands in the Uintah Basin; acreage that was taken from the Northern Utes following a federal severalty allotment scheme around 1915.

So my relatives, schoolteachers, and neighbors in towns both small (Nephi, Utah) and large (Salt Lake City, Utah) used to talk about the "Indian problem" from time

MAP 1. Location and approximate size of Ute and Shoshone reservations, 1966.

to time. Sometimes they commented about Indians with pity, wondering what could possibly be done with "them." For instance, local whites frequently asserted that Indians had been *given* tax-free reservations, food, and other annuities by the federal government, but that Indians would not work, pull themselves up, as it were. Whites frequently generalized that they could not get Indians to work in the hay or the grain for more than a day or two; that Indians were not dependable; that they could not understand how to operate a tractor, and so on. But on the whole, Indians were not thought about much at all by whites unless the whites lived in towns adjacent to reservation communities. When Indians were referred to by whites in the larger towns, such as Salt Lake City, they were characterized in stereotyped, prejudiced clichés, to wit: "As Brigham Young [an early Latter-day Saint leader] said, 'It's better to feed them than to fight them' "; or, "They're so poor and dirty, and you can't get them to work"; or, "The only good Indian is a dead Indian"; or "Those pagan bucks and squaws;" or another Latter-day Saint favorite, "There is a tribe of industrious Lamanites [American Indians] who converted and received the priesthood and they are getting lighter [in skin color] all the time"; etc. It is critical to point out that local whites were rebuking Indians for not being like whites. The Latter-day

Saints went so far as to allege that some Indians who joined the Church of Jesus Christ of Latter-day Saints (Mormons) and practiced the Protestant ethic were actually becoming white. First and foremost, however, local whites expected the Indians in Utah to observe the Protestant ethic, to compete, to be industrious, and to sever their special ties with the federal government.

My concern with Indians and Indian life waxed and waned during my youth. I attended some Ute Bear dances and an afternoon session of the Sun dance in the 1940s, and until my freshman year in college I maintained an interest in Indian ceremonialism and Indian life. During my freshman year I also became interested in Indian-white relations in Utah. This new interest was prompted by a mild furor that was created when the federal law that prohibited Indians from buying alcohol was rescinded. The local whites did not like the new law; most people I heard speak (or write) on the subject saw the law as a great setback to Indian morality and industry. It was argued that now that alcohol was freely available, no Indian would become like the local whites.

There was another force in opposition to the new federal law—the bootleggers. For years bootleggers in Salt Lake, Ogden, and Provo, Utah, had been selling Indians the keys to lockers in bus terminals where the bootleggers stored bottles of alcohol (or they would designate other hiding places). The opposition to the new law, therefore, was promoted by two factions: one saw it as a threat to Indian morality; and the other—the bootleggers—saw it as a threat to their own financial well-being. The contradictions in the arguments of the opposing forces both amused (for obvious reasons) and bothered me. I was bothered because it was unconsitutional to deny alcohol to Indians, and I was appalled to learn that some people desired to continue to deny Indians their constitutional rights. I was also appalled that some bootleggers desired to continue to exploit Indians.

Three years later another problem arose that bothered me. In 1956 the State of Utah denied the political franchise to Indians because they did not pay property taxes on reservation land. When the Northern Utes challenged this law and took it to the Supreme Court of Utah, the first ruling went *against* the Utes. The law and the litigation made the local newspapers, but did not cause a statewide furor. This unconstitutional practice was reversed later, but again the conflict was between white practices and ethics—especially Protestant ethic individualism—and Indian practices and so-called privileges. Whites insisted that Indians, too, must observe white-promoted ethics by severing special ties with the federal government and by coping with life in the same fashion as whites.

I suppose that the alcohol and voting issues got me to begin rethinking my past and thinking my way through the clichés I had heard all my life. There is, I think, a relationship among the prejudicial clichés I heard in my youth (and that are still extant in the Mountain West), the Protestant ethic promulgated by whites, laws that discriminate against Indians at the liquor store and at the polling booth, and the Sun dance. My analysis will explicate this relationship.

Between 1958 and 1964, first as an interested local white, second as an employee of the Northern Ute Tribe, and third as a graduate student in anthropology and linguistics, I attended scores of Sun dances (on all three Ute reservations), Bear dances, basketball tournaments, and the like. These events were important to me because I could congregate with my friends and enjoy their pleasures with them. On the other hand, I was not a student of these events. My scholarly interests focused on Ute history, economy, family-household organization, political organization, and language. It was not until after I had completed my doctoral dissertation (summer 1964) on the subjects mentioned above that I began to piece together what the Sun dance was, how it fitted into Ute history, and why it persisted. My attendance at Sun dances and my political-economic research on five Ute and Shoshone reservations took place in 1966, 1967, and 1969.

For instance, in the fall of 1964 I began reflecting on several pieces of research literature I had read while preparing my dissertation. In particular I reflected on Demitri Shimkin's (1953) splendid analysis of the Wind River Shoshone Sun dance. Among other things, he had treated the reworking of the dance as a response to human misery. I also thought about Marvin Opler's (1941) analysis of the Southern Ute Sun dance, in which he suggested that deprivation and dysphoria were correlated with the acceptance of the dance, and that the dance itself was only an analogue to the Sun dance of the Plains. Furthermore, John A. Jones (1955) in part explained the Northern Ute Sun dance as a defiant gesture toward white society. Although Shimkin was writing about the Wind River dance from the 1880s to 1938, Opler about the Southern Ute dance of 1938 and earlier, and Jones about the Northern Ute dance of the 1890s and 1948, I thought that there should be some overall explanation for the persistence of these dances into the late 1960s that was at least partially consonant with the explanations these men had adduced for the earlier Sun dances they had studied. The interreservation Shoshone and Ute participation made such a connection seem all the more plausible to me.

In turning to a more recent comment on the modern Sun dance I read Witherspoon's (1961: 81–82) dissertation on the Northern Ute. Witherspoon asserts that the Sun dance is broken down, although once it was a central ceremonial in Ute life. He contends that the modern version is just a "performance put on for an audience." It is no longer an activity to which everyone in the tribe contributes, and youths enter Sun dances on their peers' dares, rather than to be cured or to gain power. Although I thought when I first read Witherspoon, and know now, that initiates do not enter on dares (Witherspoon apparently had no empirical information about dancer initiation), his assertion was half right, even if unwittingly so. Among other things, youths, and adults too, dance for their peers, and I think this is a critical factor in the persistence of the dance. At any rate, Witherspoon's allegations made me want to see if they were warranted.

As I understood Ute life, there was considerable misery, considerable resistance to whites, and much more to the Sun dance than a broken-down piece of show business. I thought of the anxieties expressed by prospective initiates for months before the events; the mental and physical strain of the Sun dance; the huge crowds that attended; the castigation of whites by shamans during the course of the dance; the moralistic speeches encouraging and even beseeching Indians to follow Indian teachings that always attended the dances; the political speeches that often followed the dances; and the changes that occurred in initiates after their first dance.

After finishing the Shoshone and Ute literature on the Sun dance, I plunged into the literature dealing with social movements in preparation for the fieldwork. I read all the standard sources: Linton (1943), Wallace (1956), Worsley (1957), Lanternari (1963), Mooney (1892-3), and others. As I tried to make sense out of the common threads in so many of these analyses, I was concerned by the many exceptional cases that I could think of. All of the movements that were classified in these papers, except the "cargo cults," seemed to be born of misery and the systematic denial of access to resources; yet I could think of many North American Indian groups, long suffering in misery and long denied access to resources, that had failed to develop these movements.

In 1964–65, while I was teaching at Antioch College, Miss Sally N. Bates (a student) developed an idea of mine about who would accept and who would reject "nativistic" movements, but there was no empirical test. At the University of Oregon in 1965, Mr. Adrian Heidenreich (a student) helped me test the idea; we used the 1889–90 Ghost dance for the test. Briefly, we posited that, other things being equal, only those groups that had been structurally complex (as measured by numbers and types of kinship and extrakinship organizations, annual and sporadic rituals, levels of jurisdictional hierarchy, and so forth) would accept and perform the dance "fervently." Fervor was measured by relative number of participants, length and number of dances, etc. Heidenreich (1967) showed, for a sample of eight societies having contact with the dance, that only the least complex ones, measured by rank-order and scalogram analyses, rejected the dance or performed it only briefly. All eight societies were politically and economically deprived by his measures.

Thus, I had something else to work with. I came to think that the reason many might not have rallied around a nativistic movement was that there was no previous organization to draw the people together, no previous annual ceremonials to remember, and no joint economic and political past to want to build on. The ipso facto relation between deprivation and nativism could be summarized in either of two ways: (1) wait long enough, and a deprived group will go nativistic, or (2) charismatic leaders as well as deprivation are required to generate a movement: no leader, no movement; but all movements had to have leaders as part of the definition.

After returning from the field in 1966, I read David F. Aberle's (1966) brilliant book on Navajo peyotism. Part 5 of that book explicates a typology of social movements and a hypothesis of relative deprivation. Following Aberle, I have come to understand the Shoshone and Ute Sun dances, past and present, as a social movement, that is, "an organized effort by a group of human beings to effect change in the face of resistance by other human beings" (Aberle 1966: 315). So it is neither wholly individual nor unorganized. Resistance by human beings makes sense because human beings are, after all, the efficient actors who have subjected Utes and Shoshones and have resisted their attempts to effect changes. Ute and Shoshone subordination can be explained not only in terms of their relations to local whites, however, but in terms of the metropolis-satellite political economy in which the dominant whites and the dominated Indians operate.

I will take care to distinguish the resistance of local whites toward Indians, from national policies and multinational businesses which affect both Indians *and* the resistance of local whites toward Indians. Local white resistance, at any rate, is prejudice and bigotry on the social side; expropriation of resources on the material side; the refusal to extend credit and to make small loans, and the exploitation of Indian resources, labor, and so forth on the economic side; and domination and a refusal to share local power and state representation on the political side. Nevertheless, the major resistance is not from the local whites. Rather, it is from the political economy of the metropolis, with its Congress, its welfare bureaus, and its influential and powerful industries and lobbies.

SOME DEFINITIONS AND BRIEF DISCUSSIONS

REDEMPTIVE AND TRANSFORMATIVE SOCIAL MOVEMENTS

Aberle's (1966) definitions of redemptive and transformative movements are followed rather closely (though not completely) here because they fit quite well the social movements in Shoshone and Ute history. The Ghost dance was a transformative movement and preceded the modern Sun dance among all of the Shoshone and Ute tribes in this study. The Sun dance and the peyote religions are redemptive movements and have followed the Ghost dance among these same tribes.

The Ghost Dance, A Transformative Movement

Aberle (1966: 318–20) defines all transformative movements as having some constant characteristics and some variable features. As constant characteristics, all transformative movements consist of organized groups of people who actively seek a transformation of the social, even natural, order in their own lifetimes. Furthermore, these movements involve a radical rejection of things as they are, and some perception of the enormous force necessary to transform them.

Let us take a brief look at the constant features of the Ghost dance religion which spread among Shoshones and Utes in 1870.

1. *Time perspective.* The Fort Hall Shoshone and Bannock missionaries who carried the Ghost dance message to other Shoshones and Utes preached that the Ghost dance religion would bring about imminent and cataclysmic change. Faithful adherence to the religion would rid the world of whites, restore Indian land and the resources thereon, and resurrect the dead Indians so that Indian life could be restored and practiced unhindered by whites.

2. *Theory of history.* The Ghost dance was teleological. Adherents believed that the transformation was destined by the supernatural forces and revealed to a Northern Paiute visionary, Wodziwob. The teleological element provided strong ideological support for the Ghost dance effort.

3. *Leadership.* Little is known about Wodziwob, and it does not appear that he directed any Shoshone or Ute performances of the Ghost dance. But it was believed by Shoshones and Utes alike that Wodziwob had received a vision instructing him to perform the Ghost dance, and that proper performance of the dance would bring the promised results. Thus many Fort Hall Shoshones and Bannocks accepted Wodziwob as a visionary and a prophet. In turn, these people served as missionaries to transmit the religion to their congeners.

4. *Social disengagement.* The Ghost dance religion promised that Indians would not only be separated from whites, but that deceased Indians would be resurrected. For several reasons Shoshones and Utes even spatially segregated themselves from

whites in order to perform the ritual, usually selecting traditional territories that were not contaminated by whites.

The variable features of the Ghost dance (features not necessarily shared by all transformative movements) were that (1) the transformation would come from ritual alone (no secular means were involved); (2) the best of the Indian world would be restored (the Ghost dance did not preach for innovation or imitation of anything); (3) the beneficiaries were to be American Indians, living and dead (and no one else); and (4) the existing system, dominated by whites, would disappear (rather than living side-by-side with it, or some such).

The Sun Dance: A Redemptive Movement

The defining characteristic for Aberle's (1966: 320–22) redemptive movements is "the search for a new individual state." Whereas transformative movements seek total change to the total social or natural order, redemptive movements seek total change to the individual. It is the person, not the social order, therefore, that is transformed. Furthermore, Aberle says that all redemptive movements reject at least some features of the current society (as do all transformative movements), finding evil in the world, not merely in the individual. To this end, redemptive movements castigate society as they focus on transforming the individual. Finally, all redemptive movements have two further constant characteristics: the individual's resistance to change must be overcome, and the redeemed must change his (her) relationships with others.

In great detail we shall see how the Sun dance aims at total change in the individual by supernatural means and human effort, provides a loose code of conduct (obligations and responsibilities) for each adherent, rejects and castigates the evils of white society, and helps to resolve the conflict between Protestant ethic individualism preached by whites, and the collective ethic preached by Indians. We shall see how, through the Sun dance in particular, Indian integrity and identity can be maintained against vast odds. We shall see how and why the youth resists the dream instructions that direct him (her) to participate in the Sun dance religion, and the arduous path that must be followed once the initial resistance is overcome. Finally we shall see how the total change to individuals has a secular side and a sacred side, and how both sides merge to change the successful adherent's relationship toward others.

The variable features of the Sun dance religion (features not shared by all redemptive movements) require that candidates for redemption live in this world and struggle for the good of all, rather than withdrawing from it. Proper life in this world requires keeping a "good heart," sacrificing for others, and behaving selflessly toward family, the wider network of kin and friends, and, ultimately, the entire Sun dance community. Finally, we shall see that Sun dance chiefs vary in style, in supernatural power, and in the respect they command, but that all are visionaries and all suppress narrow individualism in favor of broad collective ends.

Origin and Persistence of Social Movements

Whereas Aberle (1966: 322–33) accounts for the origin and persistence of social movements through types of relative deprivation and reference field, I do not. Aberle (1966: 323) defines relative deprivation "as a negative discrepancy between legitimate expectation and actuality, or between legitimate expectation and anticipated actuality, or both." In my research I did not sample and administer questionnaires or scheduled interviews among the Ute and Shoshone population in order to test the discrepancy between what people have and what people say they want and can legitimately expect to receive. So I have no explicit way to measure relative deprivation.

On the other hand, I have collected the testimonies of hundreds of Shoshone and Ute Sun dance adherents over the years: that is, dancers, singers, committeemen, spectators, chiefs, and so forth. For instance, when whites have discounted Indian beliefs, I have heard Indians say to one another (and sometimes to whites), "That's just a white man's idea! They don't know everything." When Indians and whites have been drinking in white towns and when the local police incarcerate the Indians but not the whites, Indians have said to me, "Indians get thrown in jail and whites don't." The examples can be multiplied, but these are sufficient to suggest that Shoshones and Utes are relatively deprived: they see a discrepancy between life as it is (opinions of whites toward Indian beliefs; actions of white police toward Indians who drink), and life as it should be.

I pin my own explanation as to why possibly the Ghost dance and Sun dance religions came to be performed by Shoshones and Utes, and why possibly the Sun dance has persisted, to (1) the *deprivation* (not relative) these people have suffered since the beginning of reservation times; (2) to the political-economic machinery that has been a major cause of this deprivation; (3) to the sheer beauty of the Sun dance religion itself; and (4) to the religious experiences the Sun dance provides for the adherents. (The last two are causal-effects.)

In short, deprivation alone is not a sufficient explanation of the origin of the movement. Another important aspect of the Ute and Shoshone context is that these people had large summer band organizations and spring or summer rituals that drew together groups even larger than bands prior to the advent of the Ghost dance or the Sun dance; so traditions of relatively large and complex organizations obtained for all Utes and Shoshones studied here. Further, we must appeal to the thoughts and actions of agents (people) in the late nineteenth-century reservation context in order to account for how possibly the religion came to be. We must also appeal to agentive factors and context in order to account for how the religion has persisted.

At a time when fighting, fleeing, and the Ghost dance failed to have their promised effects, and when reservation Indians were greatly deprived, some specific shamans on the Wind River Shoshone reservation set about to make themselves and their community well by religious means. These shamans were not only disposed to acquire power and use the power to help themselves, but, following Shoshone traditions, they were also disposed to use the power for others. Furthermore they had a pre-reservation Sun dance tradition, and a reservation Ghost dance tradition to build on. The reasons, intentions, and dispositions of these shamans can be separated from the context in which they revised and spread the Sun dance religion to their reservation kin and friends and to their congeners on other reservations. Ultimately the explanation of the origin of the modern Sun dance must be understood as the thought and actions of several Wind River Shoshone shamans. This complex and beautiful ritual was created and has persisted among poverty and oppression, but poverty and oppression are not the final and independent causes of the modern Sun dance.

My analysis of deprivation is historical and contemporary, taking up a good portion of the book. It includes analyses of how and why Shoshones and Utes lost their strategic resources and their autonomy, and how they came to be as they are today. I also analyze the conflict between the code of conduct demanded by whites and the code of conduct promulgated by Indians, and show why the former cannot provide for Indians the goals that the whites claim adherence to their code will produce. Furthermore, strict adherence to the code of conduct promulgated by Indians is not easy. It is argued here that the Sun dance religion is the major vehicle on Shoshone and Ute reserves through which successful compliance to the Indian code is made possible and desirable.

METROPOLIS-SATELLITE POLITICAL ECONOMY

In another place (Jorgensen 1971*a*) I have defined "metropolis-satellite" political economy and explained American Indian "underdevelopment" in terms of it. The world metropolis-satellite hypothesis was originally worked out by Baran (1957) and handsomely elaborated by Frank (1967).

In brief, the metropolis and the satellite are two sides of the same coin, and they are both nexus and locus. The metropolis is nexus in that it is the center of concentration of economic and political power and influence. The satellite, too, is nexus, but it is the periphery to the center. The satellite provides resources and labor for the metropolis, and consumes the goods that are owned and produced by the metropolis, but does not share proportionately in the surpluses from its own area, nor does it concentrate political and economic power. The metropolis is also locus, as is the satellite. By and large the metropolises are cities or urban areas, whereas the satellites are rural towns and rural areas.

In my analysis I have chosen "metropolis-satellite" rather than "urban-rural" to characterize the political economy that has oppressed Shoshones and Utes so that I can emphasize the concentration-nonconcentration of economic and political power. Urban, for instance, implies a city, a locational unit filled with people: metropolis does not. It should be clear, however, that urban and metropolis are neither completely independent nor completely dependent, because the directors of the metropolis, their corporations, their research houses, and their liquid capital are located in the great urban areas. On the other hand, we know that as the economic and political power and influence of the metropolis has grown, especially in the past decade, the great urban centers have withered. That is not to say in the number of inhabitants: urban centers have generally grown in their number of inhabitants, yet they have decreased in their economic affluence, political influence, social services, and the quality of life. Ghettos have grown through natural increase and through the migration of the rural poor. Furthermore, unemployment has increased, and rebellion and repression is more and more characteristic of the largest cities in the United States (see Jorgensen 1971*a*)

The withering of the urban cores as well as the shriveling of rural areas can be accounted for through the nature of the metropolis-satellite political economy. As the resources of the satellite are expropriated by the metropolis and appropriated for the growth of the center, as labor exploitation increases and technological advances are made, fewer and fewer man-hours are required to produce more and more goods on greater amounts of land or from greater areas within mines. For the people who do not control resources or who, because their resources are meager, can no longer cope, yet who must consume the products of the metropolis, selective migration takes place from the withering rural areas to the shriveling urban cores, thus adding to the problems of the urban areas. Furthermore, the upwardly mobile are also drained off the rural areas and move to urban areas. As a partial-effect of urban decay, these people join other middle-income families in moving to the suburbs of these cities.

The metropolis-satellite economy is a single, integrated structure, therefore, in which the former grows at the expense of the latter.

NEOCOLONIALISM

In the paper mentioned above (Jorgensen 1971a), I point out how reservation Indians are different from all other American citizens in that they are subject to formal political domination that exceeds that of any other group. Reservation Indians are not only the subjects of local, state, and federal government, but they are also the subjects of tribal governments (chartered by Congress under the Indian Reorganization Act), the Bureau of Indian Affairs (a federal bureau commissioned to administer Indian land and resources, among other things), the House Committee on Interior and Insular Affairs (which appropriates budgets for the Bureau of Indian Affairs *and* approves the expenditures of tribal funds), and the Secretary of the Interior (the ultimate decisions on Indian affairs, internal and external, can be made by the Secretary).

"Neocolonial" is used here, rather than "colonial," "internal colonial," "domestic dependent colonial," or some other variant of the term, to typologize the peculiar form of internal domestic colonialism in the United States that distinguishes Indians and Eskimos, their resources, and their political niche, from all other United States citizens and dominated peoples in U.S. trust territories. Neocolonialism is a special form of domination within a capitalist democracy that is both political and economic. It began with reservation subjugation and has flourished for more than a hundred years.

Political-economic subjugation of reservation Indians has had the following consequences as capitalist democracy has developed in the United States: (1) Social ruin to the Indian, as measured in status and self-esteem, due to the rapid development of the metropolis (including the urban areas) from the mid-nineteenth century; (2) poverty as measured in access to strategic resources, the distribution of surpluses from one's own region, employment, housing, and general welfare; and (3) political oppression as measured by depletion of Indian populations through warfare, the dissolution of aboriginal polities, the loss of self-direction, the lack of access to the locus of political power, the general denial of U.S. citizenship until 1924 (with a few exceptions), and the roles of the Bureau of Indian Affairs, the House Committee on Interior and Insular Affairs, and the Secretary of the Interior in approving the conduct of Indian affairs.

This is not to say that all Indians are slaves nor that all Indians are doomed to a life of poverty in a neocolonial context. Just as some native Africans once living in colonial Tanganyika, say, could be educated at Oxford and, through one source of help or another, open bookshops in London or boutiques in Dar es Salaam, or even enter the British colonial service, so some United States Indians can move from reservations, gain university educations, and become popular authors or high ranking officials in the Indian service or any of a number of other things. The odds and the contexts in which both colonial Africans and neocolonial Indians live, however, weigh heavily against such "successes" (even if these outcomes, or "successes" from the Protestant ethic view, are desired). It is important to emphasize that *individual* successes are possible, though unusual. Tribal or group successes, on the other hand, are highly improbable.

Another way to say this is that success comes to *some* of those Indians who sever their ties with their wide networks of kin and Indian friends and leave their tribal life behind. Success, as it is defined here, is a narrow, individualistic phenomenon in which each person is besought to make his own peace through knowledge of God on the one hand, yet to enjoy achievements in society by attaining the highest niche in each personal endeavor on the other hand. Competition is, then, inherent in the life style. Each person seeks individual knowledge of God, and seeks to practice a morality and observe an ethic consonant with individual questing for self and nuclear family. Under this loose and ubiquitous code which has served capitalism so well (see Max Weber's classic *The Protestant Ethic and the Spirit of Capitalism*), the ethical person is he who earns his way, and who does so with the maximum use of his potential. The moral-ethical basis of this competitive philosophy is often used to justify unethical competitive acts and to condemn and criticize those people who do not observe the code—even as those who observe it are in competition with those who do not.

Unlike individuals, tribes are not and cannot be self-directing, do not and cannot control their own resources, and do not provide sustenance for all their members. The mechanics of the metropolis-satellite political economy explain in part why the neo-colonial reservations have suffered. Yet it is the contention here that the metropolis-satellite nature of United States capitalism only partly explains the creation and maintenance of those attributes I call neocolonialism, because it is also quite apparent that *racism*, overt or implied, also contributes to the maintenance of neocolonialism. Indeed, throughout this book it is demonstrated how racist behavior on the part of the dominant toward the dominated may be both partial cause and effect of neocolonialism. Racism, like neocolonialism, is a typologizing term, and is used throughout to classify acts of non-Indians toward Indians that are discriminatory, prejudiced, or bigoted mainly because Shoshones and Utes have different colored skins and other physical features from non-Indians. Racist assertions about Indian stupidity, lust, violence, deception, laziness, and immorality are omnipresent in white-Shoshonean history, and these assertions have allowed whites to justify personal, political, and economic subjugation of Indians.

Let us return once more to a listing of the primary attributes of neocolonialism to describe how this typological term is used here. The overwhelming majority of Shoshones and Utes live on or near reservations in a special wardship status not suffered by non-Indians. Their tribal governments have only modest amounts of control over tribal resources and tribal affairs. The House Committee on Interior and Insular

Affairs controls the disposition of tribal funds. Ultimate authority is invested in the Secretary of the Interior, and lesser authority over scores of aspects of the personal lives of the Indians—such as disposition of funds in their Individual Indian Monies accounts—is invested in Bureau of Indian Affairs employees. These special relationships to federal authority (and the special relationships of federal authority to the powerful corporations) provide the cutting edge for neocolonialism. The metropolis-satellite political economy and racist behavior coalesce to maintain neocolonialism.

A GUIDE TO THE BOOK

The following analysis of Shoshone and Ute polity, economy, society and religion is divided into four parts. The first two parts are given to an extensive, explicit, comparative analysis of Shoshone and Ute contexts. A vast amount of hard data is marshalled to lend empirical import to my generalizations.

Part I covers the period from 1800 to about 1910, beginning with a brief chapter on the history of the Sun dance among Shoshones and Utes. We then move to a comparative analysis of the political and economic causes of the depletion, forced location and relocations on, and the restrictions of the movements of Shoshones and Utes to, reservations. We will see how they fought, ran, signed treaties, latched onto transformative religious movements, fought and ran again throughout the period 1850–90. We will see how, when empirical responses such as fight, flight, and the signing of treaties failed to bring the desired effects, and supernatural responses such as the Ghost dance religion failed to have their intended effects, and when reservation subjugation was complete, Shoshones reworked and their congeners accepted a new religion, the Sun dance, to help them cope with life.

Part 2 covers the modern reservation period (1910 to the present) and includes a comparative analysis of reservation life in the greater white-reservation context. We suggest how the Sun dance provides a means for people to achieve spiritual well-being, responsibility, status, and self-esteem when these things are generally unachievable in the greater social context, or denied them by the dominant group.

Part 3 is a general description and a dialectical analysis of the modern Sun dance ritual and ideology. The generalized account of the ritual is based on a statistical analysis of hundreds of variables.

Part 4 brings together the political economic context, on the one hand, and the Sun dance, on the other. Although a considerable amount of empirical detail is presented and analyzed, there are several points where hard empirical data are unavailable and covariation cannot be demonstrated empirically. Nevertheless, interpretation seems very important to me, so I proceed to interpret under these circumstances. In this section we see what the interreservation Sun dance community is, and how it is maintained. We learn who participates, how they participate, and why they participate.

The explanations adduced here will not account for why the Sun dance was created rather than some other redemptive movement, but that does not seem to me to be a very serious problem. Moreover, my analysis employs two major types of agentive explanations (*reasons* and *intentions*), as well as the empirical generalizations about history and context. Agentive explanations often cause social "scientists" to fret, but that is usually due to their belief that social studies are sciences and that somehow agentive explanations are not scientific. I do not wish to launch a discussion of what is science and what is social science, but in the analysis I show how agentive explanations are appropriate and necessary (see Jorgensen 1971*b* for an analysis of social science).

I

HISTORY OF THE UTES AND THE SHOSHONES TO ABOUT 1910:
RESISTANCE, CONQUEST, AND DESPAIR

2 *The Sun Dance in Historical Perspective*

Except in the case of the Wind River Shoshones, the Sun dance is a post-reservation phenomenon. In an intelligent and resourceful analysis of the Wind River dance, Shimkin (1953: 436) shows that the ritual was greatly altered in purpose and practice during the early years of reservation life. The focus of the Sun dance was changed from insuring successful bison hunts and warfare to an increased concern over illness and community misery. The early Ute and Fort Hall dances (circa 1890 for Northern Ute, 1900 for Ute Mountain Ute, 1901 for Fort Hall Shoshone-Bannocks, 1904 for Southern Ute, and 1907 for Lemhi Shoshone-Bannocks at Fort Hall) stressed the same themes and had the same ritual organization as the revised Wind River dance of 1890. It appears highly probable that selective change in the Wind River ritual was a response to absolute and relative deprivation during the early reservation period, as was diffusion of the Wind River ritual to Utes and Fort Hall Shoshones during the oppressive early years of reservation existence.

Evidence suggests that the Sun dance was invented by Plains Algonquians, perhaps the Cheyenne, as early as 1700 (Spier 1921: 498; Driver and Kroeber 1932: 235; Shimkin 1953: 406–7). After 1750 this ceremony diffused rapidly throughout the Plains by channels created by the nomadic plainsmen. For instance, at times alliances were made between tribes, and they banded together to hunt and to raid. Intertribal marriages and joint participation at ceremonials were common products of these alliances. Sometimes members of otherwise hostile tribes fraternized while trading with members of the so-called village tribes of the Missouri River, such as the Mandan and Hidatsa. At still other times, especially following raids when captives were taken, the captives transmitted information about the practices of their own tribes. When captives escaped and returned to their own tribes, they took back with them information about the practices of their captors.

From the late eighteenth to the mid-nineteenth century the Sun dance ceremony was the grandest of all the aboriginal religious ceremonies performed by Plains tribes. These tribes varied greatly in how they performed, when they performed, and the reasons they gave for performing the ceremony (Spier 1921: 453–529; Shimkin 1953: 403–17). All, however, were complex group ceremonies complete with singers, dancers, musicians and spectators. It was common for a complex mythology to be associated with the ceremony. The dance was usually vowed by some individual who planned to avenge a death, lead a successful hunt, or insure a bountiful supply of buffaloes. Because dances were usually performed only after vows were made, the ceremonies were not necessarily annual affairs. In brief, men danced for three or four days and nights to the accompaniment of drumming and singing. The dancers often underwent various tortures such as ritual fasting, thirsting, and mutilations, in a quest for power, good health, success in wars and on hunts, and the general welfare of the group.

By the end of the nineteenth century this spectacular ceremony had all but vanished from the Great Plains (Shimkin 1953: 403). The Plains Indians were living upon reservations, and this intense ceremony, indeed all native religious ceremonies, had been suppressed by Indian agents, the U.S. military, and other federal employees. Why, then, did the Utes and Fort Hall Shoshones wait until 1890 or even later to sponsor the dance? And why did they begin to perform the dance at a time when it was dying out elsewhere? These questions will be discussed at length in the following chapter, but I want to make it clear here that the Shoshones of Idaho and Utah, as well as the Utes of Colorado, New Mexico, and Utah, had extensive contacts with people who sponsored the dance in pre-reservation times, such as the Wind River Shoshones, the Arapahos, the Comanches, the Kiowas, the Dakota, the Sioux and the Cheyennes, and thus they could have adopted the dance much earlier than they did. In fact, the Wind River Shoshones, who lived just north of the Utes in Wyoming and from whom the Utes borrowed the dance, had themselves learned it as early as 1800 from a Comanche, Yellow Hand, who learned it from the Kiowa. Yellow Hand joined the easternmost Shoshones and became the Sun dance leader. The leadership of the dance was retained primarily among his descendants for over a hundred years (Shimkin 1953: 409–17). It is reasonably well confirmed that the Shoshones were performing the ceremony in a rather stable form by 1820 or 1830 (Shimkin 1953: 417). From the 1820s on, the historical record is full of accounts of contacts between various Ute, Shoshone, and Bannock bands, including trade relations and inter-marriages. It is puzzling, in fact, that the Utes and other Shoshone-Bannocks did not acquire the dance from the Wind River people earlier.

In the 1820s William Ashley wrote that Utes on the Green River said they were once part of the Shoshone nation (Dale 1918: 151). In the early 1830s Warren Ferris reported that the Utes and Shoshones were at war, stealing one another's horses, women, and children (Ferris 1940: 210, 216). Rufus Sage states that both Utes and Shoshones were trading at Roubidoux's Fort Uintah (near what is now Whiterocks, Utah) in 1842. In the same year Sage camped with a village of Shoshones in Ashley Valley (near what is now Vernal, Utah), approximately thirty miles east of Fort Uintah (Sage 1846: 182, 1956: 133). And Morgan (1953: 201–2) says that Arapahos and Cheyennes attacked Fort Bridger, Wyoming, in 1843 while Utes and Shoshones were trading there.

The Wind River Shoshones began sponsoring the Sun dance during the height of its popularity on the Plains. But in the 1880s, following the last big Wind River Shoshone bison hunt and even their last warfare with other Plains tribes, at a time when the Wind Rivers had lost access to the strategic resources on which they once subsisted, when their movements were restricted, and when their death rate greatly outstripped their birth rate, a few Wind River shamans began to retool the Sun dance ritual. Shimkin (1953: 436–37) demonstrates that many war and bison-hunt features were dropped from the dance. For instance, the ceremonial bison hunt was no longer performed, nor was war divining or placing war elements in the corral. Another change in ritual acts and objects was that the Sun dancers no longer danced in place but began charging the center pole. Also, Episcopal and Catholic missions were established on the reservation and, though few Shoshones were ever more than nominal Christians, Christian-like concepts were accreted to the dance. For instance, the number of corral posts was increased from ten to twelve. Although other symbolism was attributed them, the posts came to symbolize Christ's apostles. Finally, there was a notable shift of concern toward the curing of illness and the maintenance of communal unity as the dance was reshaped. This change in focus is obviously the key to the entire restructuring of the dance: a few Shoshone shamans sought a solution to the illness, death, and petty factionalism that became pervasive in the 1870s and 1880s.

According to Shimkin (1953: 437–51), the post-1880s version of the Sun dance was sponsored by a Sun dance chief who had received a vision instructing him to direct the new dance. He appointed subchiefs and a committee to help him. The dancers and all other participants worked hard at the dance in order to nourish the public good. The dancers, for instance, suffered to achieve power and to cure the sick. Before the dancing began, the chief selected a center pole to be cut and had a hole dug for it. Often a sham battle, with Shoshones and visitors dressed in warrior clothing, preceded the erection of the center pole. Shortly after the sham battle was completed the corral was constructed. Its boundaries consisted of twelve side poles encompassing a center pole hole. The center pole was carried to the center of the corral and erected on the fourth ritualized attempt to raise it. Twelve roof rafters were then put in place, and branches were placed around the outside of the corral.

Singers and drummers sat in the southeast section, spectators in the northeast section, and dancers occupied the rest of the corral. While in the corral the men danced to and from the center pole for three days and nights without water. The singers and drummers accompanied the dancing. Some dancers, especially powerful shamans, pursued visions. If men fell in the process of the dance, they were administered to by the Sun dance chiefs. Falling often signified that a man was receiving his vision.

When the dancing terminated, the dancers received blessings from respected shamans. In turn they paid the shamans with shawls, blankets, and horses (later money) for their services. The hosts (Wind River residents) contributed gifts to the visitors, and a feast of beef and bread followed. Ghost dances were often performed as well.

The other Ute and Shoshone groups adopted this ritual while living under similar conditions to those of the Wind River people. As among the Wind River, it became the major redemptive movement on these reservations and was sponsored to promote inter- and intrareservation well-being.

The Uintah Utes had long maintained close contacts with the Wind River Shoshone. They were also the first Ute group to be forced onto reservations. Moreover, they were the first Ute group to begin sponsoring Sun dances, probably in 1889 or 1890. The Northern Utes are very clear on who the first Ute Sun dance chief was—General Grant, a Uintah—and where he learned the Sun dance—at Wind River. They are no longer clear about the date of the first performance at Whiterocks. It is doubtful that the Utes acquired the dance much before 1890 because the early and subsequent forms of the Northern Ute ritual have been quite similar to the post-1885 Wind River dance.

The Sun dance was accepted at a time when the Wind River Shoshone and Northern Ute had lost faith in the transformative promise of the Ghost dance. The latter became much attenuated among these people and was performed only as a night-long adjunct to the Sun dance and other rituals after about 1890. In earlier times, when there was still the semblance of a viable and self-sufficient native economy and polity, the Sun dance served the ends of successful warfare and buffalo hunts for the Wind River Shoshone. The major social and religious ceremonies of the Utes under similar circumstances did not include the Sun dance. Sidney Jocknick, who lived with the Utes in western Colorado from 1870 to 1883, mentions that they performed the Bear dance (which was their "most swell affair"), Tea dance, Lame-horse dance, and Dog dance. He does not mention a Sun dance and I doubt that it would have escaped his eyes or mention if it had been performed (Jocknick 1913: 292–94).

No mention at all is made of a Ute-sponsored Sun dance until 1909, when Edward Sapir learned from a Northern Ute that they received it from the Shoshones in 1890 (Spier 1921: 495). Sapir did not see a Ute Sun dance, nor did Robert Lowie, who, in 1912, corroborated Sapir's date of 1890 for the introduction of the dance (Lowie 1919: 79–80). There are, however, three photographs of a 1906 Sun dance at Northern Ute taken by J. D. Clark (see plates 1–3). No comments attend the photos, but the exterior and interior of the corral, the positioning of spectators, singers, dancers, and shaman making a speech, and the dress of the dancers is about the same as the revised Wind River dance (see Shimkin 1953: 436–50). Moreover, these features are almost identical with the modern versions of the dance. One difference that marks off Wind River Shoshone and Northern Ute dances from those performed by the other Ute and Shoshone groups is the use of twelve roof rafters, and twelve are evident in plate 2. The photographs support the argument for a Wind River origin of the dance.

After the dance was borrowed, the Wind River influence continued to be felt. We infer this from Lowie's (1919: 393) Wind River informant of 1912, Andrew Bresil, who told Lowie that he had conducted the ritual on two occasions for the Northern Utes. Shimkin (1953: 412) demonstrates that Andrew Bresil was a principal Sun dance chief during this period and that he was a grandson of Yellow Hand, the Comanche who introduced the Kiowa form of the dance to the Shoshones.

The earliest chronicle of the Northern Ute Sun dance appeared in an anonymously written account in the *Denver Republican* (3 July, 1911).[1] It is reproduced below in toto because it establishes several important points. First, many Northern Utes participated; indeed, if the account is correct, about one-third of the total tribe at that time, or three hundred "braves," *danced*. Second, the dance had been performed for several years as a prescription against "the great white plague." Third, visitors, except for agency personnel, were not allowed to attend until 1906 (when Clark took his photographs). Fourth, at that early date several whites (as so many anthropologists subsequently) prophesied the death of the dance.

As the sun set yesterday 300 Ute Indians from the Uintah and Uncompahgre valleys finished their three-day sacred sun dance which stamped out consumption among the tribesmen for another year, according to the legends handed down for ages among the Utes, and young

1. This source was located by Professor Omer C. Stewart, who graciously gave it to me.

PLATE 1. Interior of a Sun dance lodge, early summer, 1906. By J. D. Clark. Courtesy of the Smithsonian Office of Anthropology, Bureau of American Ethnology Collection.

PLATE 2. Exterior of a Sun dance lodge and groups of spectators, early summer, 1906. By J. D. Clark. Courtesy of the Smithsonian Office of Anthropology, Bureau of American Ethnology Collection.

PLATE 3. Exterior of a Sun dance lodge and groups of spectators, early summer, 1906. By J. D. Clark. Courtesy of the Smithsonian Office of Anthropology, Bureau of American Ethnology Collection.

and old alike sank to the ground to recover from the trying ordeal. Since sunrise Friday morning the 300 braves of the old school had maintained their weird sun dance which traditions and the fast-dying medicine men prescribe for the battle against the great white plague. For 72 hours the Indians went without food except such nourishment as could be sucked from a willow twig which is carried in the mouth, and incessantly pranced back and forth and around the sacred trees of the tribe at White Rock, 90 miles from Grand Junction, and in the center of the desert Uintah reservation. It has been the annual custom of the Utes for years to hold this three-day dance. They believe that it will prevent sickness and death in their lodges, and long before their white brothers knew a preventive for tuberculosis these Indians were exercising in the sunlight and carrying out methods which twentieth century scientists prescribe for consumption. Old Chipeta, the oldest living Ute squaw, who will be the feature of every celebration on the western slope this summer, has witnessed scores of these annual sun dances and her unfailing weather predictions are only surpassed by her prophecies as to which braves will be the next to die. She has undying faith in the sun dance and for three weeks before the great fete spent her time with the younger generation of braves, whipping them into line with her sharp tongue and making them adhere to the teachings of the tribe. The young braves who have attended different Indian schools throughout the country think themselves above the customs of their fathers and many refused to go through the tortuous labors of the sun dance. They were branded as "squaw men" and have been ruled out of the councils of the tribe. In late years the Indians have made a commercial proposition out of their dance. The remoteness of the sacred trees from the civilized world has kept the dance free from the greedy gaze of tourists and up until five years ago only government agents and close friends of the red men were privileged to witness the event. As the spirit of money making invaded the reservation the Utes became more and more open with their dance and this year it was viewed by scores of soldiers from Fort Duschene and by cowboys for miles around who were admitted at the rate of $1 apiece. The degeneration of the red men is not so complete, however, that they will allow pictures to be taken of their dance and before they could secure a place in the sacred area of the dance every visitor was searched for a camera. Government agents and cowboys have often tried to secure pictures of the strange rites but in vain. The dance is very simple. The braves are stripped of all clothing except a cloth about the loins and are supplied by the squaws with willow switches. These switches are grasped at both ends and the only food which the dancers take for three days and nights is what can be sucked out of the willow twigs, which are slowly moved through the mouth. To the beating of buckskin tom-toms the braves prance up to the sacred trees and back to a distance of about ten feet. This is kept up with but little variation during the entire three days and when the sun sets on the evening of the third day only the strongest of the entire tribe are keeping up to the exhorting drums of the medicine men. It will be only a question of a few years until the dance is abolished. The old braves are weakened in body and influence and the number of dancers is growing smaller each year. Quartermaster Patrick McKee of the Uintah Railway Company and distributing agent to the soldiers at Fort Duschene is interesting other government agents in a movement to secure pictures and records of the dance for reference in years to come when the Utes will no longer bow to the will of the few remaining medicine men but their success will depend upon the whim of the tribal leaders who are harder to bribe than the younger thiefs [sic].

The reporter did not understand much of the ritual, nor, it appears, Chippeta's role in preparing for the dance. Women shamans often admonish dancers to prepare themselves and to work hard for their own good and the good of the tribe. No shamans, male or female, coerce men to enter the dance as dancers; yet the statements about picture taking have always been true. J. D. Clark probably took his photographs illicitly, especially the picture of the interior of the corral (halftone 1), which seems to be taken while prone and perhaps through a break in the brush wall of the corral. The disdain for "medicine men" and "thiefs," and the naïve belief that a little education will do away with the ceremony recur again and again in the reports filed by government officials and other observers of the Utes.

Apparently Frances Densmore in 1914 was the first anthropologist to see and write about a Northern Ute Sun dance (1922: 79–80). She said that the agency superintendent had given orders that no Sun dance was to be held in 1914, but that the Ute performed one nevertheless. It seems that the government had decided to help the inevitable along, that is, the death of the dance, by killing it. The Ute response was indeed defiant. They held their dance right where it was usually held (and is still held): on the flat plains about four miles south of Whiterocks on the Neola road (Densmore 1922: 79).

It is evident from the report in the *Denver Republican* and from Densmore that the agency personnel were aware that the Utes were performing Sun dances. Nevertheless, between 1890 and 1910 no superintendent seems to have mentioned such dances in his reports to the Commissioner of Indian Affairs. In 1894 Superintendent Waugh refers to Ute dances, yet he does not specify any particular dance. In the following statement he refers to "orgies," "barbarous features," and "heathen rites." Liberally interpreted the Sun dance corresponds to each of Waugh's observations. Extra- and premarital sex relations (orgies) occur at Sun dances; ritual fasts and thirsts might be called "barbarous features"; and "heathen rites" might refer to any number of non-Christian ritual incantations which attend Sun dances. Yet a similar case for these correspondences can be made for Bear, Blanket, and Tea dances.

These Indians still love the horse-racing, the card-playing and their dances. . . . The so-called "dances" of these tribes are mere imitations of their former "orgies." Shorn of about all their barbarous features they are but comparatively innocent reminiscences of their "long ago" heathen rites and stand to them in the same relation that amusements do to people of all degrees of enlightenment. With all their seemingly superstitious amusements I have not observed that they have as yet descended to the level of the "fistic arena"! (Waugh 1894: 319)

As Waugh's quaint statement is the only mention of Ute dances between 1890 and 1911 that I have been able to locate, it seems that the Utes were very secretive about them, at least until 1906. Previously the Utes had been secretive about the Ghost dances (which, they said, had nothing to do with whites). The paucity of published information on the early dance is probably a joint effect of the reticence of the Utes to publicize a ritual created in response to white-induced deprivation, the federal policy of abolishing native Indian religious practices, and the reluctance of Bureau of Indian Affairs employees to report that native religious ceremonies were being held on the reservation.

In 1948 John A. Jones (1955: 242) was told that an Uncompaghre shot and killed a White River at the sham battle which preceded the Sun dance of 1895. He was also told that Agent Randlett and sixteen Negro troops were summoned to the Sun dance grounds from Fort Duchesne to guard against possible rioting. It is then alleged that the Ute became frightened that the government personnel would curtail their dances, and in 1896, 1897, and 1898, in response to such fears, they held them up Farm Creek in the Uintah Mountains. In my interviewing, Northern and Southern Utes have corroborated the idea that dances were held in the mountains above Whiterocks and Farm Creek at one time. They have not corroborated the unhappy event at the sham battle in 1895, but tensions between Uintahs and White Rivers, on the one hand, and between Uintah–White Rivers and Uncompaghres, on the other, were high at this time. This will be made abundantly clear in the following chapter. The event could well have happened, although not necessarily as an accident. Whether the shooting occurred or not, and whether it was accidental or intentional, Jones asserts that from 1895 on the Sun dance religion became "a symbol of defiance of the whites" (1955: 243). It is my position that the Sun dance was originally borrowed by the Utes as a reaction to whites. Their defiance preceded 1895, and the retooled dance was a vehicle through which they sought to cope with the degraded life they were forced to live.

The Ute Mountain and Southern Utes must have attended Northern Ute dances in the 1890s, though this history is somewhat murky. The current Southern Ute Sun dance chief says it was first performed there in 1904, but that it was learned from the Ute Mountain Ute. The first Ute Mountain Ute dance, then, must have been earlier. Both Northern and Ute Mountain Utes have told me that Tonapach, a Ute Mountain shaman, was the first man to sponsor a Sun dance among his people, and that he learned the dance from the Northern Utes. Tonapach, in turn, taught the Southern Ute shaman, Edwin Cloud, how to sponsor dances (Stewart 1962: 2).

Regardless of whether Tonapach taught Edwin Cloud or not, the evidence that Southern Utes had been attending Northern Ute-sponsored dances prior to 1904 is very persuasive. For instance, in 1912 Lowie (1919: 405) could learn nothing about the Sun dance from the Ute Mountain Utes and little from the Northern Utes. A Southern Ute shaman, however, gave him an account of the Ute dances, acting as if only the Northern Ute sponsored them (though Lowie obtained a photograph of a Southern Ute Sun dance held prior to 1912). The Southern Ute's account included a history of the dance which, in most important details, corroborates the historical reconstruction of the origin of the Shoshone Sun dance. He said a Kiowa originated the ceremony, and it then traveled northward to the Bannock and Fort Hall Shoshone. He added that the Northern Utes learned it from the Bannocks and Shoshones (Lowie 1919: 405). The account is correct except that the Shoshones from whom the Northern Utes learned the dance were Wind Rivers.

In the 1960s Northern and Southern Utes still related how Buckskin Charley, nominal chief of the Southern Utes from about 1890 to 1930, attended dances at Northern Ute. A sixty-year-old Southern Ute residing on the Northern Ute reservation told how each year Buckskin Charley took several men to Northern Ute to dance, and how before the dancing began the Northern Utes and Southern Utes (including Ute Mountain Utes) would perform a mock battle parade. In turn, the Northern Utes would travel to Southern Ute and do the same thing. The visitors always took the role of the Comanches (with whom the Utes battled as late as 1870). Each side would dress up in war bonnets, mount horses, and line up on opposite sides of the Sun dance field. Then, in snakelike chains, they would pass one another, singing all the time.

At the termination of a ritual held in the mountains north of Whiterocks, Utah, Buckskin Charley was asked to bless the seven horses that were given by Southern Ute dancers to people in attendance. In turn, the Northern Utes, who were hosts for the dance, gave Buckskin Charley gifts of fifty-two horses. In order to get the horses back to Colorado he had to enlist two Northern Ute youths to help him drive them.

The story is interesting because it corroborates similar stories related by Lowie (1919: 409) about mock battles and the gifts of horses, specifically to Buckskin Charley. But it also suggests, because of the mountain location of the Northern Ute dance, that Southern Utes were participating in Northern Ute Sun dances in the late 1890s or shortly thereafter.

The following generalized account, taken from Lowie (1919: 405–9) and Densmore (1922: 79–80), describes the Northern, Ute Mountain, and Southern Ute Sun dance for the period around 1910.

The dance was held annually in July and was performed (a) for the good of the community, (b) so that men could acquire shamanistic powers, and (c), so that sick Utes could be cured. Before the dancing began, the Sun dance chief went into the foothills and selected a tree to be cut and used for the center pole in the Sun dance corral. Often a sham battle preceded the cutting of the center pole, and when the pole was cut there was a proscription against letting it touch the ground. The Sun dance corral was constructed the morning that the dance was to begin. It consisted of a center pole surrounded by twelve poles which marked off the corral boundary. It usually had overhead rafters. There were special areas in the dance corral for the dancers and their stalls, for the musicians and singers, and for the spectators who encouraged the dancers. Just before the corral was constructed, the oldest Ute woman ever captured by an enemy tribe was called forth and given a horse. The lodge was then erected and the Utes pitched their camps around it. Before the dancing began, the dancers entered the sweat lodge to purify themselves.

The men danced for three days and nights without food or water. Singers and drummers accompanied the dancing. When a man became exhausted and took a rest, an old man would rise and admonish him to dance. It was thought that if the dancer did not dance, he could not expect to receive those things he desired for himself and the community—power and health. Sunrise ceremonies were held each morning, when the dancers prayed to the sun for power and when they were ritually cleansed by the Sun dance chief. On the final day of the dance, men often fell as they shuffled from their stalls to the center pole and back again. This often signified that men were receiving their visions.

When the dancing was over, but before the conclusion of the ceremony, each dancer gave away some valued item, such as a horse, to some man (undoubtedly a shaman) who, in turn, prayed for the dancer. The host group then gave gifts of horses, blankets, shawls, buckskins or other items to all the visitors. The distribution of gifts was followed by a feast of meat and bread.

Although the early accounts of the Ute Sun dance are brief, it seems clear that it was a group affair, and that the ideological purpose that was expressed for holding the dance, as well as the intentions of the dancers, shamans, singers, musicians and spectators—all of whom played some role in the production of the ceremony—was the same as for the Wind River Shoshones.

The modern Sun dance was introduced to the Fort Hall Shoshone-Bannocks in 1901 by a shaman, Bear——, who had attended previous dances at Wind River (Hoebel 1935: 578). According to Hoebel (1935: 578), Bear—— had failed to cure an ailing woman and he attributed this to an inadequacy of his powers. He dreamed to sponsor a dance and did so in 1901. Sun dances were held annually after that time.

The Lemhi Shoshone-Bannocks were moved to the Fort Hall reserve in 1907 and did not participate in Sun dances until that time. A few years later (it is not clear when), they began sponsoring their own Sun dances on the Fort Hall reserve (Hoebel 1935: 578). The early Fort Hall dances were similar to the Wind River ritual from which their own rite was borrowed; yet at some time before 1935 the oldest established Fort Hall version of the dance incorporated women as dancers and assistant chiefs. The Lemhi version did not follow suit.

The Sun dance origin myth told by living Utes and Shoshones is similar to the origin myth related to Hoebel (1935: 578) at Fort Hall. Each version involves a vision encounter between an Indian and a buffalo (or several buffaloes). The buffalo has supernatural power and is an emissary of power. Moreover, all versions include some details about how the buffalo helped the Indian, gave him instructions about how to perform the dance, and informed him of the benefits that would accrue from following the ritual prescriptions. I have chosen to relate a version of the myth told by a Southern Ute in the 1930s. It is most appropriate because it recognizes Wyoming as the place where the dance was created, and because it has some of the pseudo-Christian trappings (e.g., "God" and "twelve apostles") that were worked into the Wind River and, subsequently, other Ute and Shoshone dances.

A long time ago some Indians were camped up north, way up where Wyoming is now. They were all in a big bunch, laughing and talking. There was one Indian who was camped off to one side by himself. This lone Indian went hunting one day. He walked a long way and did not see any game. He got tired. He got thirst [sic]. His lunch gave out and he got hungry and he did not know what to do. Finally he lay down under a tree and went to sleep. While he was sleeping he had a dream. He dreamed he saw a herd of buffalo and he got up and walked toward them. He walked in little gulches and behind bushes so they would not see him. When he got close enough to shoot he stood up. The buffalo saw him and grunted and put down their heads and charged him. The man tried to run but he was so weak he could not run and he fell down and the leader of the buffalo ran right up on top of him. When the man saw the buffalo standing on top of him he fought. He fought hard. He fought with all his might. The buffalo said, "Don't do that. I am not what you think." Then the man stopped fighting and looked up at the buffalo. "Go back to your people," said the buffalo, "and tell them that you have seen God." He say, "Tell people to build corral with door facing east. Put pole in center of corral with fork on top like cross." He say, "Put buffalo skull on cross facing east." He say, "Then put up twelve poles each with fork on top for twelve Apostles." He say, "Then put long poles from each fork of little post to fork of big post." He say, "Put big end of the pole out." "Then when sun goes down let men strip naked with nothing on but britch-clout and a whistle made from bone of eagle wing. Let men dance from sides of corral up to center post and whistle while they dance so." He say, "Let other mans make drum, big drum." Then he tell 'em how to make drum. He say, "Let all mans sing and dance for four nights and four days with nothing to eat on account of Christ fasting in the desert for forty nights and forty days." He say, "Then let all mans have big feast, eat meat, eat buffalo meat, have good time and feel good." "When dance is going let all mans sing like this . . ." and buffalo show Indian how to sing sun dance song. When buffalo get done singin' he disappeared and Indian wake up. He no feel tired. He feel like he had eat big dinner and was ready to go long ways. He go back to Indian camp and talk to Indians and tell chiefs what he see. They say, "Let's have dance like that." That's how sun dance start![2]

2. This account was told by Wilson Johnson and was given to me by Professor Omer C. Stewart.

3 *Conquest of the Utes and the Shoshones*

It is my impression that the Sun dance religion, modified by the Wind River Shoshones in the late 1880s and passed to the Northern Utes, Fort Hall Shoshones, and Colorado Utes after that time, was created and sponsored as a supernatural means for Indians to solve their personal and community problems without reliance on whites. These problems, it will be demonstrated, were mostly caused—directly or indirectly—by whites.

The brief historical essay that follows shows that Utes and Shoshones lost their access to strategic resources and their self-governance as Anglo-Americans moved west and engulfed them.[1] A constellation of several reasons and motives caused the Anglo onslaught on Ute and Shoshone territory. The cumulative effect of these different impulses was disastrous for the Indians. First, men migrated to farm or to raise cattle. Others entered the Mountain West in quest of precious metals. Still others constructed railroads to connect the expanding economic metropolises west of the Sierra Nevada Mountains and east of the Rockies. Some men were primarily motivated to move west and locate in order to gain religious and political autonomy, but such men always needed strategic resources in order to live; so they too took land, and water.

The movement west, whether by pioneers in quest of land or railroaders in quest of right of way, was effected by armed force. Sometimes the armed force was the militia of the Mormon (Latter-day Saints) church, sometimes it was state or territorial militia, sometimes it was the U.S. Cavalry, and sometimes it was posses of vigilantes. As one can imagine, the Utes and Shoshones had no wish to relinquish their territories and their livelihoods, and as they resisted white encroachment they often signed treaties with the federal government, especially if whites had already squatted on Indian land, if more whites threatened to move in, and if several altercations had occurred.

Whether treaties were signed before or after Indian land was taken, and whether treaties were ratified or not ratified, they all had the same effect: whites gained access to Indian land. The treaty signings often had standard unintended consequences as well: the federal government seldom protected the rights and privileges guaranteed to the Indians by the treaties, and the federal government often failed to distribute goods promised to the Indians as payment for relinquishing their native territories.

The Ute and Shoshone responses to encroachment, broken treaties, and the limited

---

1. "Anglo" is the general term used in the west for non-Spanish whites.

access to resources that were once available to them was, generally, to resist. In the early stages this meant fighting to retain what was theirs. As the Anglo population increased and occupied the major rivers and the wagon and railroad routes, some Indians fled into the most remote and unoccupied mountainous areas. These areas, too, often became filled with whites as precious minerals were discovered in the 1860s, 1870s, and 1880s. So Indians soon had no places to which they could flee.

In 1870, at a time when the federal government was attempting to force all Utes and Shoshones, to live on reservations, the Ghost dance religion swept through these Indian populations. They adopted it in hopes of ridding themselves of whites and of resurrecting their deceased Indian ancestors. The appeal of Shoshones and Utes to this supernatural means to accomplish what they had not been able to accomplish through warfare and flight did not, however, stop further attempts by a few Ute and Shoshone groups to fight or flee. Even when the Indian populations were stricken with disease, depleted through starvation, epidemics, and warfare, and corralled on reservations, some continued to resist. After a few years the Ghost dance prophecy had not been fulfilled. All but the Fort Hall Shoshone-Bannocks were losing faith in it.

It was only after the Utes and Shoshones had been forced to live on reservations for ten or twenty years that the Ghost dance religion lost most of its Shoshone and Ute adherents and the restructured Sun dance began to spread. Its spread correlates, I think, with the resignation of many of the Indians to their fate. The Sun dance promised only that men could cope with life as it was, promised only that it could make men well and make communities happy to the exclusion of whites, yet in a white-dominated world. It did not promise, as did the Ghost dance, a world free of whites. It did not promise a radical transformation of things as they were, as did the Ghost dance.

Even the final placement of Indians on reservations coupled with the restrictions of their movements did not prove to be the end of the "Indian problem," as the whites had hoped. About the time the Sun dance began to spread, the federal government, under pressure from state, ranch, mining, and other commercial interests, passed an act which, under the guise of freedom legislation, would allot each Indian some reservation acreage. The idea was to put unused land back in the public domain and, in turning individual Indians into property owners—with proper training in agriculture—to transform them from welfare appendages to solvent petty capitalists. The result of this action was that the Indians lost even more land and became almost completely dependent on the federal government.

The expansion of the Anglos was, of course, the expansion of the American capitalist political economy. In the early years of the expansion there was an insatiable quest for land, and special interest groups garnered it with political sanction and military might. The regular fashion in which this occurred is easy to understand. After all, private capitalist influence and power was felt in Washington (the railroads and the mining industries); it dominated the early territory and state governments (the agricultural industry as well as railroads and mines) and even made itself felt on the lowest bureaucratic levels of the Bureau of Indian Affairs (BIA). Utes and Shoshones had neither capital nor power, and they seldom even influenced the BIA agents who were assigned to keep watch on them.

THE UTES

BEFORE 1850

From the mid 1600s to 1850 Utes were organized into several large hunting bands which were named for the territory they inhabited or the things they exploited on it. They hunted bison, deer, elk, and rabbits from the Rockies on the east to the Oquirrhs on the west, and from the Yampa River and Uintah Mountains on the north to the San Juan River on the south. The canyonlands of Utah in the southwestern part of Ute territory were not conducive to their big game hunting life-style, and it was sparsely populated by Payuchis—mixed Wiminuch Ute-Southern Paiutes (Jorgensen 1964; Stewart 1966*a*).

In the 1600s and 1700s Ute bands raided in New Mexico, where they stole horses from the Spanish and goods from the Pueblos (Schroeder 1965: 53–60). They harassed the Hopi villages in Arizona and regularly frequented the plains east of the Rockies to hunt bison (Schroeder 1965: 61). Ute bands raided as far south and west as Chihuahua, Mexico, and southern California in the early 1800s (Morgan 1953: 308; Heap 1957: 223–25). They also stole Southern Paiute women and children from Utah and Nevada and sold them to the New Mexican Spanish to be used as domestics and shepherds (Sale 1864: 155).

From about 1750, after the Utes had a falling out with the Comanches and after other Plains tribes, such as the Arapaho, acquired horses, Ute hunting territory in the mountain valleys was often used by hunters from the plains. So just as the Utes ventured into hostile territory on the plains and elsewhere, so was their territory infringed upon by Arapaho, Sioux, Cheyenne, and Comanche (Jorgensen 1964; Schroeder 1965).

The Utes were fine horsemen with vast herds of horses. They spent parts of the springs and summers in large encampments of 200 or more lodges. Map 2 defines Ute and Shoshone territory and the general location of the bands (summer residence groups) for the 1750–1850 period. Up to 1850 their hunting-raiding life was relatively little affected by Anglo expansion. The Ute territory had been spared from wide-scale settlement since pioneers generally had gone right past the inhospitable mountains and alkaline-bleached Great Basin, not stopping until they reached Oregon, Washington, and California. The Spanish, on the other hand, had been in central New Mexico almost continuously since 1598, and the Utes maintained contacts with them, friendly and hostile, over the entire period (v. Schroeder 1965).

The Utes had very little contact with migrants on the Oregon Trail, but they met some of them in the early 1840s as they passed through Fort Bridger, a trading post in Shoshone territory frequented by Utes and Shoshones (Morgan 1953: 201). On the other hand, when the last leg of the Santa Fe Trail to Los Angeles was opened in 1829, the Utes were quick to attack the mule trains and extort "gifts" of blankets and horses for safe passage (Bailey 1954; Sonne 1962). Somewhat earlier this practice had been initiated on the eastern part of the trail near Santa Fe by more easterly Utes and Jicarilla Apaches (Schroeder 1965: 63).

The completion of the trails to the north and south of their territory was the harbinger of worse things. Several trading posts were established in Ute territory during

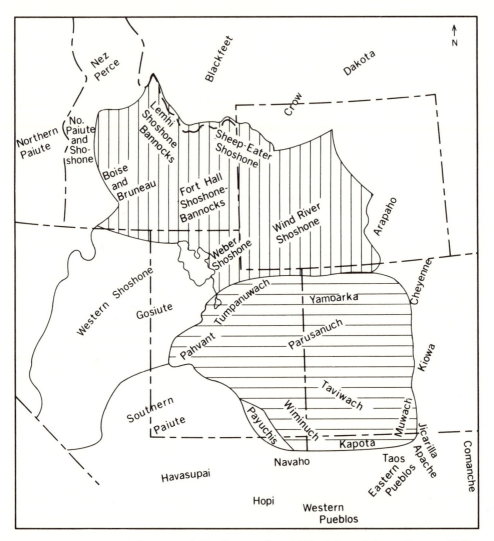

MAP 2. Distribution of Utes and Shoshones, circa 1800. Adapted from Stewart 1960a, Shimkin 1947, and Jorgensen 1964.

the 1830s, but the posts had little effect on Indian life. Since the trappers and traders were few, they did not usurp Indian land, they paid for the peltries and goods they received, and they did not press Indians into slavery. But in 1847, when the first wave of Mormon settlers passed through the Bridger Valley in what is now Wyoming, then into the Salt Lake Valley where they squatted in Shoshone territory, things began to change rapidly. Utes soon lost their land, access to the strategic resources on which they had lived, free movement between places, and the power to govern themselves. In the cataclysmic series of events that followed, the Utes were moved by legal and illegal means; their population was greatly reduced by warfare, Anglo-introduced diseases, starvation, and freezing; and they were finally corralled on reservations.

Many treaties were signed, though immediately broken by the federal government. As Utes were dispossessed, agencies and reservations were created for them. In the midst of the despair that stemmed from these latter events and the events that served to corral the Indians in the first place, the seeds of intra- and interreservation factionalism were sewn by the federal government.

The bitter history of the various Ute battles for land and livelihood, their flights from their odious circumstances, and their appeals to supernatural solutions to their omnipresent problems are briefly explicated below. Histories have been written which are much fuller than the accounts provided here. The following are recommended: Jones 1955; Jorgensen 1964; Stewart 1966b; Swadesh 1962; Parkhill 1961; Emmitt 1954. Following conventions established by the federal government around 1850, the Utah and the Colorado Utes will be treated separately. This division is somewhat artificial, for historic Ute bands did not respect state boundaries. For example, the Wiminuch, now located at the Ute Mountain Ute reserve in Colorado, inhabited parts of Utah, Colorado, and New Mexico. The Parusanuch (White Rivers) inhabited parts of Colorado and eastern Utah, and now reside on the Uintah and Ouray reserve in Utah.

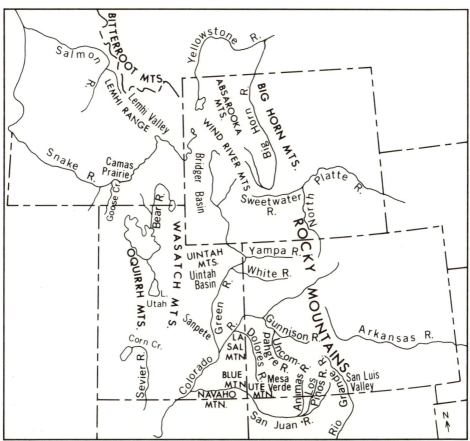

MAP 3. Some major natural features in Ute and Shoshone territory.

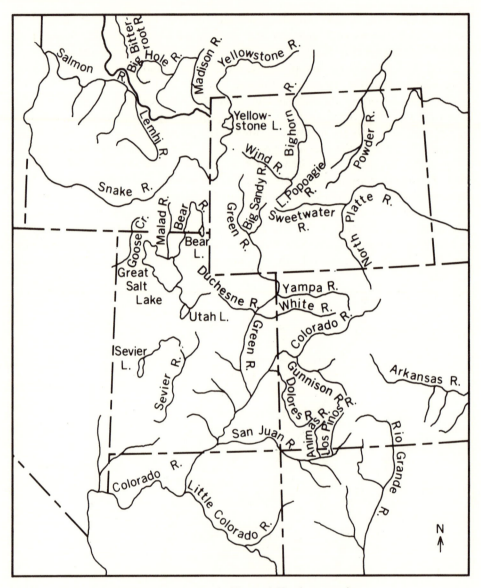

MAP 4. Some major rivers and streams in Ute and Shoshone territory.

AFTER 1850

The Utah Utes

Six years after the first Mormons squatted in the valley of the Great Salt Lake, they had expanded up and down the west side of the Wasatch Mountains for about four hundred miles, laying claim to most of the major irrigable valleys in Utah. By 1855 they had pushed into southwestern Wyoming and had begun encroaching upon the irrigable valleys of eastern Idaho, southern Nevada, northern Arizona, southeastern

Utah, and southwestern Colorado. They needed land to farm, but they also desired to protect the flanks of the State of Deseret, as the Utah territory was known to the Mormons, from hostile "Gentile" encroachment.

The movement into the Salt Lake valley, which was Shoshone territory, did not immediately bother the Utes. Indeed, in the first few years of Mormon occupancy the Utes found the Salt Lake valley a good place to trade with Mormons for European goods and to steal horses and everything else they could get their hands on from the Shoshones (Clayton 1921: 324–29). By 1848 Chief Sowiett and the infamous Ute chief Walker went to the new Mormon settlement with "several hundred horses for sale" (Church of Jesus Christ of Latter-day Saints 1848). Ute-Mormon troubles began only as the Mormons spilled over into the Utah Lake valley to the south, comman-

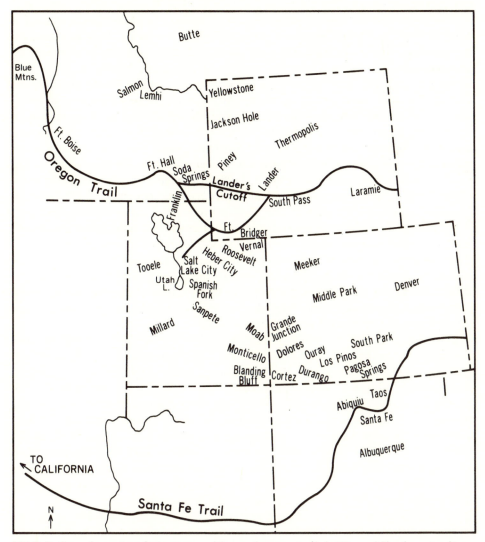

MAP 5. Some important forts, towns, cities, and wagon trails in Ute and Shoshone territory.

deering the land on which many Utes had collected roots, seeds, and berries for several months each year, and controlling access to the rivers around the lake from which Utes had collected vast quantities of fish (large suckers, catfish, and trout indigenous to the Great Basin) moving up the rivers to spawn.

In 1852 Brigham Young, the president of the Mormon Church, governor of the State of Deseret (Utah Territory), and the first superintendent of the Utah Indian Agency, was very much concerned by Ute depredations of Mormon settlements south of Salt Lake. Most of the depredations were attributed to Chief Walker. Young also wanted to put a stop to the battles between Walker's Ute band of hunters and raiders and Chief Washakie's Shoshone band of hunters and raiders from the Bridger Valley in Wyoming. So he called these chiefs to counsel in August of 1852 and got a momentary and illusory peace (Trenholm and Carley 1964: 127–41).

The reason that the peace was momentary is obvious: the Mormons continued to dislocate Utes and Shoshones from their aboriginal territories. They pushed them into conflicts with one another and with whites as Indians and whites competed for resources on which to live. That the Utes distrusted Brigham Young and his lust for all the Ute and Shoshone territory was evident in 1851 when Young attempted to send the Tumpanuwach Ute chiefs Walker and Sowiett to the Fort Laramie Treaty Council. These men refused to go because they thought it was a Mormon ploy to separate them from their band and kill them. Yet in March of 1852, a few months prior to the meeting between Walker and Washakie, some Utes and Shoshones convened at the suggestion of Indian Agent Day in central Utah, 150 miles south of Salt Lake City (Trenholm and Carley 1964: 127–28). Although Day was a Mormon in the employ of Brigham Young—the Indian superintendent, governor of the territory, etc.—the Indians did not seem to fear Day and they did want to express themselves on the matter of Mormons' commandeering their territories and the resources thereon. At this meeting Sowiett said, "American—good! Mormon—no good! American—friend! Mormon—kill-steal . . . " He was bitter about the land the Mormons were taking, the timber they were using, the animals they were killing, and so on, and he wondered why the government did not protect the Indians. The Shoshones, under Cut Nose, a lesser leader than Washakie who had not returned from the Laramie Treaty Council, also decried white encroachment.

Given these conditions, where Indians were losing everything, and given these sentiments, where Indians wanted to preserve what was theirs, it is not surprising that, soon after the meeting with Brigham Young, Walker and other Utes intensified their raiding of Mormon villages (Gottfredson 1919: 6, 18, 21, 83). Mormons disliked the Ute slave trade as well as Ute raids on Mormon communities. Brigham Young attempted to solve these problems by sending eighteen companies totalling 714 men from their "Nauvoo Legion" to destroy the Ute warriors (D. Jones 1890: 56–58; Utah State Historical Society 1854). Nineteen Mormons and probably more than a hundred Utes were killed in consequent brush fire encounters. The capitulation of Walker, who died a year later, did not terminate Ute resistance, however, as they continued to battle for their territory west of the Wasatch range.

In 1855 Brigham Young, wearing his hat as Indian superintendent, moved to confine the Utah Ute populations on farms near some of their traditional habitats in

Millard, Sanpete, and Utah counties. After establishing the farms he wrote the Commissioner of Indian Affairs that the Utes were giving up their predatory ways and learning to farm (Young 1856: 224–27). This simple, euphoric, and erroneous assertion was made regularly by agents to the Utes for decades to come, but up to 1900 practically no Utes farmed. In fact, they showed disdain for farming, and between 1855 and 1860, the only people who farmed on Ute lands were agency personnel and Mormon encroachers (Armstrong 1857: 308–9; Forney 1858: 210–11; Humphreys 1860: 170–71).

In 1860 Humphreys (170–71) reports that the Ute farms established five years earlier were surrounded by twenty-four thousand Mormons, who in many instances had begun tilling the unfenced Ute lands. (There were over forty thousand Mormons along the entire Wasatch Front at this time.) Many of the Utes who stayed near these farms during the winter of 1859–60 died from starvation and freezing. Utes were not only losing their lives and their land, but those who lived were also losing the possibility of supporting themselves on game, fish, berries, nuts, and roots. The browse forests and the taller stands of trees were being cut by Mormons for firewood, fencing and building materials, and the deer and elk were being killed for food. The streams and rivers were lined with farms, and the water was diverted by irrigation ditches. Berry bushes along the river banks were no longer accessible, and root-digging grounds were tilled or turned to pasture.

Most Utes chose not to stay in such conditions, and they moved into the east of the Wasatch range, into hunting areas they had frequented during part of each year for centuries. These haunts, such as the Uintah Basin, the Tavaputs Plateau, and the desolate and forbidding canyonlands of southeastern Utah, became the principal refuge areas for the dwindling Utah Ute populations. They attempted to maintain themselves in traditional ways, and although most of their sustenance came from the chase, they returned to the agencies on the west slope of the Wasatch for annual provisions and to beg from settlers.

In 1855, when the Mormons had more or less secured the western half of the state, they sent a group of male missionaries, well armed, to establish a colony in eastern Utah. They chose a spot close to what is now Moab, Utah, on the Colorado River. The Utah Utes, who recently had been pressed into the area, as well as the Parusanuch and Wiminuch Utes, who also frequented the area regularly, did not want to lose this territory or the resources available there. The missionaries built a fort and stockade, stored some hay and corn, and began tilling the land. Six months after their arrival a band of Ute warriors burned the fort and stockade, including the hay and corn (Gottfredson 1919: 84–87). This action momentarily arrested the Anglo expansion into southeastern Utah.

Since about 1852, following the Mexican Cession which placed the State of Deseret in the territory of the United States, Brigham Young had been at odds with several federal policies. Although he was struggling with Utes and Shoshones for territory during this same period, on several occasions he attempted to enlist these same Indians to help him, if necessary, in a war against the U.S. army. In 1857, following several years of minor altercations with Brigham Young and his territorial regime, the federal government accused the Utah territorial government of insubordination and a number of unlawful acts.[2] The army eventually marched on Salt Lake City, (the Mormon capitol), which was evacuated beforehand, and neither the Utes nor the Shoshones joined in the protection of it. Shortly thereafter the federal government decided to separate the Utes and Mormons by moving the Utes to a reservation in the Uintah Basin of eastern Utah. The basin was surrounded by mountains and arroyos and deemed to have sufficient water to support the Indians (Doty 1862: 198–200). At that time it was also isolated from the Mormon communities, the closest of which was Heber City, about ninety mountainous miles away from the proposed agency location.

Before the Utes were relocated, however, Brigham Young ordered a survey and made plans to settle the basin with Mormons (*Deseret News*, 31 August, 1861). But the survey report dissuaded him from his plans, "The fertile vales, extensive meadows and wide pasture ranges . . . were not found. . . . Rather it is one vast 'contiguity of waste,' and measurably valueless, except for nomadic purposes, hunting grounds for Indians and to hold the world together" (*Deseret News*, 25 September, 1861). There were no further obstructions from the Mormons, and by an executive order of Abraham Lincoln the 2,039,400-acre Uintah Valley reservation was established in 1861 (Walker 1872: 56).

The understaffed Indian Affairs superintendency, which had been taken out of Brigham Young's and his church's control, made no immediate effort to force the Utes to reside on the Uintah reservation. For the next few years Utah Utes continued to hunt throughout the entire eastern half of Utah, in parts of western Colorado with their eastern Ute congeners, and in Wyoming's Bridger Basin (Shoshone territory) either with Shoshones or with their permission. The old enmities between Utes and Shoshones were rapidly breaking down. Utes also returned to their erstwhile territory west of the Wasatch to harass the settlers (Hatch 1862: 208; Mann 1862: 204–5; Doty 1863: 392–96). In 1863, Ute Chief Black Hawk began raiding many of the same Mormon communities that Chief Walker attacked a decade earlier. That summer Black Hawk called a council of Utes from northern Colorado and Utah to meet in the Utah Lake valley. Utah Indian Superintendent Doty (1863: 392–96) heard of the plan and attended the meeting. So did Uriah Curtis, an employee of the Colorado Ute agency who was familiar with the Utes (Whiteley 1863: 133). Superintendent Doty was able to dissuade the Utes from waging an all-out war by promising provisions and goods to them. The promises were apparently verbal and neither was fully kept, the government never supplying all the goods that were promised and the Utes not fully refraining from waging war.

Curtis's mission was to get the Ute chiefs who had assembled near Utah Lake to return with him to Colorado, where the federal government hoped to get all Ute chiefs from Utah, Colorado and New Mexico to sign a treaty relinquishing vast amounts of their aboriginal territories. Curtis was not able to get the chiefs to travel with him, but on his return to Colorado he reported to Agent Whitley (1863: 133) his astonishment "at the wasted numbers of these bands. Chiefs who, a few years before, had led hundreds of warriors, now do not have as many as dozens."

Soon after the war council of 1863, Black Hawk's warriors and other small groups

2. A discussion of the Mormon–federal government altercation is found on page 71.

of Utes resumed their attacks against Mormon settlements. The Mormons could not effectively stop these lightning guerrilla attacks and depredations, and in 1865 they threatened a war of extermination against the Utes. At that time the new Utah Indian superintendent, O. H. Irish, got the Utes in Utah (henceforth known as the Uintahs) to agree to move to the reservation in the Uintah Basin which had been established four years earlier but which had not been used. Five well-known chiefs and eleven of lesser note signed the document which guaranteed them $1,100,000, government services, and 62½¢ per acre for all land relinquished in Utah and Sanpete counties (Irish 1865b: 144–54). The treaty was not ratified by Congress and the promises to the Utes were not kept. The Pahvant Utes assigned to the Corn Creek farm in Millard County also agreed to move to the Uintah reservation, but they never did.

In 1867 the various Ute chiefs were distraught over Ute suffering and government deceit. During the spring, Uintah Chief Tabby and his band rode to Shoshone Agent Mann (1867: 189) whose agency was located in the Bridger Basin of Wyoming, and asked why the government had not kept its promises. Uintah War Chief Black Hawk again began attacking and looting Mormon villages, this time with a group of a hundred or so warriors (Head 1867: 178). Late that same year Tabby threatened to join with Black Hawk, worrying Agent Rhodes (1867: 180–81) who thought the grievances of Chief Tabby and the other Utes were legitimate and who also thought that it was dangerous to ignore these grievances.

Conditions for the Utes only worsened through 1869. Neither the federal government, nor the territorial government, nor the Mormon Church attempted to redress the Utes' grievances. The Utes had not even received the meager annuities promised to them by treaty agreements for relinquishing their territory. Although the Utes pressed both Ute and Shoshone Indian agents with questions about why the treaty obligations were not being met, their questions went unanswered. In response to the treatment they received, several Ute chiefs issued threats to protect the land they still held (*LDS Millennial Star*, 17 July, 1869: 469). But the Utes in Utah were less and less able to make good on these threats, let alone expel the Mormons from the pre-contact territory the Utes had once occupied.

During the previous twenty years the Utes had lost their lands, their access to strategic resources on those lands, and their control over their own lives. Although they fought to maintain what was theirs, they were unsuccessful, and some Ute leaders were forced to sign treaties with the federal government. They soon found that, although they relinquished their land as their part of the treaty obligation, the federal government was not honoring its treaty obligations and was not protecting Ute treaty rights; so the Utes lost as much by the tactic of treaty signings as by those of fighting and fleeing. Disease, starvation, and warfare depleted the Ute population and made their outlook hopeless.

Early estimates vary for the entire Ute population of Utah, Colorado, and New Mexico, but they were always in the thousands. In 1839 Farnham (1841:79) said there were 8,000 Utes. In 1842 Sage (1956: 90–92) estimated that there were 15,000 Utes, Paiutes, and Western Shoshones. In 1859 Forney (363–65) estimated that the number of Utes in Utah alone was 4,500. All of these estimates may have been high, but it is my impression that around A.D. 1800 there was a minimum of 8,000 Utes in the

Utah, Colorado, New Mexico area. Forney's estimate of 4,500 Utah Utes for 1859, which is probably a little high for that late date, makes a horrible contrast with Agent Critchlow's (1877: 181–86) estimate of about 800 Utes in Utah less than twenty years later.

In 1870 the Utah Utes were miserable. They wandered between the Uintah reservation, their ever decreasing hunting grounds, and the agencies of the Wyoming Shoshones and the northernmost Colorado Utes in quest of annuities and in hopes of continuing their hunting way of life. Uintah Agent Tourtellotte (1870: 143) was vexed at the practices of the Utes under his aegis, as well as those from "Colorado and Arizona" who did not belong to the Uintah agency but who were collecting provisions there (see Jorgensn 1964 for a more lengthy exposition and analysis).

During the spring of 1870 the beleaguered Uintah Utes were reached by Bannocks and Northern Shoshones and urged to attend and participate in the Ghost dance

MAP 6. Ute reservation territories in 1870. Adapted from Jorgensen 1964.

religion, which, they were promised, would solve the ubiquitous problems facing all Utes and Shoshone-Bannocks. Thus far the Indian responses of fighting and even flight had failed to terminate Ute misery and the loss of their resources. The evidence suggests that the Utes hoped to escape their misery and reclaim their territory by turning to the Ghost dance, which had been created a few months earlier among the Northern Paiutes of Nevada. This new religion promised a solution to the Indian problems through supernatural means, rather than through war, or running away, or treaty signing.

In 1870 M. J. Sheldon, a Uintah reservation employee, reported as follows:

The Tabbywatts [Taviwach Utes from Colorado], Piemps [Weber Shoshones], and Yampa Utes from the White River [Colorado], the Uinta-Utes, Gosho-Utes [Gosiutes], Snakes [Northern Shoshones] and Bannacks, and other northern Tribes of Indians were assembling in the Bannack country fifty miles east of the Bear Lake valley [i.e., in the Bridger Basin] to perform their traditional religious rites. They meant peace and when through with their rites would disperse. [*LDS Millennial Star* 32 (21 June 1870): 25 (originally in the *Deseret News*)]

It was not, of course, a traditional rite. These groups had never jointly sponsored religious rites in the past. Another communiqué from Sheldon to Superintendent Tourtellotte in May 1870 briefly explicates the Ghost dance ideology and makes it quite evident that this gathering was not traditional. Sheldon wrote that near Heber City, one hundred miles west of the Uintah agency, he had met thirty-five Utes under the leadership of Tabby and another chief. They refused Sheldon's request that they accompany him back to the Uintah reservation. He also reported that three Indians (Shoshones or Bannocks) from the Bridger Basin were in the party and that they had brought the message that all Indians should meet in Bannock country. Several Utes had already carried the message to other Utes and to the Navajos. He went on:

They say that the word is being carried to *all the indians*, east, south west and north, to not fail to come as they *intend to resurect* [sic] *their forefathers* and all Indians who wish to see them must be there. I have spent all the forenoon endeavoring to dissuade them from going, but they say *the white man has nothing to do with this*, it is the command of the Indian god and if they do not go they will sicken and die. . . . The place selected for the grand meeting is in the vicinity of Wind River—northwest of Washakie's reservation [i.e., in the Bridger Basin]. [Jones 1955: 239–40; emphasis added]

The following spring, Utes, Shoshones and Bannocks again convened for a Ghost dance, yet this time it was held in the Bear River–Bear Lake valley of northern Utah and southern Idaho, fifty miles west of Bridger Basin and out of sight and sound of the agencies (*Salt Lake Herald* 7, 12, 18, 29 May, 14 June, 1871).

In May of 1872 the Utes convened, most probably for a Ghost dance, but this time it was held in Sanpete County (central Utah), the area in which, from 1853 to 1865, many Utes had been killed through warfare with Mormons, many more had died of starvation and freezing, and the rest had been removed through federal actions. The 1872 affair seems to have been attended solely by Utes. The reports of Uintah Agent Critchlow and Colorado Ute Agent Littlefield suggest that they were somewhat alarmed by the meeting. We learn something of the many grievances the Utes harbored, especially of their attitude toward farming and their expectations about the federal government's treaty obligations towards the Utes for taking Ute lands. The corre-

lation inferred here between Ute participation in the Ghost dance and Ute deprivation, absolute and relative, is supported by all of the evidence we have perused and
much we have not as yet assessed.

Critchlow (1872: 291–94) reported that the Utes in his charge were willing to
farm, yet that "Douglas, the White River chief, with quite a number of his band came
to the agency and succeeded in persuading our Indians . . . to give up [farming]."
Douglas told Critchlow that only white men and squaws farmed and that "President
Washington" did not intend that Utes should work. Then the White Rivers and
Uintahs left for Sanpete County, where they convened with nine hundred other Utes,
including Kapotas, Sheberetches, and Elk Mountains from Utah, Colorado, and
New Mexico (Critchlow 1872: 298; Littlefield 1872: 288).

The Ghost dance did not have its intended effect: Utes did not reconvene with
their deceased friends and relatives and they did not become free of whites. The Utes
seem to have stopped sponsoring the Ghost dance religion after 1872, probably because they were losing faith in it. Yet some Utes continued to participate in Shoshone-
sponsored Ghost dances, and bits of Ghost dance ideology were accreted to the Ute
Bear dance.[3]

It was not until seven years after the Ghost dance of 1872 that the dwindling bands
of Uintah Utes finally located permanently on the Uintah reservation. During those
seven years Critchlow (1872: 293) reported his anger that the Uintah Utes would not
stay put and that they demanded that he distribute provisions to the White River
Utes. Critchlow's counterpart two hundred miles to the east, Colorado Agent Littlefield (1872: 287–89), reported that Tabby, a Uintah leader, and his band had been
camped at his agency for part of the year. So Utes assigned to the Uintah agency were
hunting, visiting, and collecting provisions in northern Colorado, whereas Utes assigned to the northern Colorado agency were doing the same things in Utah. In 1874
no more than one-third of the 556 Utes who received annual supplies at Uintah were
on the reserve at any one time, and in 1876 only 350 Uintah Utes stayed on the reservation at any one time (Critchlow 1874: 276; 1876: 128). But in 1878–79, when the
last Ute hunting areas in Utah and Colorado were being depleted, when the white
population in Utah had grown to about 145,000, and when the Shoshones, with whom
the Utes had frequently hunted, had been pushed out of Bridger Basin, the decimated
Uintah Utes began to spend more than half the year near their agency. Critchlow
(1878: 126–28; 1879: 139–40) reported to the Commissioner of Indian Affairs that
some Utes farmed and some owned cattle which had been purchased for them by the
government, but most had nothing other than government rations and products of
the chase.

Just about the time the 800 Uintah Utes settled on their over 2,039, 400-acre reservation which, they were assured, would never be encroached upon by the whites,
several white ranchers began grazing their livestock on Strawberry Valley, which
comprised the western end of the reservation. The Utes and Agent Critchlow (1879:

3. An abbreviated and greatly modified form of "Ghost" dancing has attended many other Ute
events, such as Sun dances (Jorgensen 1964). It is a circle dance performed to bring good health
and happiness. It is not intended to bring an imminent and radical transformation to the world,
nor even to restore to life deceased ancestors.

139) were furious and made an immediate demand, which went unheeded, to move the whites and their livestock off Ute land.

The Colorado Utes

The loss of Indian territory and strategic resources to whites, population decimation, and subjection to federal government controls during the 1850–80 period was experienced by the Utes assigned to Colorado agencies just as it was by the Utes assigned to Utah agencies. The interaction between the various Ute bands was intensified and made more continuous as they were encompassed and crowded by whites, decimated, fragmented, and pushed into western Colorado and eastern Utah. Some differences in the histories of the Utes in Utah and those in Colorado are discernible, however. Utah Ute–Mormon battles began in the early 1850s and continued throughout the mid 1860s. As Mormon settlers gobbled up the land, the Utah Ute population was quickly decimated and pushed east of the Wasatch range. The Utes of Colorado, on the other hand, were pushed west much more slowly. The major battles between Colorado Utes and whites occurred nearly two decades later than those in Utah. An indication of the similarities, yet also of some of the differences, between Utah and Colorado Ute living conditions in the late 1860s, and attitudes about the future, can be gleaned from their separate responses to the Ghost dance religion of the early 1870s. The Utah Utes sponsored the dance, but no longer fought nor fled. Although members of several Colorado Ute bands participated in the Shoshone and Utah Ute-sponsored Ghost dances of 1870, 1871, and 1872, they returned to Colorado and New Mexico and continued to offer stiff resistance to whites, including one major battle. When they could no longer fight successfully, they too fled from whites.

The harbinger of what was to befall the Colorado Utes—the loss of control over strategic resources, the loss of the power to govern themselves, and the inability to exert influence over the whites who came to control them—came in 1851 when a group of New Mexican Spanish pushed for a settlement on the Conejos in the San Luis Valley of southern Colorado (Schroeder 1965: 66). Although two forts were established in the San Luis Valley shortly thereafter as the Muwach and Kapota Utes and Jicarilla Apaches began attacking the settlements, these attacks restricted the development of non-Indian settlements north of New Mexico. In 1855 Governor Meriwether negotiated two treaties with the Utes which gave them two thousand square miles north of the San Juan and east of the Animas rivers in turn for the Utes' promise to remove themselves from New Mexico (Stewart 1966*a*). The treaties were never ratified.

Between 1856 and 1861 all known Colorado and New Mexican Ute bands were assigned to northern New Mexican agencies at Taos (later Maxwell's Ranch) and Santa Fe (later at Abiquiu and later still at the Conejos in Colorado). Some, but not all, of the Muwach, Kapota, and Taviwach went to those agencies to receive the annuities promised to them for keeping peace (Meriwether 1856: 182; Collins 1857: 273–77). The Wiminuch and Parusanuch, who were located further west and north, remained either unknown to, or little seen by, the Ute agents.

A Colorado Indian agency was not established until 1861 (Gilpin 1861: 101). By that time the Colorado Utes were being pressured by mineral prospectors and miners. Many prospectors had already moved into the Durango-Dolores area. Utes were also being pressured by Arapaho, Cheyenne, Kiowa, and Dakota who entered Ute territory in quest of game, and by Navahos who were expanding northward (L. Head 1861: 102; Arny 1862: 245). As of 1863 there had been several skirmishes between Taviwach Utes and Anglo prospectors in Middle Park of the Colorado Rockies, and this prompted the government to hold a major treaty council with the Utes. The purpose of the council was to get the Utes to locate in the Four Corners area (the intersect of Colorado, New Mexico, Utah, and Arizona) and to take up farming (Evans 1863: 121–29). It was to this council that Uriah Curtis was summoning the Utes he had pursued to central Utah (see earlier this chapter).

The Wiminuch, of whom some were at Black Hawk's council, sent word to the Indian agents that they would not attend the council and would not farm. The Muwach did not attend the council nor did they send word about why they would not attend. Three Kapota chiefs attended, but would not sign the treaty. They made it clear, when it was their turn to talk, that they had no intention of farming or of being relocated. The leading Parusanuch and Yampa Ute chiefs were at Black Hawk's council in Utah. So, in the end, several Taviwach chiefs and three lesser chiefs from the White River area, either Parusanuch or Yampas, signed the treaty, which specified that all so-called Colorado Utes would relinquish all mineral rights, all mountain areas settled by whites, and the San Luis Valley. The reservation which was established for them as part of the treaty totalled about eighteen million acres.

From 1863 through 1868 the government attempted to keep the Utes out of the San Luis Valley, off the plains, away from the settlers and miners in the mountains, and out of New Mexico. The Utes refused to comply on all counts, and further refused to stay near the three agencies that were created for them in the northern, central, and southern parts of the vast reserve. In 1866 Agent Cummings caught up with some Parusanuch (perhaps Yampas) in Middle Park of the Colorado Rockies. He told them that they would have to stop hunting there as the land had been ceded to the government three years earlier. The Utes told him the land was theirs and no one had the right to sell it. Cummings (1866: 154) further says: "I persisted so long in the effort to induce them to abandon their claim and go over to the White River to a reservation in the immediate vicinity of the Tabequache [Taviwach] reserve that it seemed likely at one time to lead to unpleasant consequences, and I therefore ceased from further effort in that direction."

The treaty of 1863 is called the "Tabeguache Treaty," and it is clear why. A few Taviwach leaders seem to have been the only Colorado Ute people in favor of it. They were about the only Colorado Utes who could have been in favor of it, since they were signing away the hunting territories of other Utes but maintaining their own. The leaders of other bands, save the three lesser figures among the White Rivers, did not sign. The leading White River chiefs, Douglas and Jack, did not sign. Indeed, the resistance, culminating in a brief war, of the Ute people who were eventually located at the White River Agency in northwestern Colorado signaled the near undoing of the Colorado Utes and stands in marked contrast to the Taviwach. We will take up this matter below.

Because more whites were moving into Colorado (there were 34,000 in 1860 and

194,000 in 1880) in search of precious minerals and land, and because Ute depredations and skirmishes with whites attended this growth, a second treaty was signed by members of most Colorado Ute bands in 1868. This treaty reduced Ute lands in Colorado to about fifteen thousand acres and established two new agencies. An agency at Los Pinos, on the headwaters of the Saguache, was named "Uncompaghre," and the Taviwach Utes assumed that name. The other agency was established for the Parasanuch and Yampa Utes at Meeker and was called "White River," which name the northern Colorado Utes assumed (Oakes 1869: 269–70).

Few Indians stayed at any of these agencies. The White Rivers were unhappy about the location that was chosen for their agency. It was in a very cold canyon near the White River, and they wanted it moved to a warmer location near the Yampa (Littlefield 1871: 551). The Muwach, Wiminuch, and Kapotas simply refused to recognize the treaty and continued to go into New Mexico for annuities, which they often received although they were not supposed to. It is alleged that even Ouray, a nominal chief of the Uncompaghres (Taviwach) who generally did the government's bidding, was unhappy with the treaty and claimed he was duped (Pope 1871: 368–69).

In 1870 William F. M. Arny, former agent to the Utes at Maxwell's Ranch, was sent on a special mission to the Utes, Apaches, Navajos, and Pueblos. He met a Ute chief there who told Arny that "they wanted their country *solo*, that they intended to drive all the miners from the country, and that I must return, as they did not see any necessity of my going farther. . . . He told me that if I went and lost my life that I must not blame him as he had warned me of the dangers of going any further" (Arny 1967: 17–18).

The following day Arny (1967: 18) met sixteen Wiminuch, who cautioned him about going any farther and objected to his journey. During the next two days he ran across two parties of Kapotas, about twenty to a party, who advised him to return to Santa Fe. Finally, about a week later, Arny (1967: 23–24) met up with twenty-one lodges of Kapotas and Wiminuch on the Chama River. They were led by Wiminuch Chief Ignacio, and they told Arny the same story that he had heard earlier:

"The whites did not keep their word. They give us land and a home, where we always lived. They find gold and silver and take our land from us. They send us to Colorado and then say is not the land ours. They promise much but do little. The Great Chief our Father in Washington will do right. Tata Arny and Tata Hanson will do right, but French gave us a paper which said no white men must go into our country, then he come and say he wanted to take our land for miners, and McCook and Hunt[4] put us in a cold country. They eat the bread and give us the crust. They do not give us the cattle and sheep the Great Father sent, but we are contented without, if we are left in our own country where we have always lived." I explained to them the provisions of the treaty, and "that it was their own fault that they did not get their annuity goods, cattle and sheep which were sent to their agency for them, as they would not go there to get them."

Arny (1967: 24) told the Utes that they must stay out of New Mexico, "that the Great Father wanted his white and red children to live separate." The advice Arny offered fitted the threatening, yet paternalistic, racist form. He told them that whites

4. Lieutenant J. B. Hanson was the Abiquiu Indian Agent in 1870. J. C. French was the previous agent at Abiquiu. A. C. Hunt was governor of Colorado in 1868 and is credited with negotiating the "unpopular" Ute treaty of 1868 (Murphy 1967: 14, 22–23).

were more numerous, stronger, and more cunning than Indians, yet they were not vengeful and they wanted to be kind to the red man. Arny urged them "to submit to the will of the Government" and he promised himself that he would spend the rest of his life trying to make self-sustaining Christians out of them, because "*to civilize a whole tribe of barbarous people is well worthy the ambition of any Christian man*" (Arny 1967: 24; emphasis added).

The alleged good intentions of the Indian agents who paraded by the Utes as they were losing their resources and their control over their own lives added up to no more, at best, then kindly racism. At times agents merely kept watchful eyes on the Utes and distributed provisions to them—when and if the provisions arrived. At other times agents aided and abetted the whites who swooped in to usurp more Indian land and resources. At their worst, some Indian agents joined in with other whites in cheating Indians out of their land, their provisions, and other treaty rights. This was possible because the most influential whites in the local territories were often those who were stealing the greatest amount of land and because the federal government did not honor the existing treaties or keep close watch on the agents.

The White River Utes continued to put up the strongest resistance to white encroachment as they pestered miners and told them to get out of the territory (Thompson 1871: 555–58). Because of the actions of the White Rivers and other Utes, and especially because vast mineral deposits were located on Colorado Ute territory, the treaties of 1863 and 1868 were not considered adequate by the government of Colorado or by scores of mineral speculators.

In 1872 the federal government, under the sharp prod of various mining interests and other people of influence in Colorado, organized a commission to make a reconnaissance of the Ute. Rather than finding any economic or political factors that might have been at the root of Ute discord with one another, with whites, and with their agents, the commission adroitly reported the following: of the 5,920 Utes, 800 Uintahs were located on a reserve of more than two million acres in Utah. The 5,120 so-called Colorado Utes, on the other hand, were living on a reserve even vaster—fifteen million acres (Walker 1872: 56, 86–89).

The argument was, of course, that the Utes had more land than they could use; so the government, represented by Felix Brunot, entered into negotiations to extinguish Ute rights to the south part of the Colorado reservation. This was at the same time when Sapinavaro (Ouray's brother-in-law) and a host of Uncompaghre (Taviwach) Utes were still so angry with Ouray for signing the treaty of 1868 that they tried to kill him (Jocknick 1913: 116). Nevertheless, the Brunot Agreement of 1873 specified that Utes would relinquish their right "to a large tract of valuable mining country estimated to contain about three million four hundred and fifty thousand (3,450,000) acres" (Smith 1873: 16). Ouray was the principal signatory of the 280 who signed this "last request the government would ever make of the Ute" (Brunot 1873: 84–113). Only two White Rivers, one a nominal chief, signed, whereas five other White River chiefs refused to sign and rode back north (Brunot 1873: 84–88).

During the following six years the Utes continued to move out on the plains, to hunt in the Middle Park of the Rockies, and to deny the treaties of 1868 and 1873 (Thompson 1874: 271–72; Jackson 1959: 275, 278, 284; Bond 1876: 19–20; Russell 1876: 102–4). The Utes would not farm and many refused to take care of the livestock provided for them. Agent Danforth (1877: 46-48) at White River complained that the Indians left him in charge of the livestock and, when he did not receive the annuities that were promised to the Utes at his agency that year, the Utes stayed away and hunted.

The conflict between the Utes and the BIA agents doing the bidding of the federal government and the American economy began coming to a head in 1878. At that time N. C. Meeker was assigned to the White River agency. Meeker was determined to make the Utes acquire the orderly ways of farmers and ranchers, but his behavior and philosophy, although seemingly well-intentioned, fitted the threateningly paternalistic form. His technique was to apply stern Christian discipline, deceit, and federal troops to accomplish his goal. Meeker's story is pathetic and his tenure short-lived.[5] He thought that the Utes were stupid, filthy, and indolent. He wanted to put a stop to their gambling, horse racing, and begging. He interpreted the acceptance of rations and annual provisions as begging, rather than as treaty rights guaranteed to the Indians for relinquishing their lands. Rather foolishly he proposed to take away their race horses and withhold their government rations, hence forcing them to work (Meeker 1879: 17–19). It is my impression that the statements about the reforms that he was going to effect, as outlined in his reports to the Indian Commissioner in 1878 and 1879, were no more implicitly racist, simple-minded, morally superior, euphoric, or strongly made than the statements of the vast majority of the agents who had worked among the Utes in Utah, Colorado, and New Mexico for the preceding twenty-five years. All of these agents were *expected* to pacify the Indians, and most wrote that that indeed was what they were doing. One difference between Meeker and his predecessors was that Meeker acted upon his reform plans.

After numerous small altercations with the Utes in his charge, Meeker, who could not get them to stay at White River and farm, sounded a general military alarm. At the time a large party of Utes was out hunting. He had these hunters rounded up and returned to White River. A subsequent military investigation proved that they had harmed no one and destroyed nothing. The Utes merely had been peacefully going about their tasks of procuring a livelihood. This was drastically different from the charges Meeker had levied against them. He had told federal officials that White River Utes from his agency were out pillaging ranches, burning forests, and killing game, just for the pleasure of it.

In 1879 Meeker started to plow up a Ute race track and some of their best horse pasturage; both were located near the agency. Chief Douglas, who laid claims to the land (other chiefs such as Jack and Piah laid claim to other areas on the reservation) and whose understanding about the government's obligations to the Utes was that the Utes would receive perpetual compensation for relinquishing their land, told Meeker to stop. When he did not, the Utes fired a few rounds of ammunition over the men who were doing the plowing.

Again Meeker caused a near panic by alarming every army post and rancher in the vicinity that the Utes were on the warpath. The U.S. Cavalry was dispatched to the White River area, and the frightened Utes, upon learning of Meeker's act, rode out and met the soldiers. They tried to stop the troops from entering the agency.

5. Accounts of Meeker's foolishness, including his denigration of Ute morality, are given full treatments in Emmitt (1954) and Sprague (1957).

They asked them to surrender their arms and send only three or four officers in. The military men were unwilling to comply with the Ute requests. Instead they rode on through a narrow canyon, perfect for ambush, fully armed. A fight ensued wherein thirty-seven Utes were killed, twelve soldiers were killed, and eight agency employees, Meeker included, were massacred (Hayt 1879: xviii–xlix).

Hayt (1879) and Emmitt (1954) expose the "Meeker Massacre" for what it was, a useless war which was solely attributable to Meeker himself. Though the war was not intended by any of the parties immediately concerned, the frightened, maligned, and beleaguered Utes were fighting for what few privileges and rights, and for what little territory, they had left. The wary, skeptical military little realized that their actions would have such grievous consequences.

When the battle was still going on, a number of Ute braves from White River rode south. They tried to enlist Chief Ouray and the Uncompaghre (Taviwach) Utes to go on the warpath with them. It is said that Ouray called a general council and that the Uncompaghre Utes decided not to join the White Rivers (Hayt 1879: xxxiii). There is no doubt but that Ouray attempted to comply with the government's request to stop the battle and recover the white hostages taken from the Meeker agency. Ouray admonished the White Rivers to give up the battle, and he had the hostages turned over to the military (Jocknick 1913: 193–97).

Within three days of the massacre, the White Rivers had ridden to the agency that had been established for the Muwach and Kapotas (Southern Utes) near Ignacio, Colorado. The Southern Utes held war dances through the day and night, but the government sent in the cavalry and nipped their plans in the bud (Page 1880: 17). The war was all over and only the cleanup job remained.

There was an immediate protest throughout Colorado and a call for a war of extermination against the Utes. Colorado Governor Pitkin made the following statement to the press:

I think the conclusion of this affair will end the depredations in Colorado. It will be impossible for the Indians and whites to live in peace hereafter. This attack had no provocation and the whites now understand that they are liable to be attacked in any part of the state where the Indians happen to be in sufficient force. My idea is that, unless removed by the government, they must necessarily be exterminated. I could raise 25,000 men to protect the settlers in 24 hours. The state would be willing to settle the Indian trouble at its own expense. The advantages that would accrue from the throwing open of 12,000,000 acres of land to miners and settlers would more than compensate all the expenses incurred. [Emmitt 1954: 234–38]

Governor Pitkin followed this statement with messages to the Secretary of War asking him to send federal troops, but if that was not possible, his state troops could do the job (Emmitt 1954: 238). Pitkin's candor about extermination and the reason for it, that is, the acquisition of resources, is almost disarming. The only thing he left out was that he had extensive interests in the mining areas acquired under the Brunot Agreement as well as interests on the *extant* Ute reservation.

The talk of extermination led the federal government to round up 665 White River Utes and give them a military escort to the Uintah reservation in eastern Utah. In the same year (1880) the government called a treaty council, at which it forced the Utes of the White River reservation *and* the Uncompaghre reservation to sell all of their

land in Colorado. The same treaty council reduced the Muwach, Kapota, and Wiminuch territory to a narrow strip 15 miles wide by 110 miles long on the Colorado–
New Mexico border. The Uncompaghre inhabitants had not taken part in the war,
except to admonish the White Rivers and lead the military to the camp in which the
Meeker women from the White River agency were being kept. Many Uncompaghres
had been engaged in semisedentary pursuits such as raising sheep and goats since
before reserve times (see Heap 1957: 185–87); nevertheless, 1,360 Uncompaghre Utes
were relocated also. They were moved—under armed escort—to an area just south
of the Uintah reservation in eastern Utah. Their new locale was called the Ouray
reservation (Ute Commission 1881: 201–16; W. H. Berry 1881: 19–23).

Some idea of the immense mineral wealth of the territory Utes were forced to relinquish can be gained by looking at the mineral production of three Colorado
counties—Ouray, San Juan, and San Miguel—that were once in Ute territory. (La
Plata, Dolores, Mineral, and Hinsdale, to mention a few more counties in the Ute
area, were also fabulously rich in minerals.) Miners were working in these counties
as early as the late 1850s. They flooded into the area after 1873, and into all of Colorado
after 1880. Ouray and San Miguel counties, but only part of San Juan county, came

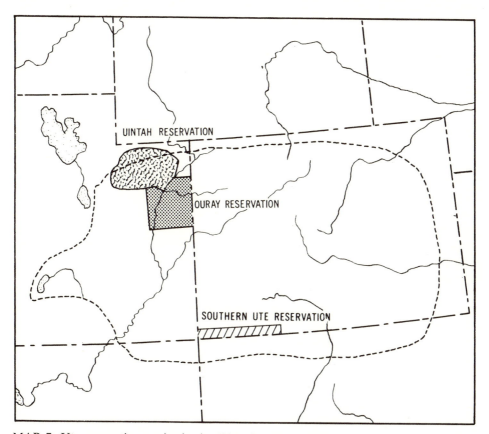

MAP 7. Ute reservation territories in 1885. Combined acreage: approximately 4,500,000
acres. Adapted from Jorgensen 1964.

under the Brunot Agreement; so the rest of San Juan, not to mention the other mineral areas, were "cleared" for *legal* occupancy and exploitation by large capitalists and smaller entrepreneurs in 1881. In the 1897–1901 interval alone, the total mineral production for these three counties was about $40 million, half of it in gold and copper (Jocknick 1913: 166). In 1902 one mine in Ouray county sold for $9 million. The movement of the Utes, attended by the threats of a war of extermination against them, was more than prodded by pressures from mining interests, as was shown earlier. This effort was well rewarded.

Chief Douglas of the White Rivers was incarcerated at Fort Leavenworth and, though later liberated, was judged "insane." He died shortly thereafter (Jocknick 1913: 200). Although no more White Rivers were killed, their punishment was harsh. Jocknick (1913: 196) wrote: "If there are any Utes left who took part in the Meeker Massacre it would appear that they have been made to pay the penalty many times over."

As of 1880 there were about 650 Wiminuch (henceforth Ute Mountain Utes) and 500 Muwach and Kapotas (henceforth Southern Utes). If we accept the tally of the Ute population as of 1872 which was provided by the Walker Commission—a federal panel charged with evaluating Ute population and land requirements—the decline over the eight-year span was precipitous. It was especially steep for the Uncompaghres, who were located in the heart of the mining district, and mirrors the trend of the Utah Ute decline about a decade earlier. The Ute Mountain Utes (Wiminuch) seem to have lost the fewest people, but they also seem to have avoided the most contact.

	White River	Uncompaghre	Southern Ute	Ute Mountain
1872	800	3000	620	700
1880	665	1360	500	650

The Uintah and Ouray Reservation

From the time that the Uncompaghre, White River, and Uintah Utes were forced to live side by side in Utah, the federal government, sometimes inadvertently, began treating the bands differently, especially with regard to allocations of land and money. The altercations between White Rivers and Uncompaghres that had begun in Colorado in the 1860s continued, perhaps intensified, in this new, depressing setting, where men were restricted to their reservations, unable to sustain themselves in the manner that they chose, and were the subjects of white bigotry.

In 1880, 665 White River and 800 Uintah Utes were placed side by side on the 2,039,400-acre Uintah reservation. As part of the agreement which was made at the council held in 1880, the White Rivers were supposed to receive per capita payments for the land which had been taken from them at Meeker, Colorado. The White Rivers received their first payment, nineteen dollars per capita, in 1880. Their new hosts, the Uintahs, received nothing. This, quite understandably, caused dissatisfaction among the Uintahs, who had been forced by the federal government to give up much of their reservation land and the game which it contained to accommodate the White Rivers (Ute Commission 1881: 332; Critchlow 1881: 157; 1882: 149–50).

The Uncompaghres had refused, in vain, to move from Colorado until compensation were paid for the land taken from them (W. H. Berry 1881: 20–21). But in

1881, 1,360 Utes from the Uncompaghre reservation were moved, also under army escort, to the Tavaputs Plateau, just south of the Uintah reservation (Minnis 1883: 137–39). Here, on 5 January 1882, the federal government, by executive order of Chester A. Arthur, established the Ouray reservation, named after the Uncompaghre chief. It totalled 1,912,320 acres. Thus, as of 1882 the total amount of land owned by the Utes in eastern Utah was 3,951,360 acres, and the total number of Utes in eastern Utah, that is, the Northern Utes, was 2,825. The two reservations shared a common border, yet had separate agencies. In dividing the residential agglomerations the federal government emphasized differences between the Uncompaghres and the Uintah–White Rivers.

The Uncompaghres were supposed to receive payments for the land taken from them in Colorado. All things being equal, the amount which was to be paid each Uncompaghre should have been the same as the amount paid to each White River. All things were not equal, because the White Rivers, out of their general fund, had to pay pension support to the families of all of the agency and military personnel who had been killed in the Meeker Massacre. Thus, each year their per capita income was about half the amount paid to each Uncompaghre. The White Rivers were angry about the Meeker debts as well as the fact that the Uncompaghres were receiving more money than they. This conflict over funds drove the wedge more firmly between the White Rivers and the Uncompaghres (see Atkins 1886: li-liii; and Byrnes 1888: 218–21).

After the government had distributed the first of the per capita payments to the White Rivers, the Uintah agent realized that the Uintahs were dissatisfied. Although they had relinquished a great portion of their land to the White Rivers, they had received no compensation in return, and agency personnel figured that the Uintahs would cause serious problems unless some equitable remedy was found. Hence the government began making annual payments to the members of both groups, compensating the Uintahs for the land which had been gerrymandered for the White Rivers. As a matter of fact, the Uintahs received slightly larger payments than the White Rivers, who were still paying their Meeker debts. But neither the Uintahs nor the White Rivers received per capita payments totalling more than fourteen dollars a year. After that time minor altercations between White Rivers and Uintahs over land boundaries and rations took place; yet it appears that they solved their problems satisfactorily. Indeed, by 1885 the marriages between White Rivers and Uintahs increased over the number of pre-1880 unions, and these new marriages helped to keep the bonds between the bands more or less secure (see Davis 1885: 180).

In 1884, Uintah Agent Davis (1884: 156) made a census, reporting that there were only 531 White Rivers and 528 Uintahs on the reservation. Thus, there were nearly 300 fewer Uintahs than in 1877 and 135 fewer White Rivers than in 1880. Davis (1884: 156) further reported that these people received one-third of their sustenance from farm products (probably mostly produced by agency-hired farmers), one-third from the chase, and one-third from rations. It is known that the White Rivers were still leaving the reservation and venturing into Colorado and Wyoming to hunt, and that the Uintahs, too, were away hunting some of the time. Perhaps the one-third figure given for support from hunting is too low.

Davis (1884: 156–57) also wrote that practically all cattle and sheep on the reservation were owned by only four or five Uintah and White River families. This is understandable, for neither group wanted to farm and few wished to give up the chase in order to raise livestock. As hunting activities were curtailed, however, the unequal distribution of property among Uintahs and White Rivers continued throughout the entire reservation period. This is not to suggest that some families were highly affluent and others were destitute. There was considerable resource sharing and labor pooling. The livestock was owned and cared for by family organizations—usually involving about three generations of bilateral kin and affines—pooling their labor and sharing in the resources.

As for the Uncompaghres, in 1885 they numbered 1,252. That is 108 fewer than the total of those who traveled to Utah four years earlier. The Uncompaghres simply refused to farm. Seventy acres were reported to be under cultivation, but these were being tilled by agency personnel (RCIA 1885: 378). The Uncompaghres spent most of their time in the southern recesses of the Tavaputs Plateau, herding their sheep, cattle, and horses, and hunting (Gardner 1885: 178). They were seldom any closer than seven miles from the Ouray agency, except on provision distribution days.

Both the Uintah–White Rivers and the Uncompaghres owned huge herds of horses. During the 1880s the Uintah–White River herds were variously estimated to contain between 5,500 and 7,000 head. The Uncompaghres were said to own 5,300 head (RCIA 1884: 316; 1885: 390). Since they treasured their horses, and because these were so numerous and required so much fodder, the number of cattle that could graze on reservation land was greatly restricted.

One of the first serious money problems for the Uncompaghres occurred in 1886, and it was soon followed by numerous critical land problems. Several distraught Uncompaghres threatened the life of their agent when he refused to distribute to them per capita money belonging to 279 Uncompaghres who were absent on annuity distribution day. He proposed to put the money belonging to the absentees in a safe and wait for them to return. The Uncompaghres in attendance, however, feared that the agent would withhold the money indefinitely. They insisted that the money belonged to them for the land taken in Colorado and that he should divide it among them. He refused and the Utes took it from him (Atkins 1886: li–liii).

During the same year the White Rivers, still angry about the Meeker debt, among other grievances, became insubordinate. The agency officials interpreted the Uncompaghre behavior and the behavior of the White Rivers as a threat, and they influenced the Indian office to incorporate both reserves under one agency and establish a military post at Fort Duchesne, which was situated about half-way between the subagencies at Ouray and Whiterocks (Atkins 1886: li–lii). Fort Duchesne was manned by six companies of troops, many of whom were Negroes. This large complement of troops frightened the Utes, who envisaged another attack by the U.S. Cavalry. Hence, they laid in a supply of ammunition and moved their families into the mountains. No fight ensued since the troops did not provoke any encounters, but considerable unrest prevailed (Atkins 1886: li–liii). The Utes, corralled and degraded, now had to fear military reprisals for any acts considered dangerous by the agency or the military command. The Negroes, whom the Utes called "Buffalo soldiers," especially frightened them (D. Freeman 1962: 2).

In 1887 it was learned that a small group of White Rivers and a large group of

Uncompaghres had slipped off the Utah reservation in hopes of fleeing from white control and of restoring their old way of life. They were hunting and roaming in their old terrain in Colorado. Western Colorado settlers, who well remembered the Meeker affair and both feared and hated the Utes, attacked and killed some of them. They also stole the herds and other property that the Utes were traveling with, amounting to 5,000 pounds of dried meat, 600 horses, 2,500 sheep and goats, and 37 head of cattle (Atkins 1887: lxxvii–lxxxii; Byrnes 1887: 201–3).

The whites were ready to kill all of the Utes who had been caught wandering in western Colorado. Apparently they were fearful that the Utes would give a performmance akin to the Meeker Massacre. The maligned Ute party, which consisted of men, women, and children of many ages, had nothing to live on, were afraid to fight, and were afraid to return to Utah. Thus they hid and waited for help. The agent at Whiterocks and the military commander at Fort Duchesne were unwilling to send Utes to assist their distressed kin, for they feared that the sight of a number of mounted Utes would precipitate an attack by the whites. The commander also wanted to keep as many soldiers at Fort Duchesne as possible. He felt it was important to control the Northern Utes so that they would not incite problems in Colorado. Finally a few Utes and a few soldiers stealthily rode into Colorado and escorted the limping Utes back to Utah (Byrnes 1887: 201–3). The stolen stock and meat were not recovered. There would be no more flights to Colorado.

Gilsonite, gypsum, and asphalt had been discovered on the southern, or Ouray, section of the reservation, while the Strawberry drainage area on the western end of the Uintah section had proved to be ideal graze and browse country for white-owned cattle and sheep. By 1887 prospectors and stockmen had moved into these parts of the reservation. This greatly bothered the powerless Utes, and each time they saw trespassers they would report their grievances to their superintendent. In turn the superintendent spent a considerable amount of his time trying to exact fines or expel trespassers from the reserve (Byrnes 1888: 217–21; 1889: 278–82; Waugh 1890: 214–16; 1891: 436–40). The superintendents alleged that they had such little success in pursuing trespassers and redressing Ute grievances that it now seemed futile to try to curb white expansion. By the late 1880s, only a few years after the Colorado Utes were moved to Utah, the BIA superintendents assigned to oversee Ute lands and to protect Ute rights favored relinquishing some tribal property. The superintendents argued that because the Indian populations were dwindling, because Indians were not exploiting their land with Protestant vigor and were standing in the way of progress, Indian land should be given to those who would use it properly. Forcing the Indians to relinquish land would also solve the trespass problem.

While mining and ranching interests were lobbying Congress to pass an act which would open the Uintah and Ouray reservation to private speculators, they received an unexpected windfall. In 1887 Congress passed the General Allotment Act (GAA or the Dawes Severalty Act), which provided for the allotment of reservation lands in severalty to each Indian on every reservation in the United States. The reservation land that was left over after all allotments had been made was to be redeposited into the public domain and opened to homesteaders and speculators. Hence, the mining and ranching interests in Utah were heartened. Shortly after the GAA was passed, Congress decided that some of the acreage on the Uintah and Ouray reservation could be sold. This was done even before allotments were made to the Indians. The Utes received some money from the sales, which was deposited in their tribal account at the federal treasury (Byrnes 1888: 218).

The GAA also called for civilizing the Indians and freeing them from their traditional subsistence economy, that is, making farmers out of them after they received their severalty allotments. But very little land on the southern or Uncompaghre-inhabited section of the reservation was irrigable. Moreover, the largest known gilsonite, gypsum, and asphalt deposits in the west were located in this Tavaputs Plateau region. Thus, steps were taken to allot lands to the Uncompaghre Utes first. Then all lands that were not allotted could be opened for homestead, mineral claims, and private purchase (Waugh 1890: 214–16; 1892: 482–87).

Uncompaghre, White River, and Uintah leaders were approached and sounded out as to whether they wanted the allotment program. None was receptive. When the subject was first broached in 1887, the Uintahs and White Rivers acted as if they did not understand the issue. In 1891, however, agent Waugh spoke to Chief Tabby of the Uintahs and wrote: "[Tabby] expressed his entire disapproval of the matter, seeming to fear the contraction of their territory and the probable sale of the surplus if they took their lands in severalty" (Waugh 1891: 436–40).

About a year earlier, as a new version of the Ghost dance swept east, again carried by the Idaho Shoshones and Bannocks, a Uintah shaman, General Grant, traveled to Bridger Basin and the Wind River Reservation. The Shoshones at Wind River had lost faith in the Ghost dance. The Sun dance, which they had altered and performed in secret for three or four years, had become their central religious ritual. The new Sun dance stressed personal redemption and the acquisition of power to cope with life—power to further good health, to cure the ailing, and to promote community well-being.

General Grant, who had seen many Sun dances in the past and had participated at Wind River, secretly introduced the dance at Whiterocks during the GAA turmoil and the pre-allotment sales of Ute land. It was taken up by the Uintahs and White Rivers according to my informants. Though the White Rivers danced, the ritual did not represent the only means left to them to cope with the whites, as we shall see below. The Uncompaghres apparently began participating three or four years later. Exactly when the Uncompaghres began is not clear. My Ute informants stress that the Uintahs brought the dance from Wind River and that the White Rivers joined in first. They do not say when the Uncompaghres began participating. J. A. Jones's (1955) informants said that Uncompaghres were participating in 1895. Feelings between the Uintah–White Rivers and the Uncompaghres were running high at that time, but their common distress in their relations with whites and in their general economic and political predicaments probably served to override their own factional disputes.

Mining interests kept the pressure on Congress to force the Indian Office to allot the Ute land in severalty; yet it was not until 1895 that a commission was appointed to survey and allot lands. Of course the commission started its survey with the Uncompaghre recluses who were roaming about on their mineral rich lands (Randlett 1895: 209–12). The commission soon found that the acreage suitable for agriculture was confined to the most northern section of the Uncompaghre territory, along the narrow flood plains of the Duchesne, Green, and White Rivers around the subagency town of Ouray. Moreover, the commission found that the available land was not sufficient to provide allotments to all Uncompaghres. It was decided that the additional acreage which was required before allotments could be made to all Uncompaghres would be taken from the Uintahs and White Rivers on the northern end of the reservation.

The furor that followed this decision held up the proceedings for two years. The Uncompaghres were upset when they learned that they would lose their hunting and grazing land in the southern area. Rumors spread that whites in great numbers were going to move onto the Ute land. The Uncompaghres were also disturbed when they learned that they would have to pay $1.25 per acre for the allotments that they would receive in Uintah–White River territory. And the Uintah and White Rivers were upset to learn that Uncompaghres were going to encroach upon their domain (see Randlett 1895: 309–12; 1896: 618–19).

Agent Browning (1896: 96–97) reports that the Uncompaghre flatly refused to pay for the acreage they were to receive from the Uintahs. He planned to move the Uncompaghres onto their neighbors' land anyway, and he planned then to revise existing treaties so that the Uncompaghres would pay for the new land from funds owed them for the land they lost in Colorado. The Uintahs and White Rivers were to be compensated with these funds. Then, in June 1897, despite all of the Ute protests to the contrary, Congress acted to provide for the allotments of lands to the Uncompaghre Utes in severalty (W. A. Jones 1897: 92).

The Uncompaghres received allotments on the basis of 160 acres per household head and 80 acres to each person over eighteen years of age. No provisions were made for future generations. Apparently 83 allotments were made on Uncompaghre territory, and 232 on Uintah–White River territory (Cornish 1898: 292–95). Another eight years elapsed, however, before the Uintahs and White Rivers received severalty allotments, and, when they did, the manner in which allotments were made and the size of the allotments were different from what they had been for the Uncompaghres.

As soon as the "excess" Uncompaghre land was turned back to the public domain, the mining and ranching interests began pressing for the opening of the northern section of the reservation. The Uintahs and White Rivers, however, had already made it very clear that they were not at all amenable to receiving severalty allotments and relinquishing more land. Agent Myton wrote:

If the consent of the Indians is necessary to be obtained in order to open the Uintah Reservation, it will be useless for Congress to pass any more laws or spend any more money for that purpose, for I do not believe there is an Indian on the reservation who is willing or favors selling any part of their land. They look with favor on leasing when they can be assured that it will not bring too many white men among them and they will not be cheated. [Myton 1899: 351]

The predatory expansion of the white-controlled economy was not to be denied by Indian will, however. All of the Utes understood this, but perhaps none understood it better than the proud White Rivers. It will be recalled that the White River Utes had received less in annual funds than either the Uintahs or the Uncompaghres. Moreover, they had not received a reservation of their own after they were relocated. They also received more strict government surveillance than the other Northern Ute groups. When the Uncompaghres were moved onto the land the White Rivers shared with the Uintahs, and when they learned that their land was going to be allotted to them in severalty and the excess turned over to the whites, they expressed their distress both to the local agency officials and to government officials in Washington. Agent Myton (1899: 352) wrote: "The White Rivers have for the last six months been threatening to go to Colorado." He thought that he had succeeded in quieting them down and had induced them to stay on the reservation, but his success proved to be temporary.

Money problems were interwoven through, and indeed were contingent upon, the land problems. In 1897 the Northern, Southern, and Ute Mountain Utes contracted the services of attorney M. K. Oldham to defend them in about one million dollars' worth of depredation suits against them stemming from the pre-1880s (Randlett 1897: 286–87). So these noncitizens who had lost their land and livelihood within the sanction of the federal government were now being tried in that government's courts of law to determine whether they should be punished for resisting white expansion and their loss of land and livelihood. To their credit, they organized into the Confederated Ute Bands and asked Oldham to bring a suit against the federal government to extract unpaid funds owed to them from the terms of the Brunot Agreement of 1873. The government had not paid for the land they took in the 1868 treaty either, and so it must not have come as a great surprise when the government refused to let Oldham take the Brunot Agreement case to court (Myton 1902: 353). Another money problem, but one which was specifically Northern Ute, began to become intense at about the same time. The White Rivers and Uintahs had not been paid for the land that they had been forced to relinquish to the Uncompaghres four years earlier, and hostilities between these factions were increasing (Myton 1901: 382). Thus, land and money problems were interlaced, and each was serving to alienate the beleaguered Ute factions from one another, as well as to alienate both still further from the federal government.

The federal government ground still more dirt into Ute eyes in 1902 when Congress acted to allot what was left of Uintah and Ouray reservation land to the Uintahs and White Rivers, to set aside a nominal amount of grazing land to be used jointly by all three bands, and to open the remaining acreage to public purchase (Report of Indian Legislation 1902: 493, 541). Unlike the larger allotments made earlier to the Uncompaghres on *Uintah-White River land* (for which they had not been paid), each Uintah and White River Ute family head was to receive only 80 acres (half the Uncompaghre allotment), and all other Indians were to receive 40 acres each (Uncompaghres 18 and over received 80 acres each) (Report of Indian Legislation 1902: 541).

The Uintahs and White Rivers never cooperated with the plan. Against their protests, allotting was begun by BIA personnel in June 1905. All Uncompaghres who had not yet received land, as well as the Uintahs and White Rivers, were allotted acreage (Hall 1905: 353–54). The Uintah and White River tracts were established around the Whiterocks agency and along the rivers on the northern end of the reservation. They were scattered from points approximately ten miles east of Whiterocks near what is now Tridell, and ten miles north of Whiterocks on what is now called Farm Creek, to Tabiona on the Upper Duchesne River some sixty miles west of Whiterocks. The Uncompaghres, on the other hand, were not awarded such disparately scattered tracts of land. In fact, all Uncompaghre allotments were clustered along a twenty-mile stretch of the Duchesne River between Fort Duchesne and Ouray as well as along the rivers that pass Ouray. Thus the federal government kept the groups separated and pleased no one.

The White Rivers were distressed that their reservation land had been allotted against their wishes, that the Uncompaghres had received White River land, and that the whites were moving onto the reservation. They urgently pleaded to be moved from the Uintah reservation to a place where they could hunt and would not be interfered with by whites (Leupp 1906: 78). When this request was not honored, a group of 365 White Rivers of both sexes and all ages left the reservation following Chief Appah.

They wandered north and east through Wyoming, living off the game they killed and some dried meat that they had prepared and stored over the previous few years. After a few months the Indian Office received some erroneous reports that the White Rivers had been killing cattle near Casper, Wyoming; so the U.S. Cavalry was sent out to round them up. They escorted them to the Cheyenne River Sioux reservation in South Dakota. Since the White Rivers did not want to return to Utah, the Indian Office arranged to lease some Sioux land at $1.25 per acre and locate the White Rivers on that land. They also received government services and rations at the Sioux agency.

The renegades refused to work, ate up all the food they had stored, ran short of rations when the government cut back their supplies, and ate up the livestock they had received. In June 1908, two years after they had left Utah, the White Rivers asked to be removed to Whiterocks, Utah. On 21 October 1908, 360 White River Utes were moved back to Utah under military escort (see Leupp 1906: 78–79; 1907: 125–31; 1908: 118–20; Hall 1906: 368).

Allotments originally made to the White Rivers on the Uintah and Ouray reservation in 1905 had been confused because the White Rivers had not identified themselves with their allotments (Leupp 1906: 77). When they returned, the White Rivers were given allotments around Whiterocks, Tridell, Alterra (or the "Bench"), and Myton. Their tracts were interspersed with the tracts held by the Uintah Utes.

In generalizing about the results of the General Allotment Act, Indian Commissioner Francis E. Leupp (1906: 77–79) looked upon the Ute case as a fiasco. He said that there were two ways in which land could be allotted—sanely and foolishly. "The Uintah Reservation in Utah furnishes an example of the rushing and haphazard method" (Leupp 1906: 77). It was allotted without proper survey and without consulting Ute desires. Leupp predicted that trouble would come from the way in which Ute land was allotted. Trouble had already occurred, not because of the way in which the land was allotted, but because it was allotted at all.

In the mid-1880s the reservation boundaries had encompassed nearly four million acres. By 1909 the size of the Uintah and Ouray reservation had shrunk to about 360,000 acres. At this time the Utes jointly owned 250,000 acres that had been set aside as grazing land, and 1,283 Indians had received allotments totaling 103,265 acres. Over 1,000,000 acres were set aside as a national forest, and a little over 2,500,000 acres were redeposited as public domain (Leupp 1909: 124).

In this theft, perpetrated against the general Ute will, the non-Ute mining and ranching interests fared best. They received good range land and mineral resources, which they leased from the government. Homesteaders found that the best land for farming was located along the rivers, and much of this had been allotted. They could not buy this land until Indians were classified as competent to sell, or until the land went out of trust status twenty-five years after allotment. As a consequence, by 1909 only 21,566 acres of land, at about $3.75 per acre, had been purchased by whites (Leupp 1909: 124). More acreage had been homesteaded, but figures were not available for 1909.

Conditions on the reservation as of about 1910 were rather grim. The Northern Ute population in 1881 was 2,825 (representing an enormous decline since 1850). By 1910, following thirty years of residence on the Uintah and Ouray reservation, the population had plunged to 1,180, or 58 percent less than it had been in 1881 (Valentine 1911: 122). The Utes were marginally existing in a mixed hunting, stock raising, and farming economy, which was supplemented by meager government rations. Ute adults had few skills and even less formal education. Out of 221 able-bodied men on the reservation, 11 held regular employment (Indian Service jobs), 75 had irregular employment (wood cutting, wagon driving, etc.), and the rest had no work. Practically all of the men, 215, were partially supporting themselves by raising stock, and 120 of these men are said to have done some farming, although they had no surplus to sell (Valentine 1911: 134–46).

The following example shows the amounts of cattle, sheep and horses owned in 1885 and 1910.

	Cattle	Sheep	Horses, Mules
1885	1,775	1,500	12,720
1910	3,565	2,554	3,695
Change	+1,790	+1,054	−9,025

There is a considerable decline in the size of the horse herds, whereas cattle and sheep increased greatly (RCIA 1885: 390; 1911: 226).

The horse herds had been depleted because the Utes no longer had range land for them and because they found that they could sell them to the whites who were moving into the territory. In 1905 and 1906 they rounded up many horses and sold them for five dollars each, which was well below what they were worth according to Hall (1906: 368). Hall goes on to say that the Utes were using the money to bootleg whiskey from the nearby town of Vernal. There was still a discriminatory law against their buying liquor, but it was circumvented.

Throughout this period of despair and confusion, from 1880 to 1910, one agent after another doggedly attempted to establish and maintain schools on the Uintah and Ouray reservation. Agent Critchlow opened a school on the Uintah reservation in 1876 that operated for three months, but it was closed because few students attended and Critchlow had no money to feed the few who showed up (Critchlow 1876: 130). This early experience set the tenor for the following years. Critchlow again tried to keep schools in session during 1878, 1879, 1881, and 1882. The longest period any of them remained in operation was eight months. Even the Presbyterians, whom Critchlow collared to operate the school in 1881 and 1882, did not have the fortitude and the wherewithal to continue after two seasons (Critchlow 1878: 127; 1879: 138; 1881: 156; 1882: 151).

Between 1883 and 1892 the schools were maintained solely by the agency. During those ten years they operated for perhaps no more than twenty months. In 1883 there were seventeen children attending, while in 1892 only about twenty pupils attended school. In the entire decade, then, there was no significant increase in school attendance (Davis 1883: 140; Waugh 1892: 483).

In 1892 the White River parents agreed to send their children to school only when the agency officials agreed to recognize as their spokesman a man chosen by the Indians. They demanded that the agent's choice be replaced by their own, and the only lever at their disposal was their children and the school issue (Waugh 1892: 483). Until 1894 the only school on the reservation was at Whiterocks, but in that year a school for Uncompaghre children was built four miles south of Fort Duchesne (Randlett 1894: 308–9). The attendance at both schools was low, as most parents were openly hostile to the program and refused to allow their children to attend (Randlett 1896: 618; Cornish 1898: 293; Myton 1900: 391).

At the turn of the century, E. O. Hughes, a recruit schoolteacher at Whiterocks, attempted to find out why students did not attend school. He journeyed all over the vast reaches of the Uintah Basin searching for White River and Uintah children of school age. An arduous two-day drive was required just to reach one of the Uintah hamlets on the northwestern end of the Basin. When he got back from his travels he reported: "I have squatted in their filthy wickiups and counseled with the stubborn savages, only to be told that they had no children, or that their children always died when they went to school, or that they wouldn't let them go" (Hughes 1901: 382).

The Utes fears seem justified. In 1901 a measles epidemic at the Whiterocks school killed seventeen of the sixty-five pupils. On the morning following the first death, "nearly all the patients were taken from their beds and carried away by their parents, and placed in the hands of the Indian Medicine man" (Hughes 1901: 382). The epidemic reached Randlett, where four children died. During the same year Superintendent Myton (1901: 381) wrote: "The health of the Indians has been very good the past year, except that there was considerable measles and chicken pox among the children and some deaths occurred because the Indian medicine men did not give them proper treatment. By the way, the medicine men are a great nuisance and hindrance to the Ute Indians." This cheap, almost detached regard for Indian lives is a hallmark of the opinions found in government and missionary reports. Throughout this book I have called such opinions "racist."

In the following years, up to 1910, the education project continued to founder. In 1904, for instance, five students died at Whiterocks and six students died at Randlett (Ewing 1904: 348; Waddell 1904: 349). Some students were sent away to boarding school. A few attended school on the reservations. Mostly, local teachers lectured to empty classrooms. Recalling now the anonymously filed article in the *Denver Republican* of 3 July 1911 (see chap. 2 at n. 1) which asserted, among other things, that the "young braves" who had returned from the various Indian schools throughout the country had rejected the Sun dance, we see that there is not a shred of evidence to support the assertion that "young braves" had been attending school. Less than a dozen Utes had been sent off to school. The local school experience, on the other hand, with the many deaths registered there and this disregard of Indian wishes, only bolsters the argument that participation in the Sun dance was more apt to increase than decrease during those years. Not only was the underfunded, understaffed, and inappropriate government education program realizing few of its intended good effects on the Utes, but the Utes were hostile toward the teachers and the agents for (1) trying to force Ute children to attend school, (2) letting the children die when they got there, (3) accusing Ute shamans of malpractice, as if they had brought about the deaths of Ute children (which the Indians attributed to the "white plague"), and (4) at the same time coercing the Utes to accept severalty allotments of land.

As for the religions of their white antagonists the Utes were heroically resistant to Christian teachings. Their resistance seems to have far outstripped their resistance to farming, and even government-sponsored educations. After 1870 there was much talk about establishing missions on the Colorado and Utah reservations. For years nothing came of the talk, and Christian proselytizing was done by agents, their wives, or sundry other zealous government personnel. Some agents were more dogged in their missionary work than others, but none had success in instilling Christian principles among their charges. Christian missionaries generally refused to work with the Utes.

In discussing Ute morality and religion, Critchlow noted that they were polygamous, unchaste, believed in a Great Spirit, believed in evil spirits, and showed little affection toward members of their own families. This veiled racism was common among whites, as we have pointed out in other examples, but again the racism was not without some paternalistic compassion. Critchlow (1875: 358–59) also said that the Utes possessed a degree of kindness, justice, and integrity unknown to many whites. These last gratuitous compliments aside, Critchlow thought that there was still room for improvement. He tried in vain to get the Utes to attend Christian services in his home (there was no church building) (1876: 130; 1877: 183). After a few years of failure he said that one could not expect the Utes to attend religious services on the Sabbath because "our services are little understood, and of comparatively little value to them" (Critchlow 1878: 127).

Critchlow seems to have been plumping to get a mission established on the reservation so that the Christian message could be made more clear to the Utes. He did not get a mission, but in 1881 he persuaded the Presbyterian Church to send two schoolteachers out to Whiterocks for a few months. According to his report, neither had sufficient time to proselytize as well as teach.

A somewhat more resourceful fellow, Ouray Subagent McKewen, induced a Unitarian minister to travel west from Boston and set up shop at Ouray in 1885. The minister lasted three weeks, and McKewen commented:

I have yet to see an Indian who professes or has any religious belief, or any idea of the Creator and the great truths of Christianity. . . . [The Unitarian minister] concluded that they [the Uncompaghres] were so intolerably stupid and sullen, and so little inclined to give him even a respectful hearing, that he took his departure . . . without accomplishing anything. [McKewen 1886: 230]

The Ute resistance to racist-sponsored Christianity is not surprising, nor is it surprising that, as the death rate increased and as Ute wishes went unheeded, these beleaguered people would suspect witchcraft and evil power on the part of whites and other Indians as the cause of many of their daily problems. The Utes continued to revere their own shamans, and not white educators, white farmers, white doctors, or white Christians. McKewen writes: "After a residence of four years among the Indians the agency physician is unable to see any appreciable progress towards the abandonment of their medicine men. There are from twenty to thirty of them, all men of influence, and including the most dangerous desperadoes in the tribe" (1886: 228–30).

It is evident from McKewen's comments, and those of practically every other agency employee from 1850 to 1900, that the shamans were considered to be the source of great problems. In the reports to the Commissioner of Indian Affairs it is often asserted that if the shamans who, after all, were dangerous men, were to be removed, the rest of the Utes could be persuaded to become Christians. It was not until about five years after the Utes took up the Sun dance religion that a mission was established on the Uintah and Ouray reservation. In 1895 the Episcopal church built a chapel at Randlett. Later they added one at Whiterocks. They did not have great success in winning more than nominal members, but they kept their doors open almost continuously until 1959.

One Christian, N. C. Meeker, died a violent death at Ute hands, partially because he overreacted when trying to implement his firm Protestant-ethic beliefs. Other Christians, after working three or four years without winning a convert, gave up and concluded that the Utes were stupid, filthy, and perhaps beyond redemption. It was not the Utes' lack of religion but rather their brand of religion that caused Christians such grief.

The Southern and Ute Mountain Ute Reservations

The Utes who had remained in southern Colorado and southeastern Utah did not fare any better than their kin at Uintah and Ouray. Their reservation was reduced to a strip on the New Mexico-Colorado border about 15 miles wide and 110 miles long. Even this was not deemed a sufficient reduction by the whites; there was a strong movement among Coloradoans and a bill in Congress to remove these people, either to the Uintah and Ouray Reservation or to Indian Territory (Oklahoma).

At a council with the federal government in 1880 the Muwach and Kapota Utes agreed to accept land along the La Plata River from Colorado into New Mexico. Yet Congress passed an act only to allot lands to Colorado Utes in severalty at the same time (Swadesh 1962: 9). The agreement made at the Ute council was not honored, but eventually the Congressional act was, at least in part.

The agency town, Ignacio, became the focal point for the Muwach and Kapotas, but the Wiminuch, who detested white encroachment and the relinquishing of lands, generally stayed farther west in the vicinity of Ute Mountain in the southwestern corner of Colorado. A few groups of Wiminuch, particularly those under the direction of Old Polk and Mancos Jim, ranged even farther west in the canyonlands of southeastern Utah. In those westernmost haunts the Wiminuch lived and intermarried with Paiutes, or the Payuchis as Utes call them. The Wiminuch and Payuchis put up the stiffest and most prolonged resistance to whites. Eventually an agency town for the Wiminuch of the Consolidated Ute agency was established at Navajo Springs (later Towaoc), and those who enrolled there became known as the Ute Mountain Utes. Those who stayed around Ignacio retained the name of Southern Utes.

The dominant leader of the Ute Mountain Utes, or Wiminuch, was Chief Ignacio.

He was disgusted with the congressional plan to allot lands in severalty and with the actual allotting which began a few years later. Ignacio held out for, and maintained control of, a 500,000-acre reserve on the western end of the Consolidated Ute reservation. This occurred around the turn of the century.

In the early 1880s the three Colorado Ute bands were still unhappy about the broken treaty promises of 1863, 1868, and 1873. According to Swadesh (1962: 10), in the 1880s the Utes knew the major outlines of their rights and obligations in *all* treaties that had been signed—by them or for them. They did not, of course, know which ones were operative, and why they had not received the money promised to them from the Brunot Agreement of 1873.

In 1881 the Denver and Rio Grande Railroad cut through the reservation from Juanita on the southeast to Durango on the northwest. Compensation was requested but not forthcoming. The towns of Durango (originally Animas City) and Pagosa Springs were growing, and the livestock operations all around them were spreading onto Ute land, destroying the graze and browse for Ute horses, livestock, and the deer and elk the Utes relied on for food (Parkhill 1961: 22, 33–35; Swadesh 1962: 8–12).

Conditions on the reservation from east to west were in turmoil by 1884. On the east, white citizens near Pagosa Springs were furious that the Indians were moving off the reservation to hunt, even though Indian land was being used illegally by some of these selfsame white stockmen. They accused the Indians of thievery and slothfulness and exerted pressures to keep them on the reservations (Swadesh 1962: 11–12). Thus the constitutional guarantees accorded to United States citizens were not extended to Utes, who were denied freedom of movement. Some Indians, however, could leave the reserve to hunt if they obtained permits from their agent (Parkhill 1961).

In the west, the Wiminuch were having constant troubles with cattlemen who used their land. One cattle outfit of twenty-one cowboys, three chuck wagons, a hundred horses, and thousands of head of cattle camped near Montezuma Canyon in eastern Utah. An incident occurred over an Indian horse that was said to have been stolen from a white. A cowboy killed a Wiminuch when he thought the Indian was going to stop him from retrieving the horse. Two more Indians were killed, two cowboys were wounded, the chuck wagons were burned, and some of the white-owned horses were shot. About two weeks later eighty cavalrymen from Fort Lewis, Colorado, attacked the Utes in the Utah canyonlands, but the latter held them off, killing two of them—one a cowboy—in the engagement (Parkhill 1961: 33–35).

Not long thereafter a family of six Utes from the Ute Mountain area were hunting near Beaver Creek above Dolores in southwestern Colorado. One night during this hunting expedition the sleeping family was slain, probably by cowboys (Parkhill 1961: 38). The massacre was allegedly retaliation for the trouble caused by the Utes a little earlier in Montezuma Canyon. In turn the Utes, near Dolores, Colorado, killed a white man and wounded his wife. This second "massacre," according to Parkhill (1961: 37–39) drew headlines in the *Denver Republican:* "INHUMAN MASSACRE BY THE INDIANS:" It prompted many petitions on the part of cattlemen and others to remove the Utes.

So in the mid-1880s the Utes were still getting it from all sides. Racist newspapers wanted the Utes moved, the state and federal governments wanted them moved, the stockmen wanted them moved, and, of course, the Utes did not want to be moved. The federal government left most Indian matters to the impotent Bureau of Indian Affairs. As furors erupted, the BIA could not, and the federal government generally did not, protect Ute Indian rights affirmed and reaffirmed in the treaties of 1868, 1873, and 1880, to wit: "If bad men among the whites or among other people shall commit any wrong upon the person or property of the Indians, the United States will . . . cause the offender to be arrested and punished according to the laws of the United States, and also reimburse the injured person for the loss sustained."[6]

No attempt was made to apprehend and punish white livestock owners for taking Ute land, nor to apprehend and punish those cowboys in 1884 for killing Utes on Ute land and the sleeping family of Utes on Beaver Creek. Partly because he did not want to alienate local whites and partly because he did not think the Indian would receive justice from local whites, the agent at Ignacio at the time of the Beaver Creek massacre did not demand a legal inquiry (Swadesh 1962: 13).

By 1885 the Utes around Ignacio and Ute Mountain were not getting any satisfaction at home and wanted to air their grievances in Washington. They received a curt "no" to their request (Swadesh 1962: 14). A year later Buckskin Charley (Muwach), Tapuche (Kapota), and Ignacio (Wiminuch) were invited to Washington to speak with Commissioner of Indian Affairs Atkins. They requested to exchange their reservation in Colorado for one in Wiminuch-Payuchi country in southeastern Utah (Jocknick 1913: 378). Their list of grievances and reasons for requesting relocation were, following Jocknick (1913: 378–80) and Swadesh (1962: 14–16), roughly as follows: They disliked white encroachment, invasions, and life style. They did not want to be forced to send their children away to school. Indeed, in the 1883–85 school years, twelve of twenty-seven children sent to the Albuquerque school died, and Ignacio's last child was one of them ("When they go away, they die, we cannot account for it"). They again refused to go to Uintah, because there was insufficient land for them. They preferred the mountains, such as the Blues and the La Sals, and especially the canyons of southeastern Utah, because the climate was relatively mild in the winter, because these were traditional hunting grounds, and because they thought that whites would not like the environment. Finally, they strongly protested the withholding of annuity payments and provisions. They very much understood that "these goods are not given to us for nothing, but come from the sale of our lands." Yet, powerless to get their annuities by argument, they had to accommodate themselves to Indian Office demands that they send their children to school in order to receive payment. Many got no annuities because they would not send children to school.

The passage of the General Allotment Act in 1887 more or less resolved the problem. The Utes could choose to be allotted, or they could maintain collective ownership of the reservation's western end. They would not get a new reservation, despite yet another plea from the Wiminuch. About thirty-two families were allotted on the eastern end, and although one of the express purposes of allotting was to create Indian farmers, only one of these families began farming. The others leased their

6. Article 6, Treaty of 1868 (Jocknick 1913: 347–55), reaffirmed in article 5 of the Treaty of 1873 (Jocknick 1913: 366–36), and reaffirmed again in the fifth provision of the Treaty of 1880 (Jocknick 1913: 370–77).

lands to Spanish and Anglos. The Wiminuch, on their part, were so opposed to allotment and farming that they threatened to burn the crops of the Kapota and Muwach should they farm (Swadesh 1962: 16–18).

In 1888, following more deaths of Ute children in government schools and the depletion of the fodder on the Indian range (McCunniff 1888: 23–24), Ignacio and other Utes again negotiated with federal officials for a new reserve to include the area from Dolores to Moab on the east and north, the Colorado River on the west, and the San Juan on the south (Jocknick 1913: 378). By this time Moab and three other Mormon communities—Monticello, Blanding, and Bluff—were established in the designated area. Moreover, cattlemen had a strong lobby to get control of the area and keep Indians out (Jocknick 1913: 378–79). When the Utes were told that Mormons were living in Moab, they said that these should be moved as the Utes themselves had been moved (Swadesh 1962: 20). When they were further told that "desert land entries" had been filed on the area by big cattle outfits, they were not fazed by that either, pointing out that Utes and Payuchis were *already* living there, *self-sufficiently* from livestock and the chase (Parkhill 1961: 17–19). They wanted to establish their own boundaries and they wanted cash and livestock if they could not. They also challenged again the practice of withholding annuities—guaranteed to them by their treaty rights for yielding the land they had subsisted on—unless children were sent to school. The commission agreed with the Indians that "good conduct" was sufficient to receive the annuities per article 17 of the 1868 treaty (Swadesh 1962: 20).

No new reservation was created by 1892, and Chief Ignacio had become such a thorn in the side of the government through his protests and his resistance to white domination that the government refused to recognize him as chief any longer (guaranteed in article 17). This action brought immediate responses from "inveterate Ute-haters" (Swadesh 1962: 23–24) in Durango and from the local agent to the Southern Ute, who feared that Ignacio would cause trouble throughout southwestern Colorado. The bureaucrats in Washington quickly relented and recognized Ignacio as chief again.

In 1895 the Ute populations were depleted, and although a majority had voted for a new and collectively owned reserve in 1888, and a treaty to that end was signed, the new reserve was never established. In fact, in 1895 an act was passed in Congress to disapprove the treaty of 1888 (Jocknick 1913: 378–80). In its stead, 375 Muwach and Kapota Utes were allotted land in severalty. Household heads received 160 acres; minors received 80 acres. Only a few women received land, but some chiefs were given double allotments.

Ignacio and the rest of the Wiminuch would have no part of it, and they succeeded in retaining acreage around and on Mesa Verde and Ute Mountain for hunting and grazing. The lands that were freed after allotting were put back in the public domain and opened to whites at $1.25 per acre.

The general trend from 1895 to 1910 saw the Utes lose more population, land, and access to water. Given the acreage allotted to them, Utes could sustain themselves as farmers only if they had access to water, wanted to farm, were content to be subsistence farmers, received proper instruction and proper farming equipment, and were not the victims of collusion on the part of local whites, agents, and ex-agents to exploit them under the indifferent eye of the government. The Utes, however, wanted to hunt rather than farm; yet during the period the game was further depleted, and except for the Ute Mountain Utes, there was little, if any, self-sufficiency. The Southern Utes lived off rations, annuities, lease income, some hunting, and even less farming and livestock raising.

In an intensive analysis of unpublished communications between Southern Ute agents, the Commissioner of Indian Affairs, and other parties, Swadesh (1962: 41-49) shows how a succession of agents accommodated themselves and the agencies to local white, rather than Indian, interests. Agents used their privileges for their own ends and—in conspiracy with traders, ex-agents, and local businessmen—to use Indian land or purchase it cheaply, and to get free access to Indian water and government-built ditches. The agents played an important role because they could declare men "competent" to sell their allotments, sell the heirship land of those they deemed incompetent, and influence the development of government irrigation ditches. In 1911 alone the Southern Ute agent sold 1,040 acres in heirship status for $4,800 and 1,400 acres of incompetents' land for $11,200. This was done in the name of Indian self-support. The sellers, it was rationalized, would receive funds with which they could manage their affairs.

The General Allotment Act, as envisaged by congressional liberals (who joined with congressional Social Darwinists and their lobbies to pass the legislation), was to make independent family farmers out of Indians and to stop them from receiving welfare. As part of the bargain of accepting allotments, Indians were supposed to learn how to farm. At Southern Ute, Anglos and Spanish, who knew how to farm and wanted to farm, leased Indian land and used Indian water. In 1902, because no surveillance had been maintained of Indian water and Indian water rights, and because whites had built ditches across Indian land, with or without government sanction, the tribe had to go to court to secure water rights. This came about when whites, who were closer to the sources, cut off water in the dry years (Swadesh 1962: 33–34). The Indians, under their many treaties, were supposed to have first title to the water crossing their land.

Through 1910 the farming instruction and equipment that they were supposed to receive was inadequate. The government allocated few funds for equipment and for instruction. The emphasis, even by most of the agents who came and went, was on hand tools and small farm plots. Of course, if Indians could not or did not farm their allotments, whites could lease it cheaply and either steal or pay half the going rate (the latter was part of a federal agreement) for water rights. Swadesh (1962: 69) shows how as early as 1884 the government refused "to sanction the purchases of labor-saving machinery on Indian agencies," and as late as 1906 government officials still refused to allow the agent to purchase sulky or gang plows because the hand plow was considered "sufficient for *their* [Indian] use" (emphasis added).

The government's promise to teach farming to the Indians came up something short of its practice, and petty white entrepreneurial interests—some agents and their local associates—succeeded in using Indian despair and loose federal controls to their own ends. All the while the agency handled Ute funds, deeming the Indians "slow of mind" and incompetent to handle their own affairs. The Utes, of course, distrusted the Bureau of Indian Affairs' handling of their money, but were unable to do anything about it (Swadesh 1962: 81–82).

As the Utes were more and more crowded by whites, the mutual hate did not lessen. On the contrary, local white fears of Utes crystallized into a general racist syndrome, and these fears were often voiced and made in protest to agents, state officials, and the military. The classic fear was that red men would molest unprotected white women, but Swadesh (1962: 67–68) shows that, except for a meal from time to time, Utes made no requests of white women. Even the meal requests stopped when the white population increased and grew more powerful—physically and politically—and the Indians adjusted to their piecemeal lives based on rations, lease income, annuities, some products of the hunt, and so forth.

The Ute Mountain Ute history veers somewhat from that of the Southern Utes. The Wiminuch around Ute Mountain preserved their segment of the reservation and continued to hunt and to raise some livestock. In 1893 these people owned three-fourths of the Consolidated Utes' 4,000 horses, 3,000 sheep, and 1,000 goats (Freeman 1893: 132–34). Unlike their Southern Ute counterparts, they did not knuckle under to white demands and they continued to resist, more or less effectively, for several years to come.

Those Wiminuch and Payuchis who inhabited the canyonlands and mountains of southeastern Utah were called "Bronco" or "Cowboy" Indians and would not settle on the reserves at all. After an agency had been established at Navajo Springs on the south end of Ute Mountain in the late 1890s, they went to Navajo Springs to collect annuities and to participate in Indian affairs, but for little else. Moreover, other Wiminuch and even Southern Utes traveled with these people as late as 1910. (see Parkhill for several interviews with Southern Utes who were directly, or whose parents were directly, involved in altercations with whites in southeastern Utah after 1910.)

The white ranchers continued to contest the Ute Mountain Utes for their land, especially for that land in southeastern Utah that was occupied by Utes, yet was not a reservation. The actions of President Lincoln (1861), Superintendent Doty (1863), and Agent Irish (1865) had caused all Ute land in Utah other than the Uintah reserve to be relinquished, so that land was not set aside in southeastern Utah. A few Utes and Payuchis under Mancos Jim took out homesteads under the Homestead Act in Allen Canyon ("White Mesa" to the Utes) west of Blanding, Utah, but others merely used the river bottoms nomadically, just as did the white ranchers. The difference was that Utes were there first.

The contest for land between the cowboys and the Cowboy Indians intensified between 1900 and 1910. About seventy thousand acres of Ute Mountain Ute hunting territory on and around the Mesa Verde just east of Ute Mountain was relinquished, under duress, in 1906 with passage of the Antiquity Act and the establishment of a national park there (HCIIA 1953: 1009). The Ute Mountain Utes were given a greater amount of "comparable" land north of Ute Mountain in compensation, but this transaction has had a hoary history, and in the 1960s Ute Mountain Utes still protested the loss of the Mesa Verde area.

Sometime between 1895 and 1904 a Ute Mountain Ute shaman, Tonapach, began sponsoring Sun dances at Ute Mountain. Along with other Ute Mountain Utes, he had attended Sun dances at Northern Ute for a few years. Just as General Grant, the Uintah, acquired the power and skills to sponsor the dance at Northern Ute, so did Tonapach acquire the skills and power to perform the dance, to cure suffering, and to bring good health to the community. It is very likely that General Grant and other Northern Utes helped the Ute Mountain Utes sponsor their first few dances. By 1904 the Southern Utes, particularly Edwin Cloud, began sponsoring the dance that they claim to have learned from the Ute Mountain Utes (Stewart 1962: 2). The analysis in chapter 2 suggests that even if the Southern Utes learned the dance from the Ute Mountain Utes, who themselves learned it from Northern Utes, they were attending dances at Northern Ute before they sponsored their own.

The Ute Mountain people repeatedly announced that they wanted to be left alone by whites, and the Sun dance was one more vehicle that allowed them to solve their own problems without white medical and religious intervention. They seem also to have continued to perform Ghost dances in abbreviated one-night sessions from time to time, much as the Northern Utes did before Bear and Sun dances. Parkhill (1961: 94) reports that in 1914 Tsenegat, a Ute Mountain Ute, participated in the Sun dance to cure his persistent upper respiratory problems. Tsenegat is said to have scoffed at a white doctor's advice about how to alleviate it in a different way. Parkhill further reports that Tsenegat participated in a night-long "Spirit dance" or "dance to the gods" two nights before the Bear dance in 1914 (Parkhill 1961: 108, taken from testimony at a federal trial). Whatever the "Spirit dance" was, the Ute Mountain Utes were still trying to maintain their health in an Indian fashion, continue with their hunting-herding subsistence economy, and stay free of whites. The last was impossible, and they were coping with disease (white-induced, directly or indirectly), death, and general misery through a modified Ghost dance and Sun dance.

Tsenegat himself was involved in one of the most sordid chapters of Ute Mountain reservation history when, in 1915, he was accused of killing a Mexican sheepherder on Ute Mountain land. The account is fully treated in Parkhill (1961). Suffice it to say that Tsenegat was never convicted, but news of the alleged murder received national attention, even as editorials in the *New York Times, Saint Louis Post-Dispatch, New York Tribune, Washington Herald, Denver Post,* and other papers. The U.S. marshal in southeastern Utah, a local Mormon, asked Tsenegat to give himself up. He would not, as he claimed innocence and as his Ute friends and relatives advised against turning himself in. Too often the whites had convicted and sentenced Utes without ever having a trial.

The marshal rounded up a posse of twenty-six cowboys in the Cortez-Dolores area on the east side of Ute Mountain in Colorado, because he could not get the local Utah Mormons to join him. He then set out to bring Tsenegat in for trial. The marshal had previously told Old Polk and Posey, the leaders of the camps where Tsenegat lived, that he would come peacefully to get Tsenegat. Actually, the cowboys, half-drunk, stole up to Tsenegat's camp at night and positioned themselves on the rocks above the canyon in which it was located. The Indian dogs heard them and began barking. The Ute families awoke and tried to flee. Without warning, the marshal and the cowboys opened fire and killed three adults and two children. A woman was drowned as she fell off her horse in the river. The posse could not catch the fleeing Utes because the Indian men from Old Polk's and Posey's camps held them off with gunfire of their own, and the posse got caught behind a barbed wire cattle fence between them and the Indian camp.

The renegade Utes, about a hundred in total, headed for the Navajo Mountain area to the west. The Mormons and the marshal held a "war council"; fugitive warrants were issued against *all* Utes who had resisted the sneak attack; and the decision was made to round up *all other* Utes in southeastern Utah. The marshal made good on the council's decision. Posses were sent out to round up Indian home-steaders and every other Indian they could find. They incarcerated and tortured some young Indian men and sent the rest, about 160, to the Ute Mountain Ute agency. The War Department became worried because the volatile situation was receiving con-siderable coverage in the national press at a time when they felt that U.S. domestic "wars" should long have been terminated. They sent General Hugh L. Scott (1928) to the scene to take command before the marshal and the cowboys could wage all-out war on the Indians and vice versa.

Scott arrived about three weeks after the posse's sneak attack, relieved the marshal of his command, and disbanded the "gunmen"—between seventy-five and a hundred of them—who had flocked to the scene. He conferred with a trader to the Navajo, John Wetherill, and with Posey and Old Polk, the leaders of the camps that had been attacked. Scott and Wetherill got these men and Tsenegat to travel with them to the U.S. attorney in Salt Lake City, where the charges against all but Tsenegat were dropped (Scott 1928).

Scott (1928) wrote that he thought the whites had been the aggressors, but that this could be proved only by Indian witnesses "whose word would not be taken against that of white men." The *Montezuma Journal* in Cortez, Colorado, soon an-nounced that "fine farm land near Bluff . . . is open to entry. . . . There is also good range close which makes it good stock country" (Parkhill 1961: 90–91). This more or less sums it up: the whites won, the Indians had no appeal. A few Utes filtered back to Allen Canyon in 1920, and by 1928 there were forty-one Utes in San Juan County, Utah. The Allen Canyon Utes were promised a new federal school in 1928 (RCIA 1928), but it was never built for them. This episode characterizes the discrepancy between federal promises to the Utes and federal practices.

As of about 1910 all the major Ute populations in Colorado and Utah had been defeated, depleted, and corralled onto areas with poor resources for farming, and they had then lost the vast majority of even these areas as they proved valuable for mineral and ranching industries. The populations that subjected the Utes had the advantage of legal and economic privilege, and they coupled these privileges with bigotry (for example, characterizing Indians as slothful and dirty) to justify their gains at the expense of the Utes. Ute treaty rights, so often denied in practice, were but a sham of their intent, and the Utes had no access to the locus of power to assure constant or even sporadic guarantees of these rights.

THE NORTHERN SHOSHONE-BANNOCKS

Before 1850

Before 1850 the Northern Shoshones were stretched from the Rocky Mountains of Montana and Wyoming on the east to the Snake River, along what is now the Oregon-Idaho border, on the west. And they were scattered from the Bitterroot Mountains, Lemhi Valley, and Yellowstone Park area on the north to the Uintah Mountains, Bear River, Goose Creek Mountains, and Snake River valley on the south (see map 2).

They hunted, gathered, and, in the extreme western and northern parts of the territory, fished. From the late 1600s on they had horses, acquired from the Utes to the south. Sometime in the early 1700s the Bannocks—Northern Paiutes from the Snake River and Blue Mountain area in eastern Oregon—joined with Shoshones and moved into the Snake River valley, Lemhi valley, and Bridger Basin. From these areas they traveled with Shoshones out onto the plains in quest of bison and on raids on other tribes. The Bannocks learned to speak Shoshone but also retained their own language, which is distinct. The evidence shows that the Bannocks were not organized into a single residence group. At any given time some might have been traveling with one or two Shoshone bands and some might have been living only with other Bannocks. It is important to note that the Bannocks were not a single tribe in a single territory. They followed several influential leaders of their own, and like the Shoshones with whom they traveled, they moved from one leader to another.

As early as 1730 the Shoshones are reported as regular hunters and raiders on the plains, known as far east as the Black Hills of Dakota and north into Canada. Throughout 1850 and even beyond, Shoshone-Bannocks were often seen east of the Big Horn Mountains in northeastern Wyoming. On the other hand, these horse-using Indians were also seen in the Snake River valley throughout the 1820s, 1830s, and 1840s by trappers and traders. When they came back from hunting and living with other bands, groups of Shoshones and Bannocks often returned to the camps of their non-horse-using Bannock and Shoshone counterparts as far west as eastern Oregon. They might reside with their less mobile congeners for as long as two years (see Stewart 1966a). Thus some people—perhaps the aged, the infirm, some of the very young, and some who simply did not desire to go on the chase—remained in Idaho, northern Utah, and eastern Oregon, hunting deer and rabbits, fishing, and gathering seeds, nuts, roots, and berries.

The flexibility of band composition is well attested, as is the mobility of bands. It appears that the more mobile and flexible hunting bands were drawn together by influential hunters, fighters, and talkers. Perhaps none was more successful in leading and holding large groups of people (150 to 300 lodges) together over a long period of time than Washakie, a nineteenth-century leader of the most easterly Shoshones from the Bridger Basin–Wind River area of Wyoming (see Hebard 1930; Trenholm and Carley 1964).

When Shoshones and Bannocks moved out onto the plains, they apparently recognized themselves as raiders. In these forays they often dealt with the Crow, Blackfeet, Dakota and Arapaho. On the other hand, when the Crow, Blackfeet, Dakota, and Arapaho ventured into the mountains, they apparently recognized that they were trespassing on Shoshone territory. As Stewart (1966a) points out, Washakie and other Shoshones attended the Fort Laramie treaty council of 1851 and, although they did not sign the treaty, they apparently gave tacit agreement to the treaty itself, which claimed that the territory *east* of the Rocky Mountains was for the Dakota, the Arapaho, the Cheyenne, the Blackfeet, and the Crow. This did not, of course, stop the Shoshones and Bannocks from going east or the eastern groups from moving west.

These were the good times for the Shoshones. Like the Utes to the south, they were splendid horsemen and hunters, had huge horse herds, and reveled in the chase. After 1850 they began more and more to feel the pinch of Anglo expansion, and good times turned to bad as Shoshones and Bannocks lost their land, their freedom to roam and hunt in the mountains, and their access to the plains. Pressures were initially felt in the 1830s as travel along the Oregon Trail thickened. The Shoshone-Bannock response to this was to harass and plunder the wagon trains, just as the Utes were doing along the Santa Fe trail. By the 1840s the movement along the trail was even heavier, and in 1847 the Mormons moved into Shoshone territory along the Platte and Sweetwater rivers to South Pass and through Bridger Basin, and then settled in the Salt Lake valley. Mormon settlers poured into Shoshone and Ute territory and commandeered the irrigable land. Gold, silver, lead, and other minerals were discovered in the Lemhi, Virginia City, and South Pass areas, and, with the influx of miners that followed, still more Shoshone land was commandeered. The building of the Overland Trail and the Union Pacific Railroad to link the expanding economic metropolises of the east and the west consumed still more Shoshone territory and gave still more access to that area which had not yet been taken from them. These developments changed forever Shoshone economic and social organizations, their religion, and their general life styles, but not without a fight.

AFTER 1850

Shoshone and Bannock resistance to white encroachment took several forms. Indeed, the Shoshones practiced all of the forms of resistance that were practiced by their Ute congeners, some of it even being carried out in conjunction with Utes. At times some of the bands fought. At other times bands fled, or fought and then fled. At other times they signed treaties. And at still other times religious movements—at first for the transformation of the entire conditions in which bands lived and later for the redemption of each religious participant—swept through the Shoshone-Bannock groups. As with the Utes, it is not suggested that resistance evolved from fight, to flight, to treaties, and to religion. On more than one occasion religion was appealed to in order to solve Indian problems, yet fighting soon followed whether or not Indians lost faith in religious solutions. On other occasions treaties were signed, only to be broken by the United States government, whereupon the Shoshones and Bannocks again began fighting to save what remained of their territory, resources, and sovereignty.

The history of Northern Shoshones and Bannocks from about 1850 on is indeed sad. As it was for their Ute counterparts, the history of the oppression and deprivation of the Shoshones has been written on several occasions and in much more detail than is necessary for my purposes here. Besides the works of Shimkin (1942, 1947, 1953) and Stewart (1960a, 1966b) cited above, I refer the reader to Hebard (1930), Brimlow (1938) and Trenholm and Carley (1964) for more complete details.[7] The interpretation of Northern Shoshone-Bannock history is mine, although it has been influenced in one way or another by my more intensive analysis of Ute history as well as by all of the authors mentioned above.

With the intent of achieving clarity rather than confusion, and following the format

7. A special note should be taken of Grace Raymond Hebard's *Washaki: An Account of Indian Resistance of the Covered Wagon and Union Pacific Railroad Invasions of their Territory* (1930). Dr. Hebard was a political economist at the University of Wyoming. She dug out many letters and reports other than those of Indian agents and also interviewed some of the early settlers in the Lander, Wyoming, area.

I established for the Utes, I will deal with the Bridger Basin or Wind River Shoshones of Wyoming separately from the Northern Shoshones and Bannocks of Idaho and Utah. The Shoshone histories are parallel in many respects, and there was indeed movement of personnel among bands; but from the 1840s on, even though Bannocks and Shoshones from the west joined him from time to time, Washakie kept the Wind River group together and signed all treaties from 1863 through 1896 to which they were a part. His strong influence surely affected the responses made by the Wind River Shoshones to a continuous series of unhappy relations with whites of power and influence, just as Douglas, Tabby, and Ignacio exerted considerable influence on the Ute people who followed them.

The Wind River Shoshones of Wyoming

In 1847 Mormon wagon trains began moving through the southern part of the Shoshone territory. By the time they reached the Bridger Basin area several mountain men, including Joe Meek and Jim Bridger, were operating the ferries on the Green River (Trenholm and Carley 1964: 105–33). Brigham Young was preparing for many more caravans of Mormons from the eastern United States, and he invited Washakie to Salt Lake City in order to make sure that the Mormon wagon trains would receive safe passage. He also wanted Washakie to stop fighting the Utes. Both groups were in the territory of his State of Deseret. In 1852 Washakie counseled with Indian Superintendent Brigham Young and Ute Chief Walker, with whom Washakie had battled, in Salt Lake City. Young thanked Washakie for his friendship, pledged to support Washakie, and influenced Walker and Washakie to make peace with one another (see p. 34).

Later in that year Young sent about forty Mormons to the Bridger Basin to settle the area and to take over control of the Green River ferries (Hebard 1930: 78–79; Trenholm and Carley 1964: 133–34). The Shoshones, who had lived amicably with the mountain men for thirty years, were angered by the squatters and their attempt to gain control of the main access through the area. So they banded together with the mountain men around Fort Bridger and chased the Mormons off.

Brigham Young, infuriated by Jim Bridger's actions on this occasion, and also by the fact that Bridger was selling rifles and ammunition to Indians within Young's State of Deseret, sent thirty-nine missionaries, well armed and commissioned as military troops, to the Bridger Basin. These men were followed by another fifty-three about two weeks later (Hebard 1930: 79). They intended to pacify the area and proselytize the Indians. As a first act they ransacked Bridger's fort, stole the livestock, and killed two of the three mountain men there. Jim Bridger could not be found (Brown 1900: 312–60). Following these acts, one hundred Mormons settled on Smith's Fork of the Green River, gained control of the Green River ferries, and slowly but surely located elsewhere in the south end of Bridger Basin from Lyman on the east to Evanston on the west (see maps 2, 3, 4, and 5).

The Mormons continued to make inroads in Wyoming, and in 1855 a group of missionaries met with Washakie and an encampment of three thousand Shoshones near what is now known as the Piney area in the extreme northern part of the Bridger Basin, over a hundred miles north of the Mormon settlements on Smith's Fork. They offered the Shoshones a *Book of Mormon* and added that they would teach them to farm. The general Shoshone response was at odds with Washakie's response, yet Washakie's position is consonant with the positions he took in most subsequent meetings with whites, and, on significant issues, his advice was usually followed. Many Shoshones requested things that they could use, such as food, knives, rifles, lead, and caps, rather than a book. One Indian man said that the book might have some value if the pages were torn out and sewn into a bag. The bag, he suggested, could have been used to carry money, if the Indians had any money. Washakie, on the other hand, lectured to the Mormons and Shoshones alike. He told the Shoshones that soon the buffalo would be gone. He then gave a peculiarly Mormon analysis of the Indian's predicament. He recognized that the whites had much greater technological skill than Indians, making such things as revolvers and pocket watches. Washakie attributed this skill, and the power to control the lives of whites and Indians alike which stemmed from it, to the "Great Father" who, out of anger, had turned his back on the dark-skinned Indian, causing his mind to go dark, and had shone his face on the light-skinned white man (Brown 1900: 350–64).

The sum of his speech was that the Shoshones would have to accommodate themselves to white men if they wished to live. He was very clear about the evidence for white superiority. He did not base his argument on Mormon philosophy alone—a philosophy he had learned from Brigham Young, James Brown, and probably a few others. He said that, whereas once the Shoshone country had been covered with deer, elk, buffalo, and antelope, and whereas once there was plenty to eat and enough hides for clothes, bedding, and lodging, this was no longer true. He stated it was no longer true because whites had made roads across Indian land and had killed off their game (Brown 1900: 360).

About a year later, after the Mormons had gained control of the Green River ferries and were expanding their settlements in southwestern Wyoming (northeastern Territory of Utah), Washakie and seven other Shoshone men rode into the northern-most ferry site near the confluence of the Green and Big Sandy rivers. According to Brown, Washakie, who had drunk some liquor, looked at the settlement with its stores, stables, and farms, and shouted that the country the Mormons had taken was Shoshone and had been for generations. He decried the usurpation of the land, the burning of all the dry wood, and the loss of game through white killing and through being chased out of the area because there was no place for them to feed or drink. Washakie said that when Indians returned from the hunt and ventured into the Mormon towns, they were often castigated and ordered out. On more than one occasion his men threatened retaliation, but violence had always been averted. He added that he was tired of white supremacy, for whites loved only themselves. Washakie then issued an ultimatum that if *any* whites were found east of the Green or north of the Sandy rivers on the following day, they would be killed (Trenholm and Carley 1964: 148–49).

After purging himself of his feelings, Washakie must have thought further about the possible consequences of his statements, for on the following morning he returned with fifteen men (the Mormons had withdrawn across the river) and told them that the Shoshones and whites could live amicably together. Thus again Washakie expressed his own feelings, analyzed the predicament of the Shoshones, and made both clear. But when he had to choose among alternatives about how to cope with white encroachment, he decided to conciliate rather than fight. He did indeed respect white power.

Washakie's attitude toward Mormon encroachment on Shoshone land can be inferred from the events of 1857. Brigham Young and the Mormon church's relationship with the federal government had deteriorated over the years for several reasons. The Mormons wanted to govern the Territory of Utah (their State of Deseret) in their own fashion. The federal government was exasperated with Brigham Young and the Mormons because of a score of incidents involving violations of federal laws, such as (1) the refusal of the Mormons to stop practicing polygyny, (2) the treasonous attempts to persuade Indians to join the Mormons in warfare against federal troops, (3) the withholding of records subpoenaed by the government, (4) the issuance of threats against a federal judge, and (5), the intimidation and obstruction of federal officers (Hebard 1930: 87; Trenholm and Carley 1964: 155). President Buchanan appointed a new governor and ordered other changes in the government of the Utah territory. He also sent 2,500 troops from Fort Laramie to pacify the Mormon state. Jim Bridger joined them and guided them into the Salt Lake area, and Washakie offered 1,200 Shoshone warriors to join in the battle *against* the Mormons (Trenholm and Carley 1964: 157).

During the later 1850s the Shoshones had problems with other Indians, such as Crows, Arapahos, and Dakotas, as well as whites; but whites directly contributed to these inter-Indian problems by usurping Indian land, killing the animals they hunted, and forcing the various Indian groups to compete for the ever-dwindling game resources. For instance, the Shoshones were involved in many battles over bison and territory with the Crows. In one battle alone, forty-nine Shoshones were killed. During the same period the government, through the Indian Office and an agency established at Fort Bridger, had promised but failed to deliver gifts and annuities to the Shoshones. As Indian resources and access to them shrank, and as inter-Indian conflicts over resources increased, the gifts and annuities took on more and more significance. Moreover, the gifts were construed as obligations on the part of the government in return for the safe passage guaranteed by the Shoshones for the Pacific Wagon crews that were cutting an overland wagon route through the area. When the goods were not delivered, Washakie informed the agent and the director of the wagon road operation that his people were being cheated. He threatened to fight. In 1858 some Bannocks and Shoshones had already acted on their threats to rid the Lander area of whites, and had burned down a wagon road supply depot (Trenholm and Carley 1964: 72).

Frederick W. Lander, the superintendent of the wagon road project, found the Shoshones bothersome and potentially dangerous. As a solution to his problems with them he requested the Bureau of Indian Affairs to give him enough money or supplies to make recompense for any damages or injuries that might be inflicted to the Shoshones, and to provide rewards for friendly cooperation as the wagon road was developed across their land (Hebard 1930: 94–95). His request for a carrot rather than a stick was granted in 1859. The benefits were to be received by the Wind River Shoshones as well as the Shoshones in Idaho and northern Utah.

The wagon road, which became the Overland Trail, was pushed on through Wyoming and eastern Idaho. Near what is now Pocatello, Idaho, one route branched south to California through the Raft River–Goose Creek area of northwestern Utah (avoiding Salt Lake City), and the other continued east to Oregon via the Camas Prairie–Snake River route. Confrontations with Indians increased all along the line as more and more wagon trains pushed through. After 1860 the incidence of depredations on these trains increased, but the depredations were generally west of Washakie's territory. It is alleged that Washakie lost some of his following because he refused to wage war against the whites during the late fifties and early sixties (Trenholm and Carley 1964: 18). Yet at the same time the Shoshone population was being depleted through warfare with other Indians and irregular confrontations with whites. It is more likely that Washakie lost some of his following through deaths incurred from inter-Indian warfare, starvation, disease, and freezing. Others were probably lost on a temporary basis as they splintered off to hunt during times of need or joined with bands engaged in minor raiding and plundering. It is doubtful that Washakie lost much of his following simply because he would not wage full-scale war.

By 1862 the Bannock-Northern Shoshones, including the Wind Rivers, were so angered by the development of the Overland Trail that they attacked all the stations on it from the headwaters of the Platte in Wyoming on the east to the Bear River in northern Utah and southern Idaho on the west. They drove off the horses and mules, left stages and passengers stranded, but killed only one person—at Sweetwater in Wyoming. The attack, which paralyzed the line, was the joint effort of several Bannock and Shoshone leaders, apparently under the direction of a Bannock, Pasheco (Trenholm and Carley 1964: 190–93).

The Bannock-Shoshones in Idaho and northern Utah were ready to wage a wider war against the whites, and tried—unsuccessfully—to enlist the Gosiutes, Western Shoshones, and Weber Shoshones to help. A battle did occur when a white, following a mock trial, executed four Bannocks and Shoshones in the Bear River, Raft River Mountains, and Goose Creek Mountains area. These populations, in turn, issued a threat of death to whites unless they stayed south of the Bear River. Some whites ventured north and were killed. This brought the military north into the Bear River area in January of 1863. In this so-called war the cavalry caught the bands of Sagwitch, Sanpitz, and Bear Hunter near Franklin, the Mormon community. They killed 224 Indians, took 175 horses, and destroyed 70 lodges (Hebard 1930: 107–9; Trenholm and Carley 1964: 195–97). The 160 Shoshone women and children who lived through it and who were found hiding, were listed as "captured" but were left there stranded, without men, horses, or lodges in the dead of winter. The military solution to the Indian problem was often more direct and final than the solutions reached by the Indian Office.

The "War of 1863," following the Shoshones' and Bannocks' relatively peaceful attempt to regain control of their territory, led to several treaty signings with the Shoshone-Bannocks during the summer of the same year. The Wind River Shoshones were not actually involved in the war on the Utah-Idaho border, but the first treaty council was held at Fort Bridger, and a thousand Shoshones attended, led by Washakie and several other men of influence. Superintendent Doty (1863: 392–96) and Agent Mann (1863: 204–5) were responsible for the treaty and for pressing, but not forcing, the Shoshones to reside on reservations. The Shoshones, on their part, had to declare perpetual peace with whites and safe passage to all who should travel on the Overland Trail. They also had to yield yet another right of way across their land for the projected transcontinental railroad. The building of the railroad was only one issue at the council; yet the railroad was soon to make obsolete the cross-continent wagon trains as well as the hunting of bison and the roaming of Indians.

The Shoshones at Fort Bridger represented a half-beaten and discouraged people, and although the treaty was signed by ten leaders, including Washakie, many young men in attendance did not want to give in to white demands and more white control of what were once Shoshone lands. They were angry with the agreement and wanted to fight. The government established the Wind River boundaries from the Platte River on the east to an unspecified point in the west, and from the Snake River–Jackson Hole area on the north to the Uintah Mountains on the south. The western boundary was never clear, but the total area was at least seven million acres. Moreover, the government promised to take care of the wants of the Bridger Basin–Wind River people by giving them $10,000 worth of annuity goods each year for twenty years.

Two more treaties were signed with Bannock–Northern Shoshone groups later that year at Box Elder, Utah, and Soda Springs, Idaho, and two were signed with Gosiutes and Western Shoshones at Tooele, Utah. Each treaty defined the territory

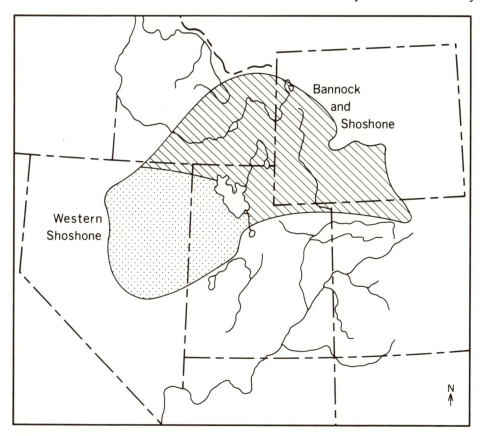

MAP 8. Area ceded to Western Shoshones and to Northern Shoshones and Bannocks in Doty's five treaties of 1863. Adapted from Stewart 1966*a*.

of the groups in question, provided annuities, and called for perpetual peace. That is, each group was promised a small amount of goods and was denied the right to defend the territory from further encroachments. Each treaty also granted the right of whites to search for precious minerals, establish mines, and lay railroads in the territory. Doty (1863) argued that these rights were necessary and could only be appreciated by those who understood and valued the "commercial-mercantile world." By omission he suggested that Indians could not appreciate the importance of the government's actions. Indeed they could not, because they were not apprised of the implications of the treaties.

The fifth treaty, that with Bannocks and Shoshones in the Lemhi area signed at Soda Springs, Idaho, violated the first treaty at Fort Bridger because it gave these people a share of the annuities promised to the Wind River people—without apprising the latter of the action—and established the eastern boundary for the Bannocks and Shoshones at the Wind River Mountains, which was only two score miles or so west of the line that was established as the eastern boundary of the Wind River area some five months earlier.

In 1865 Washakie complained on several occasions that the Shoshones were not receiving their promised annuities. The discrepancy between the government's promise and its practice was again wide. So, at Superintendent Irish's request, Washakie rode to Salt Lake in order to counsel with him. He told Irish that his people were freezing and starving to death. They needed food, not talk (Trenholm and Carley 1964: 212). During this same year the Crows, Cheyenne and Dakota, themselves being pushed from pillar to post in quest of the dwindling herds of game, tried to get the Wind River Shoshones to join them in an attack on the whites. They wanted to rid the area of whites. Washakie refused, just as he had refused similar requests from Shoshones and Bannocks; the Dakota, in turn, threatened to attack Washakie. Washakie's people were getting broken promises on one side and threats on the other; yet Washakie continued to negotiate and conciliate, rather than fight whites. The Dakota made good on their threat and attacked Washakie's camp on the Sweetwater. Washakie rallied the Shoshones after an initial loss and routed the Dakota (Hebard 1930: 111–12; Trenholm and Carley 1964: 214).

By now the gold veins that had been discovered in the South Pass–Sweetwater area of the Wind River territory were attracting attention, along with many miners and prospectors. Moreover, the Union Pacific Railroad was under construction across eastern Wyoming. In order to continue the move west, the railroad wanted title to the land, and so the government set out to extinguish the Indian title (Hebard 1930: 117–18). This meant, simply, that the treaty of 1863 had to be broken.

Informal councils were held with Taggee (a Bannock chief known to hunt and travel sometimes with Washakie, sometimes with Tendoy, an influential Lemhi chief, and sometimes only with his own people) and Washakie about establishing reservations outside the mineral areas and away from the proposed railroad routes (Hebard 1930: 118–43). When Taggee was queried by government officials about his amenability to a reserve, he asked in return why whites came into Shoshone territory without consent, and why he could find nothing to hunt. He said he would accept a reservation if it were large and had no whites, except for those whites who were supposed to provide services as part of the agreement. He wondered why the soldiers who were assigned to protect the Lemhi Shoshone-Bannocks ten years earlier had left and had not returned. In brief, the government had made promises that they had not kept. Taggee saw this as deceitful and he did not trust those who did the government's bidding at this meeting. As a condition to be met before he would accept a treaty at a future date, he wanted guarantees of free movement and right of way for his people so that they could carry on their hunting-gathering life.

This informal council set the stage for the treaty of 1868 signed at Fort Bridger. The treaty reduced Wind River Shoshone land to about 2.8 million acres temporarily shared with Taggee and his followers. It called for annuities over the next thirty years, education for Shoshones, land allotments to individual Indians, farming instruction, buildings, and so forth. Washakie agreed to the treaty *only if he could continue to go over the mountains and hunt wherever he pleased* (Hebard 1930: 123). That is, Washakie desired to travel east over the Big Horns, and west over the Wind Rivers and Tetons.

The roadbed and railroad tracks were laid, and the transcontinental railroad was completed and joined near Great Salt Lake in May 1869. The building of the railroad brought many bison skinners to the plains and mountains in quest of hides. It is estimated that there were sixty million bison in the midwest and west as late as 1860, but they were an obstacle to trains and to cattle grazing. The railroad and cattle interests solved their mutual problems by hiring bison skinners to destroy the bison (Klose 1964: 79–80). This was accomplished in the late 1860s and early 1870s. By 1885 fewer than a thousand bison remained in the United States (Klose 1964: 80). During 1868 and 1869 hundreds of thousands of bison were killed by white buffalo skinners along the eastern foothills of the Rockies in Wyoming, and Indian-Indian and Indian-white skirmishes increased. Taggee and his band had been hunting with Washakie. Now he returned to Idaho.

In 1870 the Ghost dance swept east to the Wind River Shoshones of Bridger Basin, as reported above, and the Bannocks and Northern Shoshones, along with the Utes, danced it fervently. This is the first evidence for Northern Shoshones' turning to supernatural means to rid themselves and their territory of whites. It was not the only movement to which Northern Shoshones appealed during the period, and it did not stop further resistance to white domination among the more westerly Shoshone–Bannocks. The Bridger Basin–Wind River Shoshones not only accepted and sponsored it, but proselytized Utes to join in as well. Except for the white life taken on the Sweetwater when the Shoshones paralyzed the wagon trail in 1862, there is little evidence that the most easterly Shoshones, who had put their hopes, and perhaps faith, in the treaties signed by Washakie, ever took the more violent alternative and fought their oppressors. Even the action in 1862 took only one non-Indian life. So the adoption of a religious movement in hopes of transforming Shoshone life and Shoshone context makes considerable sense among people who had followed nearly twenty years of the same advice, to wit: do not fight the overwhelmingly powerful whites.

Things got worse rather than better. The Arapaho, the Crow and the Dakota attacked white miners in the South Pass area. They also attacked the Shoshones at Wind River. Many Shoshones who received some of the annuities promised to them still faced starvation during the winter of 1871. In 1872 Felix Brunot, the man who had negotiated the deceitful agreement with the Utes to relinquish some of their most mineral-rich land in Colorado, induced Washakie and 118 other Shoshone men to make still another agreement, giving up 600,000 acres of mineral-rich land below the North Fork of the Big Popo Agie River for $5,000 worth of cattle and soldiers' rations during each of the following five years (Hebard 1930: 141–43; cf. Shimkin 1942: 453). This averted some starvation among Wyoming Shoshones for the next half-decade.

In 1874 about 125 Shoshones joined forces with the U.S. army in an attack on the Arapahos, and in 1876 they again joined with the U.S. army, this time in a battle against the Dakota (Shimkin 1942: 453). These attempts to protect their own boundaries and to ingratiate themselves with the U.S. army by attacking their old nemeses, thus providing more secure alliances with the military, are completely understandable. The Wind River Shoshones had consistently acted on the white man's treaties as if the whites were going to honor them. They also sided with the government responsible for the treaties in other instances. But the Shoshone collaboration with the U.S. army did not greatly change their circumstances, nor did it cause the federal government to live up to all of its obligations. In 1877 the Shoshones went out on the plains to hunt, but came back hungry and with few bison. Moreover, whites were spreading out on reservation land, squatting and grazing their cattle, and the government did nothing about it. Not surprisingly, the Shoshones continued to leave their agency near Lander and return to the Bridger Basin, which was no longer part of their reservation, to perform the Ghost dance.

The following year several Wyoming Shoshones joined the military in tracking down some other Northern Shoshones and Bannocks who were hiding in the Yellowstone Park–Bitterroot Mountain area following an uprising in Idaho (Trenholm and Carley 1964: 264). Coincident with their actions, on 18 March 1878 the U.S. government placed 938 starving Arapahos on land ceded to the Wind River Shoshones (Trenholm and Carley 1964: 278). The Wind River Shoshones, long the enemies of the Arapaho, did not agree to this move, and many years later went to court over it. However it came about, Arapaho preempted two-thirds of the best land and began sharing in all proceeds from the reservation as well as government rations (Shimkin 1942: 454). The federal government was extremely insensitive to Shoshone feelings and simply denied them their 1863, 1868, and 1872 treaty rights. In rather simple terms, no important distinctions between Indians were recognized, and one solution to the Indian problem was deemed sufficient in the Wyoming case: push them all together. The thought and the action were racist.

Hebard (1930: 209–10) reports that Washakie asked Agent Patten and other government officials when they intended to move the Arapahos, whom they did not want on the reservation. Hebard (1930: 211–12) also cites another of Washakie's eloquent appeals, this time to Governor Hoyt of Wyoming. Washakie had said many of the same things in his other recorded meetings with whites during the previous twenty-five years, but again he chose to trust whites rather than to lose what little he had left in battle with them, and he was able to maintain control over his followers.

Washakie told Hoyt that words could not express the grief Shoshones felt from their hunger, their misery, and their suffering at the hands of whites. He said that their desperation and bitterness often tempted them to take up arms, which they had not done. He denounced the corralling of Indians on reservations and their being denied access to old hunting grounds, while whites roamed freely, and he feared reprisals by the U.S. army should his people attempt to leave their reservation. As for the reserve, Washakie decried the encroachment of white-owned livestock on it and the liberties whites had taken in killing off the game. Throughout he recounted the promises broken by the government, and the lack of food, comfort, and implements on the reservation.

Hoyt was moved. He telegraphed the Secretary of the Interior to send supplies immediately and to keep sending supplies. Hoyt's solution to the problem, like those of Lander and several other nonmilitarists, was humane, yet neocolonialist. He wanted to keep Indians on the reservation for their own protection, and to feed, clothe, and educate them (Hebard 1930: 213–14).

The Shoshones received their supplies, but many continued to participate in the Ghost dance in 1879. During the same year another religious movement, or perhaps merely an accretion to the Ghost dance, was briefly generated when a number of Wind River Shoshone men slipped off the reservation one night and headed for Salt Lake City to be baptized into the Mormon church (Shimkin 1942: 456). The object of the baptism by immersion was to reunite Shoshones with their deceased and departed friends and relatives. The Mormons believe that baptism is one of several ritual acts that will assure reuniting of kin in an afterlife, and this belief dovetailed very well with the Ghost dance ideology prevalent at that time. The Ghost dance, however, called for reunification to the exclusion of whites. The flirtation with Mormonism was short-lived, perhaps because their ritual act did not bring the desired and promised effects.

Between 1880 and 1896 the population dwindled, as did the game, the rations, and Shoshone spirits (Shimkin 1942: 454–57; 1953: 428–37). During this time missions and agency schools were established; some Indians farmed; and, according to Shimkin (1942), rations were made available only if Shoshones sent their children to school (the same device used on the Colorado Utes). It was in this period, when Shoshone movements off the reserve were severely restricted, that the Sun dance ideology changed from that of a ritual performed to insure bravery and success in war and on the bison hunt to an ideology that allowed people to live together in an odious world and to cope with their ill health and penury (Shimkin 1953: 434–35). The Ghost dance and other native religions were forbidden by the government after 1890. Only Christianity was acceptable. So as the Sun dance was reworked and performed, it was disguised by other names (the "Sand dance" or "Half dance" according to Shimkin 1953) and became crystallized into the redemptive religious movement that still flourishes among Utes, Northern Shoshones, and Bannocks. Mooney (1892–93: 808) states that the Wind River Shoshones had "lost faith" in the Ghost dance, although they performed it a couple of times in 1889 and 1890. The major ideological change from a hope for cultural transformation, as promised by the Ghost dance, to a hope for personal redemption, some cultural restoration, and accommodation with life as it was, as promised by the new Sun dance, seems to have occurred in the 1880–95 period. The Sun dance gradually replaced the Ghost dance but, as in the Ute case, was greatly modified, and very brief versions of the latter often attend Sun dances to this day.

The practices of taking resources from the Shoshones, denying them access to those resources which they retained title to, and denying them legal treaty rights such as unimpeded movement, still flourished. Part of the white justification for the continuation of these practices was that the Indian population was getting smaller and that Indians were not using their resources. In 1896 the government got the Wind River Shoshones and Arapahos to relinquish 64,000 acres recognized as Shoshone-owned in 1863, 1868, and 1872, around the Thermopolis hot springs. This was done so that whites could own the mineral hot springs health spa, which had been used by Shoshones for over two centuries (Hebard 1930: 215–17). The Arapahos shared in the sixty thousand dollars' worth of cattle and supplies that were traded for the land. Washakie signed the treaty. In the same year the Wind River Shoshones were denied the right to travel to the Jackson Hole area hunting grounds because Indians proved bothersome to tourists (Shimkin 1942: 453). We will recall that Washakie signed the treaty of 1868 on the sole condition that his people would be allowed to hunt freely.

During 1897 more misery followed the last land cession and curtailment of their right to travel: 152 Shoshones died in a measles epidemic (Shimkin 1942: 455). In 1898, the last of the Shoshone annuities were awarded; henceforth Shoshones had to work for all rations they received. Finally, in 1900 the government began allotting reservation land in severalty under the provisions of the General Allotment Act (Shimkin 1942: 455).

Wind River Shoshone despair continued, and the population reached its nadir (877) in 1902. The allotting process continued, and in 1904, with a shrunken Shoshone–Arapaho population base, the government got the Shoshones to relinquish all of the land north of the Wind River (over 1.3 million acres). This land was put back in the public domain for homesteading and sales under the homestead and mineral land laws (Hebard 1930: 218–21). Most of the acreage that was not purchased by whites was restored to the Indians about twenty-five years later. The Wind River Shoshones still prominently display a photograph of the 1904 cession signing in the Fort Washakie community center (Rocky Mountain Hall) with the caption "How to Steal a Reservation."

Some time between 1912 and 1916 the Wind River Shoshones adopted the peyote religion, as did their Ute kin to the south. Both received it from the Dakota. It was and is an important means by which Shoshones and Utes cope with life and its vagaries. I shall not explore peyotism further, except to say that it is an important movement on all of the Ute and Shoshone reservations and that many Sun dancers are peyotists. It is also a more strictly personal redemptive movement. The Sun dance is both redemptive and restorative. Although the focus of the Sun dance is on redemption, participants also seek to restore the observances of kinship obligations and reciprocity, Indian morality, the teachings of the "old people," and so forth. For many the two are fully compatible.

The Northern Shoshones and Bannocks of Idaho

The Idaho and northern Utah Shoshones and Bannocks were organized under several different leaders, and the hunting bands themselves were flexible in membership and highly mobile. On the other hand, general territories inhabited by these bands, or to which they returned, were well recognized. The Goose Creek Mountains–Raft River Mountains–Bear River area of northwestern Utah and southeastern Idaho was Hekandika Shoshone territory associated with such men as Bear Hunter, Sagwitch, and Pocatello. Boise and Bruneau directed their hunting bands farther west along the Snake River valley, and Tambiago, a Bannock, was associated with them. Taggee, another Bannock, joined with Pocatello, Washakie, and even Tendoy; and Pocatello too joined with Washakie. Further north the Bannock chiefs Le Grand Coquin and later Tyhee, and the Lemhi Shoshone chiefs Snag and later Tendoy, operated out of the Lemhi valley and the Bitterroot Mountains of northeastern Idaho and southwestern Montana. The Sheepeater Shoshones of Yellowstone Park were often associated with the Lemhi people.

There were, then, many areas in which the Northern Shoshone–Bannocks were known to roam and to procure livelihood, and there were many persuasive and successful leaders (only a few have been named) who influenced families to join with them on hunts. The various groups that formed were recognized as coming from one or another of the areas in Utah and Idaho, but the relationships within the groups were somewhat more transitory than those within the Wind River band. The openness and flexibility of the Utah and Idaho hunting bands might well have been caused by the distances these people had to travel to get out on the plains. In some years, at least during the good times, certain people from these bands wanted to go on the hunt whereas other people did not. It is reasonable to assume that those families who went joined with some leader, not necessarily the same one always, destined for the east slope. Those who stayed back continued their residence with their non-horse-using counterparts hunting deer, elk, antelope, and rabbits, and collecting nuts, roots, seeds, and berries.

Idaho and Utah Shoshone–Bannock history parallels much of Wind River history. There are critical differences, however, especially in the responses of the more westerly groups to the loss of their territory and their mode of subsistence.

By 1855, or shortly after the Mormons had established themselves throughout Utah and southwestern Wyoming, the Saints moved into northern Idaho near what is now Salmon at the head of the Lemhi Valley. Shoshones, under Snag, and Bannocks, under Le Grand Coquin, were already there, but they welcomed the twenty-nine missionaries (Moore, n.d.: 40, 60). The Mormon missionary David Moore further reports that a hundred Indians were baptized within the year. The conversions were nominal and very short-lived, but the entrée into northern Idaho had been made. Two years later, during the crises in Utah and Wyoming, the Mormons had a further crisis in the Lemhi Valley when the Bannocks and Shoshones drove off the Mormon livestock (250 head), killed two Mormons, and injured several others (Moore n.d.: 79–90). The Mormons moved out in April 1858 and did not establish themselves again in Idaho until 1860, when they squatted in Franklin on the Bear River.

It is rather easy to understand why more people did not squat in Idaho. As wagon trains passed through in 1858, 1859, and 1860, they were pillaged all along the line, and on several occasions whites were killed (Trenholm and Carley 1964: 180–81). Depredations and battles occurred near the Goose Creek Mountains, near Bear River, near the old Fort Hall (a trading post established near what is now Pocatello, Idaho, in 1832), near Fort Boise on the Snake River close to the Oregon line, and in the Lemhi area, including the Bitterroot Valley of what is now Montana. This prompted counterattacks by the U.S. army (Trenholm and Carley 1964: 183–85).

Brimlow (1938: 27) reports that by 1863, 40,000 to 45,000 whites had moved into eastern Oregon in quest of gold. If only 25 percent of them got there via the Oregon

Trail, the traffic would have been thick over the preceding decade. Probably half or more arrived by wagons from the east, and in the remaining few months of 1863 alone the commissioner of the land office expected another 5,000 in eastern Oregon.

As the stream of migrants swelled across Idaho, Bannocks and Shoshones continued to attack the wagon trains. Because of the Civil War drain on manpower, the U.S. army could not wage full-scale war in order to stop the depredations. But after the attack on the Overland Trail in 1862, the military moved with force. There is no doubt that some Shoshones and Bannocks expected the attack, for they had moved their families north to the Lemhi area after announcing that they were going to protect Shoshone lands and kill intruders.

The private farm and ranch operators in the mountain states, and especially the wagon operators along the Overland Trail, would abide no more Shoshone and Bannock attacks. The federal government, specifically the U.S. army, was dedicated to stopping them even if it meant a war of extermination. Thus Superintendent Doty called for the five treaties with the Shoshones, just as he had called for verbal peace treaties with the Utes during the Black Hawk War. The treaties signed by the Northern Shoshones and Bannocks at Soda Springs, Idaho, and Box Elder, Utah, carried all the stipulations written into the Fort Bridger Treaty.

A year later the annuities that had been guaranteed to the Shoshones were not delivered, and Superintendent Irish, Doty's replacement, succeeded in getting some money from the government so that he could honor the treaty obligations. Irish, too, assumed that the Indians could be kept in check with gifts, and he got into almost immediate conflict with General Connor of the U.S. army, who thought hangings and annihilation were the best treatment for recalcitrant bands of Shoshones and Bannocks (Trenholm and Carley 1964: 212–13).

The Governor of Idaho, Caleb Lyon, moved to place the Boise, Bruneau, and Camas Prairie Shoshones and Bannocks on reservations in 1865. He was not successful in corralling these people. Yet in 1867 his successor, Governor D. W. Ballard, succeeded in establishing a 1,800,000-acre reservation at Fort Hall for all the Snake River valley Shoshone and Bannocks in southern Idaho, but he was not able to keep them on it. The reservation established in 1867 reduced by several million acres the land recognized as belonging to these people by the government in 1863 (Brimlow 1938: 37–43; Trenholm and Carley 1964: 214–15). It also cleared the area for railroad right of way.

The Treaty council of 1868 at Fort Bridger, which included the Bannock chief Taggee, called for land in the Fort Hall–Port Neuf–Camas Prairie area whenever Taggee's people decided to return to Idaho (Brimlow 1938: 43). Taggee, with 800 Bannocks, stayed in Wyoming for a year. When Washakie refused to share the Wind River annuities with Taggee, the latter collected four thousand dollars' worth of treaty goods from the general in charge and returned to Idaho. This irritated the 1,300 various Idaho Shoshones and Bannocks placed at Fort Hall, because they were receiving nothing and had not come under the 1868 treaty signed at Fort Bridger.

Further north the Lemhi Shoshones, Bannocks, and Sheepeater Shoshones were proving to be a nuisance in the rich mining areas of the Bitterroot Mountains. Using the excuse that the Indians had to be moved to Fort Hall for their own protection because they had nothing to eat, the government induced the Lemhi people to sign a treaty in Virginia City, Montana, in 1868. The Lemhis, however, refused to be moved to Fort Hall and were given a one-hundred-square-mile reserve in the Lemhi valley of Idaho instead. The reservation was not created until 1875, and, only four years after it had begun operating, the government tried to get the Lemhi out of the area. In 1879, following the "Bannock War," an executive order attempted to move them from the Lemhi Valley, and the government tried again in 1889, this time yielding to Idaho and Montana business interests. In the latter instance an act was passed in Congress to force the Lemhis to relinquish their land and move to Fort Hall (RCIA 1905: 106–7; Brimlow 1938: 191).

As on all other Ute and Shoshone reservations, the Indians at Fort Hall were not receiving the annuities promised to them, and they were bitter over the loss of game. Trenholm and Carley (1964: 232) report that Taggee, in council with government officials, shouted that he wanted no more of the treatment he had been receiving. In despair, yet in hopes of transforming their lives, the Bannocks and Shoshones at Fort Hall took up the Ghost dance of 1870 (Mooney 1892–93: 703–4), performing it jointly with Utes and Wind River Shoshones in 1870 and 1871.

The Fort Hall Bannock and Shoshone problems were intensified in 1871, when Taggee died. The other influential men, such as Pocatello, were not so easy for the whites to talk to, and not so willing to agree to settle on the reservation. At the very time the Indians were being pushed to settle on the reservation, whites were settling all around it and often encroaching upon it. As a response to the crowding and the trespass, and as a precaution against the threat of starvation, many Indians left Fort Hall on a hunting expedition. On route they found and killed several settlers on and about Shoshone-Bannock land. The government rounded up some of the men they thought did the killing, including a feisty Bannock leader, Tambiago. They hanged Tambiago, but before they did Tambiago warned the government officials that he had been provoked by encroachments on Indian land (Brimlow 1938: 61–68; Trenholm and Carley 1964: 262).

The hanging of Tambiago, along with the loss of Indian lands, the failure of the government to live up to its promises, and the inability of the Indians to make the whites honor Indian land, led to the brief Bannock and Northern Shoshone war against the whites in 1878. Despite a treaty prohibition, white men drove their hogs onto Camas Prairie in 1878 (Brimlow 1938: 43). The Indians who annually collected roots at Camas Prairie returned to do so in the fall of that year. When they found that hogs belonging to whites had rooted up the crops in this thirty-by-ten-mile valley, they decided to fight for what was theirs. In all, 2,500 cattle, 80 horses, and an unspecified number of pigs owned by four whites were in the valley at the time (Brimlow 1938: 76). The Indians shot and wounded two of the three whites present, but all three escaped and carried the news to the government. Soon thereafter another white who used Camas Prairie was killed, his horses stolen, and his cattle butchered and the meat dried (Brimlow 1938: 78).

Whereas the settlers treated private property as inviolable, they did not regard Indian property as private property. The settlers were infuriated with the governor for allowing the Indians to have rifles and ammunition for any purposes, and most whites feared an all-out war. In short, local white opinions and responses fitted those that I have labeled "racist." On their part, the Indians—that is, the Shoshones and Bannocks from Fort Hall and Lemhi—felt that they would all be implicated anyhow, and so several called for war (Brimlow 1938: 79). The Lemhi who had been visitors at Fort Hall went north. Buffalo Horn, a successor to Pocatello, got several men to steal some white-owned horses. The military—three companies of infantry—moved east from Boise, and those Bannocks and Shoshones so inclined made several quick strikes in the Snake River area. The warrior bands killed several whites, stole property, and drove settlers off. It is alleged that the Bannocks and Shoshones who were involved, including men from Lemhi, Fort Hall, and even the Malheur Northern Paiute reservation in Oregon, intended to destroy the railroad in their grand battle plan (Trenholm and Carley 1964: 262).

The Indians were not able to keep all of their forces together, and the Northern Paiutes, under Egan, headed west, while the Northern Shoshones and Bannocks headed north. The undoing of the warrior bands was partially brought about by the Umatilla Indians on the west, who killed and scalped Egan and three of his men on the mistaken assumption that they would receive a reward for doing so (Trenholm and Carley 1964: 264). The beleaguered Northern Shoshones and Bannocks were caught in various places in Lemhi country from the Bitterroot Mountains to Yellowstone Park. Arapaho, Crow, and Wind River Shoshone scouts were hired and used to track down the last recluses, and the Crows added a final touch to the affair by stealing the warriors' horses (Brimlow 1938: 178–87). The battles are known to have taken 78 Bannock and Northern Shoshone lives and to have wounded another 68, although Brimlow (1938: 198) estimates that three times that number were killed. At the end of the campaigns, in December 1878, 35 Shoshones were held at Fort Hall and 38 Bannocks were held at Fort Washakie and Fort Hall. By February of 1879 the total tally of incarcerated Shoshones and Bannocks at Fort Hall, Fort Washakie, Fort Omaha (Nebraska), and Fort Keough (Montana) was 131 (Brimlow 1938: 191).

The war was followed by the 1880 attempt (mentioned earlier) to move the seven hundred or so Shoshones and Bannocks from Lemhi to Fort Hall. Tendoy, one of the leading chiefs at Lemhi, was taken to Washington along with several leaders from Fort Hall. On the other hand, the federal government was successful in rounding up all other Northern Shoshones and Bannocks and forcing them to reside at Fort Hall. It was also successful in redrawing the boundaries originally established in 1867. This time around the reservation encompassed only half the original acreage.

The shrinking of the reservation was greatly influenced by the pressures put on Congress during 1879 and early 1880. Brimlow (1938: 43) argues that during this time the Idaho population, through its newspapers and congressmen, was complaining loudly that the Fort Hall Reservation was too large, and he cites a newspaper report from the *Idaho Enterprise* of 15 January 1880 as one evidence of the pressures exerted, to wit: "Here in southeastern Idaho we have an Indian reservation containing more than two millions of acres of land, the finest in the territory. On this reservation there is less than 1,500 Indians to occupy this large body of land." The new boundary line drawn later that year put about one million acres back in the public domain.

The 1880s marked the end of Fort Hall Shoshone and Bannock fights with, and flights from, whites, but it did not mark the end of their misery. The population continued to decline, and the resources available to sustain them were meager. Only thirty-two of the more than seven hundred Bannocks and Shoshones were influenced to move from Lemhi to Fort Hall during these years. They migrated in 1882, apparently to receive the benefits promised to them in 1880; but by 1888 those who moved still had not received any goods (Trenholm and Carley 1964: 271). Chief Tyhee, a Bannock leader at Fort Hall following Taggee's death, and several others went to Washington to learn why the promises had not been kept. This apparently provoked a second executive order to move all of the Shoshones and Bannocks from the Lemhi area to Fort Hall.

As for the Bannocks and Shoshones at Fort Hall in 1880, it is reported that there was jealousy between them. The agent in charge saw this as an advantage to be exploited, for the members of the two groups tended to compete for favors. He argued that those who helped themselves most would receive the most help from the agency. As an aside he complained about the reduction of rations he had been commissioned to administer (RCIA 1880: 62–64). It is doubtful that the Shoshones and Bannocks fitted neatly into two camps, as they had joined in several different bands on several different ventures for close to two hundred years, even though the Bannock people had maintained their own distinct language.

When the Ghost dance religion swept east from the Northern Paiutes again in 1889, the Fort Hall Shoshone-Bannocks and those at Lemhi, who seem never to have stopped performing the religion, began performing it with greater vigor and commitment. Mooney (1892: 805–6) merely suggests that these groups took it up simultaneously, but he also reports that the Fort Hall Bannocks and Shoshones served as the "chief medium of the doctrine between the tribes west of the mountains and those of the plains." Mooney goes on:

The agent in charge states that during the preceding spring and summer his Indians had been visited by representatives from about a dozen different reservations. In regard to the dance and the doctrine at Fort Hall, he also says that *the extermination* [of the whites] *and the resurrection* [of all deceased Indians] *business was not a new thing with his tribes by any means, but had been quite a craze with them every few years for the last twenty years or more, only varying a little according to the whim of particular medicine-men.* [Mooney 1892–93: 807; emphasis added]

From Mooney's words we can safely infer that the Bannocks and Shoshones of Fort Hall and Lemhi had not yet lost hope of ridding themselves of their white oppressors and transforming their life by bringing back their deceased relatives. The Ghost dance flickered on and off for the next few years, but in 1901 a Fort Hall Shoshone introduced the Sun dance at Fort Hall. He had learned it from the Wind River Shoshones and had received dream instructions to sponsor a dance so that he could increase his power and cure the ailing (Hoebel 1935: 578). It appears to me that, with the sponsorship of the Sun dance and the diminution in importance of the Ghost dance, the Fort Hall Shoshones, like their other Shoshone and Ute counterparts, began to shift to a religious movement that offered personal redemption, the acquisition of personal power, the curing of ubiquitous human ailments, and community cohesion. They shifted to a religion that allowed them to cope with the world as it was, a world in which their niche was controlled by whites.

At about the time the Fort Hall Shoshones sponsored their first Sun dance, the federal government decided to open land around the reservation to public settlement, and open those lands right around Pocatello, Idaho, to private purchases at not less than ten dollars an acre (RCIA 1902: 120–21). These special sales, but not the opening of all reservation lands, began at a time when only seventy-nine Shoshones had been allotted under the provisions of the General Allotment Act of 1887.

In 1905 the Lemhi Shoshone and Bannocks were still resisting relocation, and Senator Dubois of Idaho requested that they be removed to Fort Hall with "Assent to the agreement [to be] obtained *if possible*" [emphasis mine]. Otherwise the government was to proceed to remove them and, subsequently, to allot everyone at Fort Hall (RCIA 1905: 106–7). When the government attempted to move the Lemhi people, they protested to their agent that proper provisions for their comfort could not be made and that they did not want to go (RCIA 1906: 133–34). The agent pointed out that they had log cabins and some improved land at Lemhi, but that there were only shanties and unimproved land at Fort Hall. The Lemhis also did not know where they would take care of their livestock if they were to become interlopers at Fort Hall. The government countered with a grand plan. Officials suggested that the adults and livestock move to Fort Hall in the fall of 1906 and get things situated. The Lemhi children would be left at the Lemhi school and sent to Fort Hall in the spring. This infuriated the parents; so the government decided not to push for removal until the spring of 1907 (RCIA 1906: 134).

During May 1907, Chief Tendoy died; the Lemhi reservation (64,000 acres) was put under a custodian; and 474 Lemhi Shoshone-Bannocks were moved to Fort Hall. They arrived with no place to stay and no land of their own, and lived on a $10,000 gratuity plus their modest amount of livestock. The 1,200 people already there had over $32,000 to share, and $12,000 of it was from trust and treaty obligation in which the Lemhi did not share (Leupp 1907: 94–95). That year the Lemhi joined the Fort Hall people in sponsoring a Sun dance for the first time (Hoebel 1935: 578).

By 1908, a year after the Lemhi removal, the survey of Fort Hall land was still not completed, and so the Lemhi had no land to settle on. Indeed, they were unwanted guests on the Fort Hall reserve. That year the Lemhi received $11,000, all from gratuities, whereas the original Fort Hall population received $40,000, one third of which was from trust and treaty obligations (Leupp 1908: 84). So the economic discrepancy began to widen between the populations as their general resources dwindled. This continued in 1909, when the 450 or so Lemhis still had no farms or even allotments and when they received $8.20 per capita whereas the original Fort Hall people received $36.60 per capita (Valentine 1909: 91).

When all the Fort Hall people were finally allotted, the Lemhis took their allotments toward the northeast part of the reservation, and at about the same time began sponsoring their own Sun dance. A few Lemhis simply would not stay at Fort Hall, and they returned to the Lemhi valley. In 1960 between sixty and a hundred of them were still living on "non-Indian" land on the outskirts of Salmon, Idaho (Nybroten 1964: 24–25).

The history of the Fort Hall Shoshones, then, is different from the history of the Wind River Shoshones partly because the Fort Hall people were organized into more flexible bands, of which there were many. They more often fought to protect their land and to repel white squatters than did the Wind River people. When the fighting was completed, a few Shoshone-Bannocks fled, only to be rounded up by other Indians. Even before these people stopped fighting, they had turned to supernatural means, the Ghost dance, to rid themselves of whites. As that transformative movement died out, the Fort Hall people, like those of Wind River, turned to the Sun dance in order to cope with life.

When all the Fort Hall people were finally located on the reservation near Pocatello in 1907, they represented several different territorial groups, even though members from two or more of these territorial groups had joined together under prominent warriors and hunters in earlier times. The continuity and complexity of the large, year-round residence group at Wind River under Washakie's popular leadership was not matched by any of the Utah-Idaho groups before or after residence on reservations. The evidence also shows that factionalism, blatantly encouraged at Fort Hall between the various Shoshone and Bannock groups, had no intra-Shoshone counterpart at Wind River, though the Wind River Shoshones did have their problems with the Arapahos.

II

THE CONTEXT IN WHICH THE SUN DANCE HAS PERSISTED

4 *The Neocolonial Reservation Context*

The exploitative and depressing conditions that contributed to the retooling of the Wind River Shoshone Sun dance and the borrowing of that dance by the Northern Utes and, subsequently, the Ute Mountain Utes, Southern Utes, and Fort Hall Shoshones, were exacerbated after 1910. Throughout the subsequent sixty years the Utes and Shoshones have never had wholly self-sufficient subsistence economies. They have watched their tribal and personal lands dwindle, and they have watched white communities grow on what were once Indian lands. They have been consumers rather than producers, and they have seen their own lands, minerals, gas, and oil exploited by whites and white-owned and -controlled corporations. Until the late 1930s the federal government, acting through Congress and the Bureau of Indian Affairs, made the critical decisions affecting Indian resources. Since the late 1930s and the ratification of charters and constitutions under provisions of the Indian Reorganization Act of 1934 (the IRA or Wheeler-Howard Act), Ute and Shoshones tribal councils have assumed a modest amount of power in making decisions about tribal resources, but their decisions have always been subject to federal approval. In fact, federal power over all types of Indian decisions increased rather than decreased following passage of the IRA.

The Sun dance religion has flourished in this context. It is not a coincidence that Shoshones and Utes have continued to sponsor the Sun dance religion, while their economic, political, and social conditions have worsened in the past few decades.

Since about 1940, at the tail end of the great economic depression, the satellite economies of the United States have changed markedly. Small farms and ranches have been liquidated by their non-Indian owners, and purchased and consolidated by large agri-business corporations and food-processing trusts. Non-Indians have migrated to urban areas, yet many have remained in the rural areas, producing a surplus labor force. Small mines have closed because of the discrepancy between high production costs and the low value of silver, gold, and other precious minerals. This, too, has both prompted migration to urban areas and created surplus labor in rural areas.

As the white-controlled satellites have withered and as rural family income has shriveled relative to urban family income, Indians have suffered more than non-Indians. Agriculture has become less and less profitable around all the Shoshone and Ute reservations except Fort Hall. At Fort Hall, as on the other reserves, Indian land is leased to non-Indians, with the majority of all profit accruing to the non-Indians. Technologic advances, federal policies, and the Indian's lack of access to capital have coalesced to push the Indians out of agri-business and even subsistence agriculture.

The huge mining corporations, especially those engaged in oil, but also potash, gilsonite, asphalt, gypsum, and others, have moved onto the Indian reservations to exploit Indian resources. The Shoshone and Ute tribes have been counseled, by the BIA and other advisers, to allow their resources to be drained off by these industries. Control of means of production has been maintained by the huge corporations, and neither jobs nor adequate lease and royalty income has been provided for the Indians.

The Shoshone and Ute populations have been both increasing and remaining on reservations at the very time when the non-Indian populations have been migrating to urban areas. Employment in the rural areas—in agriculture, mining, or small shops—goes to non-Indians first. The consequence of this and other factors is that Shoshones and Utes have become dependent on unearned income. The Wind River population has been increasing rapidly since about 1940, and the Ute populations have grown at very fast rates since 1950. The Fort Hall rate of increase has been more regular and gradual than the others. Except for the Fort Hall population, all the Ute and Shoshone groups have become *more* rather than less dependent on unearned income as their numbers have grown. Since 1938 at Wind River and the early 1950s on the Ute reservations, local Indian groups have been the recipients of rather large amounts of unearned income from land claims judgments and from oil, gas, and mineral leases and royalties. The small, personal landholdings (allotments) have withered through alienation or have become hopelessly tangled in heirship status. The small, family farms (productivity below subsistence needs, generally) and cattle enterprises have shriveled. On the other hand, unearned income in the form of per capita payments, dividends, and welfare payments has taken up the slack created by the reduction of farming and stockraising. At first, unearned income soared to unprecedented heights; then it dropped off markedly.

The point I wish to stress here is that Indian deprivation did not occur in a vacuum. The rural economies around Indian reservations have withered as the metropolis has expanded, and Indians are merely the superexploited victims of the growth of the metropolis. In the white-Indian rural niche the Indian is a consumer in white towns. He is not a clerk or a shopkeeper. He is seldom a resident. The Indian does not participate in the local government; he is treated differently from whites by local law enforcers and judges; and he is, on the whole, discriminated against. His education, his housing, his health, and his hopes for improvements in the quality of his life are much poorer than his white neighbors'. He does, however, have legitimate expectations about what his life ought to be. Indeed, the difference between life's promise and life's practice is great for him. The Indian is pressed to observe the Protestant ethic and is taught the democratic and capitalist ideology by federal officials, BIA employees, local white businessmen, university consultants, local educators, and missionaries. This ideology is concerned with freedom, equality, equal protection under the law, and individual control of one's destiny, and it is in marked disharmony with Indian life. The evidence of the financial successes, comfortable life styles, prestige, influence, and power of local whites also is not paralleled in Indian life. Utes and Shoshones neither enjoy the power and influence of local whites, nor do they "control their own destinies," in the loose meaning of that phrase.

TABLE 1

POPULATION ON FIVE RESERVATIONS, CIRCA 1880 TO 1968

Years	Southern Ute	Ute Mtn. Ute	Northern Ute[a]	Fort Hall Sho.[b]	Wind River Sho.
ca. 1880	500	650	2,825	2,212	1,200
1890	428	530	1,854	1,925	916
1900	420	528	1,660	1,995	841[c]
1910	352	463	1,150	1,722[d]	840
1920	334[d]	462[e]	1,005	1,765	880
1930	369	485	917[d]	1,768	1,017
1940	440	493	1,000	1,900	1,200
1950	479	570	1,150	2,156	1,678
1960	679	813	1,498	2,600	1,777
1968	711	1,099	1,611	2,970	2,039

a. Adjusted to include fullbloods only. The mixed-bloods formally dissociated in 1954.
b. Fort Hall data prior to 1910 include the Lemhi population, though the people were not moved to Fort Hall until after 1905.
c. Wind River Shoshone nadir, 799, was reached between 1900 and 1910.
d. Nadir.
e. Ute Mountain Ute nadir, 437, was reached between 1920 and 1930.

POPULATION AND LAND

By about 1880 the post-contact Ute and Shoshone populations had already been greatly depleted by disease and warfare coupled with a dwindling birth rate. 1880 is taken as the point of departure because the population estimates for that period are rather reliable and because most Utes and Shoshones were corralled on reservations with no place to go from this time on. Table 1 and figure 1 demonstrate the changes in these populations over the past nine decades. The ratio scale, in particular, allows us to assess rates of population growth and decline and to interpret the major trends. It is important to note that all reservation populations continued to decrease until at least 1900. Moreover, the drop between 1900 and 1910 was more marked than the drop in the following decade, in which a major influenza epidemic occurred affecting Indians and non-Indians. It might be that the populations on all of these reserves would have leveled off sooner had it not been for the epidemic, although it is my impression that allotment proceedings and their effects served to inhibit population leveling or growth. In 1902 the Wind River Shoshone population reached nadir (799). Fort Hall did not reach nadir (1,722) until 1910, but it too began to pull out of its decline before the Ute groups. Southern Ute reached nadir (334) in 1920; Ute Mountain Ute (437) in 1925; and the Northern Ute fullbloods (917) in 1930.

In each case the initial reversal in trend is quite gradual. It is important, I think, that the Fort Hall growth rate is always more gradual than those of the other groups. Indeed, beginning in 1940 at Wind River, and in 1950 at the three Ute reservations, the rate of population increase is staggering. Between 1940 and 1950 the Wind River population increased 40 percent, whereas the Mountain States population (including Utah, Colorado, Wyoming, Idaho, Montana, New Mexico, Arizona and Nevada) increased by only 22 percent, Wyoming by 16 percent, and the entire United States by 15 percent.[1] The other four groups were at or below the national average. The ex-

1. These statistics are from the U.S. Department of Commerce, Bureau of the Census, *Statistical Abstract of the United States 1966* (p. 13). In subsequent citations from these abstracts I will use the abbreviation SAUS.

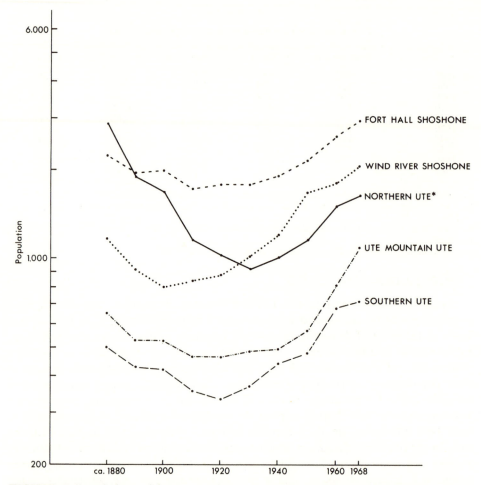

FIGURE 1. Populations of five reservations, circa 1880 to 1968. All populations are calculated between ten-year interval points. Trend lines do not allow yearly distributions; hence some nadirs do not show.

*Adjusted to include fullbloods only.

tremely rapid increase at Wind River in the 1940s correlates with the tribal acquisition and per capita disbursement of relatively large amounts of unearned income from land claims awards, gas and oil leases and royalties.

In the 1950–60 decade the Northern Ute increased at a 30 percent rate against the Utah increase of 29 percent and the national increase of 19 percent. The Southern Utes increased at a 40 percent rate and the Ute Mountain Utes at a 43 percent rate during this time. The Colorado increase was only 32 percent, by contrast; so the Colorado Utes grew 10 percent faster than the rest of the state and over 20 percent faster than the rest of the nation. Fort Hall continued to grow at about the national rate, but their 20 percent increase was greater than that for Idaho as a whole, with 13 percent. The Fort Hall Shoshones received no massive inputs (relatively speaking) of income.

In the 1960–68 interval the Fort Hall Shoshones increased by 14 percent, the Northern Ute by 8 percent, and the Southern Ute by 5 percent. All groups, then, were growing more slowly than the previous decade, but the Fort Hall rate fell off the least. Again there are some interesting corollaries. The average Fort Hall family suffered no great changes in its income, but Northern and Southern Ute families saw sharp declines in their incomes from all sources. On the other hand, the Wind River Shoshone population increased by 13 percent, almost doubling their growth rate of the 1950s, while the Ute Mountain Utes increased by 35 percent. As in our other examples, the rate of growth is correlated with per capita distributions of unearned income. Both the Wind River and the Ute Mountain per capita distributions continued throughout the 1960s. Indeed, the Ute Mountain growth rate was almost as steep as it had been in the previous decade. This was because the tribal council chose to distribute the revenue the tribe obtained from gas, oil, and mineral leases, and royalties on a per capita basis. We will take up reservation economics below and lend some empirical support to these generalizations.

Only the Fort Hall Shoshones show little drastic change. Their post-1880 decline was gradual, and they reached nadir in 1910—ten to twenty years earlier than the Ute groups. The population began to increase slowly after 1910 and, since about 1940, has approximated the national rate of increase.

Throughout the history of white relations with reservation Utes and Shoshones there have been periodic attempts to transfer lands from tribal ownership to private Indian ownership and then back to the public domain. In the case of those lands put into private Indian ownership, yet held in federal trust, states have often fought to transfer them from trust status and record them on the land tax base. The history of Indian land tenure has been marked by struggles between Indians and whites, and between state and federal governments. The record shows that it is the Indians, collectively and individually, who have lost in most of these struggles. They have seldom, if ever, had any influence on the outcome of the struggles. Table 2 illustrates the changes in tribal lands from the time that the five reservations were established through 1966. It should be emphasized that the data are conservative since figures have not been included for (a) the original Lemhi reservation taken away from the Lemhi Shoshones and Bannocks in 1907, (b) the 1863 Colorado Ute reservation territory of approximately 30 million acres, (c) the vast acreage ceded to all Shoshones and Bannocks in 1863, or (d) even the federally recognized Utah Ute acreage prior to 1861.

It is seen that the greatest amount of land was relinquished by the three Ute groups, but that overall the five reservations lost 85 percent of their total lands. The Wind River people lost the least, though at one time they had relinquished a vast amount of their land (1904), and since 1878 they have been forced to share their current reserve with the now numerically dominant Arapahos. Southern Ute lost the most and did not reclaim nearly so much as the Wind River Shoshone-Arapaho. Figure 2 graphically demonstrates the loss-gain land trends.

The acreage that was allotted in severalty between 1895 at Southern Ute and 1914–15 on the Shoshone reserves under provisions of the General Allotment Act, was to be held in federal trust for twenty-five years, after which time the allottees were expected to be able to dispose of their land as they saw fit. The nonallotted lands were to be set aside for tribal uses, or for national uses, or for homesteading and

TABLE 2

TRIBAL PROPERTY, ALLOTMENTS, AND HEIRSHIP, FIVE RESERVATIONS, CIRCA 1870 TO 1966

	Southern Ute	Ute Mtn. Ute	Northern Ute	Fort Hall Sho.	Wind River Sho.	Total[a]
Reservation land (including allotments)[b]						
Original[c]	9,500,000[c]	9,500,000[c]	3,972,500	1,800,000	3,768,500	28,541,000
1934	40,600	513,800	355,000	478,500	2,246,900	3,635,000
1950	309,500	533,900	1,061,700	524,900	2,079,600	4,510,000
1966	304,700	533,000	1,000,000	523,900	1,888,000	4,250,000
Reduction since orig. estimate	97%	95%	75%	71%	50%	Md. 75% $\bar{X}$ 85%
Allotments[d]						
Original	74,100	.....	113,000	347,300	125,000[e]	659,000
1934	40,600	.....	83,400	311,600	118,000	550,000
1950	14,900	12,000	81,300	293,600	69,700	472,000
1966	5,000	9,500	37,900	267,300	57,400	377,000
Reduction	94%	20%	67%	33%	54%	43%
Heirship status of allotments						
1934 (and % of allots. in heirship)	16,500 (40)	.....	53,300 (64)	157,800 (51)	71,000 (62)	298,600 (54)
1950 (and % of allots. in heirship)	14,600 (98)	.....	73,100 (90)	176,200 (60)	53,200 (76)	317,100 (67)
1966 (and % of allots. in heirship)	4,900 (98)	7,700 (80)	36,700 (97)	213,800 (76)	30,400 (53)	293,500 (78)

a. Rounded to nearest 1,000.
b. Southern and Ute Mountain Ute and Wind River Shoshone: 1868. Northern Ute: 1881. Fort Hall Shoshone: 1867.
c. Represents one-half of the original joint figure of 19 million for Southern and Ute Mountain Ute.
d. Southern Ute: 1895. Ute Mountain Ute (Allen Canyon only): post-1934. Northern Ute: 1905–7. Fort Hall Shoshone: 1914. Wind River Shoshone: 1907–15.
e. Wind River allotment acreage is probably high throughout. There is no precise breakdown on Wind River allotments; all totals for Wind River have been inter-polated from the grand totals for the Shoshone and Arapaho on that reserve.

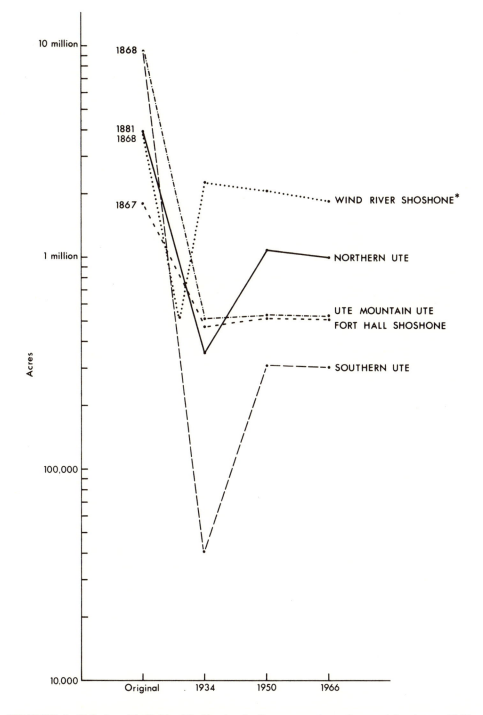

FIGURE 2. Tribal and individual Indian lands, five reservations, from origination to 1966.
*Pre-IRA survey land return, circa 1930.

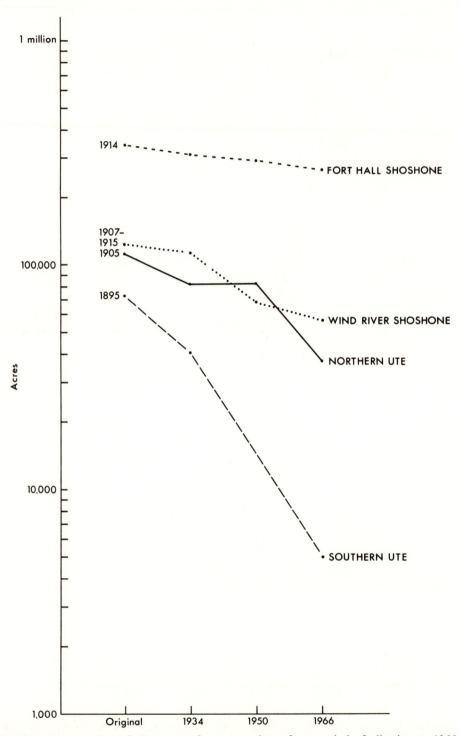

FIGURE 3. Reduction of allotments, five reservations, from period of allotting to 1966.

exploitation by whites. Table 2 shows not only that tribal lands were reduced following the GAA, but that allotments, too, had been considerably reduced by 1934. Figure 3 shows the reduction of the allotted acreage. It is clear that a large amount of severalty-allotted land was transferred out of its federal trust status and sold to whites well before the trust period was over. Until the passage of the IRA practically all land sales, either of allotments or of ex-tribal lands which had been deposited in the public domain, were made to non-Indians. The railroads received huge portions of Indian land, and they, in turn, sold acreage to farmers and ranchers. The railroads, incidentally, did not have to pay for the lands they received or for most of the costs incurred in laying their tracks. The federal government cleared the debts when they proved unpayable, but railroad financiers maintained ownership of the railroads and the right of way. White farmers and ranchers purchased or homesteaded Indian land, and mineral and oil producers claimed, purchased, or leased lands that once belonged to Indians.

Over 100,000 allotment acres alone had been alienated by sales, patents in fee, and certificates of competency by 1934 (see table 3). If we remember that all of the Ute and Shoshone populations were on the upswing by this time, whereas their land bases (severalty allotments) were decreasing, we can understand how a vicious circle was created. Indians sold land to meet the needs of their households, but they were less able to cope with the needs of their households, in the long run, as they alienated their land for immediate cash.

TABLE 3

ALLOTTED LANDS ALIENATED BY 1934,[a] FOUR RESERVATIONS
(rounded to nearest 100)

Reservations[b]	Year of Allotment	Acres Alienated by 1934	Percentage of Allotted Lands Alienated
Southern Ute	1895	33,500	46
Northern Ute	1905–8	29,600	26
Fort Hall Shoshone	1914	35,700	10
Wind River Shoshone	1907–15	9,300	7

a. Alienation by sales, patents in fee, and certificates of competency.
b. Ute Mountain Ute is not included, since lands were never allotted.

Coupled with the problems of dwindling Indian land, increasing Indian population, and the transfer of Indian and ex-Indian land to white ownership, was the problem of heirship status of allotted lands. The GAA made no provisions for the future growth of Indian populations. Moreover, by federal law each living descendant of a deceased allottee shared equally as a joint heir in the deceased's land. As the years passed and heirs raised their own families, their progeny too became joint heirs. By 1934 a single forty-acre tract often had scores of heirs.[2] Before any heir could work the land, he had to have the consent of all other heirs, and if the land was leased all heirs shared jointly in the lease income. Table 2 shows the acreage of allotments in heirship and the percentage of all acreage still in allotment status which the acreage represents.

2. See the Land Planning Committee of the National Resource Board, *Indian Land Tenure, Economic Status, and Population Trends,* part 10 of the Report on Land Planning, 1935.

In 1934, during the depths of the depression, the IRA was passed. The Meriam report of 1928 described the appalling conditions on Indian reservations, and the IRA signaled a new attack on those conditions.[3] In order for each reservation population to benefit fully from the provisions of the new act, a simple majority of the members of each reservation who turned out to vote was required to ratify constitutions and charters for their own reservations. By 1939 the three Ute and two Shoshone groups had ratified constitutions and charters (the Wind River Shoshones and Arapahos had ratified a constitution in 1930, four years before the IRA). Participation in these elections was meager, however, and it is alleged that often the results were engineered by BIA officials who induced Indians favorable to the act to go to the polls. Opponents were not encouraged to vote. The IRA ended the allotting of tribal lands and extended the federal trust period over these lands indefinitely. It made financial provisions for tribes to consolidate Indian lands and acquire non-Indian lands. The new act restricted the sale of Indian lands so that they could not be alienated to non-Indians. So the upswings in tribal land ownership from 1934 to 1950, except for some of the Wind River acreage, are accounted for by purchases made under the IRA. After 1934, allotment and heirship status acreage was purchased only by the tribal corporate bodies and often, but not always, with funds made available by the IRA. Figure 4 gives graphic comparisons of the percentages of allotments retained and the percentages of these allotments in heirship status from the time allotting was completed to 1966. If we scan the tables, ratio scales, and bar charts again, we see that private Indian land has been greatly reduced—though some land restoration took place after 1930—and that since 1930 all of the populations have grown markedly.

Among other purposes, the IRA was intended to stabilize Indian families and to get more Indians farming. The emphasis on a healthy agricultural economy made some sense in the rural Mountain West during the depths of the depression, a time when subsistence farming was commonplace. Yet even then the urban migration was extensive as small farm and ranch operators were forced to liquidate their holdings and seek employment in cities. The IRA also sought to make Indian tribes partly responsible for other things. It gave them approval or veto over the disposition of tribal assets, but it did not give complete control. It invested in the tribes the right to negotiate with federal, state, and local governments and to employ legal counsel (with the Secretary of the Interior's approval). Tribes, through their governing bodies, were also given the authority to regulate law and order, tribal membership, taxation, and several other matters critical to reservation life.[4] In many respects it made Indian tribes into small states within states. They achieved a modicum of power and control over their own lives, but the big decisions about dispositions of assets, development programs, and the like were always controlled by the BIA, the House Committee on Interior and Insular Affairs, or the Secretary of the Interior.

Even this neocolonial status of dependency with the illusion of self-control was better, in many ways, than the status of the Shoshones and the Utes during the 1900–

---

3. This is the famous report, *Problems of Indian Administration*, 1928.

4. The Indian Reorganization Act (IRA) will be analyzed more fully in a subsequent part of this chapter and in the following chapter on the Northern Ute.

Original allotment acreage

Percentage of original allotment retained and percentage of retained allotment in heirship, 1934

Percentage of original allotment retained and percentage of retained allotment in heirship, 1950

Percentage of original allotment retained and percentage of retained allotment in heirship, 1966

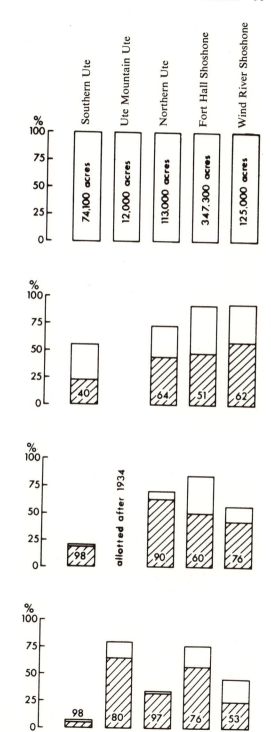

FIGURE 4. Allotment acreage, five reservations, origination to 1966.

1935 period. Throughout those years officials of the federal government declared Indians as legally "competent" or "incompetent" to manage their affairs. Indians did not directly influence local BIA personnel, and they had little access to federal government officials (though chiefs were often taken to Washington and given silver medals by high-ranking officials in the late nineteenth century). Shoshones and Utes certainly did not exercise power or influence over local and state governments. So with the adoption of charters and constitutions under the provisions of the IRA, Indians were supposed to begin to exercise *some* power over the disposition of their lands and the direction their reservation lives would take, but ultimate approval and control always rested with the Secretary of the Interior.

ECONOMICS AND SUBSISTENCE

During their reservation tenure, Utes and Shoshones, on the whole, have never been completely self-sustaining through farming, stock-raising, hunting, gathering, fishing, or earned income. Yet the evidence indicates that these people were more nearly self-sufficient, at a subsistence level, prior to and during the depression of the 1930s than afterwards. Since about 1850, Shoshones and Utes have been caught in a rural rut of the metropolis-satellite economy in which development of the metropolis has been at the expense of the satellites. Only Fort Hall land has proved to be of commercial agricultural value for small and large farming ventures. The Fort Hall area, especially with the development of the Snake River for irrigation since the 1950s, has been profitable for the raising of potatoes, hay, wheat, and cattle. The other four reserve areas in this study were never so desirable for agriculture as the Fort Hall area, and the Ute lands, with or without irrigation, were never so desirable as the Wind River lands.

For the following analysis, comparable data on all five groups for equal points in time are not available, and so most of the reference points used here will be on or around 1912, 1920 and 1927 (prior to the IRA), 1950 (following the IRA and the Indian Claims Commission Act[5]), 1962 and 1966 (following the effects of the Indian Claims Act and the movement in Congress for termination of federal services to American Indians).

During the early years following the acceptance of the Sun dance, the five reservation societies were characterized by marginal, subsistence adaptations based on stock raising, some farming (mostly alfalfa for livestock), some hunting and gathering, lease income, rations, and, for a very few people on all reserves, some part-time employment.

Tables 4 and 5 provide important information for our analysis of part of the earned livelihood of Utes and Shoshones. It is clear that by 1920 more than half of the men in all groups except the Ute Mountain Utes were doing some meager farming. The median acreage farmed was four per tribal member, and about 95 percent of these acres were planted in alfalfa or grain. Much of this land was worked by agency employees, and most of the produce was consumed by Indian livestock. Ute Mountain land was not located on good sources of water and has never been good farmland.

5. This act will be discussed below. Briefly, a Court of Indian Claims was established following the Indian Claims Commission Act of 3 August 1946 to redress Indian grievances against the federal government, especially on questions of broken treaties, unratified treaties, and other violations of dignity and property.

TABLE 4

FARMING, FIVE RESERVATIONS, 1912 AND 1920

Reservations	Able Males		Able Males Farming		Mean No. of Acres Cultivated per Farmer	
	1912	1920	1912	1920	1912	1920
Southern Ute	73	80	73 (100%)	72 (90%)	12	7
Ute Mountain Ute	60	62	20 (33%)	1 (2%)	0	0
Northern Ute	267	275	176 (66%)	218 (79%)	5	11
Fort Hall Shoshone	478	507	234 (49%)	264 (52%)	3	4
Wind River Shoshone	180	200	80 (44%)	110 (55%)	8	4
Totals and Averages	1,058	1,124	$\bar{X}^{a}$ (55%)	$\bar{X}$ (59%)	Md. 5	Md. 4

a. Means ($\bar{X}$) are weighted. Test for the significance of difference between mean percentages of farmers in 1912 and 1920. Diff. between $\bar{X}$ percents = 4; z = 3.5; $p < 0.001$

TABLE 5

STOCK RAISING, FIVE RESERVATIONS, 1912 AND 1920

Reservations	Able Males		Able Males Raising Livestock		Livestock 1912			Livestock 1920			Mean No. of Stock per Tribesman	
	1912	1920	1912	1920	Horses and Mules	Cattle	Sheep and Goats	Horses and Mules	Cattle	Sheep and Goats	1912	1920
Southern Ute	73	80	73 (100%)	80 (100%)	1,010	1,510	300	510	260	1,000	8	5
Ute Mountain Ute	60	62	60 (100%)	62 (100%)	1,065	425	1,640	360	80	2,000	6	5
Northern Ute	267	275	267 (100%)	275 (100%)	3,080	3,420	3,200	2,465	5,500	5,650	7	14
Wind River Shoshone	478	507	133 (28%)	332 (65%)	5,000	3,300	0	2,530	5,120	170	5	4
Fort Hall Shoshone	180	200	115 (64%)	180 (90%)	1,125	1,100	4,725	725	1,420	225	8	3
Total and averages	1,058	1,124	$\bar{X}$ 61%ᵃ	$\bar{X}$ 83%ᵇ	11,280	9,755	9,865	6,590	12,380	9,045	Md. 7ᶜ	Md. 5
Percentages of Totals					36%ᵇ	31%	33%	23%	44%	33%		

a. Test for the significance of difference between percentage of stockraisers in 1912 and 1920. Diff. between $\bar{X}$ percents = 22; z = 16; $p < 0.001$

b. Test for the significance of difference between the proportions of horses and cattle raised in 1912 and 1920. Diff. between Ps = 0.325; z = 96; $p < 0.001$

c. Proportional differences between medians (Md.) in 1912 and 1920 expressed in percent = 29; $p < 0.001$

In the period of 1912–20 livestock was raised on all of these reservations. The cattle and sheep were consumed by the Indians, but they were sold on the market as well. The livestock figures are interesting: in 1912, 36 percent of all stock were horses and mules—many more than were needed for farming. Indeed, most of the horses were riding ponies used for transportation, hunting, gifts (especially at Sun dances), horse racing, parades (at Sun dances), and funerary offerings. Horses were still the only source of transportation for Indians (for visiting on their reservations, to travel to other reservations, to haul game from the mountains, and the like), but the ratio of nearly three horses or mules per person was more than sufficient for their transportation needs. Indians kept horses because they had uses for them other than transportation and because they liked them, even if they were competing with cattle for fodder.

By 1920, on the other hand, only 24 percent of all livestock were horses and mules, yet the total stock owned on all reservations showed a decrease of nearly three thousand head. In 1912 there had been a median of seven animals per person, including horses and mules, and by 1920 this had dropped to five animals per person. However, the percentage of able-bodied men engaged in stock raising significantly increased in the period. By 1920 practically all able-bodied men were raising or helping to raise some livestock.

We also find that there was a decrease in the median acres farmed per person, from five in 1912 to four in 1920. This decrease too is paralleled by a significant increase in the percentage of able-bodied men engaged in farming. The Northern Utes were the only ones to show a significant gain in acres farmed and stock raised per tribesmen: both categories doubled. The variability from year to year and the general instability of the resource base and the sources of family income seem more marked at Northern Ute than on all the other reservations. Fort Hall families seem to have experienced the fewest fluctuations in their income and access to resources, but they also had less income and less access to resources than the other Shoshones and Utes. This pattern—the Northern Utes having had the greatest fluctuation of income and resource base, and the Fort Hall Shoshones the least, yet the Fort Hall Shoshones having had absolutely less income and less access to resources—has persisted since the turn of the century.

The question why the proportion of stock raised and acres farmed decreased is partially answered by the comparisons made in table 6. Here we see that there is a modest increase in the per capita ration values distributed between 1912 and 1920. But more important, we note the vast increase in least income per capita in this same period. The difference between the joint index of per family ration values and lease incomes for these two points in time is 227 percent (averaged for all reservations), and the proportional difference is highly significant. In 1920 four of five reservation groups showed an increase in their lease and ration index (per family) over 1912, whereas three of five showed a decrease in farming and stock raising (per capita) below 1912. One group, Fort Hall, showed no changes in stock raising, and because so few men farmed such a small amount of land at Ute Mountain Ute, there was no important change in farming on that reserve.

The drop in farming, and especially in the raising of horses, mules, sheep and goats, was attended by a sharp increase in acreage leased to whites for farming and

TABLE 6

ANNUAL ALLOTMENT LEASE INCOME AND RATION VALUE
PER CAPITA AND PER FAMILY, FIVE RESERVATIONS, 1912 AND 1920

Reservations	Total Ration Value[a]	Per Capita Ration Value	Total Lease Income	Per Capita Lease Income	Mean Annual Ration Value and Lease Income per Family[b]	Changes of Mean Ration and Lease Income between 1912 and 1920	
						$	%
Southern Ute							
1912	4,250	11	288	1	62		
1920	4,420	13	2,350	7	112	+50	+227
Ute Mountain Ute							
1912	5,750	12	0	0	59		
1920	4,310	9	0	0	47	−12	−20
Northern Ute							
1912	11,800	10	5,044	4	71		
1920	16,250	15	55,216	49	320	+249	+348
Fort Hall Shoshone							
1912	13,570	8	1,100	1	41		
1920	20,100	11	28,030	16	137	+96	+237
Wind River Shoshone							
1912	4,400	5	4,660	6	55		
1920	1,900	2	55,000	63	323	+268	+493
Totals and Averages							
1912		9		2	57		
1920		10		27	188	+131	+227

a. Rations and lease income are expressed in dollars and rounded to the nearest whole.
b. Family estimated at five members.
c. Test for the significance of difference between proportions of per capita lease incomes and ration values in 1912 and 1920. Diff. between Ps = 0.533; $z = 3.22$; $p < 0.001$

for cattle and sheep raising. Let us look at the relation between earned and unearned subsistence in the 1912–20 period. Figure 5 measures the relationship between farming and stock raising on the y axis, and per capita lease income on the x axis. It should be noted that the indexes measure only a subsistence level of life. The maximum unearned income (family average) in this period is only $325 per year. On the other hand, maximum acres farmed and stock raised (per capita average) is only 12 and 14, respectively. None of the three maxima belongs to the same tribe. The eta-squared value of 33 percent (N^2yx) and the freehand line shows that the relationship is not linear; rather, as unearned income increases, stock raising and farming decreases 33 percent of the time. The Northern Ute and Ute Mountain Ute are most aberrant, and they are so in different directions. The Northern Ute raised more stock and worked more acres as their unearned income increased. Both went down for the Ute Mountain Utes.

Let us now look somewhat more closely at the differences between allotted lands farmed by Indians and those farmed by white lessees. In 1912, Indians farmed more of their own land than did whites (see table 7). The Southern Utes and Fort Hall Shoshones farmed significantly more of their own lands (or agency personnel farmed significantly more of Indian lands) than did whites; the Northern Utes farmed a little more of their own lands than did whites; and the Wind River Shoshones farmed considerably less of their own lands than did whites. At that time the average lease income was 79 cents per acre, with Fort Hall land bringing in 25 percent more per unit than any other reservation.

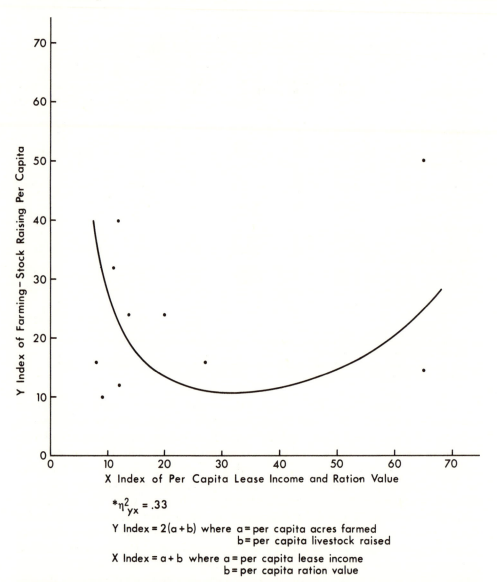

$^*\eta^2_{yx} = .33$

Y Index = 2(a + b) where a = per capita acres farmed
b = per capita livestock raised

X Index = a + b where a = per capita lease income
b = per capita ration value

FIGURE 5. Relation* between farming–livestock raising and lease income–ration value, per capita tribal members, five reservations, 1912 and 1920.

In 1920 the lease income per acre had increased by 280 percent over 1912, and Wind River land was leasing at the highest price. The five dollars per acre values for Wind River might be too high, but I cannot prove my suspicion. In any event, Fort Hall land drew 65 percent more per acre than Northern Ute land by this time, and Northern Ute land was leasing at higher fees than Southern Ute land. By 1920, then, whites were farming as much as 76 percent of the tilled Indian land as opposed to 24 percent for Indians, and this ratio has remained rather consistent since 1920.

The decrease in Southern and Northern Ute land farmed by lessees from 1920 to

TABLE 7

PERCENTAGES OF ALLOTTED INDIAN LANDS UNDER INDIAN
AND NON-INDIAN CULTIVATION, FIVE RESERVATIONS, 1912–66

Reservations	1912	1920	1950	1966
Southern Ute				
Acres cult. by Indians	88 (4,500)	35 (2,500)	43 (1,850)	. . . . .
Acres cult. by white lessees	12 (640)	65 (4,700)	57 (2,450)	55 (2,700)
Lease income per acre	$0.45	$0.50	. . . . .	. . . . .
Ute Mountain Ute				
Acres cult. by Indians	100 (20)	100 (10)	0 (0)	. . . . .
Acres cult. by white lessees	0 (0)	0 (0)	0 (0)	0 (0)
Lease income per acre	$0.00	$0.00	. . . . .	. . . . .
Northern Ute				
Acres cult. by Indians	52 (5,700)	20 (11,500)	22 (6,700)	. . . . .
Acres cult. by white lessees	48 (5,200)	80 (46,400)	78 (24,000)	56 (21,400)
Lease income per acre	$0.97	$1.19	. . . . .	. . . . .
Fort Hall Shoshone				
Acres cult. by Indians	86 (5,600)	33 (6,900)	49 (14,200)	. . . . .
Acres cult. by white lessees	14 (900)	67 (14,300)	51 (14,800)	36 (89,500)
Lease income per acre	$1.22	$1.96	. . . . .	. . . . .
Wind River Shoshone				
Acres cult. by Indians	43 (5,500)	25 (3,700)	31 (5,500)	. . . . .
Acres cult. by white lessees	57 (7,400)	75 (11,000)	69 (12,000)	30 (17,100)
Lease income per acre	$0.63	$5.00	. . . . .	. . . . .
Totals and averages				
Acres cult. by Indians	60 (21,320)	24 (24,600)	35 (28,250)	. . . . .
Acres cult. by white lessees	40 (14,140)	76 (76,400)	65 (53,250)	(130,700)
Mean lease income per capita	$0.79	$2.23	. . . . .	. . . . .

Source: Data for 1912 are from RCIA (1921: 142–46, 247–50); 1920 from RCIA (1920: 118–22); 1950 from HCIIA (1953: 1131–34, 1200–1202, 1212–20, 1264–65; and 1966 from Agency Reports. (personal communications from Consolidated Ute, Uintah and Ouray Ute, Fort Hall Shoshone, and Wind River Shoshone agencies). There are no base income figures for 1950 and neither base income figures nor raw figures on Indian allotments cultivated by Indians for 1966. It is estimated that no more than 3% of the Northern, Southern and Ute Mtn. Ute allotments were cultivated by Utes in 1966. That probably holds for the Wind River Shoshone also. In 1963 Fort Hall Shoshones cultivated 6,800 acres of Indian land to 21,400 acres cultivated by whites.

1966 is offset by the alienation of a good portion of these lands to whites. In fact, until about 1938, when the Ute tribes incorporated under the IRA, white lessees purchased the allotments which they had been leasing, as they became available. After that time allotments were primarily purchased by the tribes.

The most interesting development is the jump in farm lease acreage at Fort Hall since 1963. Whereas the farm and ranch economies around the other reservations began to shrivel in the late 1950s, the Snake River area of Idaho continued to flourish. The Snake River project made water available on upland areas of the Fort Hall reservation, enabling the rise in leased acreage between 1950 and 1966. Leasing is still very important to the Fort Hall Shoshones.

The question of allotted lands lying idle is also of interest. The majority of all allotted lands were idle through the mid 1930s because allottees died, or because they could not get credit capital to put in crops on their small acreages, or because their land has no water.

There are no comparative data on relative farming success, but the evidence at my disposal shows that white lessees *always* have been more successful than Indian farmers on Indian land. Whites have, of course, had access to capital to purchase farm equipment, and they have had an incentive to farm on Indian land because the land taxes are less than they would be if they were farming their own land. Furthermore, with leased land one has to pay only during the lease periods. That is not to say that white lessees did not farm their own land, but when leases were cheap and market prospects were good, they also leased Indian land.

For the Southern Ute between 1930 and 1948 Omer C. Stewart (1952: 82–83, reports that the Utes "regularly harvested less per acre from the land they cultivated than was obtained by 'Anglos' and Spanish from land they leased from the Indians." In 1949 an expert suggested that the best two farmers on the Southern Ute reservation had no more than a 50 percent chance of succeeding as farmers and stockmen in the competitive vocation (Stewart 1952: 83).

The Northern Ute data for 1956 suggest more of the same. Non-Indian lessees farmed three times as much Indian land as did Indians, and they also had more success than the latter (see table 8). An overall white versus Indian comparison for general farming in the Uintah Basin (erstwhile Indian land) indicates that whites had five times as many acres under cultivation and realized 32 percent greater cash values per acre. In 1956 there were 58,000 allotted acres. Fifty-three percent was leased by whites, 17 percent was worked by Indians, and 30 percent was idle.

TABLE 8

INDIAN AND NON-INDIAN FARMING
NORTHERN UTE RESERVATION AND THE UINTAH BASIN, 1956

	Acres	Crop Value per Acre (in dollars)
Reservation lands farmed by		
Indian owners, assignees, lessees	10,078	14.86
Non-Indian lessees	30,679	16.62
Nonreservation lands in Uintah Basin farmed by		
Non-Indian owners	23,209	23.67

For 1960 we have data from the Fort Hall Shoshone reservation (Nybroten 1964: 12–15). Table 9 compares the production of Indians and non-Indian lessees on Indian land. These lands are richer, more productive, and closer to markets than any of the other reservations. Yet in 1960 we see that 76 percent of all irrigable Indian land that was tilled was farmed by whites who grossed over 425 percent greater profits per acre than Indian operators. Again the reasons are quite obvious. Indian land is tied up in heirship, or allotments are small. Even if an Indian desired to farm, knew how to farm, and received an assignment (usufruct right) for irrigable land on the reservation, he would need capital to buy the seed, fertilizer, equipment, and so forth required for successful farming. The tribes do not have capital to loan, and local white creditors will not, on the whole, extend credit to Indians because they are considered bad risks (Nybroten 1964: 164–66). This holds for all of the reservations. Indeed, the major allocations of credit are made by traders and small shop owners for food and clothing.

Table 9 further shows that cultivated row crops (potatoes, beets, and onions, for example) bring considerable gross income per acre while pasturage brings very little. Yet practically all Indian land is in pasturage whereas the white lessees have only 30 percent in forage. The simple explanation is that it costs much more to put in, cultivate,

TABLE 9

PRODUCTS GROWN IN IRRIGATED INDIAN LANDS OF THE FORT HALL RESERVATION, 1961

Operators and Crops	Acres	Gross Value per Acre (in dollars)
Indians		
Cultivated row crops	30	199.70
Small grains (close drilled)	1,520	45.47
Forage, hay, tame pasture	5,037	26.85
Total	6,587	31.93
Non-Indian lessees		
Cultivated row crops	9,653	246.57
Small grain (close drilled)	5,210	48.72
Forage, hay, tame pasture	6,487	43.67
Total	21,350	136.64

Adapted from Nybroten (1964:12).

and harvest row crops (see table 10). If, in 1961, a man owned or controlled (through assignment) 174 tax-free acres (Indian land is tax-free unless alienated by fee patent), if he had about $12,000 capital and worked his land and cattle herds himself, he could support a family of five on $3,500 per year. That would be about $1,250 per year more than the average Fort Hall family of 6.2 persons lived on in 1962. The Indian, without education, capital, or access to either, leases his allotments and heirship lands and watches the tribe lease the tribal lands.

TABLE 10

CAPITAL, LAND, AND GROSS INCOME REQUIREMENTS ON FIVE TYPES OF FARMS, FORT HALL

Type of Farming	Acres Needed	Capital Needed (in dollars)	Gross Income (in dollars)	Income for Family Living (in dollars)
Beets and potatoes	143	15,015	14,141	3,500
Potatoes	252	27,999	22,497	3,500
Dairy	49	13,560	9,363	3,500
Dairy and hogs	125	13,090	10,305	3,500
Beef and crops	174	11,780	10,371	3,500

Source: Nybroten (1964:15). These figures are for 1961 and assume that the land is owned and worked by the farmer and is tax-free.

Since 1900, the Indian family farm has in fact been discouraged by the Bureau of Indian Affairs. The IRA provided for both the development of family farming and the consolidation of Indian resources. Unfortunately, consolidation negated the family farming. Furthermore, water taxes, increased capital outlay for all farm ventures, heirship problems, poor soil, and long distances from markets coalesced to make the family farm unprofitable and to work against achieving these governmental goals.

In grazing land too, the acreage used by non-Indians has been greater than that used by Indians (see table 11), at least since about 1912, when the areas around the reservations were more sparsely populated with whites, and when those whites who were there had already purchased or settled on land made available in the public domain following allotment. As early as 1905, 888,000 acres of Wind River Shoshone grazing land were leased to two men. A total of 788,000 acres were leased at an annual charge of 1¢ per acre and the other 100,000 acres were leased at 2¢ per acre (RCIA 1905: 89). In 1906 another lease was let at Wind River on 124,000 acres at 1½¢ per acre (RCIA 1906: 111). In fact, Wind River Shoshone grazing land prior to 1950 was always used cheaply and heavily by a few whites. Now we can more fully account for the marked reduction in livestock per capita (from eight to three) on the Wind River reserve between 1912 and 1920. The decline of Indian-owned stock is correlated with an incredible increase in lease income from leased allotments, but the stock reduction must be understood in the light of the uses of tribal land as well. The white use of grazing lands was briefly curtailed around 1910, but by 1920 the whites were using 94 percent of all lands. Thus Wind River use was restricted by the exploitation of Indian grazing land by whites, and the tribe did not have capital to invest in Indian ranchers. Second, the Wind River Shoshones were drawing inordinately high lease income from the same pasture and cultivation lots they were leasing to whites; so they began reducing—by sales and consumption—their own herds. Third, as allotment acreage went into heirship, lessees bought it up and again reduced the Shoshone land base.

TABLE 11

COMPARISON OF INDIAN AND NON-INDIAN USE OF INDIAN GRAZING LAND, 1912–50[a]

Reservations	1912		1920		1950	
	Raw	Percent	Raw	Percent	Raw	Percent
Southern Ute						
Acres used by Indians	5,000	100	18,000	82	.....	.....
Acres used by white lessees	0	0	3,800	18	.....	.....
Total lease income	$0		$400		.....	
Lease income per acre	$0		$0.11		.....	
Ute Mountain Ute						
Acres used by Indians	100,000	25	66,000	18	.....	.....
Acres used by white lessees	300,000	75	294,000	82	.....	.....
Total lease income	$5,900		$7,100		.....	
Lease income per acre	$0.02		$0.02		.....	
Northern Ute						
Acres used by Indians	84,000	42	109,000	47	318,000	62
Acres used by white lessees	115,000	58	125,000	53	191,600	38
Total lease income	$2,700		$1,600		.....	
Lease income per acre	$0.02		$0.01		.....	
Fort Hall Shoshone						
Acres used by Indians	410,000	100	180,000	42	200,800	48
Acres used by white lessees	0	0	245,000	58	214,900	52
Total lease income	$0		$9,240		.....	
Lease income per acre	$0		$0.38		.....	
Wind River Shoshone						
Acres used by Indians	295,000	51	110,000	6	800,000	40
Acres used by white lessees	285,000	49	1,630,000	94	1,196,000	60
Total lease income	$6,900		$79,800		.....	
Lease income per acre	$0.02		$0.05		.....	
Totals and Averages						
Acres used by Indians	894,000	56	482,200	17	1,318,800	45
Acres used by white lessees	700,000	44	2,297,800	83	1,602,500	55
Total lease income	$15,500		$181,300			
Lease income per acre	$0.02		$0.08			

Source: Data for 1912 are from RCIA (1912: 114–24, 142–46, 151–52, 233–37, 246–50); 1920 from RCIA (1920: 123–27); and 1950 from HCIIA (1953: 1131–34, 1200–1202, 1212–20, 1264–65). There are no lease income figures for 1950, nor are data available for the Southern and Ute Mountain Ute.

a. All values are rounded to the nearest hundred except for "Lease income per acre" dollars, which are rounded to the nearest cent.

The Fort Hall grazing land, like the local irrigated farm land, brought much greater lease income per acre than did the grazing land on the other reserves. The figures for Indian use at Fort Hall, if not for the other reservations, are probably a little high, but the white lessee land figures are not, for the latter were taxed and good records have been kept.

In 1950 the Northern Utes used more of their own lands than did whites, because the tribe, under the auspices of the BIA and the provisions of the IRA, bought back thousands of acres that had been alienated from them following allotment. This acreage, located primarily in the rugged Tavaputs Plateau area, had not been purchased by white ranchers, although many homesteads and desert land entries had been taken on it, and some large cattle and sheep operations were created there by non-Indians. The area just east of the Tavaputs Plateau was obtained by the mining concerns who had originally lobbied the federal government for the allotment of Ute lands in severalty. A few Indian cattle cooperatives, primarily organized along bilateral kinship lines, operated on the sparse-grass Ute tribal lands during the 1930s and 1940s.

The Southern Utes had little land to lease until the late 1930s because they had been reduced to about four thousand allotment acres with no tribal lands in 1895. After they had incorporated under the IRA, lands were repurchased for them. The Ute Mountain Utes, who maintained their lands, leased most of them, but eked out a subsistence nevertheless.

EMPLOYMENT, AND EARNED AND UNEARNED INCOME

Ute and Shoshone agriculture, except in a few extreme cases at Northern Ute, did not satisfy subsistence requirements at any time during the reservation period. This is an effect of several interrelated phenomena. First, it might be true that Indians, who heroically resisted farming during their reservation life in the late nineteenth century and who experienced many shattering defeats during that period, never generated the *will* to exploit their own dwindling resources as farmers. But into the twentieth century, and especially through the late 1930s, Utes and Shoshones had neither the technical training nor the access to funds to sustain profitable agricultural enterprises on their meager plots of land. The increase of leasing was due partly to lack of capital to develop land and partly to the heirship status into which practically all allotments had fallen. As an effect, Indians came to desire unearned income in the form of lease taxes, lease royalties, and so forth, and this desire, in turn, was constantly exacerbated by the Indians' land problems and their lack of access to significant amounts of capital both in dollars and trained workers. We should also be reminded that federal promises from the 1850s on guaranteed rations, as a carrot, to force Indians (a) to relinquish the lands for which they were contesting, (b) to settle on reservations, and (c) to give up the chase. Thus, the unearned income that was promised to the Indians was seen by them, quite rightly, as compensation for the theft of their land and the destruction of their preferred means of livelihood.

It seems evident that the average Ute or Shoshone family could not sustain itself merely by farming small acreages of alfalfa, raising a few stock, or even through rations and lease income. Men on the Northern Ute, Ute Mountain Ute, Wind River Shoshone, and Fort Hall Shoshone reservations continued to hunt deer, elk, and sage

TABLE 12

EMPLOYMENT AND EMPLOYABILITY, PERSONS AGED EIGHTEEN AND OVER, FIVE RESERVATIONS, 1912–1962[a]

Years	Total Adults	Employed		Underemployed		Unemployed		Unemployable		Est. Annual Average Earnings for Employed and Underemployed $
		Raw	Percent	Raw	Percent	Raw	Percent	Raw	Percent	
Southern Ute										
1912	201	8	4	83	41	0	0	110	55	49
1920	192	3	2	29	15	54	28	106	55	70
1950	279	15	5	10	4	104	36	150	55	.....
1962	282	87	30	45	15	37	13	113	40	2,400
Ute Mountain Ute										
1912	240	4	2	101	42	3	1	132	55	37
1920	215	9	4	37	17	61	29	108	50	340
1950	313	5	2	10	3	126	40	172	55	.....
1962	386	49	13	78	20	74	19	185	48	1,600
Northern Ute										
1912	719	41	6	66	9	219	30	395	55	112
1920[b]	612	16	2	120	20	139	23	337	55	98
1950[b]	829	83	10	166	20	131	16	449	54	630
1962	547	44	8	83	15	110	20	310	57	1,000
Fort Hall Shoshone										
1912	1,154	21	2	120	10	378	33	635	55	89
1920	1,131	18	2	137	12	354	31	622	55	124
1950	1,251	25	2	50	4	488	39	688	55	.....
1962	1,005	190	19	458	45	190	19	167	17	1,525
Wind River Shoshone										
1912	440	14	3	120	27	64	15	242	55	76
1920	484	10	2	100	20	108	23	266	55	126
1950	911	45	6	142	16	223	25	501	55	.....
1962	720	50	7	62	9	248	34	361	50	3,000
Median averages in percentages										
1912			3		27		15		55	
1920			2		17		28		55	
1950			5		4		36		55	
1962			13		15		19		48	

Source: The 1912 data are from RCIA (1912: 160–65); 1920 from RCIA (1920: 128–31); 1950 from HCIIA (1953: 1131–34, 1200–1202, 1212–20, 1264–65; 1962 from CHCIIA (1963: 168–77, 178–87, 440–43, 456–62).
a. The 1962 figures include only those persons aged eighteen to fifty-five; thus the populations show an unreal decline between 1950 and 1962.
b. Includes mixed-blood population.

chickens. Women collected nuts and berries. In order for a family to subsist, the members pooled their labor and resources. Often several families in a single household, or several families in a joint cattle enterprise, shared in the products of their joint efforts to acquire resources, earned and unearned.

What has been the employment of Utes and Shoshones since 1910, and how has wage work affected reservation life? Table 12 compares employability and employment for the five reservations at four points in time. The first generalization of significance is that unemployment has been chronic, and that regular employment has been so low as to be scandalous. In 1912, with only 45 percent of the adult population considered to be in the labor force, a median of 7 percent of employable persons were employed. The median *annual* earnings of all Utes and Shoshones, employed and underemployed, was estimated at $76. It is clear that employment was not the keystone of Ute and Shoshone subsistence, but that employment income was pooled with all other sources of family income to help make ends meet. By 1920 a median of only 5 percent of employables were regularly employed, and the annual average earnings were estimated at $124. The Ute Mountain Ute case is interesting. If we recall that only the Ute Mountain Ute of all five groups decreased in farming, stock raising, and unearned income in this period, we see that the slack was taken up with regular and part-time employment. Furthermore, part-time employment at Ute Mountain was of longer duration and paid better than comparable work on the other reservations.

It is clear that the federal government has rushed stopgap measures into operation from time to time as the exigencies of the moment have called for them. When rations are low, or stock raising is unsuccessful, or when there are no per capita payments, the government initiates piecework and part-time jobs to generate short-term income for Indians. Table 13 shows the source of Indian employment in four selected years prior to, and following, the IRA.

TABLE 13

SOURCES OF ADULT EMPLOYMENT IN PERCENTAGES, FIVE RESERVATIONS, 1912–62

Tribe and Source	1912	1920	1950	1962
Southern Ute				
Federal	100	75	40	28
Tribal	0	0	10	72
Other	0	25	50	0
Ute Mountain Ute				
Federal	100	100	100	3
Tribal	0	0	0	97
Other	0	0	0	0
Northern Ute				
Federal	99	100	43	35
Tribal	0	0	33	65
Other	1	0	24	0
Fort Hall Shoshone				
Federal	100	100	30	30
Tribal	0	0	0	5
Other	0	0	70	65
Wind River Shoshone				
Federal	100	100	30	55
Tribal	0	0	20	40
Other	0	0	50	5

Since about 1910, the meager employment available has been furnished primarily by the federal government and the tribes. The tribes gained as employers following the IRA and gained even more following claims judgments. Both gave funds to tribal corporate bodies, and these organizations were empowered to create jobs, establish and pay salaries, and so forth. Only the Fort Hall Shoshones have not received huge land claims awards or other large sources of unearned income from gas, oil, or minerals. As of 1969 they have a case pending in court with other Shoshones for the loss of large portions of Wyoming, Idaho, and Utah ceded to them in Superintendent Doty's five treaties of 1863.

The Wind River Shoshones received a huge land claims judgment in 1938, eight years before the Indian Claims Commission Act. The Wind Rivers sought and were awarded compensation from the federal government for having been forced to share their reservation with the Arapahos. They also sought compensation for encroachment on their reservation by white settlers, ranchers, poachers, and white-owned livestock, but this compensation was not allowed (Trenholm and Carley 1964: 314–15). The Shoshones were awarded about $6,400,000, against which nearly $2,000,000 were deducted as government costs for operating the reservation and other incidentals. The offsetting costs infuriated the Shoshones, as similar government acts have enraged the Utes, and the Wind Rivers sued for part of the $2,000,000 withheld by the government. They got nothing for their efforts. Nearly twenty years later (1957), the Wind Rivers settled out of court for another part of the petition, which sought restitution for the "unconscionable" treaty negotiated with the Wind River Shoshones by Brunot in 1872. They received about $530,000, from which $100,000 was again offset for government expenses.

In mid-1939, funds from the 1938 judgment were made available to Wind River Shoshones. Each Individual Indian Money (IIM) account was allocated $2,450; yet only $100 in each account could be put to immediate use (Trenholm and Carley 1964: 319). The rest of the funds ($2,350 per reservation-enrolled Indian) were controlled by the BIA, and Indians could get them only if they successfully argued a case of need, that is, only if they convinced local BIA employees that they should be allowed to use their own IIM funds. This pattern of BIA control of IIM accounts has been followed on all Ute and Shoshone reservations. The neocolonial ward is treated as incompetent until he can prove—from issue to issue—otherwise. In 1939, minors' funds, too, were deposited in IIM accounts, and $500 from each account was made available to help each minor's family. In this manner a sustenance allowance for children was provided. Adults could get access to only about 20 percent of their children's funds, except in financial crises.

Lease and royalty income from gas and oil was added to income from the land claims judgments in the 1940s. Unearned income dipped in the early 1950s, but increased in the late 1950s with new court awards, leases, and royalties. Relatively high per capita payments have been provided for Wind River enrollees since the late 1950s but the amounts often fluctuate from year to year. As is pointed out above, the Wind River Shoshone population growth has correlated, roughly, with unearned income.

The three Ute groups began pressing claims in the late nineteenth century. The Northern Utes received their first award in 1931, about $1 million. Per capita distributions were not made, and the Utes had little access to these funds because they were deposited in trust accounts in the federal treasury and controlled by the BIA. (The funds were made available to the tribal business committee following incorporation in 1938.) In 1950 the Confederated Ute Tribes of Colorado and Utah (all Utes) received close to a $32 million judgment for land taken in Colorado. By 1962 they had won almost $50 million in claims. Over $18 million was tied up in litigation with the federal government over the government's demands for offsetting costs. The funds that were made available to the three Ute groups were spent in two ways. First, they were used on tribal projects such as the purchase of land in arrears on either water taxes or improvement taxes, or both; the purchase of heirship land; and the development of recreation projects and tribal buildings. Second, they were allocated to individuals in per capita payments. These budgetary actions always had to be approved by the BIA, the Secretary of the Interior, and the House Committee on Interior and Insular affairs.

Reverting to table 12, we note that employment was always extremely low. Some employment was provided by non-Indian ranchers and farmers through the early 1950s, but it was negligible. Over the many years most employment was provided by the BIA and the various tribes. The great exception to this is at Fort Hall, where men and women often were engaged as part-time farm laborers. They also worked in local potato processing plants during the peak seasons. The Fort Hall Shoshones have lived closer to a market area than the other groups in the study, and they have picked up other odd jobs in this area from time to time.

There was little fluctuation in the sources of Indian employment in 1912 and 1920, but great fluctuation in 1950 and 1962 (see table 13). Overall it is clear that Shoshones and Utes have long suffered from job instability. Federal agencies were directly, and tribal governments indirectly, dependent on federal funds to provide employment. There has been no viable economy on any Shoshone or Ute reserve to provide regular and stable employment.

The paucity of "outside" employment has been caused by several factors. It is evident that whites have not extended jobs to Indians and that there has been prejudice in hiring practices, but very few jobs have been available in any of the local white towns. The available jobs usually have gone to relatives of the employer, and practically always to whites. Moreover, the jobs often required skills that Indians did not possess, except for the highly exploitative farm and ranch labor (part-time). The Indian has been a consumer, and not a clerk, or any other type of employee, in white towns.

In brief, the rural unemployment problem has worsened since 1950 as the farm and ranch economies around all but the Fort Hall reserve have shriveled. Mechanization of farm and ranch work has reduced the labor time needed for production in agri-business. As production has increased, the average farm size has grown and more capital has been required for farmers to keep the land in production. As a corollary, fewer and fewer Indians in an ever-expanding population have sought jobs. Furthermore, fewer Indians have raised their own cattle and crops. Increased unearned income from land claims judgments has helped them to meet their domestic needs, while the great changes that have come about in agri-business have contributed to the Indians' demise as farmers and ranchers. The distance from markets, poor soil, small and complicated landholdings, and lack of access to credit capital have discouraged Indians and helped sustain their apathy.

Let us contrast Shoshones and Utes with the national population on employment. These statistics will shed light on how the Indians have been integrated into the labor market. In 1950, 70 percent of the noninstitutionalized adult Americans (that is, those not in the hospital, in school, in penal institutions, or in mental institutions) were classified in the labor force, against 45 percent for the Utes and Shoshones. In 1962, 77 percent of the total adult population was considered to be in the labor force against about 52 percent for the Utes and Shoshones. The 25 percent difference between Indians and the total population for these periods is not a coincidence; nor are the unemployment statistics a coincidence. In 1962 unemployment was 5.6 percent for the nation and 37 percent (a median) for the Utes and Shoshones (all national statistics are from SAUS 1966 [1966: 218]). As to skills, only 51 percent (median) of all employed and underemployed Utes and Shoshones possessed anything approaching a skill, and 49 percent had no skills (see table 14). We can infer from these percentages that the employable segments of the Ute and Shoshone populations were severely handicapped in the early 1960s. They had few skills to sell on a market which was glutted with labor and controlled by non-Indians.

TABLE 14

EMPLOYMENT AND SKILLS, FIVE RESERVATIONS, 1962

Skills	Percentages of Employed Tribesmen				
	So. Ute	Ute Mtn. Ute	No. Ute	Ft. Hall Sho.	Wind River Sho.
Semi-skills and skills, including skills of "self-employed"	70	33	55	45	51
No skills	30	67	45	55	49
Total	100	100	100	100	100

These percentages are based on all employment, i.e., permanent, temporary, full-time, part-time, "self-employment," piecework, etc. The data are from CHCIIA (1963: 168–87, 440–43, 456–62).

The rough correlation that we have noted among population growth, unearned income, and the decline in Indian agriculture is reflected in Indian household composition and size. In table 15, for instance, we see how family size varies with amount of income, and how amount of income varies with source (earned and unearned). The 1950 data represent the Ute reservation economies just before the time when land claims awards and relatively large oil, gas, and mineral income became available to them. The Wind River Shoshones had been receiving large amounts of unearned income for eleven years at this time. The Fort Hall Shoshones, similar to the Ute groups, were not the recipients of unearned income in 1950. The 1962 data represent the reservation economies during the period since large sources of unearned income have become available to them. All but Fort Hall were receiving large amounts of unearned income at this time. The two Shoshone groups are important in our analysis because one received relatively large amounts of unearned income at both ends of the period, and the other never received large amounts. The three Ute groups are

TABLE 15

ANNUAL AVERAGE FAMILY INCOME AND RATIO EARNED/UNEARNED SOURCES OF THE INCOME,
FIVE RESERVATIONS, 1950 AND 1962

Reservations	Average Family Size	Average Family Income $	Percentage of Income Earned	Percentage of Income Unearned
Southern Ute				
1950	6	900	80	20
1962	5	5,900	41	59
Ute Mountain Ute				
1950	6	900	90	10
1962	5	8,400	18	82
Northern Ute				
1950	6	1,525	60	40
1962	5	4,000	25	75
Fort Hall Shoshone				
1950	6	2,255	65	35
1962	6	2,260	67	33
Wind. River Shoshone				
1950	5	4,900	35	65
1962	5	5,000	34	66
Averages (unweighted)				
1950	5.8	2,096	66	34
1962	5.2	5,112	37	63

Source: These data are from HCIIA (1953: 1131–34, 1201–3, 1212–20, 1264–65); and CHCIIA (1963: 168–86, 440–43, 456–62).

important because they shifted from very little unearned income to large amounts of unearned income during the period.

We see that as family income increased between 1950 and 1962, family size decreased. We also see that the ratio of earned to unearned income was reversed. Closer inspection shows that the Shoshone groups changed very little during the period, whereas the Ute groups changed markedly. In both 1950 and 1962 the Fort Hall Shoshones maintained large family households on minuscule incomes, most of which was earned. In both 1950 and 1962 the Wind River Shoshones, however, who had been receiving per capita distributions from land claims judgments, oil, and other leases and royalties since 1939, maintained their relatively high incomes (unearned) and their relatively small family sizes. The Utes, who began receiving land claims, lease, and royalty income after 1950, experienced increases in their family incomes (unearned) and decreases in their family sizes. By 1962 the Ute groups were dependent on unearned sources of income.

The Wind River Shoshones, who became dependent on relatively large amounts of unearned income before the Utes (1939), also seem to have decreased the size of their family households before the Utes. On the other hand, the Fort Hall Shoshones, who had never received large amounts of unearned income, maintained their large family households throughout the entire span. Fort Hall household income in both 1950 and 1962 was meager but predominantly earned. It is of interest to our analysis that dominant sources and average amounts of income for Fort Hall families at both ends of the period are similar to the sources and amounts of Ute incomes in 1950. We can infer from these data that household size varies with the amount of income and, in the Shoshone and Ute cases, the amount of income varies with whether the income is earned or unearned. Paradoxically, the greater the ratio of earned over unearned income, the less the income and the larger the family household. This is a feature of a highly exploited population on an unstable resource base. Households increase in membership as resources become less stable and less predictable. Near kin, affines, and often distant kin, join together under the same roof to pool their resources and share their skills. When resources are more predictable and when income is relatively high, independent nuclear families tend to form separate households. This topic will be discussed in greater detail below. It is important here to note that the highly exploited Ute and Shoshone populations have been more stable when they have been dependent on unearned rather than earned (exploitative underemployment) income.

The relationship of the amount of family household income to unearned sources of income is illustrated in figure 6. We see that 63 percent of the increase in family household income is explained ("caused") by the increase in unearned income. In brief, the Shoshone and Ute populations have grown and family households have proliferated since 1950. In the same period there has been an increased dependence on predictable (if only for a few years) and unearned income on all but the Fort Hall

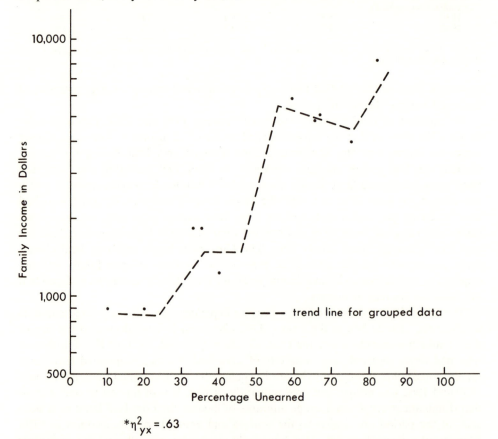

$$*\eta^2_{yx} = .63$$

FIGURE 6. Correlation ratio* of unearned income and family income, five reservations, 1950 and 1962. Unearned income = percent approximation of unearned income contribution to total income. Family income is standardized on five persons.

reserve. The shaky nature of the entire reservation economic situation in the past is obvious. The reservation economic structure is still shaky. A change here or there, such as termination of federal services to Indians or the drying-up of unearned income from leases, royalties, and land claims, could create instant and catastrophic problems for Indian families.

Although Ute and Wind River Shoshone incomes (for family households) increased from 1950 to 1962, the incomes only allowed them to consume, not to create businesses or investments. Indeed, the family incomes of the Utes in 1962 and the Wind River Shoshones in both 1950 and 1962 were not *real* in the sense that the gross (see table 15) was immediately available for use by the household heads, for IIM funds and minors' funds were stringently controlled by the BIA.

Let us make a few comparisons of Shoshone and Ute family incomes with those of non-Indians for about 1950. The state incomes in our data are for 1949; all of them are medians and all of them represent *money*. Indian family incomes, too, are medians, but in addition to money the figures include other sources of income. For instance, Indian income figures include BIA estimates of the cash value of animals procured in hunting and consumed by Indians, the cash value of crops and livestock that are raised and consumed by Indians, and the cash value of timber and other resources that are procured and used by Indians. In 1949 the average income for the Colorado family was $3,080, or nearly 230 percent greater than the family income for Southern and Ute Mountain Utes. The Idaho family income was $3,055, or about 36 percent greater than the Fort Hall Shoshone family income. The $3,300 income for the Utah family was nearly 120 percent greater than that for the Northern Ute family. The Wyoming family income of $3,525 was, however, topped by about 38 percent by that of the Wind River family. (The state figures are from SAUS 1966: 337–38).

In 1962 the average income (all sources) of all Ute and Shoshone families ($5,112) was $1,800 less than the average income (money) for all families in the western states ($6,928). Only the Ute Mountain Utes topped the western states' average in 1962. These comparisons do not show the great fluctuation in amount of income, sources of income and household size, and they do show that even in the peak income period for Shoshones and Utes, Indian families had less income than local non-Indian families.

RESERVATION ECONOMIC CONDITIONS, 1966

1966 was the year in which Sun dances were observed on all five reservations; so the 1966 economic conditions are selected for special attention here. We shall also discuss some of the options available to Utes and Shoshones to cope with life, and the prospects for economic conditions on the reservations as the satellite economies shrivel.

Tables 16 and 17 reflect the same grim statistics that obtained in previous years. Here the adult age is lowered to sixteen, and an employable person is classified as someone who is not a student, a housewife, a woman for whom no child-care substitute is available, or a person who is physically or mentally disabled, retired, or institutionalized. There are proportionately (about 3 percent) more employables than in 1962; yet only the Fort Hall Shoshone adults are more than 60 percent employable. The Fort Hall employable population is nearly 10 percent higher than the next closest Indian group, yet nearly 10 percent lower than the national average.

TABLE 16

EMPLOYABILITY OF PERSONS AGED SIXTEEN AND OVER, FIVE RESERVATIONS, 1966

Reservations	Total	Employable[a]		Unemployable	
		No.	Percent	No.	Percent
Southern Ute	368	166	45	202	55
Ute Mountain Ute	505	222	44	283	56
Northern Ute	856	411	48	445	52
Fort Hall Shoshone	1,809	641	35	1,168	65
Wind River Shoshone	1,104	530	48	574	52
Total	4,642	1,970		2,672	
$\bar{X}$			42		58
Median			45		55

Source: Data are adapted from the Report of Labor Force submitted semi-annually to the BIA by the superintendent at each agency.

a. Tests for the significance of differences among employability rates on the five reservations follow. Probabilities are derived from z score differences between percentages.

So. Ute	U. M. Ute	No. Ute	F. H. Sho.	W. R. Sho.	
X	N.S.	N.S.	.001	N.S.	So. Ute
	X	.05	.001	.05	U. M. Ute
		X	.001	N.S.	No. Ute
			X	.001	F. H. Sho.
				X	W. R. Sho.

TABLE 17

EMPLOYMENT OF EMPLOYABLE PERSONS AGED SIXTEEN AND OVER, FIVE RESERVATIONS, 1966

Reservations	Total Employable	Permanently[a] Employed		Under-employed		Unemployed	
		No.	Percent	No.	Percent	No.	Percent
Southern Ute	202	77	38	81	40	44	22
Ute Mountain Ute	283	103	36	64	23	116	41
Northern Ute	445	94	21	48	10	303	69
Fort Hall Shoshone	1,168	334	29	221	19	613	52
Wind River Shoshone	574	173	30	247	43	154	27
Total	2,672	781		661		1,230	
$\bar{X}$			29		25		46
Median			30		23		41

a. Tests for the significance of differences among permanent employment rates on the five reservations follow. Probabilities are derived from z score differences between percents.

So. Ute	U. M. Ute	No. Ute	F. H. Sho.	W. R. Sho.	
X	N.S.	.001	.001	.001	So. Ute
	X	.001	.01	.01	U. M. Ute
		X	.001	.001	No. Ute
			X	N.S.	F. H. Sho.
				X	W. R. Sho.

The employment percentages are also familiar: employment is rare, and underemployment and unemployment are chronic. Seventy-one percent (median 64 percent) of all employable Utes and Shoshones either have been out of work, of *all kinds*, for a year or more, or they have been engaged in short-term jobs. Short-term employment includes fighting fires, building fences, thinning beets, or putting up a white man's hay. All are highly exploitative, providing low wages, no job security, and no benefits.

By contrast, the national rate of unemployment was only 4 percent in 1966, and the rate in rural areas about 18 percent. The median and mean for Ute and Shoshone unemployment, on the other hand, was 41 and 46 percent, respectively (USPNACRP

1967: x).[6] National underemployment for farm workers ran as high as 37 percent in 1966, whereas the Southern Utes and Wind River Shoshones were underemployed at rates of 40 and 43 percent.

The permanent employment figures for Utes and Shoshones include any employment that engages a person for a year or more, even if that person works less than forty hours per week. Thus, these "permanent employment" statistics include Indians who work two days a week in a tribal garage, three days a week in a tribal arts and crafts shop, and so forth. Even with this liberal definition of permanent employment, only 29 percent of employables are permanently employed. (The median is 30 percent with a tight, low range of variation from 21 to 38 percent.) As in 1962, practically all jobs are provided by the tribes or the federal government. Again only Fort Hall is an exception; the Shoshones and Bannocks at Fort Hall get some employment from private sources.

These statistics indicate dire poverty. But in the United States many rural poor live in chronically depressed, poverty-stricken areas. Because there are vast areas of rural poverty in the United States, it might be assumed that Utes and Shoshones live in a depressed area in which all inhabitants, regardless of race, ethnicity, or religion, are equally impoverished. If this were true, Indians would be absolutely deprived, but the contexts in which they live would not contribute to their relative deprivation.

On all five reservations the Indians are surrounded by, and interspersed among, people who are either average or better on a national ranking of rural poverty-affluence (USPNACRP 1967: 4–5).[7] These rankings hold special interest for us because the Indians were *included* in the poverty-affluence measures for each county, and only rural populations were measured (cities such as Idaho Falls and Pocatello in Idaho were excluded from the county analyses). In these rankings the Southern and Ute Mountain Utes are located in counties which are ranked in the middle fifth of the affluence-poverty continuum; the Northern Utes and Wind River Shoshones are located in counties which are ranked in the next highest fifth; and the Fort Hall Shoshones are located in counties that rank from the highest fifth to the middle fifth. Yet each of these reservation populations rate extremely low on the measures used (see n. 7). The discrepancy between Indian and non-Indian in the same area is, indeed, marked.

With Indian unemployment, underemployment, and unemployability so high, we again ask the question, how do Shoshones and Utes cope with life? It is evident that these Indians are coping as they have for the past several decades. Unearned income is very important, as is income from part-time and full-time work. A modest amount of stockraising for Indian consumption, products from hunting and fishing, and commodities from welfare doles are also critical. Equally important with the income and the goods is *how* goods (such as automobiles, tools, livestock, deer, trout, and federal

6. National and rural employment data are from the U.S. President's National Advisory Commission on Rural Poverty (USPNACRP).

7. Counties were rank-ordered in 1960 in terms of dependency ratio of rural persons under 20 and over 65 to those between 20 and 64, number of rural families with less than $3,000 annual income, percentage of rural families with less than $3,000 annual income, percentage of persons 25 years and older with less than seven years formal schooling, percentage of dilapidated and deteriorated rural housing.

surpluses of rice, butter, wheat, etc.), money, and skills are pooled and shared within and between households.

Indian households in which there are no stable wage earners and little cash income must rely on the pooling of unstable income (from part-time work), low income (from welfare), and goods from relatively diverse sources. A single composite household, for instance, might include an aged person receiving welfare benefits from Old Age Assistance, children on Aid to Dependent Children, a man in his twenties or thirties working part-time when employment is available and hunting when it is not available, and so forth. Perhaps no one in the household owns a car, but an automobile is borrowed from a relative residing in another house so that trips can be made to the store. In return, the borrowers contribute services, labor, or even goods such as venison from a hunting venture, to the lender.

Table 18 shows the variation in the sources of Shoshone and Ute unearned income for 1966. It is clear that all of the groups rely heavily on unearned income of which the two major sources are welfare and per capita payments. The Ute Mountain Utes and the Wind River Shoshones show the greatest amount of per capita income; the Northern Utes and the Fort Hall Shoshones show the greatest dependence on welfare income; and the Southern Utes take an intermediary position.

TABLE 18

SOURCES OF INDIVIDUAL AND FAMILY UNEARNED INCOME, FIVE RESERVATIONS, 1966

Reservations	Annual Per Capita Payment or Dividends	Percentage of Enrolled Members on Welfare—Tribal, County, Federal	Percentage of Families Receiving Commodities	Percentage of All Allotments on Lease (Heirs and Allottees)
Southern Ute	$240	4	. . . . .	55
Ute Mtn. Ute	$1,200	3	. . . . .	0
Northern Ute	$150	25	40	57
Fort Hall Sho.	$0	33	40	40
Wind River Sho.	$780	7	29	32

We can now account for variation in the means of economic maintenance among the five groups shown in table 17. The Northern Utes and Fort Hall Shoshones have the least employment and underemployment as well as the greatest dependence on welfare. The Southern Utes have the greatest employment and underemployment, and so they supplement their meager per capita income with some income from tribal and federal jobs. The Ute Mountain Utes and Wind River Shoshones have less employment and underemployment than the Southern Utes, but greater per capita income than all other groups.

The 1966 data used in tables 16–18 do not show unearned income that was deposited in IIM accounts in the 1950s and is currently available to the Southern and Northern Utes in the form of allowances drawn from the IIM accounts of children. Furthermore, the 1966 data do show funds deposited in the IIM accounts of Ute Mountain Utes and Wind River Shoshones that these people cannot expend without BIA permission. This especially applies to funds belonging to children. So the real income for Northern and Southern Utes is higher, and the real income for Ute Mountain Utes and Shoshones is lower, than is apparent from these tables. Of all five groups, only Fort Hall income and its sources are accurate as reported here. And only Fort Hall people have not received per capita payments. Since 1912 all our measures show that the Fort Hall Shoshones have been the most impoverished of the five groups, yet have had fewer ups and downs in population, employment, income and access to resources.

Indian Agriculture and the Metropolis: An Overview

The federal government, working through the BIA, has long attempted to encourage Utes and Shoshones to embark on an agriculturally based life. Various agricultural education programs were conducted, such as training Indians for farming with nothing more advanced than hand tools. Indians were denied access to water, yet Indian funds were used to develop land and water sources used by non-Indians. Indian lands were purchased by non-Indians, and other Indian lands were simply taken away from Indians following the GAA. In brief, petty entrepreneurs—farmers and stockmen—expanded onto Indian land, either expropriating or exploiting it, and began supplying the metropolis, with the complicity of the federal government.

Still, it made some sense to encourage Shoshones and Utes to engage in agriculture in the 1890s. In fact, it made some sense to encourage Indian participation as late as the 1920s, although the majority of Ute and Shoshone-owned soils were poor, the reservations were considerable distances from markets, the allotment lands were increasingly tied up in heirship status, and allotments and heirship lands generally could not be used by Indians because they lacked capital. Since 1950, however, it has not been wise to pursue agriculture on the three Ute and Wind River Shoshone reservations. It has been especially unwise for allottees, assignees, or heirs to try to farm small tracts of land in the past two decades. The land requirements and capital outlay to meet subsistence requirements alone have been beyond the reach of a majority of Indian families. This is not a fortuitous circumstance but the result of the consolidating and monopolistic development of the American agri-business working hand-in-hand with federal farm policy. Nevertheless, even since 1960 government and university experts (engaged by the tribes) have encouraged small ranch operations on some reservations (notably Wind River; see Wind River Agency 1965) and large tribally run operations on others (notably Northern Ute, as we will see in the following chapter; and Southern Ute, see Johnson 1963: 186–89).

It is abundantly clear why these livestock operations have not succeeded and it is highly improbable that they ever will succeed. Stock raising has been encouraged at a time when thousands of small ranch operators are going bankrupt every year, and when large operators are controlling more and more of the market. In fact, in a monopolistic fashion large super market chains are buying feeder lots and packing plants. Thus the chains themselves control almost all facets of production through vertical integration. Only calves are needed in these operations, and they can be purchased at nominal costs from producers located close to the feeder lots. It must be recognized that Ute and Shoshone cattle enterprises are located hundreds of miles (often mountainous) from markets. Distance from markets can increase costs as can mode of transportation. The Northern and Ute Mountain Utes must travel considerable distances to get to railroads, making stock-raising success less probable.

Furthermore, range-fed beef does not bring a good price on the market. This is related to technology, monopolization, and consumer preferences. The packing industry has been revolutionized by technological innovations. Currently most of the slaughtering and packing process is mechanized. The engineering of the machinery, however, requires standard-size animals. Beef, cattle, for instance, are desired at 700–900 pounds liveweight. Feeder-lot beef can be fattened on hybrid crops in a very short time. When the animals attain standard size, they are slaughtered. Range-fed beef cannot be controlled nearly so well. Their sizes vary and they do not grow as rapidly as the less active animals confined to feeder lots. Many large animals are not wanted at all by the biggest packing plants.

The second reason that range-fed beef are not desired is that informal cartels are beginning to control all means of beef production. Costs are reduced and profits increased for these informal cartels as they centralize ownership. In the process of growing larger, the corporations acquire access to greater amounts of capital and can increasingly control both wholesale purchase prices and market distribution prices of beef. While they are beginning to dominate the industry, it becomes more difficult for the small operator who produces range-fed beef to make a profit. Not only can the packing houses set the purchase price, but the big packers can demand feeder lot beef only. It is even a more closed market when the packers also own the feeder lots. Indeed, the current demand is increasingly for calves that can be quickly fattened on the feeder lots. To make a profit, the owner of range-fed animals is more and more dependent on his calves. In order for this operator to stay in business, he must withstand both the expenses of maintaining a large breeder stock and high transportation costs from the annual sale of the calves the breed animals produce. Only the largest operators survive.

The third cause of the demise of the range-fed beef industry is the consumer preference for well-marbled meat. High-intensity feeding (corn, sorghum, bran) of inactive animals on lots produces marbling. It also justifies the large packers when they refuse to buy range-fed beef, or when they bid very low for such beef because it is not well-marbled and tender.

The Northern Utes in particular are bitter because they were encouraged to invest in a relatively large and extremely expensive cattle enterprise in the early 1960s. They were told that it would be a growth enterprise well adapted to the reservation environment, Ute interests, and Ute life-styles. In fact, stock raising in range areas in the Mountain West was already on the decline, required few personnel, and was inappropriate for the environmental-economic niche occupied by the Northern Utes. In nearly ten years of operation the Ute enterprise has never shown a profit.

If stock raising is inappropriate as a tribal enterprise on a relatively large basis, it becomes even more difficult for small operators to compete, as production costs (transportation, hybrid crops, etc.) increase. The small entrepreneurs often cannot get the capital they need to see themselves through the calving seasons.

In the past decade, farming has not been profitable on any of the reservations except Fort Hall, where non-Indian lessees are operating very successfully. Bean farming in the area near Ute Mountain has been successful, but not on Ute Mountain land. The major farming on the three Ute and the Wind River Shoshone reservations has been in alfalfa (fodder), yet profitable alfalfa farming requires vast acreage for production as well as livestock to consume the product. Alfalfa is expensive to transport because it is bulky. Bulk can be overcome by reducing the hay to pellets, but this is expensive and represents a capital outlay over and above water taxes, seed, tractors, bailers, elevators, and trucks. Stock raising and farming (agri-business) are clearly related in the Mountain West, and they have been dying together on and near all of these reservations, save Fort Hall.

Since 1920 the farm population of the United States as a whole has decreased by two-thirds, and its percentage of the total population has plummeted from 30 to 6. Although the acreage of all land in farms has increased, the number of farms has been reduced by much more than half, and the average size of farms in the United States, since 1940 alone, has increased by well over 200 percent (SAUS 1966: 613–24; 1967: 608). Between 1954 and 1964, the number of farms in the mountain states was reduced by over 25 percent, and the average size of farms was increased by over 27 percent— from 1,450 acres to 2,000 acres (SAUS 1966: 617; 1967: 608). Moreover, in the mountain states only the producers whose farm products were valued at over $40,000 per annum in 1959 and 1964 showed an increase in the value of their products. The average for all other producers, i.e., all who sold products whose total values were less than $40,000 in 1959 and 1964, showed a decrease in the value of their farm products ranging between 3 and 4 percent for the $10,000–$40,000 bracket, and between 1 and 2½ percent for the $2,500–$10,000 bracket (SAUS 1967: 610). Finally, because of feeder lots and sundry technological innovations, the man-hours (labor time) necessary to produce beef (measured in liveweight) have been cut nearly in half since 1935, and one-half of that reduction was effected between 1960 and 1964 (SAUS 1967: 629).

In the President's National Advisory Commission Report on Poverty (1967: 142), we read:

Today's farm policy is dominated by acreage control and price support programs. Well over two-thirds of the federal cost of assistance to farmers, including export subsidies, is associated with efforts to balance supplies with demands for individual farm commodities. This is a commercial farm policy rather than a policy to alleviate rural poverty. Farmers receive benefits from this assistance approximately in proportion to their contribution to total farm output.

If farming must be large and is dominated by price supports, why not have a large operation employing many Indians? The most obvious reason is that employment goes down as the size of the operation increases and as mechanization becomes a more efficient labor-time producer. From the same source:

We believe technological advance in agriculture will continue at such a high rate that problems of adjustment from farm to non-farm employment will be continual. This advance in agriculture will not assist the rural poor. In fact, most of the burden of this adjustment will fall on them.

Indian Industrial Development

As of 1966 the reservation economies had provided few other prospects for employment, especially employment under Indian control. Although agency personnel at each Ute and Shoshone reservation spoke of the possibility of enticing small manufacturing firms to move onto the reservations and provide jobs, none of the reservations had been successful except Southern Ute, which got a private trade-technical school to establish itself there in the mid-1960s.

On other reservations around the West, the pattern has been to expend Indian capital to provide the "private enterprises" with a building or buildings, to lease the building at a low annual rate, and to provide a cheap labor force for the industries involved. The industries do not come under Indian ownership, and Indians do not control the means of production. The employed tribal members benefit from salaries that allow them to consume in local white towns (see Steiner 1968: 124–35). Approximately ten thousand new jobs have been opened by private industries on American Indian reservations since 1960; yet six thousand of these jobs have gone to non-Indians. So the better-trained non-Indians living in the shriveling rural areas are occupying the jobs ostensibly made available for Indians (see BIA 1968). It is clear that the surplus, extremely cheap labor force in the withering satellite sectors of the economy are being exploited while the Indians are being superexploited.

Since the 1930s all but the Fort Hall Shoshones have reaped some income from the mining of coal (Wind River), oil (the Ute groups), gas, uranium, phosphate, gypsum, potash, and gilsonite (the Ute Groups and Wind River). Yet Indians have not controlled production, or even gained employment from the operations. Multinational corporations have surveyed the land, tendered bids, drilled the wells, extracted the resources, and transported, refined, and marketed the products. The multinational corporations have profited from the special use tax (allowance) applicable to the exploitation of Indian lands, as well as from the tax depletion allowances offered to oil, gas, and mineral producers generally. The carrots given to the reservations are lease and royalty income. The BIA has not encouraged the tribes to develop their own minerals, and the tribes have neither the expertise nor the capital to do so alone. Judging from the influence wielded by the mining lobbies prior to the passage of the General Allotment Act, and the influence wielded by the multinational oil and mineral corporations in maintaining the privileged tax depletion and protective import laws that have sheltered them for decades, it is doubtful that the government will make available massive loans for the Utes and Shoshones to use in exploiting their own resources in the so-called "free enterprise" American economy. In mining, too, Indian resources are being drained from the reservations while the profits go to non-Indians.

The development of commercial recreation was begun at Northern Ute on a tribal basis and at Wind River on an individual basis. Neither has provided many jobs or much income. The short life history of the Northern Ute venture is discussed in the next chapter. It is important to note here that recreation, the sale or leasing of mountain lands to affluent whites for summer retreats, is possible on all of the reservations, but each of these possibilities has created legitimate skepticism and grievances at Northern Ute, where Indians see white men moving on to Indian land once again and exploiting Indian resources for white pleasure. Nationally, nearly 50 percent of all non-Indian capital used for reservation industries that are neither mineral nor agricultural has been spent on recreation enterprises (see BIA 1968). The Indian, of course, does not have sufficient income to vacation on his own reservation.

Indian Employment in Urban Areas
With few job opportunities on or near the reservations, and little prospect of developing viable reservation economies, with the tribal corporate bodies themselves heavily dependent on unearned income, and the BIA representing a special form of

the federal welfare enterprise which offers some services but little hope, it seems that one possibility for a better life for Indians is to seek employment in urban areas. Some Utes and Shoshones did so, especially during World War II. Since the early 1950s the BIA's Employment Assistance Program (EAP) (formerly the Navaho-Hopi Rehabilitation Program and then the Relocation Program) has been developed to help the transition from rural to urban life. Yet the EAP has never been successful with Utes and Shoshones, and it provides a classic example of how Indians become sensitized to their deprivation as they are moved from pockets of rural poverty and placed in pockets of urban poverty.

There are no complete records on how many Utes and Shoshones relocated between the early 1950s and 1966, but officials on all of their reservations doubt that anyone has ever stayed on relocation longer than two or three years. Relocatees from such reservations as Northern and Ute Mountain Ute seldom stay away over a few months.

The few relocation statistics available are most enlightening. In 1962 four people left the Ute Mountain reserve under the EAP. None stayed on relocation. The Southern Utes sent two adults on relocation. Both returned before the year was out. In 1962 there were nineteen relocatees from Northern Ute (families included). All returned. Through 1961, at Fort Hall, only fifty-three persons had enrolled in the program, but because more than 50 percent dropped out before they had completed their training, the program was terminated. It was reopened in 1962, and five young people relocated. It is thought that another twelve might have gone on their own (without BIA assistance). At any rate, it is alleged that the middle-aged and elderly Fort Hall Shoshones put extreme pressures on the younger people to stay on the reservation, maintain Shoshone ways, and help the family. At Wind River there were about seventeen relocatees under the EAP in 1962 and perhaps four others who moved to urban areas on their own.[8]

Why do so few go on relocation? And of those who go, why do the majority return? Indians I know who have been encouraged by BIA officials to relocate in Denver, Chicago, Los Angeles, and Oakland usually give somewhat similar answers. They go to get a skill and a job because there is nothing for them on the reservation. They return because they get lonely for their friends and kin. They get lonely for the reservation. They allege that they get paid less than whites for the same kind of work and, moreover, that they cannot make ends meet in the city. As despair creeps in, they often begin drinking. And when they get drunk, failing to show up for work, they often get laid off. The despair and dysphoria increase. The Indians have no savings, and their ghetto counterparts have no savings either, so other Indians cannot be turned to for help. At this point Indians have few options. The two that are taken most frequently are return to the reservation, or suicide.

The Indians who return to the reservation do so to get support from their kin. Paradoxically, the kin who have remained on the reservations have constantly urged the urban migrants to return because the reservation dwellers, particularly the aged and the female household heads, themselves need support from the relocatees. That is, although the relocatees might be employed full-time in the city and would not be employed full-time on the reservations, they do not earn enough money to support

8. These data are from my field notes and from the chairman, House Committee on Interior and Insular Affairs (1963) (henceforth CHCIIA).

themselves and to help support their reservation-based kin while they are working in the city. When the relocatees return to the reservations they might find part-time work. Or they might hunt, fish, raise a couple of calves, and provide automobiles for trips to the agencies, to the trading posts, and to the white towns. In return for the support they provide, they receive support from their kin in the way of a place to live, mutual sharing of welfare income and commodities, lease income, and so forth.

Some idea of why the EAP has not worked and why Indians, after the EAP practice does not live up to the euphoric BIA promise, are often bitter about the program when they return can be culled from the following example from the Seattle program.

Reservation Indians from the western United States who locate in Seattle are placed for three weeks in modern apartments with carpeted floors, draperies, an all-electric kitchen, private bath, and living room. The "Indian appreciation of contemporary living may motivate him to excel in his trade *so that some day he may be able to afford similar luxuries for his family*" (Brophy and Aberle 1966: 104; emphasis added). After his three-week "indoctrination" period the Indian and his family move off to an urban slum and are given a poverty-level subsistence income while the potential wage earner (male or female adult Indian) acquires the skills to become a body-fender re-pair man, diesel mechanic, hair stylist, or something of the sort. The family moves from comparative opulence back to squalor, but this time in a new and ugly urban setting. Until they find their way to the local Indian center, they will make few friends and might begin drinking to escape from despair or to "have a good time" (see Steiner 1968: 175–92; Brophy and Aberle 1966: 102–5; Nader 1968: 14–15).

The results of the EAP are not well understood. The BIA has no adequate records of how many people acquire skills and jobs and stay in cities once they move there, although there is little doubt but that the absolute number of Ute and Shoshone re-locatees is small relative to the number of their congeners who remain on reservations. Furthermore, of those who relocate, few stay in cities or acquire skills. On a national scale, Ablon (1964: 297) guesses that no more than 17 percent of the first two hundred families to relocate in the San Francisco-Oakland area during 1954–55 stayed there until 1963.

A more recent study of Indians in Los Angeles (Price 1968: 170) shows that only 19 percent of all Indians in that city were born in the same state as their fathers, that the vast majority of them arrived there since 1955 (the beginning of the relocation program in that city), and that the median year of arrival of relocatees was 1961. Price reports that in recent years (circa 1962–65) the BIA in Los Angeles assisted approximately 1,300 Indian relocatees annually. His report does not delve into reserva-tion life or the reasons for which Indians leave the city and return to their reservations, although he mentions a survey made by the Navajo Tribe covering their nine-year involvement in the EAP. About 37 percent of all Navajo families (555) who were relocated during this period returned (Young 1961: 236). Price's (1968: 168–75) own survey demonstrates that relocatees are young (median age, twenty-five years), have resided in Los Angeles for two years (median), have incomes of $4,000 (median), live in central Los Angeles (59 percent), speak native languages, associate primarily with American Indians, and would return to their reserves if they could get comparable employment there.

The above figures are revealing in that they show that Indians locate in ghettos and earn low incomes. The income of the Indian family in Los Angeles matched the national *non-white* family median income for 1965, was $700 *lower* than the average income of families in Chicago's black ghetto in 1965, and was $3,000 below the national white family median income for 1965 (see Steiner 1968: 211; SAUS 1967: 333). Since leaving the reservation the Indian migrants' expectations have risen, and the discrepancy between what they have and what they have been promised has been widened. Price's survey turned up only thirteen Utes and nineteen Shoshones (included are Western Shoshones from reservations and rancherias other than Fort Hall and Wind River). Since Los Angeles, San Francisco-Oakland, Denver, and Seattle are the major relocation centers for these people, it is safe to infer that very few Utes and Shoshones have ever gone on relocation, and fewer still have stayed on relocation.

Welfare Responses to Economic Deprivation

As the reserve economies have foundered and promises for solvency have remained empty, the federal government has responded with welfare measures. The BIA alone grew in employees from 9,500 in 1955 to 16,000 in 1968, and their budget increased from $49 million in 1949 to $241 million in 1969. The increase in budget and employees to administer to Indian needs is a characteristic welfare response to poverty. This response has not been sufficient to the task at hand. In 1964 the federal government's "War on Poverty" reached the reservations with the intention of solving Indian problems. In 1969 about $430 million were spent on various federal programs (including the BIA's) to benefit Indians.

The Office of Economic Opportunity (OEO) and the Community Action Projects (CAP) are two instruments which have been used in the War on Poverty. As in most governmental welfare programs, only symptoms are treated. On each reservation a few Indians receive federal largesse through salaries from jobs made available in OEO and CAP. In turn, they use their salaries for daily consumption. Soon after the programs were initiated, Indians got into several squabbles with white bureaucrats from OEO, and with welfare experts from various universities over how funds should be allocated (see Steiner 1968: 193–214, for a fact-filled essay on the War on Indian Poverty). As funds were made available and as the Indians who were drawn into the OEO and CAP programs increased their expectations about what ought to be done and what could be done, they found that they could not achieve their expectations. Whereas the federal government was happy with the progress that was made, the $4 million allocated in 1964 amounted to about $10 per Indian, and the $12 million allocated in 1966 amounted to about $30 per Indian. Even during 1968–69, when $430 million (all federal programs) were spent on Indian programs, the national average family income of Indians was only $1,500. As a contrast in priorities and allocation of resources, from 1966 through 1969 the federal government spent about $30 billion per year on the Vietnam war.

The five Ute and Shoshone reservations received the OEO and CAP in the mid-1960s, and each of these organizations offered a few full-time and part-time jobs to Indians. CAP newsletters were circulated, beginning in 1966, on all of these reserves, apprising Indians of community work projects, counseling services, trips, work opportunities, welfare rights organizations, and the visits of EAP officers. The War on Indian Poverty is but one more stopgap, which has provided modest funds for some

Utes and some Shoshones. Most of these funds, however, have made their way to white shop owners in the local areas. If anyone uses the funds to generate more capital, it is the white shopkeeper and not the Indian consumer.

HEALTH AND PRINCIPAL CAUSES OF DEATH

Indian health problems have been monumental since white contact. The Shoshones and the Utes were greatly depleted by disease, starvation, and freezing, not to mention warfare, from the 1850s through the turn of the century. As for diseases in the more recent period, table 19 shows that the incidence of trachoma (contagious inflammation of the conjunctiva and cornea of the eye) and tuberculosis (all forms) alone was staggering. Although the range of positive cases of trachoma and TB per examined population was reduced between 1912 and 1927, the average (22–24 percent) remained almost unchanged: *nearly one-fourth* of the Shoshones and Utes had these diseases. This was higher than the all-Indian average rate for these two diseases in 1912 and 1923 (Committee of the National Tuberculosis Association 1923: 48). The incidence of other diseases was also high—out of all proportion to national rates—especially childhood diseases such as rachitis, mumps, chicken pox, and measles; diseases that afflict people of all ages, such as dysentery and pneumonia; and general malnutrition.

By contrast, during the 1920s a report was submitted to the Senate which stated that during the colonial period the TB rate was not as high among Indians as it

TABLE 19

TUBERCULOSIS AND TRACHOMA, FIVE RESERVATIONS, 1912–27

Tribes and Years	Percentage of Population Examined	Individuals With TB (Raw)	Individuals With Trachoma (Raw)	Percentage of Individuals Examined Found to have TB and/or Trachoma	Estimated Percentage of Population Having TB and/or Trachoma
Southern Ute					
1912	23	24	56	95	41
1920	27	28	50	87	32
1927	63	10	35	13	. . . . .
Ute Mountain Ute[a]					
1912	28	1	66	49	41
1927	43	10	37	24	. . . . .
Northern Ute					
1912	63	27	40	9	14
1920	48	59	110	32	30
1927	68	10	246	32	. . . . .
Fort Hall Shoshone					
1912	33	44	5	8	5
1920	32	54	15	12	41
1927	13	37	40	32	. . . . .
Wind River Shoshone					
1912	37	60	135	33	47
1920	40	19	37	10	77
1927	99	10	92	11	. . . . .
Averages					
1912	40			24	21
1920	39			23	45
1927	51			22	. . . . .

Source: Data are from RCIA (1912: 170–74, 1920: 131–35, 1927: 58–60).

a. No data are given for Ute Mountain Ute in 1920 since they had no physician.

TABLE 20

MAJOR ENDEMIC DISEASES AND CAUSES OF DEATH, FIVE RESERVATIONS, 1945–50

Reservations	Major Diseases in Order of Frequency	Major Causes of Death in Order of Frequency
Southern Ute	Diseases of childhood TB Upper respiratory inf. VD	TB Cerebral hem. Cirrhosis Prostatitis Accidents
Ute Mountain Ute	Dermatitis Diseases of childhood Diseases of the eyes TB	Senility TB Gall bladder Accidents
Northern Ute	Dermatitis Upper respiratory inf. Diseases of childhood	TB Pneumonia Accidents Heart disease
Fort Hall Shoshone	Malnutrition Dermatitis Diarrhea TB Diseases of the eyes Pneumonia VD Diseases of childhood	TB Pneumonia Diarrhea Infection and neglect Gall bladder Accidents Heart disease
Wind River Shoshone	Malnutrition TB Upper respiratory inf. Diseases of the eyes Diseases of childhood	TB Pneumonia Diseases of childhood Accidents Heart disease
All reservations	Gastroenteritis including malnutrition, diarrhea, etc. Dermatitis including all forms of skin infections Upper respiratory infections including TB, pneumonia, etc. Eye diseases of all kinds including trachoma, glaucoma, conjunctivitis, etc.	Upper respiratory infections, especially pneumonia and TB Interrelated effects of malnutrition and neglect Accidents, including deaths caused by freezing, alcohol-related deaths, etc. Heart disease

Source: Data are adapted from HCIIA (1953: 1132–34, 1200–1203, 1212–20, 1264–65). Most of these data represent chronic diseases over the 1945–50 period. Neither raw figures nor percentages were given.

TABLE 21

CAUSES OF REPORTED DEATHS, FOUR RESERVATIONS, 1968

	Total Deaths	Accidents, Violence	Respiratory Diseases	Digestive and Nutritional Diseases	Infections and Parasitic Diseases	Circulatory Diseases	Other or Unknown
Southern and Ute Mountain Ute	18	7	2	3	2	3	1
Northern Ute	24	6	4	2	2	1	9
Fort Hall Shoshone	33	8	4	5	3	7	6
Totals in 100 percent	(75)	29	13	13	9	15	21

Source: Indian Health Service (1969).

a. Southern and Ute Mountain Ute data are combined by the Indian Health Service. Data were not available for the Wind River Shoshone.

was among whites (Committee of the National Tuberculosis Association 1923: 38). So Indians were not always afflicted with this disease. Then, as now, TB is correlated with several factors other than the tubercle bacillus (*Mycobacterium tuberculosis*). The organism appears among populations where there is a lack of food—in quantity, or quality, or both—worry, chronic fatigue, and other diseases or unhealthy conditions. TB is an infectious disease which is excerbated by the general conditions of poverty but which can be partially controlled by the medicine isoniazid. There is no firm evidence that any populations, Indian or not, have developed immunities to TB.

It is not surprising that the diseases and major causes of Ute and Shoshone deaths in 1950 and 1968, diseases which occur at rates hundreds of times greater than among whites, have not changed much in kind since the early reservation period.[9] Their high incidence reflects the Indian's environment: his insufficient sanitation facilities, poor and crowded living conditions, and poor nutrition.[10] On top of all this, there is an unusually high incidence of "accidental" deaths and suicides among Utes and Shoshones. The accidental deaths are usually attributed to freezing, drowning, fires in the home, and auto accidents.

HOUSING

During the reservation period Ute and Shoshone housing has, on the whole, been abominable by American standards as well as the standards in the Mountain West states. From table 22 we can infer how the housing conditions of these people have contributed to their unusually unhealthy history. In 1920 (roughly fifteen years before the IRA), 73 percent of Utes and Shoshones were living in tents, tepees, and other floorless dwellings. They were, of course, no longer on the chase; so their dwelling sites were more or less permanent, and they remained close to their refuse. Though they located near streams, rivers, and springs, the water they used was not so clean as it had been thirty or forty years earlier before whites and livestock began sharing the use of the area. Only at Southern and Northern Ute did a significant number of people live in dwellings with floors. This is not to suggest that floored housing among the Utes was comparable to local white housing in those areas. The best Ute housing was log cabins, which were (and are) dark and damp, yet durable. Most floored housing, however, consisted of clapboard shacks, walled tents, and the like.

In 1950 (roughly fifteen years after the IRA), the only place where tepees or floorless tents were still occupied year around was at Fort Hall. The impoverished Fort Hall people have had the worst of it (for the five groups) on all of the measures we have seen so far. Yet in 1950 the majority of all Shoshone and Ute housing was substandard by local white comparisons: only 37 percent of all Utes and Shoshones lived in log cabins, and this was the *best* Indian housing. Frame houses were usually worse than the log cabins and were inhabited by about 50 percent of all Utes and Shoshones.

9. The Public Health Service, Indian Health Facilities, report by geographic area—such as Phoenix, which includes Northern Ute—rather than by reservation; so I could not get specific information on each reservation. See U.S. Department of Health, Education, and Welfare, Public Health Service (1963).

10. See the comments of C. J. Wagner in U.S. Department of Health, Education, and Welfare, Public Health Service (1963).

TABLE 22

TYPES OF HOUSING, FIVE RESERVATIONS, SELECTED YEARS

Year and Type of Housing	So. Ute Raw	%	Ute Mtn. Raw	%	No. Ute Raw	%	F.H. Sho. Raw	%	W.R. Sho. Raw	%	Total Raw	%	Percent Range
1920													
Permanent, all forms from log cabins to clapboard shacks with floors	55	47	0	0	158	63	80	18	25	13	318	27	0–63
Permanent, all forms from log cabins to clapboard shacks without floors	63	53	0	0	7	3	70	15	35	18	175	15	0–53
Tepees, tents and other impermanent structures without floors	0	0	148	100	85	34	300	67	135	69	668	58	0–100
											1161	100	
1950												$\bar{X}$	
Log cabins		35		30		51		17		50		37	
Frame, clapboard, etc.		45		55		47		78		47		54	
Stone, earth and misc.		20		15		2		1		3		8	
Tents, tepees		0		0		0		4		0		1	
												100	

Data are adapted from RCIA (1920: 131–35), and HCIIA (1953: 1132–34, 1200–1203, 1212–20, 1264–65).
a. Percent mean is not weighted.

In one major Northern Ute community, Lang (1953: 32–35) reports for 1948 that of all the houses he surveyed only 8 percent had doors, insulation, and windows, and these were usually log cabins. Another 43 percent were army surplus shacks or clapboard houses with broken windows and ill-fitting doors. The remaining 49 percent were wall tents with floors, or single-room structures made of cardboard, refrigerator casings, and other scrap materials.

As for household conveniences, the water supply for 89 percent of these Northern Ute homes was taken from ditches and streams. Only 11 percent had water piped inside. As for cooking and heating, 96 percent had nothing but coal-wood stoves. Only 11 percent of the homes had electricity.

By 1965, housing at Northern Ute had improved considerably by the 1950 standards but not by adjacent white standards. Though houses were still predominantly frame or log cabins in a poor state of repair, in 1965 only 45 percent lacked running water. Moreover, 50 percent of the homes had septic tanks, 50 percent had gas or electric stoves for cooking or heating, and 90 percent had electricity (Christiansen, et al. 1966: 13). In the early 1960s the federal government and the tribe began a sewer pipe and water project to get clean water and plumbing to most homes. The project was still in progress in 1969 (*Ute Bulletin*, May 1969: 3). There were some notable additions in Ute homes: 79 percent had television and 78 percent had radios. Not all of them worked in 1965 because Utes were short on finances to get damaged sets repaired. But the radio and television sets had worked within the past decade. This is important, for it has been my experience that Utes play their television and radio sets for the better part of the day and into the night. In so doing, they are constantly apprised of consumer products and the amenities of American life. Only 13 percent of Northern Ute homes have telephones; to make a call, the majority must get to the public telephone at the community trading post in their area.

At Fort Hall the housing and conveniences had not improved as much in the early 1960s as at Northern Ute. Whereas about the same percentage of Fort Hall and Northern Ute housing was comparable to white housing in their areas (5 percent), 82 percent of Fort Hall housing consisted of box cars, substandard frame houses often in need of renovation, or tentshacks. Only 13 percent were log cabins (Harmsworth and Nybroten 1964: 80–83). Only 19 percent of the Fort Hall houses had indoor plumbing, and 18 percent had indoor bathrooms (50 percent of the Northern Ute homes had both). Sixty-four percent of Fort Hall homes had electricity, and 56 percent had television sets. Only 6 percent had telephones.

TABLE 23

DWELLING UNITS BY NUMBER OF PERSONS PER ROOM, FORT HALL SHOSHONE,
NORTHERN UTE, UTAH, AND IDAHO, 1960 AND 1965.

	Fort Hall (1960) Percent	No. Ute (1965) Percent	Utah (1960) Percent	Idaho (1960) Percent
No. of persons per room				
One or less	21	29	74	78
1.01 or more	79	71	26	22
	100	100	100	100
Median no. of persons per room	2.03	1.5	0.80	0.74
Av. size of household	6.12	6.60	.....	3.25

Data are adapted from U.S. Department of Commerce, Bureau of the Census (1967: 4, 36–40); Christiansen et al. (1966: 13); Harmsworth and Nybroten (1964: 71–73).

Table 23 provides us with a final set of comparisons on Ute and Shoshone housing. Comparable data are not available for the other groups. It is clear from these data that Ute and Shoshone households are overcrowded and much different from the averages in their respective states. Whereas only about 25 percent of Utes and Shoshones live in houses with one person or less per room, about 75 percent of the residents of Utah and Idaho live in houses with one person or less per room. The general populations of Utah and Idaho are significantly different from the Utes and Shoshones also in the average size of households. Whether the Indian goes to the city or not, he sees the differences between his own home and his own conveniences and those of the whites around him. Plates 4–9 depict Indian and non-Indian (including BIA employees) housing on the Northern Ute and Wind River Shoshone reservations.

EDUCATION AND LITERACY

The data in table 24 account for Utes and Shoshones eighteen years of age or older in 1950. The illiteracy reported for the groups is extremely high, although data are not complete for the Southern and Ute Mountain Utes. Only Wind River has a low illiteracy rate, but like all of the other groups, practically none of the Wind Rivers had a twelfth-grade education, and the college graduate was unique.

In 1947, 2.7 percent of the total United States population over fourteen years of age was illiterate. In 1950, 31 percent of the entire United States population over twenty-five years of age had completed high school, and 9.4 percent of the same population had graduated from college. The median school years completed for all races was 11.8 (SAUS 1966: 113). The Indians' tiny percentage of high school graduates,

PLATE 4. White man's home, owned by Bureau of [Indi]an Affairs, on Wind River Shoshone reservation, [For]t Washakie, Wyoming. May 1969.

PLATE 5. Indian's home on Wind River Shoshone reservation, May 1969.

[PL]ATE 6. Two Northern Ute homes on Whiterocks [Roa]d, Northern Ute reservation, close to Sun dance [gro]unds. May 1969.

PLATE 7. White man's home on Whiterocks Road, Northern Ute reservation, close to Sun dance grounds. May 1969.

[PL]ATE 8. Four Northern Ute homes, Randlett, Utah. [Ma]y 1969.

PLATE 9. White-occupied home owned by Bureau of Indian Affairs, Northern Ute reservation, Fort Duchesne, Utah. May 1969.

TABLE 24

ADULT ILLITERACY AND EDUCATION, FIVE RESERVATIONS, 1950

Reserve	Total Adults	Illiterate (Percent)	12th Grade Educ. (Percent)	College Graduates (Percent)
Consolidated Ute:				
Southern and Ute Mountain	(592)	.....	(27) 5	(0) 0
Northern Ute[a]	(829)	(450) 54	(54) 7	(4) 0.004
Fort Hall Shoshone	(1251)	(700) 56	(50) 4	(3) 0.002
Wind River Shoshone	(911)	(70) 7	(75) 8	(1) 0.001
Av.			(206) 6	(8) 0.002

These data are adapted from HCIIA (1953: 1131–34, 1200–1202, 1212–20, 1264–65). Southern Ute data were merged with Ute Mountain, and the Wind River data had to be interpolated from the Shoshone—Arapaho totals.
a. Includes mixed-bloods, whose 490 members were dissociated from the tribe in 1954.

their gross lack of college graduates, and the high rates of illiteracy give some indication of how they were handicapped in relation to whites. Shoshones and Utes had meager educations and a paucity of skills. Indian education was usually acquired in all-Indian schools, generally did not go beyond the eighth grade (only 27 percent of all Utes and Shoshones had even reached the eighth grade). Utes and Shoshones, therefore, were not prepared to compete for jobs other than unskilled farm-ranch labor, even if other work had been open to them. For the 1960–66 period some data are available on Southern Ute, Northern Ute and Fort Hall Shoshone education. There have been modest quantitative improvements in adult education since 1950, but these data say nothing about the quality of education. It is generally understood that after about the second grade Shoshone and Ute students begin to drop behind whites in academic performance and never again close the gap (Witherspoon 1961; Berry and Nybroten 1964: 113–138; Jorgensen 1964). The dropout rate for Indian students is great after the eighth grade. The following statistics, scanty as they are, confirm the generalizations about the quantity of education.

In 1965 the median years of school completed for all Northern Ute household heads and homemakers was 8.7 against 7.7 for all Fort Hall Shoshone household heads in 1960 (Christiansen et al. 1966: 9–10; Harmsworth and Nybroten 1964: 74–75). The median years completed for all U.S. household heads in 1960 was 10 (SAUS 1966: 339). It is presumed that the median years completed by non-Indian household heads in the Mountain West is even higher than the national figure, because the median school years completed by everyone in the Mountain West over twenty-five years of age was 12 in 1960 compared to the national median of 10.6. The median school years completed by Fort Hall Shoshones twenty years of age and over was 9 in 1960 and for Southern Utes it was 10.1 (The Southern Ute statistics are based on a sample of 157 [64 percent of the total] adult Southern Utes, adapted from Johnson [1963: 33]).

Whereas since 1950 there has been a modest improvement in the number of years Utes and Shoshones attend school, a modest improvement in their housing and, perhaps, a modest improvement in their health, the white communities around them have progressed faster in all of these areas, have maintained control of the local polities and economies, and have treated Indians, generally, as a pariah caste, even as they have exploited them. Utes and Shoshones have not increased their access to strategic resources with their new educations, nor have they gained control over their own lives.

POLITICAL PARTICIPATION

In 1924 the Citizenship Act gave the political franchise to all United States Indians. A few Indian veterans of World War I had been granted citizenship under an act of 1919, and as early as 1887 some Indians had received citizenship following the General Allotment Act if they (a) voluntarily established residence in the United States apart from their tribes, taking up "civilized ways," or if they (b) received "patents" to their allotted land, i.e., converted their land to alienable and taxable status (Haas 1957: 12–30).

The General Allotment Act rather candidly gets at the nub of the "citizenship problem." It focuses on land ownership and tax obligations. The GAA was enacted on the assumption that property ownership creates responsible citizens; but responsibility entails paying taxes on the land, and paying taxes means that land owners have to work their land for a profit so that they can pay their taxes. Indeed, Indian land (because it has been held in trust) and land taxes (because they have not been paid) have always provided reasons to discriminate against Indians at the polls, even though *all* United States Indians received the political franchise in 1924. As late as 1938 seven states did not allow Indians to vote. In 1948 Arizona and New Mexico courts ruled that there would be no more discrimination against Indians at the polls in those states. But as recently as 1956 the State of Utah denied the vote to Utes, Paiutes, Gosiutes, Shoshones, and Navajos (Peterson 1957: 116–26).

Over the years attempts to justify the discrimination, either in state statutes or in constitutions, have centered on one or another of the following points: (1) Indian exemption from real estate taxes (considered unfair, undemocratic, and anticapitalist); (2) maintenance of tribal affiliation (considered a mark of an uncivilized and irresponsible people practicing "savage" customs); and (3) federal guardianship (considered unfair coddling by the federal government, making Indians less responsible and unqualified for participation in local, state, and federal politics). All three of these points were made in a ruling by the Supreme Court of Utah in December of 1956. Under legislative pressure from the Northern Ute Tribe and the National Congress of American Indians the restrictive state statutes were eventually revised.

Yet even as late as 1969 the land tax issue was still very much alive in Utah, though the vote was no longer denied to the Indian inhabitants. In the *Uintah Basin Standard* (a newspaper in Roosevelt, Utah), a woman wrote of her displeasure that Ute Indians had all the benefits of citizenship—too many, in fact, when it came to questions of state welfare assistance—though Ute names did not appear on any tax record. A Northern Ute replied in the *Ute Bulletin* (the tribal newspaper) of March 1969 that Ute names appear in the name of every white person leasing Indian land, because the lessee pays a special, reduced use tax on leased Indians lands, thus lowering white operating costs.

This conflict is old and of long duration on all of the reservations, though until the late 1950s Indians seldom responded to the taunts of local whites who leased their land, grumbled about their tax-free status (land tax only), and denied them their franchise. Stewart (1952: 84) reports that in the 1940s the Anglos and Mexicans discouraged Southern Utes from voting in local, state, and federal elections because they did not pay land taxes. In fact, some Indians told Stewart "that they did not vote because they had been told that they would have to pay full land taxes if they did." About 4 percent of the eligible Southern Ute voters exercised their franchises in 1944 and 1946, and neither Democratic nor Republican organizers attempted to register Indians.

Table 25 accounts for Indian registration in local counties, and Indian voting in tribal elections during the 1952–54 period. It is evident that very few Indians participate in either tribal or local politics, but the difference between participation in the two is highly significant.

TABLE 25

LOCAL AND TRIBAL POLITICAL PARTICIPATION, FIVE RESERVATIONS, 1952–54

Reservations	Indians of Voting Age	Indians Reg. in Local County		Indian Participation in Tribal Elections	
		Raw	Percent	Raw	Percent
Southern Ute	252	28	11	125	50
Ute Mountain Ute	263	10	4	105	40
Northern Ute[a]	591	50	8	118	20
Fort Hall Shoshone	1,123	. . . . .	. . . . .	169	15
Wind River Shoshone	650	316	48	273	42
Totals and averages	2,881	404[b]	23	790	27

$d = 11\%$ between local registration (23%) and tribal participation (34%) excluding Fort Hall; $z = 7.2$; $p < 0.001$.
Source: HCIIA (1954: 202, 204, 229, 244). Wind River local and tribal participation may be high as it was interpolated from Shoshone-Arapaho totals.
a. Northern Ute data include mixed-bloods.
b. No data were available for Fort Hall; so average is determined for other four groups only.

Thus, thirty years after ratification of the Indian Citizenship Acts, 23 percent of Utes and Shoshones were registered in their counties (not necessarily voters), and sixteen to twenty years after the Indians had ratified their tribal charters and constitutions, only 27 percent were voting in their tribal elections. Nevertheless, 35 percent voted in tribal elections, whereas only 23 percent were even registered to vote in local, state, and federal elections (figures exclude Fort Hall because of incomplete data).

Southern Ute, the smallest reserve, participated at the highest rate in tribal elections. Wind River Shoshone, the second largest reservation population in this study, participated at the next highest rate. As for local registration, the Wind Rivers were registered at rates ranging from 430 to 1,200 percent greater than the Utes. The Wind River data might be somewhat misleading because they were interpolated from the joint Shoshone-Arapaho figures. Whatever the case, the more literate and *perhaps* better educated Shoshones seemed to be registered at a higher rate to participate in local elections than the other groups, but even their registration rate is well below the voting rate for Wyoming as a whole. The voting age populations of the following states voted in the national elections of 1960: Wyoming 74 percent, Utah 79 percent, Idaho 81 percent, and Colorado 72 percent (SAUS 1966: 381).

The meagerness of political participation in local and other nontribal elections is not simply a result of the land tax question. Indians are discriminated against and exploited by whites in white towns near all of the reservations. Furthermore, the BIA, which has controlled Indians for over a century—ipso facto denying the Indians power over many key decisions in their own lives—is known to be staffed with racists of many persuasions (see excerpts from the secret report of the President's Task Force on Indian Affairs, 1966). For the 1940s Stewart (1952: 86) writes that non-Indian government employees and the local whites both held that Indians were biologically inferior. He cites a non-Indian adviser and coach who told Southern Utes, "I am better than any Indian who ever lived, and any white man is better than any Indian." At Southern Ute and elsewhere this kind of bigotry is noticed by Indians and any casual observer. Bigotry toward Indians is also observed in simple measures such as the differences in employment practices in the local areas, the differences in salaries and positions of those who are hired, the differences in the exercise of power and influence over local white *and* Indian affairs, and so on.

The despair often becomes sullenness or apathy, sometimes bitterness; the deprivation persists nevertheless. Stewart (1952: 86) writes that the nominal Southern Ute chief of the late 1940s "said with bitterness that the Indians were always cheated. He added: 'It doesn't do the Indians any good to get a college education because they can't get a decent job if they do.'" When BIA policy was disapproved of by Indians in the past, the Southern Utes, Ute Mountain Utes (Euler and Naylor 1952), and Northern Utes (Lang 1953; J. A. Jones 1955) either refused to cooperate, perhaps offering passive resistance, or railed bitterly about the Bureau's actions. Often the Indians thought it would do no good to protest BIA decisions. More often, however, Utes either feared reprisal from the federal government if they protested, or they did not know how to form pressure groups for effective action, or both.

In 1953, even though Utes and Shoshones were dissatisfied with their relationships with the BIA, they overwhelmingly disapproved of terminating their relationship with the federal government (HCIIA 1954: 202–7, 229–31, 244–46). This was to be expected following seventy-five years of domination in which the Indians were dependent on dole administered through the BIA, and in which the BIA was their sole link to the locus of power. The panic created by termination proceedings, following the Indians Claims Commission Act, had not subsided by 1966, even though the Utes and Shoshones were not terminated. These Indians have lived in constant fear that their relations with the federal government—through the BIA—will be drastically altered. Furthermore, Shoshones and Utes have little power or influence to exercise in effecting federal policies so that their relations will not be altered. Whether on the local or federal level, Indians are recipients, the people for whom decisions are made. Generally, those who make decisions for Indians do not even request Indian advice about the decisions made for them.

In 1962 the same general pattern of nonconfidence in the BIA on the part of Indians is reported for the Fort Hall Shoshones. Federal policies and their interpretations had created considerable frustration over the years, and those well-meaning federal employees who had attempted to implement the policies merely exacerbated the frustrations (Harmsworth and Nybroten 1964: 104).

There is very little information on the participation of Utes and Shoshones in local, state, and federal elections since 1954, save the move on the part of the Northern Utes to gain their political franchise in Utah in the late 1950s. We know, however, that Utes and Shoshones do not serve in elected or appointed offices in the counties or states in which they reside.

Johnson (1963: 41–44) reports that by 1960 the registration of Southern Utes for nontribal elections was up to 15 percent (4 percent over 1954). Nevertheless, the Ute percentage was 61 percent less than for the Spanish-Americans and 69 percent less than for the Anglos in the local counties (Rendon 1962: 1–110). We can infer from Rendon's analysis that Southern Utes are very marginal participants in local non-Indian politics. This is true for the other Utes and the Fort Hall Shoshones. The Wind River Shoshones might be an exception. In the early 1960s a much greater proportion of Southern Utes were registered as independents than of Spanish-Americans and Anglos; registered Southern Utes voted much less often than the Spanish-Americans and Anglos; and among the Southern Utes, but not the Spanish-Americans and Anglos, fewer on welfare voted than those not on welfare (Rendon 1962: 1–110). There is some evidence that Anglos have stopped discouraging Indians from voting, but it is doubtful that they have begun encouraging them to vote. Apathy and disillusion better account for the lack of Indian participation in non-Indian government.

The participation in tribal politics is even more interesting. In the late 1930s the Indian Reorganization Act was adopted by all Ute and Shoshone groups except the Wind River, who already had a constitution. Table 26 shows (a) that a majority of voting eligibles turned out to vote only among the Northern Utes, Southern Utes, and Wind River Shoshones; and (b) that constitutions were ratified by majorities of the eligible voters only among the Southern and Northern Utes. The Northern Ute vote included the mixed-bloods who were later dissociated from the tribe.

TABLE 26

VOTES ON RATIFICATION OF CONSTITUTIONS WITH BYLAWS UNDER THE IRA,
FIVE RESERVATIONS, 1934–35

Tribes	Eligible Voters	Votes Cast		Votes "Yes"		Votes "No"	
		Raw	% of Elig. Voters	Raw	% of Elig. Voters	Raw	% of Elig. Voters
Southern Ute	129	95	74	85	66	10	8
Ute Mountain Ute	225	12	5	9	4	3	1
Northern Ute	634	354	56	335	53	21	3
Fort Hall Shoshone	971	406	42	375	39	31	3
Wind River Shoshone	1,032	808	78	339	33	469	45

Data are from Haas (1947: 13–20). Northern Ute figures include mixed-bloods. The Wind River Shoshone-Arapaho rejected the IRA, but they were already operating under a constitution ratified in 1930.

The perplexing thing about all of these votes, except at Wind River, is that the overwhelming majority of voters favored reorganization. The charge has frequently been made that local BIA personnel on many reservations escorted voters favorable to reorganization to the polls, and did nothing to encourage the participation of the voters who were not favorable. The IRA was important to the Commissioner of Indian Affairs during the New Deal era, John Collier, and his close associates. They wanted to completely revamp Indian life. Many lower-level bureaucrats are said to have worked hard to deliver the appropriate votes for ratification of constitutions and charters, but data to support these allegations are scanty and unreliable. The charge against the BIA for tampering will be explored in the Northern Ute case (see chapter 5).

Whatever the case, we know that the proportions of Indians voting on all reservations in 1952–54 were significantly lower than the proportions of Indians who ratified constitutions in 1935. We also know that tribal charters were ratified by much smaller votes than were the constitutions (ratified two or three years earlier). This is especially interesting because charters granted tribal committees the authority to conduct tribal business. It is highly probable that following two or three years of tribal government the Utes and Shoshones were either apathetic and did not bother to vote, or were disgruntled and refused to vote for ratification. Only Ute Mountain Ute showed a dramatic increase in tribal election participation. This was the reservation with the least factionalism, which fact might partially account for the political participation.

The IRA, after a fast start in appropriations and programs in the mid- and late 1930s, was soon undercut and failed to live up to its promise. When World War II began, many BIA employees as well as young Indians went into the service; there was a reduction in BIA appropriations with concomitant deterioration of reservation physical plants, schools, roads, and hospitals. Retrogression, if that seems possible, took place on the reservations (Brophy and Aberle 1966: 21). Moreover, as the IRA and the BIA faltered, Indians became more aware that the IRA actually *increased* the power that the federal bureaucracy held over them, especially that of the BIA and the Secretary of the Interior. In their minor states within states, Utes and Shoshones learned that the Secretary of the Interior, as provided for in their IRA constitutions, was required to review nearly all ordinances they passed, whether they were financial, legal, or other (see Jorgensen 1964; Brophy and Aberle 1966: 34–35; Steiner 1968: 250–67).

The effects of these changes in federal policy and the new legal restrictions placed on Utes and Shoshones were (and are) exacerbated by the attitudes of many BIA personnel. They socialize with each other and with local whites, not Indians. They belong to predominantly white churches, usually located in nearby white towns. Generally they work to increase rather than decrease the social distance between themselves and their Indian wards. My impressions, and those of others cited above, are adequately reflected in the Report of the President's Task Force on American Indians, which was completed in 1966.

Too many BIA employees were simply time-servers of mediocre or poor competence who remained indefinitely because they were willing to serve in unattractive posts at low rates of pay for long periods of time; ... too many had unconsciously anti-Indian attitudes and are convinced that Indians are really hopelessly incompetent and their behavior reflects this assumption. [Cited in Nader 1968: 14]

To return to the participation in tribal elections: the relatively high participation at Wind River can perhaps be explained by the fact that the Shoshones share their reservation and the governing of it with the numerically superior Arapahos. The Arapahos had constituted only 49 percent of the reservation population in 1900, yet were up to 58 percent by 1966. So the interloper Arapahos, who have neither the same native language nor the same cultural heritage as the Shoshones, and who have

maintained their distinctiveness—geographic separateness and almost no intermarriage—from the Shoshones (Hebard 1930; Elkin 1940: 231; Trenholm and Carley
1964: 281), have outstripped them in population growth. The evidence marshaled
above indicates that population growth is closely related to financial betterment.
The Arapahos may have stabilized their resource base and bettered themselves somewhat earlier than the Shoshones. It may also be that the competition between these
two distinct groups has stimulated participation in tribal and nontribal politics.

As for the other Shoshone and Ute reservations, most have some important social-
political features in common with Northern Ute (described in some detail in the
following chapter). In brief, there is a pervasive, often low-keyed, factionalism on all
of the four reserves. The parties to the various transitory factions on the three Ute
reserves share a common culture heritage and a common native language. The factions are somewhat fluid in membership. They are not divided into fixed camps and
are not firm in their opposition on all political issues. The composition of the factions
changes from issue to issue. Sometimes people align, more or less, along historic band
lines—or some combination of them—and sometimes they align along "nativist" versus "not-so-nativist" dimensions (Johnson 1963; Jorgensen 1964). There are no reported formal factions or political segments at odds with one another at Ute Mountain.

At Fort Hall three different groups are known to line up against one another on
some issues and in various combinations on others. All speak the Shoshone language,
and the Bannocks speak Bannock (Northern Paiute) as well. The Bannocks, as we
know, also share a common culture heritage with the Shoshone. So the factions do
not always oppose the Bannocks to the other groups, but usually tend to split along
the Lemhi-Hekandika-Bruneau or Boise lines.

Fort Hall has the least intratribal political participation of all the groups in this
study, and one cannot help but think that the meagerness of their participation is
related to the paucity of everything else in Fort Hall Shoshone life except underemployment, disease, illiteracy, poor housing, and discrimination (see Collier 1970:
28–30, 32–35). Fort Hall people do not even have land claims money to generate
tribal jobs, or to create dissension by unpopular allocation. In 1962 only 8 percent
of 130 Fort Hall household heads said they would go to the tribal council for advice
on financial matters, and 3 percent on educational matters. The Shoshones and Bannocks felt that the council did not do anything very well, and they complained that it
was "undemocratic." When asked what they would do if they were on the council,
most household heads responded that they would improve housing first. Then, although not necessarily in this order, they would improve the water supply, the government, and their public relations with local whites (Harmsworth and Nybroten
1964: 105). It seems quite clear that the wants of the Fort Hall people were very simple
and basic. They were not simply quibbling over who had power.

Again, the factionalism that occurs on all of these reserves is usually the transitory
or will-o'-the-wisp sort. Tribal members participate very little in the formal processes
of government, but they take sides on various issues and question the decisions of
their tribal councils or the relations of their tribal councils to the BIA. The pervasive-
ness of factionalism and the often amorphous nature of the alignments makes analysis
of the specific problems difficult. Indian participation patterns in tribal governments
seem to fit in well with the general wariness Indians exhibit towards the white gov-

ernment (Congress and the BIA) which created the Indian governments and has maintained de jure control over them. One factional dispute among the Northern Utes that was rather clear-cut and linked to several intratribal and extratribal interests will be assessed in the following chapter.

RELIGION: NOMINAL CHRISTIANITY

On each of the Ute and Shoshone reservations Christian proselytizing still occurs, and on each reservation some Indians are nominal members of Christian churches. Until about 1950 most Northern Utes born since 1900 had been baptized as Episcopalians. Through the 1920s many Southern Utes were baptized as Presbyterians (Nelson 1963: 23–32). No single church ever held great sway at Fort Hall, although many Shoshone-Bannocks have been nominal Protestants of one type or another (Harmsworth and Nybroten 1964: 78–79). Perhaps a third of the Wind River Shoshones were nominal Episcopalians in the 1930s (Shimkin 1953: 467).

Other Christian denominations have made some inroads into these populations over the years, but on the whole Indian membership in the various denominations has meant only that some Indians were baptized at some time. The proselytizing Mormons (whose missionary network covers most of the white-populated world), have been in constant contact with all of the Ute and Shoshone populations since 1847. They have, however, won almost no converts to Mormonism among the Southern Utes (Nelson 1963: 33–43), Northern Utes (Jorgensen 1964), Wind River Shoshones (Shimkin 1942: 451–62), or Fort Hall Shoshones (Harmsworth and Nybroten 1964: 78). Their *Book of Mormon* doctrine about the racial inferiority of Indians (whom they call "Lamanites") probably has not helped their cause. The Catholics have done no better than the Mormons on most of these reservations, although they won a few converts among the Wind River Shoshones. The Utes, however, who have had intermittent contact with Catholics since the sixteenth century, have not joined the church except in some important and rare instances (see following chapter).

An enlightening analysis of contemporary Fort Hall Shoshones who have Christian religious affiliations and those who do not shows practically no significant differences between them on such factors as divorce, delinquency, welfare, intact homes, economic status, or the average number of children per mother (Harmsworth and Nybroten 1964: 78–80).

It is clear that Utes and Shoshones have resisted Christianity in the form in which it has been offered to them. The white practitioners of the Christian religion, especially the Mormons (because they are dominant around most of the reserves), are the same people who do not extend credit to Indians, except for small amounts of food, clothes, appliances, and perhaps auto purchases. Credit is extended only when the white shopkeepers know that income will be made available to the Indians through per capita payments, welfare checks, dividends, and the like (see Bennett 1961: 159–63; Jorgensen 1964; Johnson 1963; Witherspoon 1961; Nybroten and Farmer 1964; 164–67). The local Christians are the same people who have discouraged the Indians from voting in nontribal elections, who control the local governments, and who have taken Indian land (or who now use it cheaply). Furthermore, year in and year out, the local Christians have enjoyed more consumer comforts than the Indians, they have controlled the local schools and shops, and they have discriminated against Indians in many ways.

SOME EFFECTS OF EXPLOITATION AND DOMINATION

The Sun dance has persisted in Shoshone and Ute reservation contexts in which Indians have been exploited, dominated, and discriminated against. Modest changes have occurred in these contexts from time to time, and we have seen how and why these contexts have changed and why each reservation is different from every other reservation in many particulars. The interreserve variation is of little consequence, however, because almost all of the Indians on all of these reservations have remained in the same relative position to the dominant whites in their midst since the turn of the century. It is important to point out that because the Sun dance is a large-scale ritual in which the vast majority of all Shoshones and Utes participate, there is no correlation between Sun dance participation and Christianity, education, or political activity. There are practically no well-educated, politicized Christians among the Utes and Shoshones. Of the very few who have high school educations, who participate in tribal and nontribal politics, and who attend Christian churches, some are avid participants in the Sun dance, some are average participants, and a few do not participate.

As a final measure of difference between Indians and local whites, let us assess the residence patterns of Utes and Shoshones in the early 1950s and the mid-1960s. In table 27 we see that about 90 percent of all Utes and Shoshones lived on their home reservations in the early 1950s, and about 88 percent in the mid-1960s. The difference is not significant. Furthermore, in 1966 approximately 5 percent of all Utes and Shoshones lived on reservations other than their home reserves, and there was very little variation between the five groups in the percentages of their memberships living on reservations. Since 1950 the on-reservation populations increased from about 6,000 to 7,500. For the general population of the Mountain West states, on the other hand, the rural population decreased from 45 percent to 33 percent of the total population, and decreased absolutely from 2,290,000 to 2,256,000 (SAUS 1967: 17). The rural out-migration pattern for the Mountain States does not hold for the Ute and Shoshone populations within them.

The data show, then, that practically all Utes and Shoshones live on reservations, and very few Indians leave their home reservations for any significant length of time. Those who leave often take up residence on another reserve. Aside from relocation programs aimed at pushing Indians from the reservations, since 1950 many Shoshone and Ute males have been inducted to military service. The Indian populations are youthful (32 percent of all Utes and Shoshones in 1966 were males twenty-four years of age or younger), undereducated, and unemployed. Where we have proper records, we know that more Southern Utes per capita (14 percent) have served in the military than have the dominant groups—Anglos (10 percent) and Spanish-American (8 percent) (see Alfred n.d.: 29a). It is relevant that Anglos and Spanish-Americans control the local draft boards. Indeed, Anglos control the draft boards for all of the reservation areas, and draft calls on all of the reservations have increased with the preparation for, and prosecution of, wars abroad. Indians who cannot avoid the draft in the normal

TABLE 27

Percentage of Enrolled Tribal Members Living on Home Reservations, Other Reservations, and Elsewhere, Five Reservations, 1950–66

Tribes and Years	Total Enrolled	Total at Home	Percentage at Home	Percentage on Other Reserves	Percentage in Military, at School, or Other
Southern Ute					
1950	479	479	100	0	0
1953	541	449	84	. . . . .	. . . . .
1962	685	631	92	. . . . .	. . . . .
1966	695	598	86	7	7
Ute Mountain Ute					
1950	570	570	100	0	0
1953	622	576	93	. . . . .	. . . . .
1962	922	877	95	. . . . .	. . . . .
1966	1,050	1,008	96	4	0
Northern Ute					
1950	1,150	1,150	100	0	0
1953	1,247	1,165	93	. . . . .	. . . . .
1962	1,565	1,370	88	. . . . .	. . . . .
1966	1,600	1,328	83	10	7
Fort Hall Shoshone					
1950	2,156	2,156	100	0	0
1953	2,250	2,049	91	. . . . .	. . . . .
1962	2,700	2,150	80	. . . . .	. . . . .
1966	2,800	2,464	88	4	8
Wind River Shoshone					
1950	1,678	1,512	90	. . . . .	. . . . .
1953	1,700	1,540	91	. . . . .	. . . . .
1962	1,825	1,643	90	. . . . .	. . . . .
1966	1,970	1,773	90	4	6
Totals and averages					
1950	6,033		$(\bar{X})$ 97		. . . . .
1953	6,360		$(\bar{X})$ 91		. . . . .
1962	7,697		$(\bar{X})$ 87		. . . . .
1966	8,115		$(\bar{X})$ 88		93[a]

The 1950 data do not record who, among those living off their home reserves, live on other reserves. Though figures are high, they are from a point in time before many in the youthful Indian populations were of draft age, before the Korean War call-up, and before the relocation program.

The 1953 data do not show who lived where off their home reservation, yet they might reflect the Korean War call-up. At this time all reserves but Fort Hall had fixed post office addresses for *all* enrolled adults, and all of these tribes were distributing per capita payments. Fort Hall had fixed post office addresses for all but thirty-five adults.

The 1962 data probably should show an average of about 4 or 5 percent enrolled Indians living on reserves other than their home reserve.

The 1966 data are more complete as they come from the labor force surveys on each reserve and my own field research on each reserve.

a. This figure represents $\bar{X}$ at home and on other reserves.

ways—school deferments, critical occupations such as farming, and so forth—are inducted. Of the 7 percent off-reservation population (see table 27), probably 30 percent were in the military, 40 or 50 percent were in Indian boarding schools, and the remaining 20 or 30 percent were living in urban areas (either on relocation programs or on their own initiative).

Contradictions between Forces Influencing Indian Life

The history of Shoshone and Ute economics, politics, housing, and health since 1910 offers an ample explanation of why the Sun dance has persisted. Shoshones and Utes have had their territory expropriated, their labor and resources exploited, and their lives dominated by whites. As Indian conditions have worsened, they have been treated to dole by state and federal governments. Since their subjugation on reservations, Shoshones and Utes have been beckoned in two directions by the federal government: individualism and collectivism. They have been beckoned to collectivism also by the Indian communities, and to individualism by their hedonic impulses. The conflict between collectivism and individualism, whether stirred up by federal policy or by intra-Indian ethics, has continued unabated since the 1870s.

During the 1850s, '60s, '70s, and '80s, selected Shoshone and Ute chiefs were coerced to sign treaties binding for *all* people in their bands. Furthermore, reservations were established, and bands—often more than one—were placed on them. The Shoshones and Utes were restricted in their movements off the reservations and were kept separated from non-Indians. They were not citizens of the United States and were collectively denied the constitutional guarantees in the Bill of Rights. This collective treatment of Shoshones and Utes encouraged them to maintain their collective similarities.

On the other hand, the federal government urged Shoshones and Utes to forget their chiefs and their communal land, to narrow their responsibilities to themselves and their immediate families, to work hard, and to assume civilized ways. In the 1890s and early 1900s, native Indian religions were forbidden, and collective land was allotted in severalty. In 1924 Shoshones and Utes became United States citizens and were further encouraged to move to the cities, work hard, and leave the Indian life behind.

The conflict between collectivism and individualism promoted by federal policies took on a new dimension in the 1930s, when Shoshones and Utes organized tribal governments under the IRA. Reservations were collectivized again, this time by the purchasing of individual allotments and alienated land. Indian corporations were formed to direct tribal enterprises. Yet, while the federal government was urging this collectivism, Congress and the BIA were negating it by enrolling Indians in white schools (Johnson-O'Malley Act, 1935), taking Indian health care from BIA control, and encouraging family subsistence agriculture. Furthermore, the Secretary of the Interior and the House Committee on Interior and Insular Affairs increased their powers over decisions made by Indian tribes.

In the late 1940s and throughout the 1950s the push toward individualism was reintroduced, this time through programs which would (a) sever the ties between Indians and the federal government (Termination), (b) settle any outstanding debts owed to Indians (Indian Court of Claims), and (c) force Indians to sever their relations with the reservation and their Indian friends (Relocation and Employment Assistance).

In the 1960s, much as in the 1930s, federal policies were modified, and Shoshones and Utes were again caught between both collective and individual impulses from the federal government. On the one hand they were told to stay on their reservations and develop tribal economies. On the other hand they were told to move to the cities and sever their reservation ties. The collectivism that is urged by Shoshone-Ute ethics focuses on responsibilities first to the immediate family, then to the wider network of kin and affines, to the reservation community, and finally, to the Shoshone-Ute community. Kinship obligations and obligations to the Indian people are emphasized. It is expected that each Indian will "help out" others, and that donors will receive support in return when the exigencies of the moment so dictate.

Hedonic individualism, on the other hand, tempts Indians to abandon all responsibilities, seek pleasure, do not work, and become totally dependent on others.

Our analysis of the growth of the metropolis-satellite economy has made it clear why federally-urged collectivism has not achieved its economic goal, and why, paradoxically, the growth of the metropolis has increased the need for intra-Indian collectivism. It is also paradoxical that even if Indians put all their energies to collectivism in the federal sense, they could not achieve the collective goal. By federal law, Indian polities do not exercise full political and economic power over Indian resources, and this alone negates the form of Indian collectivism envisaged by the federal government.

If Indians stay on their reservations and pursue individual economic ends, however, it is evident that most are doomed to failure. The political economy has denied the role of Indian as producer. If Indians move to the city, they are pressed into urban poverty, but they are also encouraged to stay in the city by crumbs of wealth which they did not have on the reservation.

A final contradiction in federally-urged individualism exists between the philosophy and the practice of the bureaucrats. The BIA officials who urge the Indians to sever their kinship and reservation ties, to get off the welfare rolls, and to make their way through hard, productive work, are themselves dependent on the greater welfare enterprise for their sustenance and status. The bureaucrats need both the Indians (to provide a justification for the existence of the BIA) and the federal government (to provide salaries for BIA positions) in order to cope.

The tug of Indian collectivism is strong. Indians beckon each other to observe the teachings of Indian elders, and to put some social distance between the dominated (Indians) and the dominant (whites). Shoshones and Utes return from the city, perhaps giving up full-time employment, in order to "help out" at home. On the reservation they probably are underemployed at best, but by pooling and sharing skills and resources many people—the collectivity—are better able to cope than they were when the workers were in the city. Hedonism is avoided out of fear of death and because the collective ethic is unalterably opposed to it.

The Indian can acquire status, create a feeling of esteem, and legitimize his behavior by turning to the Sun dance religion. In the religion both collective ends and individual ends are served. The desirability and correctness of Indian ways are validated in an Indian context, and each participant in the religion is recognized for his personal contributions, his personal sacrifices, and his personal gains—that is, redemption in which a new state of grace is achieved.

The redeemed—many people in the Ute-Shoshone community—work for the good of all Utes and Shoshones. The Sun dance community is spiritually and socially separated from the white community, the nonredeemed. Even though oppressive conditions persist on and near the reservations, and flight from the obligations imposed by the Indian community is tempting (momentarily, at least), the conflict is in part resolved by adherence to the Sun dance religion.

The road to redemption is not easy, however, and many adherents falter en route. The causes of the faltering lie in the reservation context and the metropolis-satellite political economy which maintains it. Let us analyze the Northern Ute case to gain a more complete understanding of the causes and forms of deprivation.

5

Deprivation at Northern Ute

We shall analyze the Northern Ute case more intensively than the other four. There are two reasons for this: (1) I know the Northern Ute history, people, and contemporary context more intimately than the histories, people, or contexts of the other reservations included in this study; (2) the histories and contexts of the five groups (including the current age profiles, job distributions, family organizations, relative positions vis-à-vis local white communities, control over strategic resources, and general access to the locus of power) do not vary significantly from reservation to reservation. The Indian populations in the past and present are much more similar to one another than they are to whites in the areas they jointly occupy.

A BRIEF HISTORY OF RECENT NORTHERN UTE POLITY AND ECONOMY

From 1881, when the people who are now called Northern Utes were relocated in eastern Utah, to 1938, when the Northern Ute tribe completed reorganization, the majority of the political decisions affecting Ute life were made by BIA employees at the local agencies, at regional offices, and in Washington, D.C. Except for the local agents, Utes had little physical access to, and even less influence on, the men who made decisions for them. For instance, because the Utes had no political power, no access to capital, and meager educations throughout the pre-IRA period, it was very difficult for Utes to maintain ownership and control of their land. Indeed, following federal policies their overseers encouraged them to alienate their land. Since reorganization, the tribal government, the BIA, the Secretary of the Interior, and the House Committee on Interior and Insular Affairs have wielded considerable power over Indian lives. The tribal government is not organized in the traditional Indian fashion whereby influential headmen try to persuade Indians to follow their lead, and decisions are consensual. It is modeled, instead, after a collage of federal (including the federal bureaucracy), state, and local government features. In fact, the tribal government duplicates agencies of all three forms of government. Because of the duplication of forms and the manner in which decisions are made and power is distributed, the Indian is often at a loss to know who, among those allegedly in power, can and do make decisions.

As viewed by tribal members, many political abuses are perpetrated by the BIA and the tribal government. Let us look at some decisions made by these bodies which have affected key aspects of Ute life—their land and money—and assess the response

Utes have made to these decisions. When the Northern Utes were threatened with allotments in the 1890s, their response through their headmen was to resist. In 1906, one year after Uintah and White River lands were allotted, one renegade group of 365 White River Utes led by influential headmen (Chief Appah, Andrew Frank, Sapponose Cuch, and others) made good on an often lodged threat to the agent and left the reservation. The White Rivers had made it clear that they (a) did not want allotments in severalty, (b) did not want whites moving onto unoccupied lands which had been redeposited in the public domain, (c) were unhappy that Uncompaghres had received allotments on Uintah–White River territory, and (d) wanted to take up the chase again. That is, they wanted to restore their aboriginal collective life if they could not preserve their federally-urged collective life on the reservation.

In the same year the Uintah Irrigation Project was begun. It had been rejected by the Indians, but was desired by the BIA and settlers who claimed the unallotted Indian lands. The goal of this collective project was to make *family* farming successful. Liability and responsibility were intended to be individual (to each allottee), whether or not the individual Indian wanted to participate in the project. Congress authorized $600,000 for this major subjugation project, which would make cultivation of Uintah reservation lands possible. After thirty years, this sum, and many others which were subsequently poured into the project, were to be reimbursed by the Indian allottees. In making this decision for the Northern Utes, the federal government assumed that the project assessments would be paid from profits earned from crops, from the sale of Indian lands, or from whatever means the Utes possessed (HCIIA 1953: 1007). Little thought was given to the way in which Utes would pay the bills incurred in this project (initiated against the Utes' protests), and almost no attempt was made to resolve the conflict between collective and individual programs sponsored by the government through the BIA.

By 1908 some $330,000 had been spent on the irrigation project. Less than $7,000 (2 percent) had been paid to Indian laborers, "as it was almost impossible to induce the Ute Indians to work on canal construction" (RCIA 1908: 55). Approximately 42,000 acres were reached by canals at this time, of which only about 11,000 acres were being farmed. Furthermore, "the greater part of this [acreage was] being cultivated by white lessees of Indian allotments" (RCIA 1908: 56). Utes refused to dig the canals or to farm. They wanted to maintain their collective life on the reservation. They wanted to hunt, fish, collect nuts, seeds, and berries, raise horses, and receive the benefits that had been promised them by the federal government for relinquishing their major resource areas and way of life.

The Northern Utes received about $1,200,000 in 1930 for nearly one million acres of reservation land which had been appropriated for a national forest in 1905. In 1933 the funds from the settlement three years earlier were deposited in trust (federal treasury) in pro rata shares for each Northern Ute. Although an equal fraction of the money ostensibly belonged to each Ute, and each Ute knew it, all the funds were controlled by BIA officials (ultimately by the Secretary of the Interior). Funds belonging to household heads were made available to Ute household heads for land improvements, house construction, and other purchases that would help the individual (HCIIA 1953: 1008). Collective schemes other than those initiated by the BIA were discouraged.

In the depths of the depression, in 1937, it was time for Ute property owners to pay for the services and improvements (Wright 1948: 335). By this time ditches and canals had been dug, individual allotments had been leveled and plowed, regardless of whether the services were requested, water had been diverted onto Ute lands, 26 percent of all allotments had been alienated, and 64 percent of the nonalienated allotments were tied up in complicated heirship status. Most Utes could not pay off the debts against their allotments or heirship land, and some allotments had accrued as much as $1,600 in debts against them (Wright 1948: 335). The reservation area itself had been reduced by 91 percent to 360,000 acres from nearly 4,000,000 in 1885 (see map 9).

The tribal Business Committee was formed in 1937 and began administering tribal political and economic affairs. The committee's authority was restricted by provisions

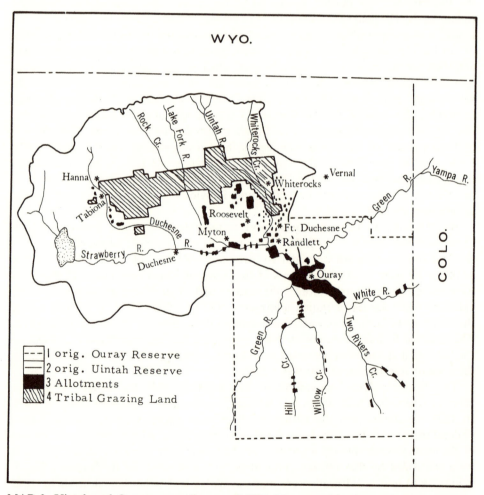

MAP 9. Uintah and Ouray reservation as of 1937. Ute-owned lands as of 1885: approximately 4,000,000 acres; Ute-owned lands as of 1937: approximately 360,000 acres. Modified from Wright 1948 (p. 329) and Jorgensen 1964.

in the IRA which delegated authority over financial expenditures and jural punishments to the BIA, Congress, and the Secretary of the Interior. One of the committee's first acts was to draw $100,000 made available by the IRA, and $100,000 from tribal funds to purchase allotments (whether or not in heirship) as a means of settling old debts (HCIIA 1953: 1002). The BIA and the Secretary of the Interior approved the expenditures and Congress authorized the purchases. Thus the tribe's Business Committee had no real power. It followed the BIA's plan and began coercing allottees to sell. The tribal corporate body was an instrument of the federal government and was used to implement another reversal of federal policy from individualism back to collectivism, although this time collectivism was of a corporate nature. Within the new collectivism the federal government urged the establishment of farm and livestock cooperatives. Some allottees did not sell and merely plunged further into debt. One of the economic abuses in this process was that tribal funds that had been obtained from the Brunot Agreement and from payment for expropriation of land under the General Allotment Act, and deposited in the federal treasury, were being used by the tribe to settle old debts incurred by individual tribal members. This was often done against the will of the tribal members, and the abuse did not go unnoticed. Utes were paying debts they had not wished to incur, with Ute funds, to the Ute tribe. The debtors never touched the money, of course. The tribe was buying back Indian land from Indians and using Indian money to do it. Furthermore, the Business Committee used tribal and federal funds to purchase acreage that was being liquidated by local white entrepreneurs who were bankrupt. Utes, therefore, were also purchasing acreage that until 1850 had been their unrestricted domain and later had been their ceded territory (federally-created reservations of 1861, 1881). They were allowed to repurchase their land because the rural economy was shriveling.

The tribe had not supported reorganization enthusiastically. It is alleged that the fullbloods were against it and the BIA was for it (J.A. Jones 1955: 229–32). It is further alleged that the BIA and the mixed-bloods were responsible for ratification, and that the mixed-bloods got control of the tribal Business Committee. Although the vote was overwhelming in favor of establishing a committee (213 for, 8 against), only 30 percent of those eligible voted. The mixed-bloods may well have been instrumental in the vote. There were about 300 of them of all ages at this time. Legally dissociating the mixed-bloods from the tribe in 1954 was an indication of the anger of many fullbloods (see Bennett 1961: 159–63).

During the period 1937–48, money trickled into the tribal coffers from mineral and land leases. During the same period allotted Utes were assessed by the BIA for maintenance charges, and by the state for irrigation water (Lang 1953: 31). Whether or not an allottee farmed during the period, indebtedness automatically accrued from the project costs. Moreover, it was stipulated that landowners who did not pay off their irrigation project debts could not work their land. Hence a vicious feedback system ran most Utes hopelessly into debt. In 1946, with the intent of redressing some of their grievances over the Uintah Irrigation Project, the Uintah and White River bands filed a suit in the U.S. Court of Claims for "compensation for wrongful and wasteful use of tribal trust funds [in the] Uintah Irrigation Project" (HCIIA 1953: 636). This grievance was not satisfied, but it is a poignant example of Ute attitudes toward a federally-urged scheme that they did not want and which was ill conceived.

Family farming could not be successful, given the unfavorable rural niche the Northern Utes occupied, and the direction the metropolis-satellite economy was growing. At best, the long-run land acquisition, land subjugation, and irrigation programs created jobs for local whites, further developed water resources for local whites, developed Indian land so as to make it more desirable for white lessees, and gave the struggling, white farmers and ranchers a buyer for the land they wanted to liquidate. The tribe reacquired land, but because individual Utes had no capital, they had little access to the land.

From 1948 to 1951 the tribe began receiving royalties from oil, phosphate, and gilsonite leases. Although $1,500,000 had been received, in June of 1951 the tribal treasury showed a balance of only $46,500. The more than $2,000,000 received in one form or another since 1937 had been spent on land acquisition, land subjugation, payment of Uintah Irrigation Project costs stemming back to 1906, and salaries for Business Committeemen and other tribal employees. Following incorporation, but especially in the late 1940s, the destitute, poorly educated, and unskilled Utes argued at General Council meetings that they could not pay the charges levied against them for the Uintah Irrigation Project and still farm. They resented having to pay for water that was once free and that they felt was rightfully theirs (Ute Indian Tribe 1949: 8). Utes were bewildered and aggravated by the events that occurred around them, but especially by the state's control of their water, the tribal and federal control of their land, the federal control of their individual funds (IIM), and the Business Committee's nominal control of their tribal funds (real control was federal). They were unhappy, too, with their inferior status in the white towns in the Uintah Basin.

In 1948, 1949, and 1950 the Northern Utes began to decry BIA–Business Committee policies of communal land ownership, and federally-urged cooperative schemes for land usage (Lang 1953: 31; J. A. Jones 1955: 253). The cooperative livestock associations, for instance, were developed so that Utes (not necessarily networks of kin) would share the costs of bulls, scales, and corrals; but each association member was supposed to act as an independent entrepreneur. While the federal government pushed this scheme, the Business Committee (aided and abetted by the BIA) consolidated individual land under tribal ownership. The federally-urged collective scheme conflicted with the federally-urged individual scheme, and both were opposed to the collective Indian ethic that prevailed. That is, the stock association ownership units formed by the Utes were primarily large kinship units. Observing the collective Ute ethic, kinship units pooled their labor, skills, and resources in order to cope. Each nuclear family was not an independent entrepreneurship. Few could have survived if they had been. Indeed, these were consumption units that consumed most of what they produced. By the late 1940s it was difficult for these cooperative kinship units of the larger associations to persist. They needed capital for bulls, breeder stock, and general operating expenses. Utes began making requests to the Business Committee, but the committee was not responsive to many Ute requests because (a) their ultimate control over Ute finances was nil, and (b) there was little the committee could do about many of the recurrent demands: the satellite economy—at least the role of the small operators and entrepreneurs within it—was shriveling.

When the Confederated Utes received nearly $32 million from their first large land claims payment in 1951, there was considerable unrest and apprehension among the Ute people. The record of the Business Committee up to that time had not been good from the impoverished Ute point of view. Since 1937 the committee had acted to buy up individual allotments from allottees or their heirs to settle old debts. By 1950, 90 percent of all nonalienated allotments were tied up in heirship status, about which the committee could do little other than purchase the heirship land. The committee had paid some of the expenses of the Uintah Irrigation Project (both the project and payment for it were disapproved by the fullbloods), and had created further land subjugation projects on tribal, not individual acreage. The committee, under its charter, had also created jobs for its own members and others, most of which were filled by mixed-bloods, and paid the salaries with tribal funds. These actions had antagonized the majority of fullbloods to the point at which they would make no effort to cooperate with the tribal government (Lang 1953: iii, 46; J. A. Jones 1955: 238–39).

On the other hand, the federal and tribal governments set about repurchasing unoccupied lands and some white-owned land in the area for the Ute reservation. The Indian and tribally-owned property grew from 360,000 to about 1,000,000 acres, or to 25 percent of the original reservation. The Utes were pleased over the reacquisition of land, but not with the use of their meager tribal funds to achieve it.

With the allocation of the $32 million land claims award to the Confederated Utes (about $18 million was the Northern Ute's share), there was a huge apparent increase, and a large real increase in unearned income for each family. There was a concomitant movement among the fullbloods to expel the mixed-bloods from the tribe. This was accomplished in 1954 with federal approval. Indeed, the BIA pressed this action as the first step in terminating both fullbloods and mixed-bloods from federal obligations.

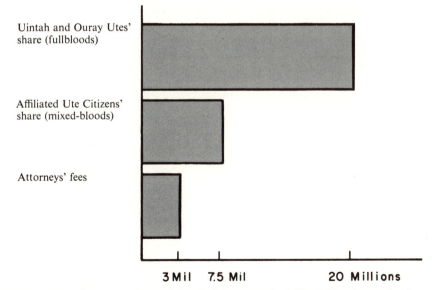

FIGURE 7. Northern Ute share of Land claims award, 1950–62. Total awards of approximately $47,700,000 were shared by Confederated Ute Tribes (Northern, Southern, and Ute Mountain Ute). Northern Ute share is about $30,500,000.

The 490 mixed-bloods became the Affiliated Ute Citizens, taking with them 27 percent of the 1951 award and 27 percent of all subsequent claims awards. They also received the large Rock Creek section, that is, the northwest portion, of the reservation. The mixed-bloods were willing to dissociate, for the years of bickering had drained them of their desire to remain a part of the fullblood group. Furthermore, the mixed-bloods anticipated that they would improve themselves socially and economically if they dissociated. This was, of course, the promise of the termination program. The mixed-bloods accepted the first stage of termination when they dissociated, and termination was completed for them in 1960. The fullblood population (over 50 percent Ute blood) in 1954 was 1,314 and growing rapidly.

Thus, in 1954 the Business Committee was fully controlled by fullbloods for the first time. Two committeemen were to be elected from each of the three reservation bands (Uintah, White River, and Uncompaghre) (Ute Indian Tribe 1956). As early as 1954 a group of Utes (later to be known as the True Utes), predominantly members of the White River and Uintah bands, wanted the Business Committee and tribal government disbanded (Jorgensen 1964). The leaders of the group argued that nothing good could come from anything that had been so bad in the past. It was not sufficient in the True Ute view merely to rid the committee of the mixed-bloods; they did not want the Uncompaghre Utes to share in Uintah–White River judgment claims or to participate in the tribal government. The True Ute leaders feared the role that the Uncompaghres might assume in directing the tribal government (because an Un-

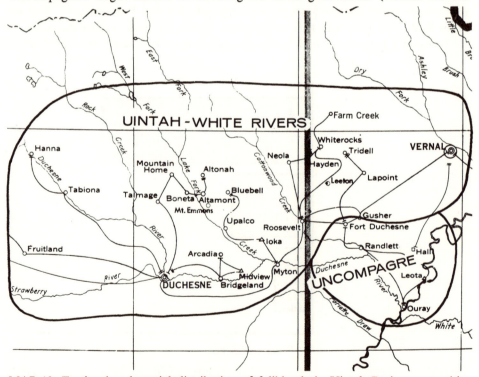

MAP 10. Factional and spatial distribution of fullbloods in Uintah Basin communities, 1906–66. Adapted from Jorgensen 1964.

compaghre had been the most influential fullblood on the committee), and they feared that the committee would continue to spend tribal funds on unpopular projects rather than allocate them to individual tribesmen. They argued to disband the tribal government and to allocate all funds on a per capita basis.

The True Ute leaders had many reasons for wanting to dissociate from the Uncompaghres. The seeds of dissension were planted in the 1860s and 1870s when the Uncompaghres were the principal signatories to three treaties which relinquished practically all Ute lands in Colorado and New Mexico. In 1879 the Uncompaghres refused to join the White Rivers in warfare following the Meeker battle. In 1880 the Uncompaghres received their own reserve in Utah (the White Rivers did not), and larger per capita cash payments than the White Rivers (who were forced to pay debts incurred as a result of the Meeker battle) for relinquishing their Colorado land. In 1897 the Uncompaghres took Uintah–White River land when their own reserve was allotted. Between 1937 and 1954 an Uncompaghre was the dominant fullblood on the Business Committee, and he was in the process of passing his mantle on to his nephew (a person of Ute-Navajo parentage, and the only college graduate in the tribe).

The True Utes were not successful in dismantling the tribal government, and for five years committee business was conducted rather tranquilly. During this period the powerful Uncompaghre committeeman died, and his nephew gained de facto control of corporate Ute affairs. The young Uncompaghre allocated jobs to Uncompaghres and introduced most of the legislation that met the approval of the committee. He met some opposition from some well-educated White Rivers, but, on the whole, the Uintahs and White Rivers elected committeemen who were influential spiritual leaders. Often these men had meager educations and very feeble knowledge of English, which made it difficult for them to operate effectively in committee meetings attended by white business advisers and BIA personnel. The Uintah and White River committeemen extolled the collective Indian ethic of Utes' responsibilities to observe the teachings of the elders, to maintain family and kinship integrity, and to help out kin and other Utes. They knew misery and they desired to alter BIA–Business Committee spending patterns and priorities to meet the collective expectations of the Indian ethic and to reduce Indian misery. The White River–Uintah committeemen were not successful, and they often resigned their posts before their terms were completed (Jorgensen 1964). The conflict between the Indian collective ethic and the federally-urged (and -overseen) form of collective control was obvious.

Although committeemen were elected every other year, Utes were not active participants in the electoral process. Often twelve to fifteen votes were sufficient to get a committeeman elected, and, until 1964, only about 15 percent of the eligible voters went to the polls. As for legislative functions of government, a General Council of all eligible voters in the tribe is held once each year. The Ute voters can pass and repeal any legislation they desire at this time as long as seventy-five eligible voters attend and a simple majority favors (or opposes) an issue. Very frequently the specified dates for the council had to be changed because a quorum could not be convened— even when intra- and intercommunity gossip would lead one to believe that most Utes were vitally concerned about tribal legislation.

So, relatively unhindered by legal checks, the fullblood Business Committee assumed many of the attributes of a state within a state. The committee negotiated with federal, state, and local governments, employed legal counsel, established a police force and a tribal court, and appointed tribal judges. It continued the policy of repurchasing allotments and allotments in heirship status, continued the development of tribal subjugation farms (which never showed a profit), and created many projects with the hope that they would better Ute life. Except for the tribal farm, none of the projects could be called "investment" expenditures. All others merely consumed tribal funds. As one ex-committeeman aptly put it, however, the committee was investing in the individual: programs in counseling, preschool education, recreation, youth camps, and even a tribal newspaper were begun. Large recreation halls were built in three communities so that people could get together for shows, games, and parties. Although some Utes were unhappy about the expenditures of vast sums, they seemed to agree that many of the programs had some merit.

Tribal attitudes began to change as early as 1956, however. At that time the five-year-old practice of directly awarding per capita payments to Utes from tribal coffers was terminated. Future payments were placed in the IIM accounts and administered by tribal Family Plan officers and BIA personnel instead. Utes would appeal to Family Plan personnel for funds to buy appliances, improve their homes, or some such project. The Family Plan officer in turn, would make a decision about the request and pass it on to a BIA employee. The BIA official had the final authority on whether or not IIM funds would be released for the request. When funds were awarded, they were given directly to the supplier of the goods rather than to the Ute, for a basic distrust of the Indian's financial abilities had been the reason for the creation of the Family Plan. Although Bureau officials were convinced that Utes were "squandering" their per capita funds during the five-year period prior to initiation of the Family Plan, they did not cut off all individual Indian handling of Indian funds. Each family was allocated a modest food and clothing allowance each month to spend as it saw fit. To get extra cash, Utes often had to plead for new refrigerators, washing machines, or the like. A check to cover the purchase would be sent to local white merchants, who often never delivered the appliance. Rather, the merchants would buy back the uncrated appliance at less than the wholesale price from the Indian (see Witherspoon 1961).

The Family Plan lasted for three years, and its termination signaled a change in tribal expenditures worked out several years earlier. The amount of unearned income deposited in the IIM accounts fell off drastically, whereas tribal expenditures for large projects and for maintenance of the tribal government increased.

From the Ute point of view one of the most irritating aspects of the Family Plan was that the Business Committee and the BIA forced payment of back debts from these funds. Some of the debts extended back more than four decades, such as those from the Uintah Irrigation Project. In any event, 21 percent of Family Plan expenditures ($737,000 in the 1957–59 period alone) went to settle debts involving the Uintah Irrigation Project, Revolving Credit Fund, tribal assistance, and purchases from local merchants.

After unearned income had plummeted, the True Ute faction announced its plans to dissolve the government. Several times during the spring of 1960 the True Utes had been unsuccessful in gaining popular support for their plan, including one attempt at the General Council in early June. On 28 June 1960, the True Utes armed themselves and attacked the tribal offices, chasing the administrators from their desks. The disgruntled True Ute organization, which included two Sun dance chiefs and an ex-committeeman among others, was, in turn, repelled four days later. The attackers were incarcerated, but because the tribal jail could not hold all of them, some were placed in local white jails. The abortive revolutionaries were freed two weeks later to attend the Sun dance.

The True Utes sought to bring immediate and far-reaching change to Ute society. They preached that the ruinous trend which Ute society had taken under successive business committees would be reversed when the True Utes gained power and dissolved the old government. They wanted to increase the social, political, and economic distance between Utes and non-Utes, and they wanted to cease relying on non-Ute advice about how Ute funds should be spent. The True Utes saw an enormous discrepancy between things as they were and things as they ought to have been. When they acted on their desires, first within the legal context of the General Council and later in abortive, illegal (revolutionary) fashion, they made clear to a generally angry but politically inactive tribal populace the intensity of their own deprivation and of their quest for change.

General dissatisfaction continued to increase in the following years, and in 1962–63, when the average Ute was the recipient of the fewest funds he had had for over twelve years, political pressure groups under True Ute sponsorship grew and exerted considerable pressure on the committee, tribal employees, and the BIA. Ute families were forced to join into larger household units, and the household units were forced to "help out" and, in return, receive help from an even wider network of kin and affines. Utes increasingly preached and practiced the collective Indian ethic. Indeed, the exigencies of the moment forced them to observe it.

BIA employees, particularly those in the social service (welfare) division, were dismayed over the Ute practice of sharing money between households and throughout wider networks of kin. The reciprocity networks among kin greatly alarmed the (white) director of BIA social services at Northern Ute when he learned about them in the early 1960s. The welfare director had preached the federal line of family independence and self-sufficiency. When he learned how Utes shared their resources—particularly how elderly people took youngsters (usually their grandchildren) into their homes—the local social service director issued a statement in the tribal newspaper (*Ute Bulletin* 1962). He pleaded with the elderly people not to take children into their homes, arguing that the old folks were being duped and that the young people did not "contribute to the support of the household . . . and have actually taken funds from the elderly individuals."

The protestations of the BIA employee did not stop the Utes from joining together in larger households and pooling their skills, labor, and resources. Nor did they stop Ute adults from badgering tribal and BIA social service officials to turn over control of their IIM accounts to each Ute adult. In 1963 the BIA capitulated, but by that time most adult Utes had spent all of their funds so that the concession newly won from the BIA had no great effect on their lives (*Ute Bulletin* 1963, October).

In the summer of 1963 the destitute Northern Utes convened with Shoshones, Colorado Utes, Southern Paiutes, and other Indians (about 1,500 in all) following a Sun dance to discuss a land claims judgment. The judgment had been won by the

Confederated Utes, but funds were withheld by the federal government while off-setting costs were being determined (see Jorgensen 1964). Although the meeting had no effect on federal or Business Committee decisions about how the funds would be allocated once they were deposited with the tribe, the Indians met and listened to the influential leaders. The main point made by most speakers was that Utes, Shoshones, and Paiutes were one people—*nuc*, in the Ute language—before the federal government tore them apart. The collective ethic preached throughout the meeting was that *nuc* had to stay together, had to help each other. The Utes even suggested that one group (the Pahvant from Millard, Utah) were being unjustly treated by the federal government because the Pahvant had been denied plaintiff status with the Northern, Southern, and Ute Mountain Utes in the award that was under discussion at the 1963 meetings. The Utes argued that the Pahvants were legal plaintiffs and should share in the award.

These examples from the early 1960s are only a few of the many conflicts between federal government policies and the collective Indian ethic, between Indian needs and the nature of the political economy that created Indian problems. For instance, the Protestant ethic individualism encouraged by the federal government has been contradicted by the nature of the satellite economy, and by the corporate collectivism pushed by the federal government through the BIA and the Business Committee.

Let us focus on the composition of the Ute tribal organization in 1963–64 to get a better idea of the intra-Ute dissidence that was created and maintained by Business Committee policies. Figure 8 allows us to infer the cause of some of the Ute problems and the reason that Utes would turn on some of their elected officials. Quite simply, Utes wanted money, but could not get any. On the other hand, the tribe initiated a livestock enterprise (which has never shown a profit or employed many Utes) and a hunting enterprise (which has shown modest profits, but has not generated many jobs or much income) just at the time when most Ute families began living on the unearned income in their children's accounts.

Both whites and mixed-bloods served in many tribal posts (see fig. 8). Moreover, advisers from Utah State University and the University of Utah were retained by the tribe. Mixed-bloods and whites occupied roughly 20 full-time jobs and 40 part-time jobs (summer employment) and paid advisory positions throughout the year. This was from a total of roughly 45 full-time jobs and 60 to 80 part-time jobs (60 part-time jobs in 1963). On top of this, three influential Ute families occupied 12 of the 25 full-time jobs not filled by whites or mixed-bloods. Very few jobs were available for the vast majority of Utes.

In late 1964 the tribe went through a financial crisis. The 1951 land claims funds and subsequent royalties had been almost totally drained, and the federal government had not paid the tribe its 1960 and 1962 land claims awards. The judgments were still withheld because of litigation over offsetting costs claimed by the federal government for operating the reservation. The Business Committeemen and other Utes were not only unhappy about the government's actions, but they did not want to pay for services they had not requested, services such as the Uintah Irrigation Project which had squandered their funds (see *Ute Bulletin* 1963, March).

The Uncompaghre committeeman who had been the most influential individual in the tribal government since the late 1950s became persona non grata. He left the res-

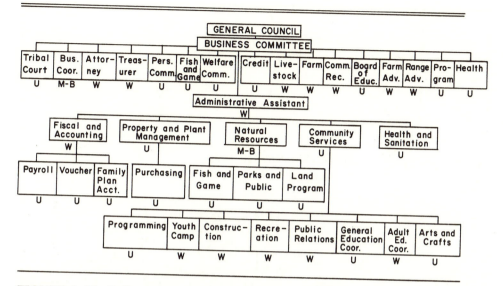

FIGURE 8. Ute Indian Tribe organization, 1962–64. The letters below the boxes indicate whether Utes or others occupy the positions referred to: U = Utes; M–B = mixed-bloods; W = whites. Adapted from Ute Indian Tribe (mimeo., n.d.).

ervation and the tribal government. In mid-1964 the committee fell into new hands (again Uncompaghre). The committee dropped most of its education and community recreation programs and retained those programs that it hoped would generate jobs and income—cattle and recreation hunting (as opposed to hunting done by Indians for subsistence), in particular. The 1960 and 1962 award funds were received by the tribe in 1965. The committee deposited the funds in local banks and has attempted to operate on the dividends that have accrued from bank interest on the capital. It has been reshaped through the election of three True Utes since 1964. Furthermore, it has become more responsive to the expressed concerns of the electorate. Over two hundred adults have attended the more recent General Councils, whereas quorums could not be mustered in the late 1950s and early 1960s. The electorate also has taken a more active part in legislating for the tribe. A viable economy has not yet been created, and divisiveness on most economic issues is still the norm. Nevertheless, these beleaguered people have begun to work to weld themselves together on many issues.

For instance, in late 1968, somewhat beyond the research period for this study, the Utah State welfare office in Vernal decided to withhold the welfare checks for December. The rationale was that, since the Utes were going to receive their annual $150 dividend that month, $150 should be deducted from their welfare payments. The welfare recipients organized a pressure group and headed for the state capital in Salt Lake City. The tribal attorney, the agency superintendent, and other tribal officials joined the group, but not as official spokesmen or official representatives. In this case the state welfare agency was the body with immediate control over Ute finances. The Utes, collectively and through individual initiative, pressured the state welfare bureaucrats to make a concession and relinquish the funds the Utes had been counting on.

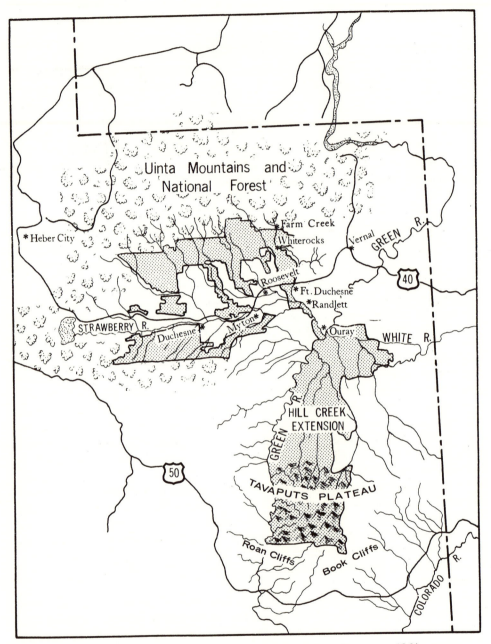

MAP 11. Uintah and Ouray reservation, 1966. Adapted from Jorgensen 1964.

For its part, the welfare establishment told the Utes how they could spend their dividend funds. The state welfare office served notice that, if the Utes could not prove that they had spent their dividend funds on appropriate goods and services, it would deduct the unproven amounts from subsequent welfare payments.

The examples marshaled here on Ute political economic history should make it clear that the Utes seldom have participated in, or have influenced the making of, the major decisions that affect their lives. Utes have attempted to be heard on many issues, usually unsuccessfully. Sometimes their struggles to be heard by people of power and influence, and to control their own destiny, have been tragic indeed. Utes have fled from the reservation, attacked the tribal government, and withdrawn into bickering factions. Only the primitive means of using pressure groups has had any success at redressing grievances. Utes are operating in a neocolonial, welfare-dependent setting. The tribal government—pushed and pulled by the conflicting demands of collectivism and individualism—is itself subservient to the BIA, and the BIA is subservient to Congress and the Secretary of the Interior. When tribal members have attempted to exercise greater external controls on their own government, they have seen the futility of the venture. Nevertheless, when Utes look at their immediate money and land problems, they are well aware that the tribe and the BIA have immediate control over both, and that decisions encouraged by the federal government about the disposition of such resources often worsen the problems.

RECENT ECONOMIC DEPRIVATION

Since 1945 Northern Utes have been unemployed, underemployed and unemployable at very high rates. Households have lived off bits of earned income pooled from several sources: unearned income derived from land claims awards, oil and land leases, and state welfare. Most housing has been poor and crowded. We have seen how transitory political factions have developed to challenge the tribal government, and how political pressure groups have formed on various issues to force the BIA to relinquish their authority over IIM accounts. Generally Utes have no individual

TABLE 28

AVERAGE HOUSEHOLD SIZE AND INCOME (ALL SOURCES),
NORTHERN UTE RESERVATION, SELECTED PERIODS

Years	Major Sources of Income (in order of importance)	Approx. Average Household Income per Year	Average Household Size
1945–50	Part-time labor; piecework; "self-employment"; state welfare; regular employment; lease income	$1,500	6.2 (1950)
1951–59	Unearned income from land claims, leases; regular employment; part-time labor; "self-employment"; piecework	$6,750	4.4 (1957)
1960–62	Unearned income from claims, leases; part-time labor, piecework; regular employment; tribal assistance	$4,000	. . . . .
1963–66	State welfare; unearned income from land claims, leases; part-time labor; piecework; regular employment	$2,600	6.6 (1965)

access to strategic resources, and they are greatly removed from the loci of local, state, and national economic and political power. Drinking has persisted at an alarming rate, and its effects on Ute life have been unsettling.

Table 28 shows how Ute households in the late 1940s[1] were large and subsisted on an average of about $1,500 per year, which was pooled from part-time farm labor and general labor, "self employment" (usually subsistence farming and ranching), state welfare, and, in a very few cases, regular employment with the tribe and the BIA. Men did not work full time on white farms or ranches, and they did not work at all in the white-owned mines, small industries, and stores in the areas adjacent to the reservation.

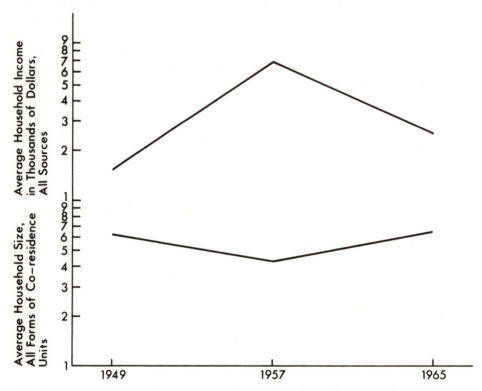

FIGURE 9. Average household size and income, Northern Ute reservation, 1949, 1957, and 1965.

During the 1950s the Northern Utes became almost wholly dependent upon unearned income derived from land claims judgments against the federal government and distributed first as per capita payments and later as "Family Plan" funds. Indeed, between late 1951 and mid-1959, over $11,000 was awarded to each enrolled Northern Ute. During the same period the population grew from 1,200 to 1,600 fullbloods, the household size decreased from about 6.2 to 4.4, and the household apparent income increased from about $1,500 to about $6,750 a year. Whereas on the average

1. 1945–50 survey data are from Lang (1953) and HCIIA(1953).

there was about $242 per person per year in 1949, there was about $1,535 per person per year in 1957.[2]

As the larger multiple-family households broke up into nuclear family households, and as more and more youths got married, the joint cattle enterprises broke up as well.[3] Furthermore, fewer and fewer men engaged in subsistence farming for themselves or in part-time ranch and farm labor for surrounding whites. At the same time the tribal government purchased original allotments, especially those in arrears on Uintah Irrigation Project payments and those hopelessly entangled in heirship status. Tribal jobs, full-time and part-time, were opened and made available to Utes as the tribe spent vast sums from their land claims awards on various noninvestment projects.

From 1960 to 1963 the unearned income deposited in the IIM accounts dwindled. This was part of a ten-year plan, which called for a gradual shift in emphasis from partial individual allocation of land claims funds to complete tribal expenditure of these funds. The brief, three-year interval was attended by a marked decline of household income, the bulk of which was still provided by land claims award funds, oil and land leases (CHCIIA 1963: 440). As the land claims monies for personal use dwindled, and as people expended everything in their accounts, some households began growing in size as multiple families, linked through either the male or female line, took up co-residence and pooled their resources.

In 1963 no funds were deposited in the IIM accounts, and many people became destitute, especially the aged. By late 1962 the tribe had awarded $60,000 in tribal assistance loans, and, because their own funds were dwindling, they urged needy Utes to apply for state welfare. From 1963 to 1966 state welfare became the major source of funds for the Utes. The average household increased to 6.6 persons by 1965 and was living on a per capita income of about $395, or $2,600 annual income for each household. The income figures represent a drop of over $1,100 per year per person over the average 1951–59 figure.

In 1965 the tribe finally began receiving funds from the two Confederated Ute land claims judgments made in 1960 and 1962, minus government offsets. The Northern Utes' share totaled $13 million. The tribe deposited some of these funds in a local bank and began paying an annual dividend of $150 to each enrolled Northern Ute in 1966. That amounts to an average of $990 per year per family. By 1966, fully 25 percent of *all* enrolled Utes were also receiving some form of state welfare.

The inverse relationship between income and household size shows how volatile the Ute households were over the 1945–66 period. As the Utes shifted from welfare income to per capita income from tribal sources, the population grew markedly and the large households fragmented into self-sustaining nuclear families. When the tribal funds were nearly exhausted and the tribal spending program was greatly altered so that funds were no longer allocated on a per capita basis, Indian families shifted

2. "Apparent" is used here because Utes did not handle all of their monies and could not get all of their monies, and many of the funds deposited in their IIM accounts went to pay off previously incurred debts. Sometimes the Utes would not acknowledge the debts. In many instances Utes did not know debts had been incurred.

3. See Jorgensen (1964) for an extensive analysis of the breakdown of family subsistence farming and joint household cattle enterprises in the 1950s.

TABLE 29

EMPLOYABILITY OF NORTHERN UTE PERSONS AGED SIXTEEN TO FIFTY-FIVE, 1956–66

Year	Total Adults Aged 16–55	Employable Adults		Unemployable Adults	
		No.	Percent	No.	Percent
1956[a]	466	224	48	242	52
1962[b]	547	237	43	310	57
1964[c]	598	260	43	338	57
1966[d]	641	300	46	341	54

a. Data are adapted from Ute Tribe (1956: 81). Age intervals are adjusted to exclude people over 55 years of age.
b. Data are adapted from Indian Unemployment Survey (1963: 440–443).
c. Data are from Jorgensen (1964: chapter 4; 1964 unpub. field notes).
d. Data are adapted from Uintah and Ouray Agency Report of Labor Force (1968), Bottenfield (personal comm.), and Jorgensen (unpub. field notes).

TABLE 30

EMPLOYMENT OF EMPLOYABLE NORTHERN UTE PERSONS AGED SIXTEEN TO FIFTY-FIVE, 1956–66

Year	Total Employable Adults Aged 16–55	Permanently Employed		Underemployed		Unemployed	
		No.	Percent	No.	Percent	No.	Percent
1956[a]	224	.....	.....	113	50	111	50
1962	237	44	18	83	35	110	46
1964	260	45	17	115	44	100	38
1966	300	83	27	48	16	169	56

a. Temporary and permanent employment are lumped together in the 1956 data (Ute Tribe 1956: 81). It is most likely that the majority of employment was temporary. Sources are same as for table 29.

back to welfare income. Furthermore, many nuclear families split up through divorces and through loss of custody over children.[4] The people from these broken families joined the households of their kin. Sometimes separate households were occupied, but labor, skills, and resources were shared.

The data on employment used in tables 29 and 30 and in figure 10 generally show that the relative size of the labor force (employables) for adults between the ages of eighteen and fifty-five changed very little during the 1956–66 period (about 45 percent of adult Utes were "employable"). Approximately 20 percent of the employables were "permanently" employed, and about 50 percent were usually unemployed. The composite percentages for "underemployment" (part-time, piecework or temporary employment), "unemployment," and "unemployability" average around 90 percent of the adult Northern Utes for the four intervals.

The BIA's definitions of employable and unemployable are the same as in the preceding chapter. These definitions allow for easy manipulation so that embarrassing unemployment percentages can be depressed by classifying the unemployed as unemployable. Permanent employment does not mean full-time employment. It only means that a person has been employed for more than twelve months. Temporary

4. Between 1957 and 1959 alone there were 138 *recorded* divorces (including adoptions and guardian assignations). The number per year increased during the 1960s.

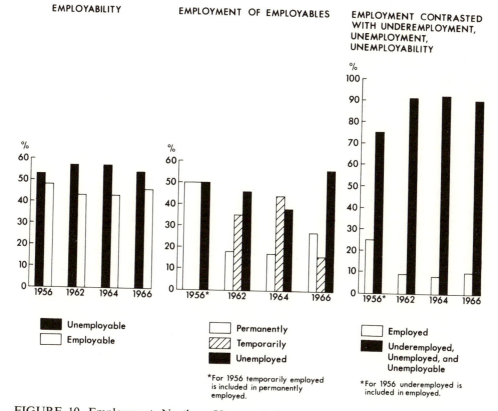

FIGURE 10. Employment, Northern Ute population, ages 18–55, selected years 1956–66.

employment means that at some time during the year in question a person has been hired to do seasonal work or piecework. The category has been expanded to include "self-employment," which usually means something less than subsistence ranching or farming. In the fourth column of table 30, temporary employment is referred to as "underemployment." Unemployment means no employment during the year.

The data for 1956 are slightly misleading because permanent employment is not distinguished from temporary employment. Graphically this probably has the effect of inflating the former and deflating the latter. It is my impression that permanent employment was lower in 1956 and 1966. Whatever the case, the data do not depart markedly from the other figures for the decade.

From 1951 to 1959 the tribe and the BIA were the major employers of both permanent and temporary personnel, although in the first half of the period about thirty men, belonging to four joint-family enterprises, continued to raise cattle and sheep. By 1962 the tribe supplied 60 percent of all jobs (permanent and temporary), the BIA supplied 32 percent, and 8 percent were from either self-employment or other federal employment. The self-employment included one small cattle enterprise, one sheep enterprise, and one small mixed cattle and sheep enterprise. The armed forces provided the majority of federal employment not provided by the BIA.

Only two years later, in 1964, the tribe had run out of most of its funds and had begun struggling through a reorganization crisis. Jobs were eliminated, and the BIA became the major employer of Northern Utes, providing 53 percent of the employment. Most of the employment provided by the BIA was piecework such as fence construction and fire fighting. The percentage of employment provided by the tribe dropped from 60 to 40. Seven percent was provided by other sources, including the armed forces, self-employment, and part-time farm and ranch labor. It is apparent that the BIA stepped in to fill the gap with piecemeal jobs during these very dispiriting years.

In 1966 the employment structure had changed again: the Bureau and the tribe each provided about 35 percent of the employment. The tribe finally had received the claims funds that had been withheld by the federal government, and was expending some of them on jobs. By this time, too, the federal government's poverty program made its way to the reservation. The Office of Economic Opportunity and the Community Action Project, two instruments of the program, provided more permanent and full-time jobs than had ever been available on the reserve in the past. Figure 10 demonstrates the changes in the ratio of permanent to temporary employment brought about in this year. The poverty program provided 23 percent of the employment. The remaining 7 percent was provided by self-employment (3 percent) and part-time farm and ranch labor.

Overall it is quite clear that the Utes have been dependent for employment on federal governmental funds made available to them in one form or another. Their livelihood, generally, has been culled from government funds either earned (the smaller portion) or unearned (the larger portion). Indeed, full-time employment is negligible. White-controlled industries in the area (such as oil and gilsonite) and white shopkeepers do not employ Utes. In 1962–63, when some Utes again began doing part-time work for white ranchers and farmers, the Indians had plunged back into an economic and social context that was worse than that of 1950 in many respects.

The full-time jobs available to Utes have not been equitably distributed throughout the tribal households or throughout the adult age groups. During the very late 1950s through 1965, women occupied about 12 and men about 33 of the approximately 45 full-time jobs available to Utes. Furthermore, the jobs provided by the tribe were controlled by three families with considerable influence in tribal affairs. Twelve of the 25 full-time jobs as well as 3 of the part-time jobs were taken by members of these three families.

Temporary employment provided by the tribe was made available primarily during the summer seasons. Men were hired for building-construction crews, truck driving, and general labor in the tribal cattle and recreation operations. Women were hired as part-time secretaries, clerks, and cooks for summer tribal enterprises as well. The BIA also offered some part-time employment, and it, too, was primarily summer work. For instance, between November 1962 and January 1964, when conditions on the reservation were extremely bad, 75 jobs were made available. They were, however, short-time piecework, such as fence building, road repair, forest fire fighting and forest reclamation projects, which amounted to only 150 man-months of work.

Other "part-time and piecework" employment was provided by local ranchers and farmers who enlisted male Indians to mow and put up their hay and wheat, or to work their cattle and sheep. Much, but not all, of the "employment" was carried out without real cash remuneration to the Indians. For example, whites often paid fines ($15 to $50) for Ute men serving sentences for drunkenness at the local jails. In turn, the Indian put up the white man's hay. The work expected from the Indian requires about ten hours a day for three or four days (sometimes a week). An insult was added to this exploitative arrangement when the alfalfa harvested was raised on land leased from Indians. The Indians, either allottees or heirs, could not farm the acreage because they had neither the equipment to farm it efficiently, nor the funds to pay for irrigation water or to pay subjugation debts owed to the tribe and the BIA (another prerequisite to farming). The Utes who helped the whites in the harvests were supposed to be grateful for the favors rendered them by the whites. When Indians raised alfalfa on Indian land (assigned or allotted), they often had to borrow white-owned tractors, for the use of which they handed over one-fourth of their crops, and that fourth was selected by the white owner.

About thirty women were active bead and leather workers. They averaged about fifty cents an hour for their work, although none of them support themselves or their families from these pursuits alone. There were very few local outlets for their beaded bags, moccasins, Sun dance belts, and other products. Most of the goods produced by the Northern Ute women were purchased by trading posts and restaurants in Vernal and Roosevelt, and by the tribal arts and crafts division.

The facade of Protestant ethic individualism was there, exemplified in the nuclear family household, but it soon gave way as Ute financial conditions changed. As incomes began dropping in 1960, preciptiously so in 1963, kin and affines in sundry combinations established co-residence and pooled their resources. The family compositions of households took many forms: some were joint families (e.g., sisters, their spouses, and their offspring); some were stem families (e.g., a conjugal pair, the unmarried offspring of the pair, and one or more married offspring of the pair, including their spouses and children); but most were composite families (e.g., a woman, her divorced or unmarried children, grandchildren, and miscellaneous collateral relatives). In 1964 one household of Northern Utes had seventeen members sharing a three-room house.

As of the late 1960s the great majority of Ute households and even wider networks of kin were pooling the funds available in the IIM accounts of their members, income from the state welfare agency (Aid to Dependent Children, Old Age Assistance, and Aid to the Blind), and income from federal welfare assistance and tribal loans (the last are repayable).

Unearned income, of course, was not sufficient to maintain many households, so earned income from temporary work was also pooled, as were welfare commodities, game, nuts, and berries. Young men hunted deer, sage hens, and rabbits, distributing the products within their own households and among their kin in other households. Women collected nuts and berries, preparing both pemmican (with venison) and berry cakes and sharing them within their own households and among other kin. The gainfully employed Utes lent their automobiles to their kin for trips to the store. The borrowers did not have to repay the favor, but usually provided some service (e.g., labor) or some good (e.g., venison) for the help received.

The rate of employment (all forms) in 1956 for men between the ages of 31 and 60

TABLE 31

MALE EMPLOYMENT BY AGE, NORTHERN UTE ADULTS, 1956 (N = 291)

Ages	Frequency	Employed	Unemployed
18–20	13	23% (3)	77% (10)
21–30	75	33% (24)	67% (50)
31–60	160	54% (87)	46% (73)
61 +	43	44% (19)	56% (24)
N =	291	134	157

was much higher than for younger and older men. Table 31 demonstrates that the 31–60 age group was employed at a 54 percent rate, whereas the 18–30 age group was employed at a 31 percent rate (percentage is interpolated). On the other hand, the more youthful group had a 22 percent larger population then men between the ages of 31 and 60.

Nearly a decade later, in 1964, the 18–30 age group had grown markedly; yet the employment rate was about 15 percent below the 1956 figure for all forms of work. The 31–50 age group was employed at about a 50 percent rate, getting the bulk of the piecework and short-term jobs provided by the BIA. The 51–65 age group had about 45 percent employment. For the group older than 65, only men with skills were employed. The differences in employment percentages between 1956 and 1964 are greatest for the youthful segment of the population, particularly for people less than 31 years old. In 1964 permanent employment was down, temporary employment was up, and the population had grown markedly.

In 1956 (see table 32), males with semi-skills and skills were employed at a 63 percent higher rate than men without skills, and fewer (proportionately) young men than old men had semi-skills or skills (see table 33). Skills are loosely defined as "painter,"

TABLE 32

MALE EMPLOYMENT BY SKILLS, NORTHERN UTE ADULTS, 1956 (N = 291)

Alleged Skills	Employed	Unemployed	Totals
Semi-skills and skills	84% (97)	16% (18)	100% (115)
No skills	21% (37)	79% (139)	100% (176)

$\phi = 0.62 \; p < 0.001$. The rate of employment is 63 percent higher for men who are semi-skilled or skilled than for those who have no skills.

TABLE 33

AGE DISTRIBUTION OF SKILLS, HAPHAZARD SAMPLE, NORTHERN UTE ADULTS, 1956

Age	Frequency	Semi-Skills, Skills (%)	No Skills (%)
18–25	59	10	90
26–39	87	39	61
40–49	54	56	44
50–64	65	52	48
65 +	26	42	58
N =	291		

The data in this table are meant to be interpreted for heuristic purposes only. The 1956 sample represents all Ute males in the age group (Ute Tribe 1956:81).

that is, someone who has done some painting; "farmer," meaning someone who has done some farming; "truck driver," and so forth.

For the 1963–66 period comparable information is not available, but in 1965, 42 percent of household heads were semi-skilled or skilled whereas 58 percent were not, and 51 percent were employed (all forms of employment) whereas 49 percent were not. We can interpolate that, when employment was available, it was often given to household heads whether or not they possessed skills. Furthermore, employment is a partial determinant of who will direct a household. The permanently employed household member is nearly always the household head, especially if that person also has a spouse. Employment for Utes in 1965, as it had been in 1956, was still way below the farm, state, and national averages.

Meager data are available on the age distribution of skills in the late 1960s. Yet, as in earlier years, the primary fashion in which Ute youths acquire skills is through on-the-job training (in the employ of either the BIA or the tribe). Youth are much less apt to be hired than people in their thirties, forties, and fifties (with family responsibilities). Semi-skills and skills are, however, still rare, and there are no employers to hire those who possess them.

WHITE CONTACTS AND UTE DEPRIVATION

We now turn our attention to local white-Indian relations and the immediate sources of Ute status and self-esteem deprivation. These forms of deprivation are clearly linked to the political-economic conditions which have obtained throughout Ute reservation history, and to the Protestant ethic promulgated by the white majority. Whites have beckoned Utes to dissociate from the tribe and from federal supervision, and to assume the individualistic and "civilized" life-style that whites presume characterizes the white family. Yet, as we have seen, Utes could not be successful "individualists" even if they tried. The white response to the Indians' failure to meet white expectations has been to discriminate against Indians. It is paradoxical that the very people who helped to create and maintain the oppressive conditions of Ute life also discriminate against Indians because they have not altered those conditions (or left the reservation) to satisfy white expectation.

Northern Utes have not participated in the politics of county and local governments. When Utes have gone to white towns it has been as consumers, to purchase food, clothes, appliances, entertainment, alcohol, and so forth. The young men, lacking work, have often got drunk and been thrown in the local jail. If some kin, or perhaps friends, have had some money, they have bailed him out. If not, the incarcerated Ute has cleaned and repaired the streets and done other odd jobs as an unpaid city employee.

A common complaint made by Utes in the late 1960s was that the police in the white towns treated Indians and non-Indians differently. The Indian was accused of drunkenness by the police and taken to jail. There was *no* successful appeal. The white, often the obstreperously drunk cowboy, drinking in the same bar with the Indian, was neither accused of drunkenness nor taken to jail. Statistics have not been marshaled on this phenomenon, but I have seen such situations frequently. It would serve no useful purpose to spell out this indecency in any greater detail.

We can see in table 34, however, that Utes paid about $70,000 in fines in local white towns during a six-year period in the 1950s. The percentage of fines for alcohol-related crimes assessed in the local white towns was approximately 90 percent ($63,000) of the subtotal. It cannot be denied that these fines were an important source of revenue for the small towns. The beer halls and restaurants also profited from the business. The Ute Tribe levied considerable fines also—more than were paid and than appear in the table. About 65 percent of the total fines listed in table 34 were assessed for drunkenness or some alcohol-related act, usually drunken driving. The tribal police chief is white and he has enforced the reservation drinking laws somewhat *less* stringently than his counterparts in the adjacent white towns. Nevertheless, the majority of crimes committed by Utes on the reservation have been alcohol-related.

TABLE 34

FINES PAID BY UTES

Courts	1952	1953	1954	1955	1956	1957
Duchesne and Uintah county towns	9,108	11,528	5,670	16,649	14,450	22,685
Ute Tribe	. . . . .	9,490	12,928	13,385	7,583	10,493
Totals	9,108	21,018	18,598	29,964	22,033	33,178
Grand Total	133,901					

Adapted from Ute Indian Tribe (1954: 15; 1958: 42)

That many Utes drank, were hauled into court, and paid many fines during the height of the unearned-income period is apparent. In the late 1960s, drinking was still a problem on the reservation, and the tribe had established its own alcohol studies program to help correct it. An Alcoholics Anonymous center was opened in Roosevelt, and Utes were invited to stay there in order to help them stop drinking. It is interesting that when unearned income dwindled, drinking did not. Yet Utes could no longer pay their fines in white towns; so they were then encouraged to cease drinking by white agencies as well as by an agency established by the tribe.

In the 1960s most Utes thought that alcohol was a destructive influence on the home and the community. Some, even among those who drank, thought that it should be outlawed on the reservation. Others, including those who did not drink, thought that it was a personal matter that should involve no government intervention. This does not mean that these Utes considered alcohol a positive factor in Ute life.

These views are wholly consonant with some 1965 survey research results obtained by Christiansen and others (1966: 14–15). Unfortunately the survey team mixed their response categories so that mutually compatible opinions about the solution to drinking problems were treated as separate and exclusive opinions. Nevertheless, we learn from Christiansen's report that 25 percent of 150 Ute respondents thought nothing should be done about drinking on the reservation, while 37 percent believed alcohol should be outlawed. Another 27 percent of the respondents believed that the Indian drinking problem would be *automatically eliminated* if employment and income increased and discrimination by whites decreased. The final 11 percent said that Alcoholics Anonymous would solve the problem. It is obvious that a person could believe that drinking is harmful to the individual, his family, and his community, but that drinking is personal nevertheless; that it is made worse by white discrimination and by the lack of jobs and income; and that joining Alcoholics Anonymous would help solve the drinking problem.

It cannot be denied that most Utes feel discrimination is a core problem in their relations with whites. Discrimination is mentioned in reference to jobs, to drinking, to attitudes about Ute beliefs and Ute moral life. In Christiansen's 1965 study, 85 percent of the adult Utes sampled said that "discrimination" was the major source of their dissatisfaction with whites. The term "discrimination" represents a composite index to account for the general Ute perception of white behavior toward them. In the following pages the nature of white discrimination toward Utes will be amplified. The data on which the discussion is based are primarily from my observations.

It is to whites that Utes have had to appeal, and it is the local white community which has created in Utes the feelings of status inferiority, behavioral inferiority, and a sense of low self-esteem. Discrimination, which takes so many forms, has intensified the drinking problems of many Utes.

Drinking, it has been noted, is considered by Utes to be aggravated by the refusal of whites to accept Indians. Other examples of discrimination will help us better to understand Ute deprivation. For instance, in private conversations Utes decry white skepticism of Indian accounts of their own history. Utes also decry the behavior of whites who make light of Ute knowledge and skills.

Every white in the Uintah Basin does not ridicule or challenge native accounts of Ute life, but that is because very few whites are sufficiently interested in, or acquainted with, Utes to obtain information about which they could become skeptical. The insidious general nature of white discrimination is that of an indifference toward Indians which is based on a stereotyped disapproval of Indian life. Utes are accustomed to the indifference and the stereotyped responses; yet more threatening responses occur when whites listen to Indians and then challenge the validity of the Indians' statements. A few white employees of the tribe and the BIA, four or five missionaries, and several schoolteachers are about the only people who have enough face-to-face contacts and discussions with Utes to directly challenge Ute beliefs. On occasions my own skepticism (and that of other whites) has been received very coldly. When Utes know the white challenger well enough to be critical, they usually say something like, "That's the white man's idea. You don't have any knowledge of these things, and it won't do any good to try to explain them to you."

Utes have voiced a more general hostility toward white BIA personnel, especially the higher-ranking officials. Utes criticize BIA bureaucrats at General Council in front of all Utes in attendance, and sometimes, especially recently, criticisms are made directly to the officials. The Sun dance provides the forum for Utes to make their most general criticisms, and these criticisms are not restricted to BIA personnel. Throughout the dance, shamans lambaste those whites who have little respect for Ute behavior, and they repeatedly counsel Utes to follow collective and cooperative Ute ways, not individualist and competitive white or corporate collective ones (many BIA-Business Committee Programs).

It is difficult to imagine any white working among the Utes for any length of time and failing to understand how Ute intelligence, beliefs, and life styles have been ridiculed—perhaps, worse still, dismissed—by whites. Ute responses to ridicule, to stereotyped rebuffs, and to indifference are evident in personal conversations with whites, Sun dance orations, and in the counsel Ute adults give to Ute youths. In the *Ute Bulletin* for 1960–64, but especially for 26 January 1963 and 2 May 1964, Utes castigated educated whites whom they had hired to provide them with counsel in legal affairs, education, and economic planning. The Utes had purchased advice, but they wanted to make it clear that they had not hired the counselors to tell the Utes how they had to act on their counsel. One bitter article said that Utes were not "stupid savages," after all, and that Utes could and would make the final decisions about whether they would act on the advice that they purchased from whites.

Perhaps one of the most transparent examples of discrimination is the following. In and around Roosevelt, Utah, nearly six thousand whites live side by side with the Northern Utes. The two populations have been in constant contact since whites moved to the area in 1906. Between 1958 and 1968 I met no more than two dozen local whites who knew the names of more than half a dozen Utes. These whites were the chief of police, a restaurateur (who served lunches to prisoners in work gangs), the owners of two local bars, the owners of two auto dealerships, and a few ranchers. In the Duchesne area to the west and the Vernal area to the east, also former Ute territory, there were thirty or so whites out of seven thousand who knew the names of as many as six Utes. These whites, too, were the police chiefs, etc. In Vernal, the state welfare officers also knew the names of many Utes. On the reservation the white traders, tribal employees, BIA employees, missionaries, and a few resident Mormons knew the names of more than six Utes.

Utes began attending integrated schools off the reservation in 1950, when the BIA closed the schools on the reservation. At that time the BIA began awarding grants to the Duchesne and Uintah counties to build schools that would serve whites and Utes. The Bureau, under the auspices of the Johnson-O'Malley Act of 1935, and following the termination policies established by Congress in the late 1940s and early 1950s, was attempting to force all Ute children to attend white schools and to acquire white educations, skills, and values. The rationale was to integrate Utes into the local communities near the reservation. With this action the BIA intended to dissociate the young Indians from tribal ways and to prepare them for termination from special federal obligations.

While serving as the tribe's education coordinator in 1960, I often met with superintendents, principals, counselors, and teachers from the Uintah and Duchesne school systems. With one marked exception, they all spoke condescendingly about Ute children, allowing that they would tolerate the Indian students in class if they were quiet. The educators would even allow Indian children to sit in the back of the classroom (as the Indian students desired), if they would keep still. To a person, however, they all thought that the unobtrusive Ute children sitting in the backs of the rooms whispered to one another in Ute too much. Moreover, the educators were convinced, almost to the point of obsession, that they were the subjects of the whispering (in Ute, no less). Thus, Ute children were made to understand that little was expected of them, and were constantly suspected of ridiculing their teachers in Ute. To put it in the local idiom, the whispering was a sneaky act by a sneaky, lazy, and stupid people.

In the same vein, it is of more than incidental interest to note that Uintah and Duchesne counties formed a community education council in the late 1950s. It was composed of educators, civic leaders, and law enforcement officers, and among other things the council was charged with solving delinquency problems involving all students in the school system. Although juvenile delinquency problems for both Indians and whites in the area ran the gamut from stealing to drunken brawls, the council was concerned only when white delinquents were involved. As cases were introduced, council members were assigned to go to this or that parent, this or that law agency or judge, and to report the findings at the next council session. On the other hand, Ute delinquency was considered to be a Ute problem and not a community problem, even though the local criteria for delinquency were met by several Ute youths. Whites did not care to work with the recalcitrant youths, since it was their opinion that nothing could be done to solve the "Indian problem."

Phenomena of this kind are widespread, and the stereotype of Indians as lazy, dirty, stupid (or infantile), and immoral underlies the prejudice and the indifference. In the past and in the present a double standard of interest and justice has prevailed in Ute-white relations. Utes have been accepted in white towns as consumers, but not as producers or even employees. Utes have attended white-dominated schools only because the BIA contributed to the schools' construction and helped defer all other education expenses. Yet in school Utes have been expected to do no more than remain quiet, attend fairly regularly, and advance from grade to grade. Performance has had little to do with advancement (Witherspoon 1961). Where "Indian problems" have arisen, they have been treated differently from white problems. The Indian accused of drunkenness in a white town has been summarily incarcerated; from the Indian point of view and from my own observations, the white has not. There has been little effort to treat problems of Indian youth in the same fashion as problems of white youth. The foregoing, I submit, are causal effects of racism—effects which have become self-perpetuating, or causal. In short, Indians have been denied access to resources and power. As wards of the federal government, they have been forced onto the welfare dole and denied the power of self-governance. Local whites, in turn, have rebuked Indians for living on the welfare dole, for not observing the Protestant ethic, and for not being like whites. As a causal effect, whites discriminate against Indians; Indians remain disillusioned and apathetic; and Indian apathy rationalizes white prejudices.

Comments about Indian slovenliness, unwillingness to work, immorality, and drunkenness have been commonplace. Rather than refer to Indian males and females by name, local whites usually have called them "bucks" and "squaws." The belief that Indians are inferior is widespread in Utah communities. The Mormons hold that Indians ("Lamanites") are the progency of Laman, a *Book of Mormon* profligate. Laman and his progeny were cursed by God with dark skins and slovenly ways because of Laman's behavior. Indian unemployment, drinking, substandard housing, school performance, and so on, reinforce the Mormon belief, and vice versa.

The white communities in the Northern Ute area are predominantly Mormon, as are the educators, businessmen, and civic leaders. In spite of sixty years of Ute-white physical proximity, adult contacts between the two groups are usually confined to business transactions—the Utes buying and the whites selling—and sessions in local courts and jails. There has been little or no fraternizing. Whereas Utes usually refer to white restaurateurs, traders, BIA personnel, missionaries, auto dealers, judges and police chiefs by name, they refer to most other non-Mormon whites as "white guys." Mormons, however, are referred to by Utes as "Mormons." The referent is derogatory.

CHRISTIANITY AND THE NORTHERN UTES

In their 1965 survey of a haphazard sample of 150 adult Utes, a team of Brigham Young University interviewers, all of them Mormons, learned that 51 percent of the Indians claimed to be Episcopalian, 22 percent Mormons, 7 percent Catholic, 5 percent Native American (peyotists), and 15 percent other (Christiansen, et al. 1966: 12). The statistics are surprising in one sense: through 1964 there were only two Mormon Ute families. In 1965 three Uncompaghre Ute men around twenty years of age were recruited to Mormonism and sent to proselytize among other Indians in Montana. In 1966 these young men and the two families were still the only active Mormon Utes known to me.

It is probable that the 22 percent listed as Mormons in the survey conducted by Mormons were influenced—wittingly or unwittingly—by the interviewers. The respondents were asked to declare membership in some religion. If the Utes did not wish to reveal their membership in the Native American Church, and if they were not Catholics or nominal Episcopalians, they probably declared Mormonism. The Episcopalian and Catholic percentages fit my expectations. The Native American figures are way too low. Whatever they mean, the percentages reflect nominal membership only, and by these standards some Utes belong to several religions, for example, Episcopalian *and* Native American. Except for a couple of Episcopalian families in Whiterocks, the Mormons in Roosevelt, Randlett, and Arcadia, and about four Catholic families, only the members (declared and undeclared in the 1965 survey) of the Native American Church are active church participants.

Concerning religious activity, most of the respondents in the 1965 sample said that neither they nor any member of their household had attended a church service in the month prior to the interview. This meets expectations, but I suspect that no member of the household had attended a church service for "the year" if not for "the decade" prior to the date the interview was conducted. Questions probing beyond one month were not asked, but my data and the testimony of resident missionaries confirm the suspicion about attendance raised here. Membership is indeed nominal; both attendance and membership are stressed by the white Christians, but the Indians are not concerned with attendance.

Northern Utes have been in frequent contact with Mormons since 1847 and in constant contact since 1906. Throughout most of Ute-Mormon history, Utes have not joined that religion.

Since the 1940s the Southern Baptists and Jehovah's Witnesses have been proselytizing among the Northern Utes. Each sect has won a few converts from among the mixed-bloods, but no fullbloods have been active in either denomination.

In the early 1950s the Catholic church organized a parish in Roosevelt, Utah; it had long been established in Vernal. Some of the agency employees, including the superintendent and the assistant superintendent (1960–64), the director of Land Operations (1958–65), and others, attended mass. In the late 1950s the formidable Uncompaghre committeeman became Catholic, as did three other gainfully employed fullblood men and their famiiles. Each of these men has said that the Catholic church does not discriminate against Indians because of color (whereas the Mormon church does), and that Catholics accord Indians the respect that they desire. The Catholics, however, like other churches, have had no success with most Utes.

The Episcopal church, which has a small membership throughout Utah, established a mission among the Northern Utes in 1897. It was in continuous operation until 1959, when it was closed for three years. Many Utes have been baptized as Episcopalians, especially those born up until 1950. Yet the pre-1959 and the post-1962 pastors have lamented that Utes do not visit the Episcopalian or any other Christian church, except to attend funerals or, occasionally, weddings.

Conversions of Utes to Christianity have never been numerous, membership has always been nominal, and participation of converts has never approached anything which might be deemed a wholesale religious movement. Indeed, contact with Mormons, the dominant sect in the area, effectively kept Utes from joining that sect for nearly 120 years. The recent male converts to Mormonism are youthful. Interestingly, their conversions correlate with the most severe economic deprivation the Utes have experienced since 1950, certainly the most severe economic crisis in the lives of these young men.

Utes have long emphasized the role of the individual in seeking visions. Furthermore, Utes have accepted the claims of vision recipients, and have accorded each of them respect. No single vision recipient has been recognized as the sole possessor of all truth and all power. These expectations and dispositions of the Utes may have disinclined them from accepting the claims of a Mormon prophet, or of those missionaries stumping for the truth of one Christian sect over all other religions. Utes rejected missionaries who came to them on a temporary basis in the nineteenth century (see chap. 3), resident missionaries who have been in their midst since the 1930s, and the Mormons who have occupied their lands, helped to corral them on the reserve, and have denied them status and self-esteem. Even the Christian elements which have accreted to Ute religious beliefs and practices seem to have been passively, if not unwittingly, accepted. Utes received the peyote religion and the Sun dance as ritual packages which already had some syncretized Christian elements in them—elements which Christians might not recognize as being Christian at all. If anything, the Christian elements lessened in importance in the Ute versions of the rituals.

III RELIGIOUS ACTS, OBSERVANCES, AND BELIEFS

6 *The Modern Sun Dance Ritual*

A knowledge of the main details of the Sun dance ritual, and of the variation between the reservations in the manner in which each performs the ritual, is critical to my subsequent analysis of the religion. The generalized account demanded by the format of my study cannot, unfortunately, convey much of the beauty, vitality, and deep redemptive, religious significance of the ritual. I shall have to leave it to another author—probably not an anthropologist—to furnish the narrative that can describe the drama and brilliance of the Sun dance.

The religious focus of the three-day, three-night ritual is on the acquisition of power (*puwa* in Ute, *poha* in Shoshone). Spectators crowd in and around a large corral to lend encouragement to the dancers inside. The dancers forego food and water, experiencing considerable pain and privation, as they pursue power for their own good health, for the commonweal, for helping the bereaved whose close friends or kinsmen have recently deceased, and to make themselves shamans. Sun dance committeemen (nondancers) assist the Sun dance chief in conducting an orderly ritual by tending the ritual fires, preparing the ritual water, policing the corral, and exhorting the dancers and singers to remember their obligations to their dream instructions (or the power that bestowed the dream instructions), to themselves, and to their kin, friends, and the entire Indian community.

Singing teams provide accompaniment while the dancers charge and retreat from a center pole in the heart of the corral, blowing eagle-bone whistles as they dance. The singers concentrate on the songs and the dancers, and they meditate about power and the quest to obtain it. The dancers, too, concentrate on power, and in the rest periods between dance sets, the dancers meditate about the meaning of the religion and the orderliness of life.

Throughout the dance, spectators collect bundles of willows and other green plants and offer them to the dancers. These gifts comfort and cool the dancers when they are pressed to the body. Spectators also provide damp cloths each morning so that dancers can freshen up, and other spectators build stalls of saplings within the dance corral so that dancers can escape the hot glare of the sun during the rest periods.

At specified times, invalids are brought into the corral. The chief, or some other renowned dancer, diagnoses the ailment and treats (shamanizes) each invalid to make that person well again. As dancers themselves become faint, they too are treated by chiefs or other dancers (possessors of considerable power) in order to regain their strength. All the while singers sing and spectators meditate to help make effective the shaman's cure, and to help the invalid receive the power that is being offered.

On the final day of the ritual the members of the host reservation offer gifts, in the name of the dancers, to the visitors from other reservations. And on the day following termination of the dance, the host community provides a feast for all dancers, committeemen, singers, and spectators from all reservations.

Although I have attended many Sun dances since my youth, and although Utes and Shoshones have explained the religion to me in considerable detail, I must make it clear that (1) I have never danced, (2) I have never asked a chief to divulge his sacred, personal visions (not that a chief would divulge such information if asked), and (3) I have not reported or analyzed any information (especially beliefs) that Utes and Shoshones hold to be inviolable.

The following account is based on a statistical analysis of ritual acts, observances, and beliefs, on the five Ute and Shoshone reservations in 1966.[1] The religion is not identical on each reservation, and aspects of the ritual performances vary on the same reservation from year to year depending on the chief and his dream instructions.

Analyses of the dance ideology and religious experience will be made in chapter 7. Analyses of the underlying factors which motivate people to participate in the religion, and of the Sun dance as a redemptive religion, will be treated fully in part 4.

THE SHOSHONE AND UTE SUN DANCE RITUAL: A GENERALIZED ACCOUNT

In 1966 the five rituals showed marked similarities with one another, as one might expect: the Ute and Fort Hall dances stem from the Wind River dance, and at present people from each of these reservations attend and participate in the dances of every other reservation. There are differences nevertheless. Some of the differences are attributable to the Sun dance chiefs, some to the various reservation contexts in which the rituals occur, and some to the specific dream instructions and intentions of many of the dancers. Let us reconstruct an impressionistic general form of the Shoshone-Ute Sun dance of the late 1960s. The reconstructions will be based on several statistical analyses (one table summarizes the relationships at the end of each section; also see the appendix).

Pre-Dance Activity

Throughout the winter and spring evenings, practice singing sessions are held in the homes of Sun dance chiefs, Sun dance committeemen, and other good singers. Singing teams that will perform in Sun dances during the summer are formed by respected leaders or renowned singers. The singers for each team are usually drawn from the same bands or the same communities on each reservation. Singing practice is considered very important to staging a successful dance, and the participation of good singers is actively sought on each reservation.

Prospective initiates to the dance begin to prepare themselves during the winter and spring as well. Among the Utes the process is usually triggered by repetitive dreams. The dreams are interpreted by shamans, such as a Sun dance chief, as meaning that the dream recipient is supposed to dance. Among the Shoshones dreams are not required, and encouragement from friends, relatives, or shamans is often sufficient

---

1. The definitions of the 374 variables and the ratings (practices, beliefs, objects, and observances) for each ritual are listed in the appendix.

to motivate a person to dance. Dancers do not join formal fraternities or sodalities.

The prospective initiate usually seeks the counsel of a Sun dance chief sometime in the winter or spring. The dancer-to-be is instructed to dance in twelve dances. The prospective dancer is further instructed to dance a minimum of two times (an even number), preferably four times, if the full twelve-dance prescription cannot be fulfilled. He (or she) is also counseled (1) not to dance too hard or too vigorously, lest he dance out of control; (2) to acquire power (supernatural) slowly over the years, learning to control each dose of power that is acquired before more is sought; (3) to abstain from alcohol because alcohol and Sun dancing do not mix; (4) to abstain from peyote because only the strongest men can get power from both peyote and the Sun dance; (5) to guard against extra- or premarital sexual practices after dancing, because as a dancer with newly earned powers he will have become unusually fertile; (6) to be extremely cautious in the use of the power acquired in the dance; (7) to be of "good heart," that is, generous and kind; and, entailed with this, (8) to be aware of his obligations to kin and friends, especially the "old folks," and to maintain the integrity of Indian life.

In these special sessions, and in other conversations with dancers, the prospective initiates are told why they cannot eat or drink during a dance, and why they must dance with restraint until that time (usually the twelfth dance) when they should pursue their vision.

In the late spring the tentative dates for the Sun dance cycle are set. Northern, Southern, and Ute Mountain Ute chiefs meet at a Northern Ute Bear dance and establish the plans for the dates of the Sun dances. The chiefs follow previous conventions in the order in which dances are performed. The dates that are established at this meeting are conveyed to the Shoshone Sun dance chiefs (who may be in attendance). The Southern Utes sponsor the first dance, which is followed, in order, by the major dances at Wind River, Fort Hall, Northern Ute, and Ute Mountain Ute.

Whether among the Utes or the Shoshones, the head chiefs receive dream instructions to direct Sun dances. Each spring the chiefs, after receiving such dreams, announce their intentions to direct dances on their reservations. The position of head chief is quasi-permanent among the Shoshones, but is temporary and determined anew each year, at least hypothetically, among the Utes. (In recent years, however, one man has directed most of the Southern Ute dances.) Assistant chiefs may cosponsor dances. Among the Utes the assistant chiefs are drawn from the local reservations.

Sun dance committees are selected by the chiefs shortly after they announce their intentions to sponsor a dance. All committees include a gate keeper, fire tender, waterman, lodge policemen, and, among the Shoshones, a camp crier. The committees and their chiefs begin their preparations for the summer dances they will direct by sending formal and informal invitations to specific men on other reservations, especially chiefs and dancers, to attend their dance.

About one month before the dance is held, the committee makes plans for a feast to follow the dance. At about the same time the chief goes out to select a forked willow tree to serve as the center pole. It is located and marked, but not cut down at this time.

Two or three days before the center pole is cut, the chief and some members of the committee move to the dance grounds and erect their lodges. Singers, their families,

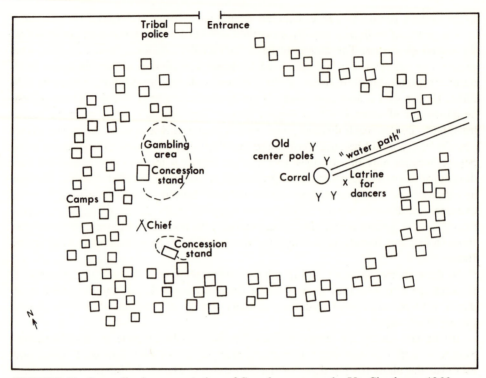

FIGURE 11. Generalized representation of Sun dance grounds, Ute-Shoshone, 1966.

and other visitors begin moving to the dance grounds a day or two before the corral is built. There is considerable fraternizing between people from different reservations, and there is also considerable singing practice.

Before dawn on the day the corral is to be constructed and the dance is to commence, the chief and some of the dancers go to the tree which has been selected to be used as the center pole. The tree is prayed over by the chief and, at dawn, cut down by the chief using a steel ax. The felled tree is stripped of its branches. It is then pulled along, usually by means of some mechanical device such as a winch or a come-along, and lifted onto a waiting truck, where it is "nested" or cushioned on the truck bed.

Twelve side poles and twelve side rafters for the lodge, preferably willows for poles and conifers for side rafters, are selected and cut by members of the tribe. This work is accomplished from one day to one week before the lodge is constructed, usually with chain saws. The poles are not moved to the dance grounds until after the center pole is moved. The lodge poles and rafters, too, are put on truck beds, but they are not cushioned. The trucks are driven to the Sun dance grounds and unloaded a couple of hours after sunrise.

Table 35[2] expresses the coefficients of association for the five dances on fifty "pre-

2. The coefficient of agreement used here is Driver's G (Driver and Kroeber 1932). The formula is
$$G = \frac{a}{\sqrt{(a+b)\,(a+c)}}.$$ Driver's G has several features that are appropriate for my purposes.

TABLE 35

ORDERED G MATRIX, PRE-DANCE ACTIVITY, FIVE UTE AND SHOSHONE
SUN DANCES, FIFTY VARIABLES, 1966

	SU	UM	NU	FH	WR	Av. of Diagonals
SU	.....	.94	.78	.74	.64	
						.640
UM	.94	.....	.84	.80	.68	
						.710
NU	.78	.84	.....	.68	.78	
						.787
FH	.74	.80	.68	.....	82	
						.820
WR	.64	.68	.78	.82	.....	
Column Av.	.775	.815	.770	.760	.730	

A difference between *G* scores of about 10 (in percentage) is significant at the 5 percent level. The only significant matrix error is NU-FH. NU is closer to WR than to FH, but FH is significantly closer to UM and SU than is WR.

dance activity" variables.[3] It is clear that no two dances are exactly the same, and even the Ute Mountain–Southern Ute association shows some differences between the two. The Ute groups are more similar to one another than they are to the Shoshones. Some of the most interesting differences will be assessed in a later section of this chapter.

Preparation, Construction, and Meaning of Corral
The Sun dance corral, whose Ute and Shoshone names mean "thirst house," is

It is always positive and varies between .00 (zero) and 1.00 (unity). The former is complete lack of association and the latter is perfect association. (2) When the *b* and *c* cells of a conventional fourfold table are equal, as they are in every table in this analysis, *G* = percent. Thus the *G* values can be understood as *percentages* of agreement between each pair of rituals. (3) *G*'s sampling error has been proved, and a test for the significance of difference between *G* coefficients is available (Ellegard 1959). Therefore, it can determine whether the difference between *G* scores from two pairs of rituals, say Wind River–Fort Hall and Wind River–Northern Ute, are significant or within the range of values expected from sampling error alone. Because the bulk of these data are interdependent, that is, the dances are historically related and are not independent of one another, the significance tests will only be used as plausibility measures which will help us to understand the differences and similarities in the relationships. The matrix positions of the tribes in table 35 and all subsequent matrices of *G* scores are ordered in terms of "best fit" scaling along one dimension. The measure of "best fit" here is a simple one. The averages of the diagonals (righthand column) should decrease from the diagonal of self-relationship to the uppermost diagonal in the matrix, or that diagonal which is furthest removed from the line of self-relationship. The first diagonal above the line of self-relationship should have the highest values and the highest average value. The next higher diagonal should have equal or lower values than the preceding diagonal, and so forth. Thus the lowest values, or most distant relationships, should be located away from the line of self-relationship toward the upper righthand corner of the matrix. Table 35 fits the model except for the relationships of Northern Ute with Fort Hall and Wind River. Northern Ute is more similar to Wind River (.78) than to Fort Hall (.68). The difference in units of *G* between the two (.10) is significant at the 5 percent level; yet, because Fort Hall is more similar to Ute Mountain and Southern Ute than is Wind River, the ordering here yields the best fit. The column averages also support the "best fit" nature of the ordering obtained. The averages should be smallest on either end and largest in the middle of the matrix. Thus the dancers which share the most features with all other dancers are placed in the middle of the matrix and those that share the least are placed on the extremities.

3. The variables on which the coefficients of similarity for this table are obtained are listed in section 1 of the appendix.

constructed during the morning and afternoon following the transporting of the materials to the dance grounds. The construction is overseen by the Sun dance chief, who has the hole for the center pole dug first. There is no ritual involved with digging the hole. Before the center pole is erected, it is partially decorated by attaching scarves to each fork, by placing a bison robe and a bundle of willows (a "nest") in the crotch, and by painting stripes around the trunk (or some combination of these things). The pole is then moved into position near the hole by the chief and anyone who wishes to help. The center pole is supported with the use of several crossed poles tied together with strands of rope, one person holding on to each pole. Then follow four separate thrusts of the center pole, each preceded by songs and prayers and each followed by feigned exhaustion and blasts on an eagle-bone whistle. Some workers push the center pole while others, nestling the pole in the crotch of their forked sticks, direct it upwards. The pole is erected on the fourth thrust.

The position for each corral post hole is then measured from the center post by the chief. Working rapidly as possible, teams of men dig the twelve post holes at the designated spots. The westernmost corral post—the "backbone"—is lined up with the center post so that both directly face the rising and setting sun. This is the first corral post to be erected. The rest are erected in no particular order. When the side posts are in place, side rafters are laid on and between each of the side posts. At the Northern Ute and Shoshone dances, and sometimes at the Colorado Ute dances, roof rafters are also constructed. At least four rafters are used, one for each cardinal direction. The "east-running" rafter is considered most important. It is decorated with feathers; all of the pine boughs except those on the very top of the east-running rafter are stripped, and the pole is placed on and between the crotches of the backbone and the center pole. The exterior of the corral is then covered with sapling cottonwoods, willows, aspen, and brush, leaving only the east-facing doorway open.

The corral is usually finished by late afternoon, and the dancers and chiefs retire to their lodges to prepare for the dance. The committeemen must collect firewood, prepare the drums, contact the leaders of the singing teams to lay plans for the services of the singers throughout the dance, and carry out the wishes of the chief. As dancers arrive who have not previously informed the chief of their intentions to dance and who have not participated in the corral construction, they usually notify the chief of their intentions to dance.

The center pole and other ritual items of the corral have several meanings for the dancers. At base, however, is the belief that the center pole is the medium through which supernatural power is channeled. The center pole is also believed to have supernatural power of its own. Power comes in the form of the sun's rays, but need not come only in this form. Power can also be channeled through the pole at night, either through the moon or through the sacred fire. In all instances, day or night, sun's rays or moonbeams, power is equated with water. The center pole has many meanings, often referred to by the same person as "God's brain," "Jesus," "the Crucifix," and other names. The willow nests placed in the crotch of the center pole represent a "nest of water," or "Jesus' body," or power; the bison head or stuffed eagle attached to the center pole on the second day (just below the crotch) are other channels through which power flows as well as being themselves possessors of power which they can dispense rather than merely channel from another source.

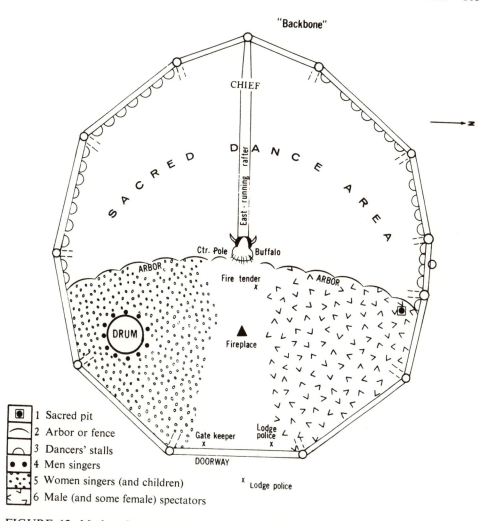

FIGURE 12. Modern Sun dance (on third day of dance). Adapted from Jorgensen 1964.

The center pole is frequently painted with bands which are said to represent the days of the dance; God, Jesus and Mary; the three months that the pole will have "water"; and so forth. Whatever the specific interpretation offered by any Sun dance adherent, the meaning of the cardinal directions, the east-running rafter, the center pole, the doorway, the entire corral, can vary somewhat from individual to individual and chief to chief. The sources of this variation come from dreams, borrowings from other tribes, and borrowings from other rituals and religions. But meanings are widely shared as well. The chief explains to the dancers what the features of the corral mean, and shamans, in their orations during the dance, often present their understanding of what the features of the corral mean. All of the interpretations are usually accepted and treated as compatible with one another. Indeed, dancers, ex-dancers, chiefs, committeemen, and spectators agree that "no one knows the 'complete' meaning of the dance" or even the complete meaning of the features of the corral. Dreams and visions are important in expanding knowledge and conferring greater insights about the dance to the believers.

As the dance progresses, several regular changes are made in and to the corral. A very low dirt altar is built up around the base of the pole. It represents the "life-giving" soil. On the second day stalls of saplings are usually built for the privacy of each dancer by the dancer's friends or anyone who wishes to help the dancer in his ordeal. Decorated sheets are usually hung between the saplings, and favorite colors are chosen to paint each sapling. The painting is said to both "dry out" and "cool" the sapling, just as a dancer is "dried out" and "cooled" by paint. Dance paths are cleared of rocks for the dancers by their friends, and a fence or arbor is constructed to separate the dancers from the singers and spectators.

A large drum is moved into the southeast section of the corral during each dance session and suspended off the ground. The singers position themselves around the drum. The male singers and drummers sit immediately around the drum on benches or chairs. The women sit on the ground. Saplings cut down during the morning are often placed upright with their leaves intact in the singers' area on the last day to help attract power. The saplings, like the willows and many other green things, are said to be life itself.

From the second morning on, a sacred pit is dug in the northeast section of the lodge. A juniper fire is built and the smoke is inhaled by the dancers. The ashes are removed and buried and the hole is filled after each use. Each evening, beginning on opening night, a sacred fire is built directly east and in front of the center pole. The fire and the moon represent the sources through which power is channeled to the center pole during the night sessions. The sacred ashes are scraped up and buried following each sunrise ceremony.

Table 36 demonstrates that there is about as much variation in the preparation, construction, changes, and meaning of the Sun dance corral as there is in the pre-dance activities.[4] This section is brief because the "meaning" of the ritual features of the corral, as well as the acts and observances to be described below, will get an extended analysis in the following chapter on Sun dance ideology and religious experience.

It should be noted, however, that Northern Ute is still central in the matrix. On these variables, at least, Northern Ute is more closely related to Wind River than to other Ute groups. Wind River, in turn, is more closely related to Northern Ute than it is to Fort Hall. The Fort Hall–Wind River relationship is again a bit puzzling as both are relatively close to Northern Ute practices, but Fort Hall is closer to the Colorado Ute practices than is Wind River. This is rather similar to the relationships on pre-dance activities.

DANCERS: THEIR INTENTIONS, INSTRUCTIONS, AND EXPERIENCES

In the late afternoon the dancers begin assembling at the chief's lodge, which is located directly west of the Sun dance corral and which is in line with the rising and

---

4. The 75 variables on which the coefficients of association for table 36 were obtained are listed in section 2 of the appendix.

TABLE 36

ORDERED *G* MATRIX, CONSTRUCTION CHANGES THROUGHOUT THE DANCE, AND MEANING
OF THE CORRAL, FIVE SUN DANCES, SEVENTY-FIVE VARIABLES, 1966

	SU	UM	NU	FH	WR	Av. of Diagonals
SU	.....	.87	.77	.65	.64	
						.640
UM	.87	.....	.81	.73	.69	
						.670
NU	.77	.81	.....	.79	.85	
						.783
FH	.65	.73	.79	.....	.79	
						.815
WR	.64	.69	.85	.79	.....	
Column Av.	.733	.775	.805	.740	.743	

A difference between *G* scores of about 9.5 (in percentage) is significant at the 5 percent level. As in previous tables, the NU/WR relationship is closer than the NU/FH relationship; yet FH is closer to SU and UM than is WR. This time, however, NU/WR is *closer* than FH/WR. There are no significant reversals (errors) in this matrix.

setting sun. If the dancers have not already done so, they tell the chief of their intentions to dance. Some of the men have taken ritual sweat baths before they gather at the chief's lodge. Most, however, have prepared for the dance by eating a fare of saltless meat and fried bread, and have gone with as little water as possible for a few days. The dancers feel that this spartan fare will prepare them for their ordeal. It is also "Indian food," which will direct their cravings away from other food and will put them in the proper frame of mind to abstain from food altogether while pursuing spiritual ends. The last meal and last drink is taken either with the chief or with a few friends an hour or so before the dance begins.

The dancers enter the dance for many reasons, but practically all are following prescriptions to complete twelve dances. Moreover, all of the dancers intend to acquire power and, eventually, to put it to useful purposes, that is, to give themselves good health, to bring good health and well-being to the community, to bring comfort to the suffering, to dispel the ill will of ghosts, or to prepare themselves to become shamans.

After entering the dance, the dancers take no food or water until the dance is terminated.

Table 37 demonstrates that the relationship based on ideology and some ritual practices of the dancers are very close and similar.[5] They show much higher agreement than do the pre-dance practices and the construction and meaning of the features of the corral. The high level of the relationships suggests, of course, that the core of dancer ideology is very similar. Two distinct clusters are obtained nevertheless: the Ute groups show perfect unity with one another, and the Shoshone groups show the same internal unity. The differences between the groups turn on two issues: the Shoshones emphasize dream instructions for initiates less than do the Utes, and the final drink and meal among Ute dancers at Ute dances are more apt to be taken with the Sun dance chiefs than they are among the Shoshone.

Again, the overall similarity in the dancers' intentions and reasons for dancing,

5. The 35 variables on which these coefficients are based are listed in section 3 of the appendix.

TABLE 37

ORDERED *G* MATRIX, DANCERS: THEIR INSTRUCTIONS, INTENTIONS, REASONS FOR DANCING,
AND THEIR EXPERIENCES, FIVE SUN DANCES, THIRTY-FIVE VARIABLES, 1966

	SU	UM	NU	FH	WR	Av. of Diagonals
SU	.....	1.0	1.0	.89	.86	
						.860
UM	1.0	.....	1.0	.86	.86	
						.875
NU	1.0	1.0	.....	.86	.86	
						.907
FH	.89	.86	.86	.....	1.0	
						.965
WR	.86	.86	.86	1.0	.....	
Column Av.	.938	.930	.930	.902	.895	

A difference between *G* scores of about 13 (in percentage) is significant at the 5 percent level. There are no reversals in this table.

their beliefs about power and power acquisition, and their beliefs about the ends to which power can be put is striking and suggests that ideology is less apt to vary than other aspects of the dance. It also suggests the importance of ideology in integrating the dance, for the ideas are clearly less variable than the many ritual acts and objects we have assessed thus far. This topic will be pursued at length in chapter 7.

DANCERS' DRESS: CHANGES AND MEANING

The Sun dancers wear skirts of cotton, satin, velvet, nylon, or wool. They are often decorated with sequins or embroidery and may have geometric designs, figures of animals, or even facsimiles of Indians or Jesus on them. They are changed at least once a day and represent an important part of the dancer's dress. Sometimes breech-clouts or aprons are worn over the skirts, and they, too, can be decorated.

In the dance corral the dancer never wears shoes, although some don moccasins and all cover themselves with sheets when they leave the corral to relieve themselves.

As a standard accoutrement, each dancer carries an eagle-bone whistle around his neck, usually with a white feather attached. The whistle is often borrowed or inherited. Some are purchased. No matter how they are acquired, those that have been owned by shamans or successful dancers are preferred. Dancers also wear pendants or beaded necklaces and broaches, satin cloth, and ermine skins. The pendants are changed at least once a day, as are the skirts and aprons. Belts, usually three inches wide or more and preferably elaborately beaded, are worn around the waist. They are tied with a thong and cover the top of the skirt. Beaded bags often are attached to the belt at the hip, but sashes that are drawn around the waist and left hanging off one or the other hip are equally popular. Many dancers will alternate the uses of sashes and beaded bags or pouches. Prayer horns are no longer carried or used.

As the dance progresses, the dancers change their ritual dress. During night dancing sessions many participants will wear T-shirts, and during day sessions many will protect their eyes with sunglasses. Some dancers will wear sunglasses day and night when they have had special dream instructions. After the first day, dancers will attach small down feathers to the tips of their fifth fingers. Beginning on the second day, ermine skins are often woven into the hair or dangled around the necks of the older dancers, and, the longer the dance progresses, the more probable it is that renowned and powerful dancers will carry special eagle feathers, or fans made of eagle wing or eagle tail. Ritual objects which include eagle feathers are especially useful in controlling power and, in shamanistic practices, passing power on to other dancers as well as to ill spectators. On the last day of the dance many of the dancers carry small willow wands in order to draw the "water," or power, to themselves.

Usually beginning on the second day of the dance, a member of the Sun dance committee will mix a paint and distribute it to those who want to cover themselves with it. Each day more dancers use body paints, and some add special designs to the face and chest. The body paints are said to "dry up" a dancer and "cool" him. The opposition of thirsting and quenching the thirst, or of suffering in order to cleanse the body and make ready for the benefits that will accrue when power is acquired, is expressed in the body painting just as it is in the painting of the center pole and the saplings for each stall.

The decorative paint motifs used on the body, as well as the motifs used on the beaded belts and pouches, the sashes and pendants, and the skirts and aprons, become more elaborate the longer the dance progresses. Within broad limits, each dancer develops his own wardrobe and paraphernalia. The decorative motifs, however, can be learned in dreams, borrowed from other dancers, or created and bestowed by kins and friends.

TABLE 38

ORDERED *G* MATRIX, DANCERS' DRESS: CHANGES AND MEANING,
FIVE SUN DANCES, FORTY-TWO VARIABLES, 1966

	SU	UM	NU	FH	WR	Av. of Diagonals
SU	. . . . .	.90	.90	.76	.76	
UM	.90	. . . . .	.95	.79	.79	.760
NU	.90	.95	. . . . .	.83	.83	.775
FH	.76	.79	.83	. . . . .	.98	.840
WR	.76	.79	.83	.98	. . . . .	.915
Column Av.	.830	.858	.878	.840	.840	

A difference of about thirteen units of *G* between pairs is significant at 5 percent or less. Pattern is the same as for the preceding matrices except that FH/WR are more strongly related to one another here and both are equally similar with NU, UM, and SU.

Table 38 takes a position intermediate among the highly similar relationships noted for dancers' intentions, instructions, and ideology (table 37), and the somewhat lower relationships that obtain between ritual acts and items associated with the construction of the corral (table 36), and the pre-dance activity (table 35).[6] It demonstrates again that Sun dance ritual paraphernalia, in particular, are rather more variable

6. The 42 variables on which the coefficients of association in table 38 are based are listed in section 4 of the appendix.

than Sun dance ideology; but it also demonstrates that dancers' dress, partially because some some of it is inherited, some borrowed, and some stimulated by the dress of other dancers, is somewhat less variable than the ritual paraphernalia and acts associated with construction of the corral or the pre-dance activities. Pre-dance activities and corral construction are more apt to be participated in by nondancers and ex-dancers than active dancers, and this might help to account for the greater variability in these phenomena. Sample error may also contribute to lowering the relations between reservations for the activities prior to the dances and in the construction of the corrals. The relationships obtained for these two subjects are based on more variables than are the relationships for dancers' intentions, etc., and dancers' dress. The orderly direction of the relations throughout the four matrices assessed so far, however, suggests that the relationships are real and not products of sample error.

The Fort Hall–Wind River relationship again is strong, as are the relations among the Ute groups. Northern Ute forms a clear bridge from the Colorado Utes to the Shoshones.

PERFORMANCE OF THE DANCE

The reader should keep in mind that, as the dance progresses, certain features are added to the corral, and changes are made in the dancers' dress.

After nightfall, and preferably before the moon is overhead, a large dance drum is beaten near the chief's lodge. When the moon is overhead the drum is beaten again, representing the "last call" for dancers and notifying the singers and other spectators that the dance is about to begin.

The dancers assemble west of the Sun dance corral, lining up in single file behind the chief. As they blow on their eagle-bone whistles, the dancers march clockwise three times around the corral before entering. They usually line up near a friend or relative so that they can be next to one another throughout the dance.

The chiefs are the first dancers to enter the corral. They take their positions directly in front of the "backbone" or the westernmost corral post, so that they will face east directly in line with the center pole. The dancers position themselves around the back of the corral on either side of the chiefs. (Most of the dancers enter during the first night, but during four-day dances some dancers enter during the second night. These participants have usually had dream instructions to participate in three-day dances.) After the dancers have positioned themselves, the gate keeper, the rest of the committeemen, and the drummers move into the corral. The spectators and singers are the last to move in, and the spectators are kept back as far as necessary by the corral police.

Opening songs, usually led by the chief, are sung, and each is followed by whistle blasts. The chief then offers a prayer to the center pole. Before the dancing begins, but following the songs and prayer, the gate keeper calls for the bedrolls and personal effects of the dancers to be carried into the corral by their friends or relatives or whoever else is serving as their sponsor. When this is completed, the first "rest" song is sung. It is followed by four loud beats of the drum, and then the dance songs commence. The chief is the first person to begin the dancing in the first set.

During the first dance set the fire tender starts the sacred fire directly east of the center pole and just outside the sacred dance area. The fire tender and his aides nourish the fire throughout the first few hours of the night, but they let it burn down to a pile of charcoal, ash, and embers for the sunrise ceremony.

The dance sets during the night are composed of four songs each, and each set lasts about three to five minutes. The dance songs are played at about 180 beats per minute. Each dance set is terminated with a rest song that lasts about one minute and is sung at between 120 and 160 beats per minute. The drum is beaten loud four times at the end of each rest song to signal the next dance set.

In subsequent dance sets any dancer can be the first man to begin dancing. If some prefer to stand at the back of the corral, they may do so. If some prefer to sit, they may do so. As they dance, perhaps no two dancers use exactly the same dance step, though each dances in a path that he (or she) makes with his feet as he goes forward and back to and from the center pole. Sometimes a person's step will change during the course of the dance. The steps are learned in dreams or borrowed from other dancers. Generally the younger dancers bob and gyrate somewhat more than the older dancers, but they are cautioned to keep themselves under control lest they expend too much energy and get knocked down by an angry and challenging spirit.

Dancers can bed down for the night whenever they wish. They merely roll out their bedrolls, take off their ritual paraphernalia, and climb into their sleeping gear. On the first night most of the dancers usually bed down at about 1:00 A.M. The singers sing as long as dancers want to dance, however. By one o'clock most spectators have left the corral as there is little for them to watch and to participate in.

About half an hour before sunrise the gate keeper rustles the dancers out of their sleep and tells them to get up. The pre-dawn cold is painful, but the dancers must get up for the sunrise ceremonies that terminate the night dancing session.

The sunrise ceremony is conducted by the chiefs. The dancers are lined up in four lines behind the center pole. They stand and blow their whistles while the singers sing the sunrise song. Then, as the sun rises, the dancers raise their arms to catch the sun's rays. They follow this by patting their bodies with down feathers that they have been holding. this action is intended to capture the sun's beneficial rays, which are synonymous with power and water.

The sacred fire has been allowed to burn out, and the fire tender shapes the ashes into a circular mound representative of the moon and sun. The chief summons the dancers to sit around the fire's ashes. They do so, covering themselves with sheets or blankets. Four special sunrise songs are then sung by the chief or chiefs, sometimes accompanied by the dancers, and each followed by blasts on the eagle-bone whistles. The head chief then composes and offers a prayer, sometimes following this by blessing each dancer individually (verbally while using eagle feathers). The ashes from the sacred fire are carried out of the corral and buried by the fire tender.

When the sunrise ceremony is completed, the spectators, especially the women, go to their camps or to their trucks and bring shave cream, razors, mirrors, and towels to the dancer or dancers they are "helping." The women also bring moist rags with which the dancers can wash up. The dancers rest for a couple of hours before the "first day" session begins.

At about 9:30 A.M. the first call is made on the drum to signal that the dancing will shortly begin. The Sun dance committeemen roust the dancers from their naps, and the people on the camp grounds are notified of the proceedings. By about 10:15 A.M.

the dancing resumes. Male singers have positioned themselves around the drum. Other spectators, mostly men, sit in the northeast section of the lodge. The gate keeper and corral police spend much of their time keeping the "doorway" or "water path" to the east open, that is, they do not let spectators press in around the east side of the center pole and block the path of the morning sun's rays into the corral.

The dance songs are sung at about four songs per set, and the beat is quickened to 190–200 beats per minute. Moreover, the dance sets themselves are stretched out to from twenty to thirty minutes. Each set is terminated by a rest song, which is usually sung at 160 beats per minute and lasts about one minute.

During the dancing the dancers are expected to stay in their own paths to the center pole, especially early in the dance. If dancers wander out of them, they are apt to be ridiculed by spectators and directed into their own paths by adjacent dancers. Later, say during the second afternoon or the third morning, a dancer may wander out of the path in pursuit of a vision; then he is not ridiculed, but encouraged. If a dancer drops something while dancing, he must wait for a rest song before he can pick up the fallen object.

Some dancers chew the indigenous "bear root" in order to make them salivate, but they are not allowed to eat or drink. They watch one another closely on this score, and are also watched by the corral police. Dancers can leave the corral during rest songs to relieve themselves. They usually go in pairs and they always cover themselves. The corral police do not watch them closely when they go to the latrine, but stories are told about how dancers have bolted from the dance grounds in quest of water in the past. The corral police are said to have given chase, capturing the renegades at the water's edge. Invariably the recalcitrant dancers are said to have been mixed-bloods or whites, or perhaps even Indians from other reservations.

As the morning wears on, committeemen and other respected shamans (usually elderly, either men or women, former dancers or not) move up close to the center pole and exhort the singers to sing and the dancers to dance. They stress the importance of acquiring power and the marvelous uses to which it can be put.

Generally there is very little shamanizing in the corral on the first day. There is a proscription against it on one reservation, and on two others chiefs are allowed to shamanize dancers only. The dancing is often cut off at midday for about an hour, then resumed until about 5:15 P.M. Sometimes dancing is uninterrupted through the noon period and terminated around 3:30 P.M. A "quitting" or "flag" song usually ends the day session.

The first call for the second night session is sounded at about 6:30 P.M., and the dancing begins at about 7:30 P.M. The "evening song" is sung first, and no one dances. Although the dancing begins before sunset, the sacred fire is not lighted until after the sun goes down. The ritual proceeds along much the same lines as the first night. Most dancers bed down a little later, usually between 1:00 and 3:00 A.M. Some men dance intermittently all night long, however.

About half an hour before sunrise the dancers are again raised from their sleeping or napping for a ceremony similar to the previous sunrise ceremony. During this morning, the singers, drummers, and spectators join in with the dancers in patting themselves with the sun's rays. They also pat themselves when the ceremony is over.

Following the chief's prayer and blessings to the dancers, a sacred fire pit is dug just outside the dance area in the northeast section of the corral. The gate keeper fills it up with fresh, green juniper boughs and starts a smoky fire with some embers from the sacred fire pit in front of the center pole. Dancers are then called over in groups of three to huddle over the pit, where they are covered with sheets and instructed to inhale the cleansing and fragrant smoke. When all dancers have breathed the smoke, the ashes are buried and the pit is filled.

During the interim between the ceremony and the day session, stalls are built, paths are cleared, and arbors are constructed.

The second day session begins about 10:00 A.M., following a call thirty minutes earlier. A "morning song" is sung before the dancing begins. The dance session on this day is not interrupted, and it lasts until 5:30 or 6:30 P.M., ending with a "quitting song." The dance sets last from ten to thirty minutes and increase in tempo from about 200 beats per minute in the morning to 210 beats per minute in the afternoon. Rest songs do not occur at regular intervals, and when they are sung, they are as brief as thirty seconds or as long as one minute.

Orations are made throughout the day, but especially in the morning and early afternoon. Committeemen and respected shamans, Indian guests, and others do the orating. During the same period invalids enter the corral and request Sun dance chiefs or famous dancers specifically selected by the clients to shamanize them. In the shamanizing (curing) procedure the invalid is brought into the corral and up to the Sun dance pole, where the invalid's shoes are removed. The chief, or whoever is selected by the client, diagnoses the problem and then performs his (or her) curing techniques, using those that are appropriate for the problem as diagnosed. Powerful dancers can and do shamanize themselves when they feel faint, but they often request the services of the chief when they feel especially weak. Younger and less prominent dancers, too, request to be shamanized by older and more powerful dancers during the course of the dance. At Wind River there is considerable family shamanizing and blessing on this day, and this practice sets Wind River off from the other dances.

The third night session begins at about 8:00 P.M. with the "evening song." The Ute rituals are about the same as for the first two nights, but there is both shamanizing and blessing during the third night of the Shoshone dances. As during the day, spectators—either invalids who wish to be cured or families seeking blessings—will select a chief to shamanize them. They approach the center pole while the singers and dancers continue to sing and blow their whistles. All participants, through their singing, dancing, concentration, and maintenance of "good hearts," work to help the chiefs in their cures and blessings.

The dancers again bed down sometime between 1:00 and 3:00 A.M., but a few get up and dance throughout the night. As before, they are rousted before dawn from their sleep in preparation for a sunrise ceremony similar to that of the preceding day except that a juniper smoke fire is not built.

The "last day" of the dance (either the third or fourth day depending on the chief's intentions), begins about 9:30 A.M. with the "opening song." Four dance songs still comprise a set, but they now run as long as thirty-five minutes at from 200 to 220 beats per minute. It is during this session that the older dancers, particularly those who are participating in their twelfth dance (but perhaps anyone who has danced for several years and feels he ought to pursue a vision), will dance vigorously and without rest in quest of visions. During these periods the tempo quickens to 220 beats per minute, the dance sets lengthen to thirty-five minutes (at a dance in 1963 a set went an hour and a half at 220 beats per minute), the other dancers stand in their stalls and blow their whistles in encouragement, all of the women in attendance beat rhythm with willow wands and join in the singing, and the male spectators make war whoops and shout encouragement. Respected shamans orate and challenge the dancers to "take" some power away from Buffalo, or the center pole. They preach about the importance of the dancers' callings, the beauty and importance of Indian ways, and the necessity to maintain the integrity of Indian life. They also rail against the devilish ways of white men, who, though powerful, do not possess Indian power. For some of the lengthiest orations, especially if they are given by highly revered Indians, the dancing and singing is stopped. The lengthy orations do not interrupt the vision quest dancing, however.

If a dancer receives his vision, he is "hit" by a jolt of power which lifts him from his feet and brings his feet up to a level with his head before he falls to the ground.[7] The vision recipient lies on the sacred dance ground "stone cold" as his body is filled with power (cold water). At this time his soul is off somewhere being counseled. His fellow dancers move his body to his stall, cover him with a sheet, and position his head toward the center pole and his feet toward the perimeter of the corral. When the vision recipient gets up, after an hour or so, he will dance completely "refreshed," that is, he has been cooled, and his thirst has been quenched by power (which is water).

During this day there is considerable shamanizing of dancers by themselves, dancers by other dancers, and invalid spectators by renowned dancers. At Wind River, family blessings are also performed.

The "last dance" is determined by the chief, and his decision is relayed to the gate keeper. The decision is made on the basis of the length of the dance (three or four days), the weather, the singing, whether the dancers are pursuing visions, and so forth. It can be terminated at any time between 11:30 A.M. and 5:30 P.M.

About one hour before the "last song" is sung, gifts from donors on the sponsoring reservation are collected by the Sun dance committeemen. A buckskin or sheet is placed on the spot where the sacred fires have been burned each night, and as the gifts are donated they are placed on the buckskin. The chief's final prayer is made toward the center pole and over the gifts.

While the dancers are still in the sacred area, several respected shamans appear in the spectator area. Each dancer selects either a Sun dance chief, a fellow dancer, or one of the respected shamans in the crowd (male or female), to administer a final blessing to him (or her) and to validate and cement the power that he has just won throughout the course of the dance. The blessing is given in the dance area, and the recipients of the blessings pay the donors for their services.

Following this, the sacred water is brought into the corral and blessed by a committeeman—either the gate keeper or the water chief. The person who gives the blessing takes the first drink and spits it out at the base of the center pole. The dancers retire

---

7. The religious experience is analyzed in the following chapter. To satisfy any questions the reader might have about whether or not visions are received, and whether or not recipients receive them in the fashion prescribed here, I have seen several dancers receive visions in precisely this fashion.

to their stalls and hang their sheets between the stall saplings so that they are obscured from view. The sacred water is then carried to each dancer, one man starting on either end of the corral. The dancers spit out the first drink, and take very modest second drinks.

When this is completed, the gate keeper fans himself and the center pole, and the dancers file out of the corral in a single line headed by the chief. The spectators then line up to get a drink of the sacred water that was not drunk by the dancers.

The dancing is over, but the distribution of the gifts, collected as the dance neared termination, and the feast are yet to be performed. The gifts are chiefly money, cloth, and Indian handicrafts, and they are distributed to the visiting Indians by the Sun dance committeemen. Those who have traveled the farthest receive the most elegant gifts. At the feast, which is held on the following day, the visitors are the first served and receive, along with all others who attend, a meal of boiled meat, corn, fried bread, and fruit. The gift giving, feast, and several aspects of spectator participation in the dance and the extracurricular activities that attend it are analyzed at length in part 4.

TABLE 39

ORDERED *G* MATRIX, PERFORMANCE OF THE DANCE, FOUR RESERVATIONS, 172 VARIABLES, 1966

	SU	NU	WR	FH	Av. of Diagonals
SU	.....	.79	.69	.71	
					.710
NU	.79	.....	.87	.76	
					.725
WR	.69	.87	.....	˙.78	
					.813
FH	.71	.76	.78	.....	
Column Av.	.730	.807	.780	.750	

A difference between *G* scores of about 7.2 (in percentage) is significant at the 5 percent level. There are no significant errors in the matrix. SU and FH are most different from NU and WR. Each has fashioned its own dance. WR and NU are most similar. NU is next closest to SU, whereas WR is next closest to FH. The difference between NU/FH and WR/FH is not significant, but the difference between NU/SU and WR/SU is significant. Thus, NU again is most similar to most dances. With the omission of UM, the NU/WR ordering is adjacent as it is under similar circumstances in table 42.

Here let us look at two tables of coefficients of similarity based on the ritual acts and observances in the performance of the dance proper. Table 39 is based on 172 ritual act and observance variables that occur during the performance of the dance.[8] The most striking feature of the table is the high relation that obtains between Northern Ute and Wind River Shoshone. The two are more similar to one another than any other pair. This relationship shows that the central part of the ritual—the performance of the dance proper—is most similar between the two groups who have performed the dance for the longest time. It also shows that the Wind River Shoshone practices have influenced the Southern Ute less than the Northern Ute practices have influenced the Fort Hall Shoshone practices. Nevertheless, the Fort Hall Shoshones and the Southern Utes have fashioned their own dances after borrowing them

8. The 172 variables on which these coefficients in table 39 are based are listed in section 5, *A* through *H*, of the appendix.

directly from the Wind River Shoshones, in the Fort Hall case, and indirectly from the Wind River Shoshones and the Northern Utes, in the Southern Ute case. The overall relations among the four groups are very high, but the Wind River–Northern Ute relationship stands out.

When the variables on the performance of the dance are reduced to the fifty-five observed among the Ute Mountain Utes, we see that the order remains the same as in most of the tables above, with Ute Mountain Utes positioned between Southern Utes and Northern Utes, and Fort Hall Shoshones positioned between Northern Utes and Wind River Shoshones. Table 40 demonstrates this ordering.[9] We see that Northern Ute and Ute Mountain rituals are identical on these variables, and the relation of the latter to the Wind River Shoshone ritual is also high.

TABLE 40

ORDERED G MATRIX, PERFORMANCE OF THE DANCE,
FIVE SUN DANCES, FIFTY-FIVE VARIABLES, 1966

	SU	UM	NU	FH	WR	Av. of Diagonals
SU	.....	.82	.82	.75	.78	
						.780
UM	.82	.....	1.00	.84	.80	
						.775
NU	.82	1.00	.....	.84	.80	
						.820
FH	.75	.84	.84	.....	.78	
						.835
WR	.78	.80	.80	.78	.....	
Column Av.	.793	.865	.865	.803	.790	

A difference between G scores of about 10 (in percentage) is significant at 5 percent or less. Fort Hall and Southern Ute are most distinct from the other rituals on these variables.

OVERALL RELATIONSHIPS

As a final pair of measures of Sun dance similarities let us assess the relations among the five reservations based on 257 variables (table 41), and the relations among all but the Ute Mountain Utes based on 374 variables (table 42). (Exclusion of the Ute Mountain ritual from the second measure is explained below.) Both tables are presented here because they give us somewhat different information about the dances, even though every variable included in table 41 is also included in table 42. What is important is that the Wind River and Fort Hall positions are reversed in the two tables (as they are in tables 39 and 40). This allows us to focus on the reversal for a brief, but special, discussion that will have relevance throughout the chapter.

The relationships measured in table 41 pertain to all aspects of the Sun dance. As we know, these aspects include the preparatory and ritual activities engaged in by singers, dancers, committeemen, chiefs, and the community at large before the Sun dance is performed each year. These activities are stretched out over several months, and the assessment of these activities above has been instructive in our

9. The 55 variables on the performance of the dance on which these coefficients are based are listed in section 5 A and H, of the appendix.

TABLE 41

ORDERED *G* MATRIX, AGREEMENTS AMONG FIVE SUN DANCES, 257 VARIABLES, 1966

	SU	UM	NU	FH	WR	Av. of Diagonals
SU	. . . .	.89	.83	.75	.67	
UM	.89	. . . .	.91	.79	.77	.670
NU	.83	.91	. . . .	.79	.83	.760
FH	.75	.79	.79	. . . .	.85	.817
WR	.67	.77	.83	.85	. . . .	.860
Column Av.	.785	.840	.840	.795	.780	

A difference between *G* scores of about 5.7 (in percentage) is significant at the 5 percent level. There are no significant errors or reversals in this table. NU is more closely related to WR than FH, but not significantly so. FH, on the other hand, is significantly closer to SU and not significantly closer to UM than is WR.

understanding of the involvement of the members of the reservation communities in the dances they sponsor and the dances sponsored elsewhere. The relationships here (coefficients of agreement) are also based on variables that account for (a) the formal design, construction procedure, and meaning of the Sun dance corral and its parts; (b) the initiation of novice dancers, their dream instructions, and their intentions for dancing; (c) the ritual preparation of dancers for each dance, and the ritual paraphernalia they wear throughout each dance; (d) the performance, or sequence, of ritual acts and observances in each dance, including the order and variability of these phenomena from beginning to end; and (e) the ritualistic behavior of spectators. These coefficients do not reflect similarities or differences on extracurricular events which attend these rituals. Extracurricular events are treated separately in chapter 11.

The relationships reflect spatial, linguistic, and historical differences. The Southern and Ute Mountain Utes in southwestern Colorado are most similar to one another and least similar to the Wind River and Fort Hall Shoshones. The differences are significant at less than 5 percent. The overall agreement of Ute Mountain with other groups is inflated by the close historical, spatial, and administrative (BIA) relationshp between Ute Mountain and Southern Ute. The Shoshones are most similar to one another, although Fort Hall is significantly closer to Southern Ute and absolutely, yet not significantly, closer to Ute Mountain than is Wind River. The Northern Ute ritual takes a strong intermediate position showing high relationships with the other four rituals. Northern Ute is most similar to the Ute Mountain Utes, in equal agreement with Southern Ute and Wind River Shoshone, and least similar to Fort Hall Shoshone. Even this last relationship is quite high, however.

It is interesting that the original donors of the ritual, the Wind River Shoshones, have the lowest overall agreement with the other rituals. The Northern Ute, with the highest overall agreement, were also the first among the Utes and Shoshones to borrow the ritual from the Wind River, and remain the most centrally located of all the groups. These factors have probably helped to create the general nature of the Ute dance; that is, the Northern Ute location has facilitated borrowing and lending of features with the two Shoshone and two Ute groups over a sixty-year period. The

Northern Ute dance is, indeed, the focal point of the Sun dance cycle, and the Northern Utes attend and participate in more dances than the members of the other reservations.

Table 42 is based on 374 variables and excludes the Ute Mountain Ute ritual. The additional 117 variables included in these coefficients pertain to the ritual acts and practices of the first two days and all three nights of the dance. The data for these aspects of the Ute Mountain dance are too sketchy and incomplete to be included here. The Ute Mountain Utes are more disposed to be apprehensive and suspicious of whites than is any other reservation group in this study, as is borne out in the preceding historical and contextual analyses. As a consequence, and because I did not wish to antagonize these people, I left the Sun dance grounds frequently during the performance of the dance proper, except for the first night and last day. My presence was tolerated, perhaps, because I did not badger the Ute Mountain Utes with questions during the performance of the dance. Yet my presence was disconcerting because no other Anglos attended and because the Indians knew I was studying the ritual and the Sun dance community.

TABLE 42

ORDERED *G* MATRIX, AGREEMENTS AMONG FOUR SUN DANCES, 374 VARIABLES, 1966

	SU	NU	WR	FH	Av. of Diagonals
SU	. . . . .	.82	.70	.72	
					.720
NU	.82	. . . . .	.85	.77	
					.740
WR	.70	.85	. . . . .	.83	
					.830
FH	.72	.77	.83	. . . . .	
Column Av.	.750	.810	.790	.770	

A difference between *G* scores of about 4.5 (in percentage) is significant at the 5 percent level.

The ordering in the second matrix aligns Wind River next to Northern Ute and pushes Fort Hall to the edge. This ordering has one matrix error or reversal (not significant). Again Northern Ute shares the most features with the other rituals, but, with the addition of the acts and observances of the dance proper, Wind River has the second highest score of shared features with the other groups. Thus, Wind River and Northern Ute are moved to the center of the matrix. This arrangement reflects the influence of ritual acts and observances on the overall orderings and the intensity of the contact relations that have obtained in the Sun dance community over the past five or six decades.

The Northern Utes and the Wind River Shoshones are most similar. This is to be expected, given the Sun dance history as we know it at present. We recall that the Northern Utes acquired the dance from the Wind River Shoshones around 1890 and that they have attended one another's dances since that time. In 1901 the Wind River Shoshones passed the Sun dance along to the Fort Hall Shoshone bands, and at about the same time the Northern Utes passed the dance along to the Ute Mountain Utes, thence to the Southern Utes.

Since the early 1900s, but especially in the 1960s, more people from more reserves in the Sun dance community have attended the Northern Ute dances than all other dances, and currently more dancers (per capita) and more visitors (per capita) from Northern Ute and Ute Mountain Ute attend more dances than dancers or visitors from any other reservation. The religious and economic implications of these generalizations, and the evidence for them, are spelled out in part 4.

ATTENDANCE AT THE DANCES

Let us now assess the flux and flow of attendance at the Sun dances of 1966. At a glance we can see that attendance is heavier at night (when the employed can attend) than during the day, heavier from the second night through the third morning than at other times (and heavier on weekends, again when the employed can attend), and heavier during the times when the dancing is most vigorous and dancers pursue visions (when interest quickens and spectators arrive to lend encouragement to the dancers).

The attendance data in table 43 were collected at several spot checks at each dance. The figures do not account for total attendance at the dances (see chapter 11 for a complete analysis of attendance and participation). There are some overall similarities in the attendance patterns at the various dances determined by these spot checks, but the patterns are sufficiently different to warrant a few comments in the next section of this chapter.

TABLE 43

SPECTATORS IN SUN DANCE CORRALS AND TOTAL SPECTATORS ON CAMPGROUNDS,
FOUR RESERVATIONS, SELECTED PERIODS, 1966

Periods	So. Ute Colorado 2–5 July		W.R. Sho. Wyoming 8–11 July		F.H. Sho. Idaho 26–30 July		No. Ute Utah 5–9 Aug.	
	Cor.	C.G.	Cor.	C.G.	Cor.	C.G.	Cor.	C.G.
First night	100	800	250	900	325	700	350	1,300
First sunrise	70	450	110	800	75	700	150	900
First morning	80	450	150	800	80	520	120	1,000
First afternoon	80	450	150	800	80	520	200	1,000
Second night	150	700	170	1,000	300	1,000	300	1,400
Second morning	100	500	170	1,800	175	900	180	1,200
Second afternoon	150	500	300	1,800	225	900	225	1,200
Third night	200	700	500	1,900	300	1,250	300	1,600
Third morning	170	450	200	800	300	1,300	200	1,000
Third afternoon	.....	.....	.....	.....	.....	.....	400	1,600
Fourth night	.....	.....	.....	.....	.....	.....	400	1,700
Fourth morning	.....	.....	.....	.....	.....	.....	350	1,500
Termination	400	700	400	900	300	1,300	500	1,800
First night following dance		1,000		1,000		1,900		1,800
Total Enrollment 1966	695		1,970		2,800		1,600	

All totals are smoothed.
Cor. = Inside corral
C.G. = Camp Grounds

Overall, the smallest crowds of spectators around the corral and on the dance grounds occur during the sunrise ceremonies. Larger crowds convene during the day sessions, and the largest crowds convene at night. From day to day, too, there is an overall increase in attendance, except at Wind River, where maximum attendance is reached on the third night. Proportional to the reservation populations, all of the dances draw vast crowds of spectators. Some are camped on the dance grounds, some are not.

SOME SPECIAL CHARACTERISTICS OF EACH DANCE

The statistics above, as well as the ratings of the variables in the appendix, demonstrate that the rituals are very similar on the whole. The greatest variation occurs in pre-dance activities and in certain specific ritual acts and paraphernalia. The least variation obtains in Sun dance ideology, in the conduct and meaning of the ritual acts and observances of the dance proper, and in the intentions of dancers. Further, I have certain impressions about the special characteristics of each dance that are supported by my observations but not necessarily by my statistics.

The Northern Ute dance is characterized by its grandeur and activity. It draws large numbers of dancers and vast numbers of spectators. The spectators jam into the corral and contribute to the electric atmosphere in which much of the ritual is performed. Each dancer seems to be free to pursue power at his own dance pace, and the individualism spreads to the shamanistic practices, wherein many invalids request cures from one or another dancer or from the Sun dance chief. The curing of invalids seems to be more prominent at the Northern Ute dance than elsewhere.

The Wind River Shoshone dance is also a large dance with many dancers and many attenders. The chief plays a relatively minor role in this ritual, especially when compared to the role played by the chiefs in the Ute dances. The prominence of "family blessings" during the last two days of the Wind River ritual is also unique to the Wind River dance.

The most notable feature of the Bannock Creek dance at Fort Hall is, of course, the participation of women. The women dominate the proceedings, dancing hard and relentlessly. The male head chief at Fort Hall seems to have much less control of the ritual than the female chiefs, although the male and female chiefs jointly direct the proceedings. There is some shamanizing of invalids and some blessing of families at Fort Hall, but the former is less prominent than at Northern Ute, and the latter is less prominent than at Wind River Shoshone.

The Southern Ute dance is small and serene. It has absolutely fewer participants and fewer spectators than the other dances (though there are many spectators in proportion to the population). The chief is an exceedingly strong figure and exercises a marked control over the dance. Several elderly shamans also have noticeable effects on the dance, particularly in their orations. There are several Christian overtones in the dance, especially in certain motifs on the dancers' paraphernalia and in speeches given by one or two of the shamans. The singing is not as strong as it is on the other reserves. Often it is performed by only a handful of men.

The Ute Mountain dance impresses me with its secretive nature. The Ute Mountain people are especially hostile to whites, and so few whites ever attend. The mood of the dance is very intense, and the dancers themselves are very athletic. They seem to dance harder and longer than their counterparts at other dances. Fewer non-Ute Mountain people attend this dance than the other dances, but it usually has more dance participants than the Southern Ute dance. The constant emphasis at Ute

Mountain Ute on performing the dance the "proper way" gives the Ute Mountain dance a rather self-righteous quality. (The emphasis on proper conduct is made known to all dancers and participants at all other reservations as the Ute Mountain Utes are great travelers as well as afficionados of the ritual.) Although every Shoshone and Ute group thinks it performs the "best" dance, only the Ute Mountain Utes seem to hold this opinion self-righteously.

SOUTHERN UTE

The pre-dance activities at Southern Ute are rather more elaborate than at the other reservations. At the ritual cutting of the center pole all dancers are expected to participate in the felling (though not all participate), and only a steel ax can be used. When the tree is felled, it is stripped of all branches at the cutting site. This is not true for the other dances. The rest of the poles and rafters are selected and cut by men whose services have been specially requested by the chief and who are paid by the tribe (from a special allocation for the Sun dance). At the Sun dance grounds only the Southern Utes continue to stage a parade to move the center pole to the corral site. Women, horses, tambourines, feather headdresses, and singing accompany this brief morning ritual.

During the erection of the corral a buffalo skin robe is placed over the willow bundle (nest) and placed in the crotch of the center pole before it is erected. The Southern Ute also tie on eight scarves (rather than two), four to each fork of the pole, before the pole is erected. Each scarf is a different color. The center pole is lifted at the end of three feints and thrusts rather than four as in the other dances, and three sets of songs, followed by whistle blasts, accompany the procedure.

The Southern Ute ritual varies from the others in that the dancers' stalls are constructed on the first morning rather than on the second, and all stalls are painted the same reddish-brown color. The same paint that is used as the basic body paint is used on the stall saplings.

During the dance the dancers cannot use painted designs until the second day, but all are painted with the reddish-brown body paint on the first day. When individual designs are allowed, red, white, and blue paints are preferred. On the third day of the dance all of the dancers are instructed to carry willow wands. The chief is instrumental in maintaining all of these features and in exercising considerable control over the form of the dance.

When the dance commences, no opening songs are sung. The gate keeper offers the first prayer to the center pole and the chief offers the second. The latter includes a pipe ritual to the cardinal directions. Then, before the dancing begins, the sacred fire is lighted.

Instead of song sets, only one song is sung at a time. Fewer and smaller singing teams participate at the Southern Ute dance than participate at any other dance. The sunrise ceremony is directed solely by the head chief, and his imprint on the ceremony is unmistakable. The chief sings and leads the dancers in six special songs, followed by one, two, three, four, four, and four whistle blasts respectively. During the first sunrise ceremony the chief asks all spectators to leave following the opening songs. The sacred ashes are moved out by means of a wheelbarrow, and the chief then sings more songs and offers a prayer so that the dancers will be successful in their pursuit of power, and all Indians will experience good health and happiness.

The morning dance sessions begin about an hour later than the sessions at the other reservations, owing mainly to a paucity of singers. The songs, generally, are brief (three to five minutes), and one to a set. Just before the end of the dance session of the first day, the chief lines up all dancers behind the center pole and shamanizes the group as well as each dancer separately. No other chief does this.

During subsequent night and day sessions the length of the dance sets increases somewhat, and more people join in the singing. On the second night several men and women sing all night long in order to get special spiritual help in overcoming some malady. The chief instructs them to do so and then gives them special blessings during the subsequent sunrise ceremony. During the sunrise ceremony of the final night the chief gives a special blessing to the person who prepares the paint for all dancers. This, too, is unusual.

At the termination of the dance the chief and two members of the committee take turns showing special ritual objects that dancers on other reservations do not possess. The chief shows a Sun dance doll which was stolen from the Kiowa in a period before the Southern Utes performed the Sun dance. He also shows a sheet with "Jesus' footprints" on it. A buckskin with a Sun dance painting and a sheet with mixed Christian–Sun dance symbols, that is, Jesus and a buffalo, are also shown.

The final drinks are given to the dancers by visitors who have been chosen to circulate the pitch-lined basketry containers of sacred water. The use of visitors to pass the water to the dancers, and the use of pitch-lined receptacles for the water, are unique.

Following convention, the Southern Ute dance was the first in the cycle of Shoshone and Ute rituals held in 1966. It was unique, however, in that 150 whites who called themselves "Bizarros" attended the ritual, camping on the dance grounds. These people introduced themselves to whoever asked as a colony of psychedelic religionists, many of whom resided near Washo, Nevada (close to the Washo Indian reservation). This astounding number of white cultists made their presence felt at many points during the ritual. We shall assess the influence exerted by the Bizarros in several places below.

A final interesting point about the Southern Ute dance is that there is more commuting on the part of Southern and Ute Mountain Utes to this dance than is noticeable on the part of any other local group or groups to other dances in the Ute-Shoshone cycle. This is explained partly by the high percentage of employment at Southern Ute (78 percent of employables enjoy some form of employment—part-time 40 percent, full-time 38 percent), the close proximity of the Ute Mountain Ute reservation, and the relatively high unearned income enjoyed by the Ute Mountain Utes (allowing many of these people access to automobiles to move back and forth to their homes).

UTE MOUNTAIN UTE

Traditionally the Towaoc dance is the last to be performed in the Shoshone-Ute cycle. The Ute Mountain dance has no unique features which separate it from the other dances. It shares some unusual features with Southern Ute, many with Northern Ute, and a few, such as stripping the bark off the center pole from the ground up to the buffalo head (mounted just below the crotch), with the Fort Hall Shoshone. It seems quite evident that the Ute Mountain Utes and the Northern Utes have held more rigidly to the early twentieth-century form of the dance than have the Wind River Shoshones, the original donors, or Southern Utes and Fort Hall Shoshones, the most recent recipients. The historical integrity with which the Ute Mountain dance has been preserved may justify the opinions of Ute Mountain Ute people who say that theirs is the correct dance.

Northern Ute

The Northern Utes sponsor two dances a year. Their second dance is considered the major Northern Ute dance, and it is the fourth ritual performed in the cycle. The Northern Ute dance is different from the others in that a larger number of chiefs serve from dance to dance than at any other reservation in the cycle. Usually there are no more than two chiefs at any dance, however. The composition of the Sun dance committees also changes markedly from dance to dance, depending on who serves as chief. A special feature in the Northern Ute pre-dance activity is that the chief ritually kills the center pole by shooting it before it is felled. The other Ute groups assign the task to a World War II veteran. The Shoshones do not shoot the center pole at all.

In the construction of the corral the Northern Ute also differ from the others very slightly. The fence between the sacred dance area and the spectator-singer area is made of upright forked sticks topped by stripped saplings, as opposed to logs, willows, and other barriers among the other four groups.

During the course of the dance proper the Northern Utes are distinct in that no shamanizing is done on the first day, whereas in some form or another there is shamanizing at all other dances on the first day. The Northern Ute dance is also distinct in that some men pursue visions on the third night, whereas at the other dances the vision quest is usually restricted to the third day. Other than these few distinctions, there is nothing of interest in the ritual that the Northern Utes do not share with other groups. We will see below how certain distinctive sets of attributes mark the Ute cluster, some mark the Northern Ute–Wind River relationship, and some set off the Wind River–Fort Hall relationship.

Fort Hall Shoshone

The Fort Hall dance is most distinct in that women not only dance but two of them serve as chiefs. One serves as head chief and one as assistant chief, and both seem to exercise greater influence on the dance than do their male counterparts. There are several other features which also serve to set Fort Hall off from the other dances. Traditionally the Bannock Creek dance at Fort Hall is the third ritual to be performed in the cycle. (In recent years performances of dances other than those at Bannock Creek have been irregular at Fort Hall.)

The head chiefs direct the committee members and helpers to select four roof rafters, one for each cardinal direction, rather than twelve or none at all. During the construction of the corral the female chiefs participate, as do all other women who wish to help. Throughout the dance several changes are made in the corral. A dirt mound is built up at the base of the center pole on the second night. On the third day willow bundles are placed on top of the mound on the east side of the center pole, and at the termination of the dance a "digging stick" is thrust into the base of the dirt mound to ritually kill the center pole. The saplings used for the dancers' stalls are painted white, and this is consistent with the basic body paint the Fort Hall Shoshones prefer. The fence that separates the dancers from the spectators and singers is made of aspen posts and willows tied to the posts.

During the performance of the dance there is a certain "looseness" that is not observed at the other dances. Whereas other groups have a mild prohibition against whistling—because of a belief that ghosts whistle—in 1966 some of the dancers whistled in the corral on the first night before the dancing got started and before the fire was lighted. As spectators laughed, more dancers whistled. Also, even after the opening ceremony and during the first night of a three-day dance, late dancers were allowed to enter the corral. (They did not seek permission to enter, however. They merely walked in.) Late entrance to a three-day dance is not allowed elsewhere. Further, after dancers enter the corral and begin to dance, they are allowed to change their positions vis-à-vis one another around the back of the lodge. This practice is not allowed at the other dances.

The opening songs and sunrise songs are sung by the drummers and singers rather than by the chiefs and dancers. Chiefs have not delegated this responsibility to drummers and singers on any other reservation. Although this special feature may draw nondancers more deeply into the ritual, it may also be a result of the chiefs' faulty knowledge of these special songs. Fort Hall has no special "quitting songs" at all. When the dancing begins, the dancers open up very fast, and women, in particular, charge the center pole. The dance songs and the length of the dance sets are slightly longer at Fort Hall than anywhere else and they seem to have been prolonged by the aggressive, nearly indefatigable dancing of the women. Indeed, the hard-dancing women offer constant challenges, sometimes verbally and sometimes by their deeds, to make men sing and dance.

All of the rituals include a taboo against menstruating women being present in the Sun dance corral. The Fort Hall Shoshones tell stories about how women, even female dancers, have been chased from the corral if their menstrual period occurred while they were in the corral or in the dance. Although women are discriminated against in these situations because of the dangerous properties of the menstrual flow, they are still extremely important in the dance. Indeed, the female chiefs are more active in shamanizing "fevered" dancers than are the male chiefs.

During the night sessions, special "fire songs" attend the building of the sacred fires, and, at the same time, the female chiefs shamanize all dancers. The male chief then offers a prayer to the center pole.

Throughout the dance there are a few other details that are different from the other dances, usually in some ritual practice performed by a woman rather than a man. For instance, on the second day women often rush to the center pole and hug it. It takes great confidence in one's own power to do such a thing, for the belief is that if a person hugging the pole did not have control of a considerable amount of power, he (or she) would be struck down. If one *has* power and can control it, one will merely harness more power by hugging the pole. (As on the other reserves, the pole is believed to be a possessor of power [water], and a channel through which power flows. When a person hugs the pole, he [or she] will be "cooled" by the water [power] within the pole.)

On the final day of the dance, the first drink of ritual water is offered to the center pole, and this too is slightly different from the practices at the other dances.

WIND RIVER SHOSHONE

The Wind River Shoshones normally sponsor two dances a year. Their first dance is considered to be the major Wind River effort in the cycle. In the Wind River ritual a tribal dance committee hires and directs the teams who cut down the rafters and poles for the corral, making sure that the poles are cut the day before the corral is erected. After the corral materials are moved to the dance grounds, the crier chief moves all of the poles into place by dragging them behind his horse. He continues to use his horse to ride about disseminating news throughout the camp during the course of the dance.

During the construction of the corral the center pole is the last pole erected rather than the first. Though there is no special ritual associated with the digging of the center post hole, it is dug first, and a "digging stick" is placed in it until the center pole is erected. This is the obverse of the Fort Hall practice. At Fort Hall the stick is plunged into the dirt altar at the base of the pole at the end of the dance. The Ute groups, on the other hand, do not use the stick at all. A bison head, sometimes a stuffed eagle or a strip of cloth, is put in place below the crotch of the center pole *before* the dance begins. As for the base of the pole, a dirt mound is constructed, but willows are not placed on it or in it. This, too, is different from all other practices where the relations between willow and water, willow and earth, and earth and "life-giving" substance are emphasized. The preferred color for stall saplings and basic body paint is yellow, and this sets off the Wind River ritual from both Fort Hall and the Ute groups. The fence used to separate dancers from spectators is made of two logs laid to rest on the ground.

During the performance of the dance there are a few notable features about the Wind River ritual. The dancers form two lines, one behind the head chief and one behind the visiting chief (see chapter 8 for an analysis of chiefs and visiting chiefs). In their approach, one line circles the corral clockwise and the other circles the corral counterclockwise. The entry into the corral emphasizes the role of the visiting or guest chief. (Guest chiefs are not distinguished in this fashion at Fort Hall, and guest chiefs are no longer summoned to share the responsibilities of directing the dances on the Ute reservations.) During the opening song all of the dancers kneel. This act has a pseudo-Christian overtone. There are other such features that are peculiar to this dance. For instance, the guest chief in 1966 was a mixed-blood Ute (Affiliated Ute Citizen) from Utah with a Mormon and an Indian heritage. This man salted his prayers, which were recited in English, with typical Mormon prayer phraseology, for example, "Heavenly Father, we ask that your spirit be with us today . . . "

A most striking feature is the family blessing. None of the local Christian churches sponsor such blessings, although Mormon patriarchs are known to give blessings to their own families. Shoshone blessings are certainly not identical to the Mormon practice. The Shoshone family blessings are consummated through a technique that is essentially different from that for curing. A family or group of relatives (sisters; a man and wife; a father, son, and daughter, etc.) are brought together near the center pole, and the chief gives them a collective blessing. The chief uses his feather wand to brush all of them, and he is paid for his services. Shamanistic cures are the same at Wind River as elsewhere.

The importance of the family blessings can be measured simply from the attendance figures for the Wind River dance. The peak attendance in and around the corral at Wind River is on Sunday (the second day and night), rather than on Monday (the third day and termination) as is the case on the other reserves. The attendance peak correlates with an expectation among Wind River people that Sunday is the day to receive a blessing, or to "help" (by attending and meditating) others receive their blessings.

A slight difference in the Wind River Shoshone sunrise ceremony is that the dancers do not raise their hands to greet and channel the sun's rays as it rises. Another difference is that the Wind River Shoshone chiefs open the ritual to shamanizing of dancers and nondancers on the first day. The other rituals allow for the shamanizing of dancers only, or else no shamanizing at all. On the other hand, at the termination of the dance very few dancers take final blessings, so that the role of the Sun dance chief, which is so emphasized during the family blessings and shamanizing throughout the course of the dance, is not important at all at the close of the dance.

SHOSHONE-UTE DIFFERENCES AND THE POSITION OF NORTHERN UTE

The Ute groups perform Bear dances in the spring; the Shoshone groups do not, though some Fort Hall and Wind River Shoshones attend the Ute Bear dances, especially if they belong to families in which there is a Ute-Shoshone marriage. The prospective Ute Sun dance chiefs announce their intentions to direct Sun dances at the termination of the Bear dances. The Shoshone chiefs usually announce their intentions to sponsor a Sun dance on Memorial Day (not at a Ute Bear dance).

The dream instruction–dream interpretation syndrome for dancers is a more prominent feature of the Ute than it is of the Shoshone dances.

Other features that distinguish the Ute dances are their emphases on willows and the ideology that attends them; their painting of stall saplings and bodies reddish-brown; and their changes of clothing and ritual paraphernalia, which surpass those of the Shoshones.

In pre-dance activities the Shoshones differ from the Utes in that they hold "Baby" dances on the eve of the Sun dance. These are dances for the chiefs and their special guests and serve as a warm-up for the Sun dance ritual. Utes participate only when at Shoshone dances. There is no evidence that Baby dances were ever sponsored by Utes.

In the construction and features of the dance corral it is interesting that the Northern Ute and Wind River practices are more similar to one another than either is to the practices of Fort Hall Shoshone or of the other two Ute groups. Whereas all of the Utes paint their center poles with stripes, the Shoshones do not. If Shoshones paint the poles at all, it is with a whitewash. The Northern Utes and Shoshones use roof rafters, especially an "east-running" rafter, to channel the power into the corral; the other Utes do not.

Many of the corral features which distinguish Northern Ute and Wind River Shoshone dances from the others can be explained by their relative access to resources. For instance, these groups stress the importance of roof rafters, pine boughs, on the tips of the rafters, and the ideology that attends these objects. The Fort Hall Shoshones do not stress a need for these objects as elements vital to the proper performance of the ritual nearly as much as do the Northern Utes and Wind River Shoshones. The Southern and Ute Mountain Utes do not stress a need for the objects at all. It happens, however, that the Northern Utes and Wind River Shoshones have much easier access to conifers than the other groups, and, according to dancers and spectators alike, this availability is the reason some dances have roof rafters and the attendant ideology.

Whether the availability of similar resources influences the similarity between the Northern Ute and Wind River Shoshone dances is not especially important. On the other hand, it is interesting to get opinions of dancers about the similarities and differences of the rituals. More than a dozen Northern Ute dancers have told me that the Wind River dance is more similar to the Northern Ute dance than the Northern Ute dance is to the Southern Ute dance. They also say that they know better what to expect at Ute Mountain than at Southern Ute. The opinions held by Northern Utes about the Ute Mountain and Southern Ute dances may stem from the strong, innovative role assumed by the current Southern Ute chief (see chapter 8).

Shoshones at Wind River identify their dance with the Northern Ute dance and not with the Bannock Creek dance at Fort Hall. This is probably a result of many factors, but foremost is the role of women in the Bannock Creek version of the dance. As for the Arapahos, who share the reservation at Wind River, the Shoshones point out that few of them ever participate in the Shoshone dance. And the Shoshones say that the Arapaho Sun dance is "more like those people up north, the Cree, than ours." In their description of the differences between the dances they practically always mention that Arapaho dancers do not move up to the pole; they just stand in their stalls and blow whistles. They also point out that the spectators at the Arapaho and Cree dances eat and drink in front of the dancers. None of these are Shoshone or Ute practices.

The high agreement between Northern Ute and Wind River dance performances shows that the two have maintained many similarities since the Ute borrowed the dance from the Shoshones. And their sustained contacts have contributed to the maintenance of the similarities. A recent innovation that has caught on at Wind River and Northern Ute is the "flag ritual," which includes special songs for raising and lowering the United States flag before and after each daily dance session.

In the Shoshone ritual scarves are not tacked to the center pole by dancers on the final day of the dance as they are in the Ute ritual, and there are no other offerings to the "old people." Moreover, orations do not interrupt the dancing on the final day. At the Shoshone dances, speeches must await the termination of the dancing, at which time special sessions are held for them.

7 *Ideology and the Religious Experience*

Our analysis in this chapter will partly focus on religion qua religion. All Sun dance participants know the religion in the religion's own terms. We cannot hope to understand the enduring appeal of the religion unless we, too, learn something of its composition and meaning, and of the fulfillment that comes to each individual from participation in the ritual. At the very least we can attempt to comprehend the religion qua religion. We can attempt to know the beauty and the dignity of the Sun dance, epitomized, perhaps, by the vision quest. In particular, we shall analyze the meaning of supernatural power, the opposing yet compatible forms in which power is evidenced, the meaning of the ritual acts and objects, and the manner in which the preceding are explained by the ideology—a communitarian ideology that synthesizes oppositions, that makes compatible the discrete, the particularistic, and the diverse with the whole.

IDEOLOGY

IDEOLOGY AND POWER

Sun dance ideology centers on power and power acquisition. The power concept of twentieth-century Utes and Shoshones is the same concept of power that was held by Utes and Shoshones of the nineteenth century and, perhaps, by generations of Utes and Shoshones who preceded them in the Great Basin and Rocky Mountains. Indeed, the Ute-Shoshone concept of power is homologous to the belief in a diffuse, impersonal, supernatural force that was held by the vast majority of North American Indians at contact.

The Ute word for this diffuse, supernatural force is *puwa*, and the Shoshone word is *poha* (or *box, buha*). As it is envisaged by these people, the force is everywhere, and everyone and every living thing needs a little of it in order to live. During a Sun dance, power in amounts beyond that which is required for life itself is pursued. The power is "called" into the corral by dancers, singers, committeemen, and spectators. The ways in which it is called by the various participants—dancers and nondancers—and the intricate web of ideas that explain the relationships between power and ritual acts and objects of the Sun dance will occupy us here.

Often when Utes or Shoshones talk about power they are talking about major depositories of power rather than power itself. *Puwa (poha)*, the term(s) for power, is often used synonymously with the "Great Spirit," *sinawaf* (animal creator), God, "That Man," and the center pole. The attribute that makes each of these "beings" similar is that they all have great amounts of power. Appeals to these various sources of power for different reasons, at different times, following different instructions, then, becomes understandable. All have in common the attribute of power.

The beliefs that are basic to the ritual, that is, those beliefs about power and how it is acquired, are woven into a complex fabric. On certain issues Utes and Shoshones distinguish the religious symbol from the thing symbolized. On other issues the two are merged.

The key symbol in Sun dance ideology is the dichotomy of "dry-hot" : "water-cool." This dichotomy represents power in various forms, which are both symbolic and literal. Thus, power *is* dry and hot, as well as wet and cool. Furthermore, power is *symbolized* by dry and hot, wet and cool things. The dance is the "thirst dance" or the "heat dance" (dry and hot), and a dancer thirsts, going without food or water, so that his thirst may be quenched (water and cool). The ideology of power, then, is an ideology of opposing but compatible forces. One can gain power only by synthesizing the opposites. Figure 13 schematizes the relationships between power and the synthesis of the competition between them.

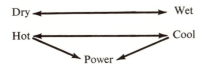

FIGURE 13. Synthesis of competing forces.

The sun plays a very special role because it is a localization of great power that it emits through its rays, rays which are both hot and cool, which both cause a person to dry up and to slake his thirst. Yet the sun is not the sole locus of power, because power is diffuse. Furthermore, at night power is emitted from the moon, whose rays are both hot and cool, and by the sacred fire, whose flames are hot and whose ashes are cool.

Throughout the first three nights and two days of each dance the rays that dominate the dancers, singers, and other participants, are those that are hot and dry. The competing rays, those which are cool and wet, effect the participants toward the end of each dance when the meditation, the enduring, the sacrifice, and the courage is rewarded. At this time the thirst that has been created by the hot and dry rays, is quenched by the wet and cool rays. The oppositions are united, and power is bestowed upon the adherents as a result of the synthesis. Thus, the sun's rays are both hot and cool, dry and wet; they cause a person to dry out and to slake his thirst as well. The competition, with the resulting synthesis of the oppositions, is always experienced in the same sequence: first a person dries out; then he is cooled with a drink of water. The competing forces test a person's willingness and courage to endure. When courage and personal merit have been established throughout the course of the dance, the worthy are rewarded.

From the Indian view, a person literally gets hot and dry and literally gets cooled and has his thirst quenched. Literally a person gives himself to the pursuit of power. In the process, and as a condition for obtaining power, he purges himself of his evil:

the spirit causing disease or sickness and errant ways. He is literally cleansed and his power is rejuvenated. In a dancer's case, power is also increased. The participant, dancer or not, is ready to take on life anew.

The center pole itself is equated with a man or anything else that must have water or life-giving power. Throughout the course of a dance, the pole too must dry out; it too must sacrifice. Yet as the pole dries out it also channels power to those who can control it. The center pole is often stripped of its bark and painted, and the paint serves to help dry the pole out so that it can channel the life-giving power.

The life of the pole is short, but its role of giving power to worthy Sun dance adherents during its life is immense. Just as the "old people" (deceased Shoshones and Utes), who knew so much about the religious truths and who controlled so much power, passed on when their power was depleted, so must the pole pass on when its power is depleted. The pole gives its cooling power, which is necessary for life, so that humans may live. On the other hand, from death comes life. From the death of the center pole comes not only the extension of human life, but the birth of new center poles, poles that are cut and used at subsequent dances. From the death of Shoshones and Utes—those who become the "old people"—comes the birth of new generations of Shoshones and Utes.

Although the Sun dance pole expires while helping others, the benefit to new generations of trees or to new life generally is immediate. Human rewards are twofold: first, life is prolonged in the here and now, and the human recipients of the pole's power use it to help others, just as the pole did. Second, those human recipients, too, will die eventually so that others may live. From individual sacrifice and individual reward comes collective life.

Paint is applied on dancers and also on their stall saplings. The paint helps to dry out both dancers and saplings. In the drying process, however, the dancer receives help from the saplings in his quest for power. Indeed, the saplings provide shade and support for the dancer; that is, they offer their power to the dancer while the dancer endures the thirsting process. So the relation of sapling to dancer is similar to that of the center pole to dancer. The sapling liberates its cooling power (the water and coolness needed for life), as it endures the challenge of hot and dry power. This is done out of generosity in order to help the dancer.

Although the sapling dies when all of its power is depleted, the reward for the sapling's death is twofold as it is for the center pole: (1) the death of the sapling gives birth to a new generation of saplings; and (2) the help offered to the dancer allows the dancer to live and, in turn, to help others. In the long run, the dancer, too, dies. At that time, the dancer becomes revered as one of the "old people," and through the dancer's death a new generation of dancers is born. Furthermore, the "old people" are propitiated at each dance, and it is believed that they can bestow power to the living as a means of helping the living to cope. They help the living win power, health, and solace.

So the courage and sacrifice of both sapling and dancer is recognized, both are individually fulfilled, both help others with their life-giving power, and both die in order that others may live. The human outlives the sapling, carrying on the good work made possible in part by the sapling's sacrifice. The community survives because of individual sacrifice, and that sacrifice is recognized and approved.

The saplings that are erected to provide shade in the singers' area on the last day also dry out as they withstand the hot power from the sun's rays. As is the case for the stall saplings and the center pole, it is believed that the saplings in the singers' area bestow their cooling power to the singers—the power the saplings need for life itself. The cool, wet power from the saplings moistens the throats of the singers as the singers themselves dry out.

Thus we see that the competing powers "hot-dry" and "cool-wet" are linked to life and death. When all the "cool-wet" power of a being has been dissipated, that being dies. Yet through sacrifice and death—which results from the bestowal of one's own "cool-wet" power on others—others can live. New generations are born (all living things), and the Indian recipients of power have their lives prolonged so that they can help other humans to live. Power for life is earned only when the competing forces of "hot-dry" and "cool-wet" are fused. The center pole, the stall saplings, the saplings in the singers' area, the dancers, the singers, and the attentive spectators undergo the same physical suffering—drying and thirsting—to gain the same physical rewards—cooling and quenching the thirst. Spiritual rewards include the gaining of power and the satisfaction that supernature is beautiful and can be helpful. Indeed, one is satisfied that sacrifice and death yield plentitude and life.

Even the low dirt altar at the base of the center pole dries out during the dance. The dirt too needs power through a fusion of "hot-dry" and "cool-wet" forces, so that living things can come from the earth. One dancer put it this way: "Each year things are born and things die; all of them things get their power from the dirt—that's where life comes from. That's why those doctors take the dirt from around *sinawaf*[1] [center pole]. It gives good health to everybody and cures the sick people who need new life."

The buffalo head, or whatever else is attached to the center pole, is believed to contain power, much as the dirt contains power in and of itself. It is also believed that the buffalo is like dirt in that it is a channel through which one receives power from other sources. In these two senses Buffalo is very much like any shaman, or Indian doctor; Buffalo has power of his own to dispense; yet he gets power from other sources.

Dancers say, "Just as when the buffalo is thirsty he can dig water out of the dust where no one can see it, *nuc* [Indian] can get water from Buffalo when he is thirsty." They mean that in the Sun dance each dancer thirsts and sweats. When he has sweated himself dry and it seems that he cannot get water from any place to quench his thirst, he then receives water either *from* Buffalo, who gives the dancer some of his own water, or *through* Buffalo, who gets water in supernatural ways himself. The fusion of the competing powers, hot-dry versus cool-wet, quite literally means that power is awarded in the form of water, the real substance, to rejuvenate the dancers and to cool their "fevers." Power is won as a synthesis of the opposites.

Buffalo, then, is not conceived as an omnipotent god, although he is one of the leading characters in the Sun dance. Indeed, the willow nest in the crotch of the center pole, directly above the buffalo head, both symbolically represents and literally means water from God, or from *sinawaf*, or from the sun. The nest, in turn, feeds its water

1. *Sinawaf* refers to the center pole here. *Sinawaf* is the "creator" in animal form, a locus of great power.

to Buffalo and the center pole. The nest, which is also often equated with the body of Jesus, sacrifices its own power so that others may live.

It is again relevant to point out that all men and all things do not have equal amounts of power, and this is very evident in the course of any dance. A dried out dancer might hug the center pole for the cooling sensation it gives him. The dancer says that it gets the "fever" out. This sensation is experienced even though the center pole is also drying out. The explanation of why the dancer would have the "fever" whereas the pole would not is simply that the center pole has more residual power, that is, water, than the dancer, so that it can cool those who are confident enough to hug it. On the other hand, the hot and dry competing power will soon win out. The pole will shortly die so that new life can emerge.

Some dancers, too, have more power than other dancers, and a dried-out dancer might choose to have another, more powerful dancer, cool him off. The client who seeks such help is not apt to hug the center pole because he does not control sufficient power or sufficient confidence to do so. The dancer whose help is requested is also "drying out," but he has residual power. Moreover, the very powerful dancer can exercise his control of power by drawing water from the center pole through his whistle, or through his hands, or through his feather fan, or even through his head. He passes it to his client by blowing it into his chest through his whistle, or by pressing his head, hands, or feather fan against his client's head or chest. He then fans the client from head to toe with sacred dirt scooped up with his fan, or he spits on his hands and places them on his client (even though he is dry, he can produce water). The dancer, man or woman, chief or nonchief, who can do this has power in con- considerable quantity, confidence in his techniques, and the confidence of his clients.

IDEOLOGY AND THE DIVERSITY OF SYMBOLS

In symbolic representations or religious objects and acts which are meant to represent things of religious importance, we encounter considerably more variation than is evident in beliefs about the nature of power and the way it behaves during the dance. For several years I was perplexed by the many interpretations I heard about the meanings of such things as the center pole, the corral posts and rafters, the fire and its ashes, the buffalo head and various ritual objects which are hung from the center pole, and other acts and objects integral to the ritual. My puzzlement was solved only after I began asking whether alternative interpretations of such features as the twelve corral posts were in opposition or whether they were equally correct. I had received two different interpretations from the same person at different points in time.

The cause of the variety of interpretations is partially explained by the following comment from a middle-aged Northern Ute dancer: "No one person knows the true meaning or what the whole dance means. Even the chiefs who have danced for a long time know only parts of it. They are always learning more about it through the dreams that that Man gives them." These new interpretations, revealed in dreams, are additive rather than replacements for old interpretations. The interpretations introduced by a chief or other person at one dance on one reserve are carried to other reserves in the Sun dance cycle.

The following represent the most frequent interpretations of the symbolism of features in the corral. The center pole represents life, the sacrifice of power so that others may live, a man, a man's heart, Jesus Christ, Jesus' crucifix, God's brain, power itself, water, *sinawaf*, and probably several other things to which I am not privy. The willow nest in the crotch of the pole represents water, life, Jesus' body, and the sacrifices of him who dies so that others may live. The stripes on the center pole represent the number of days that the dance will last (yet four-day dances have been performed while there has been only one painted stripe on the pole), the trinity of Mary, God, and Jesus (never the Holy Ghost), and the three months that the pole will have water before it dies. The green branches and leaves at the top of the pole represent the "miracle of life." The scarves tacked to the forks of the pole represent offerings made to the "old people," and they are requests to the "old people" to give aid to the living or to all those who seek power and good health. In fact, in these offerings they are also asking the spirits to refrain from hindering the health or obstructing the desires of the dancers.

The corral post directly west of the center pole is the buffalo's "backbone," though the east-running rafter that rests between the center pole and the westernmost corral post at Shoshone and Northern Ute dances also represents the backbone. The eagle-tail charm that is tied to the east-running rafter in order to catch power and channel it into the lodge is said to represent the three or four days of the dance, to be a request for Mother Mary to be present, and to be a request for "good luck."

The corral posts and rafters at the extreme northern, eastern, and southern points represent the three remaining cardinal directions. The four cardinal directions represent the sacred number four as well as the four dances some dancers should take part in before receiving a vision. The eight remaining posts, along with the original four, are said to represent the twelve apostles of Jesus Christ, the twelve [sic] commandments, the twelve [sic] days of Jesus' fast, the twelve dances each dancer should participate in before he receives his vision, a man's twelve ribs, the twelve months of the year, the twelve tail feathers "all" birds have, and probably several other things.

There are, of course, interpretations of the corral that integrate every structural aspect into a single analogy. For instance, the corral represents a human being in the following way: the twelve posts are the ribs, the north- and south-running rafters are the ears, the east-running rafter is the backbone, the center pole is the brain and the heart, the boughs and needles on the tips of the rafters represent the hair, the east-facing doorway is the mouth through which the sun's rays enter.

The mixture of pseudo-Christian and non-Christian symbols should not be interpreted as representing a transition from traditional religion to Christianity. The pseudo-Christian symbols were, for the most part, syncretized with the Sun dance ritual when the Wind River Shoshones passed the religion on to the Northern Utes and Fort Hall Shoshones. The ritual has changed little since that time and does not fit into any niche of modern Christianity.

The focus of the Ute-Shoshone Sun dance religion on the acquisition of power has gone relatively unchanged for over seventy years. The role of dream and vision instructions has been a constant source of minor, but new, ritual acts, observances, and even interpretations of features of the dance over these same seventy or more years. The changes have been mostly cumulative, and the "truth" of each addition is readily recognized. In fact, most interpretations are passed from Sun dance community to Sun dance community through joint participation at rituals.

RELIGIOUS EXPERIENCE

The Sun dance provides a context wherein Shoshones and Utes of all ages and both sexes—singers, dancers, committeemen, orators, and spectators—can have a religious experience. This religious experience can have lasting value because the recipient acquires power to help him cope with everyday life in the future, and to understand better how life and death are complementary and how suffering is a necessary part of life. In the process of participation in the dance, some of the sick are cured (if only temporarily), mourners are pacified, the "old people" are propitiated, good health is assured, and initiates to the dance are given new responsibilities commensurate with their newly acquired power. Furthermore, pursuit of the religious experience briefly separates the adherents from the mundane and oppressive problems of everyday lives.

THE VISION

The ultimate form of a Sun dance religious experience is the vision. Everyone in the corral participates in the acquisition of a vision for the recipient, and they also participate in the benefits. A generalized account follows because the vision quest, the context in which it occurs, the general features of the vision, the manner of the recovery of the recipient, and the response of the people in the corral are very similar from dance to dance and reservation to reservation.

There is intense excitement during the third day of a dance, which day is considered the propitious time to receive a vision. If a dancer is to receive one, it will come then. A few minutes before the third day's dancing begins, the gate keeper and the fire tender shout instructions to the dancers to get up and dance.

After the session begins, old men and women shamans move up close to the center pole and orate, beseeching dancers to dance for the good of everyone. The most respected old people, especially at the Ute reservations, harangue the dancers and tell them that they are acquiring special responsibilities to lead an "Indian" life and to remember and practice the ways of the "old people." They are told that their new powers will require care and should not be abused by drinking, carousing, or practicing the ugly traits that have stemmed from white culture. Usually at least one shaman will stand up beside the large drum and offer a long prayer emphasizing Indian life. ("Indian" is not restricted to "Ute" or "Shoshone" but includes all Indians in the Sun dance community.) The prayer focuses on the desirability of marrying Indians and preserving Indian integrity, the need to acquire power to cure the sick, the need to treat one another as relatives as the "old people" used to do, and the need to honor the obligations and duties of family life.[2] Thus, orations, harangues, and prayers stress obligations and responsibilities to family, wider kinship affiliations, and the entire Sun dance community. So whereas participants pursue individual ends, they are also admonished to pursue collective ends. Furthermore, the satisfaction of individual ends serves to satisfy collective ends, and the former cannot be accomplished without the latter, as we shall see.

These orations, harangues, and prayers are offered intermittently throughout the

---

2. One old and highly revered Ute Mountain Ute man gave prayers and speeches emphasizing these themes at dances on every reservation in the 1966 ritual cycle.

session.[3] By 11:00 A.M. or so, the spectators are jammed so tightly into the corral that there is barely room to move. The corral police constantly move people out of the doorway so that a clear path, two or three feet wide, will lead from the center pole directly out of the corral.

As the excitement builds, the dancers are encouraged to dance hard, to seek a vision, although it is by no means thought that all dancers will receive visions. Most dancers avoid overextending themselves in their first eleven (sometimes three) complete dances and attempt to conserve their energies so that they will not fall. Many dancers conserve their energies because it is believed that each succeeding dance is more difficult than the one that preceded it. As a consequence, the more one dances, the dryer one becomes, or the more difficult the task as the hot-dry power challenges the dancers. Older dancers think that young dancers are more than a little presumptuous when they seek visions too soon.

Great power, when localized in one person, entails great responsibility on the part of the recipient. It is argued that youths are often frivolous and run great risks when they accumulate power. Moreover, to fall in a Sun dance does not necessarily mean that a dancer has received a vision, or even a dose of power that he can control, but it does mean that he has been hit with a jolt of power. A novice might receive more power than he is prepared to handle properly, and most recruits to the Sun dance guard against receiving power in large doses. As a consequence, the novices follow the advice of their elders and those who counsel them during the dance to rest during some dance sets. They also make sharp retorts to the old shamans who tell the young men to get up and to dance harder in the course of their orations or harangues.

Dancers think that they have to be literally knocked down by the buffalo, or the eagle, or the center pole to receive a vision. A vision is not a prerequisite to the acquisition of power and good health, however, for both come from participation alone, whether or not the dancer is knocked down. Participants also think that they earn more power each time that they dance; that is why the adherents get "dried out" faster with each performance. Thus the competing forces of dry-hot and wet-cool are synthesized for each dancer at each dance. The power acquired by each individual at each dance is dissipated as it is used to combat the evil spirits and to help oneself and others. Hence many continue dancing to keep their power strong, or to keep their power pantry full. The individual power acquired is used not for narrow individual ends but for broad individual and collective ends (at a minimum to help sufferers and mourners as well as oneself).

Some dancers reach physical and emotional points where they believe that they are indeed "knocked down" by Buffalo.[4] If the dancer is unconscious for a short time only and yet does not immediately dance again, it is assumed that he is afraid of Buffalo and has rejected his power. Old shamans jump up from among the spectators at these times and shout at the exhausted dancer. Above the din created by the spirited

3. The third day orations and prayers yield to family blessings and shamanizing at Wind River, though the former are given as well.

4. Further references to being "knocked down" by Buffalo can just as well refer to being hit by a jolt of power from Eagle, a ribbon attached to the center pole, or from the pole itself. It depends, of course, on what, if anything, is mounted on the pole. That, in turn, is contingent upon the Sun dance chief's dream instructions.

dancing and whistling and the deafening singing, drumming and willow rattling, they yell something like the following (freely translated): "You can get what you're looking for. You've got to go get it. If you want to be a doctor[5] you've got to work for it. You've got to take it away from that buffalo. He wants to give it to you, but it isn't going to be easy." As is expected of him, the avid young believer usually attempts to dance again. All of his life he has heard his friends and relatives ask, "Did everybody make it?" or "Is there anybody who didn't make it?" The youth does not want to be someone who did not make it. The question asked by Shoshones and Utes mean did anyone collapse in front of Buffalo and then fail to muster the courage to get up to dance and again to meet Buffalo head on? Buffalo knocks down those who violate customs, or pursue power too fast, or who cannot withstand the hot-dry force. Those who are knocked down must get up and dance again, showing that they have the courage to withstand Buffalo's jolts of hot-dry power.

On this final day the singing picks up to about 220 beats per minute. Songs are stretched out to as much as fifty minutes when it appears a dancer is "going for it," that is, when he is seeking his vision. Those who pursue visions are usually older dancers who have danced for many years. Often they have not taken a single rest during the entire dance, aside from the ritualized rest periods. They lunge forward and backward from their stalls to the pole, looking into Buffalo's eyes all the while. When a dancer begins to waver out of his own dance path, the other dancers retreat to their stalls and blow their whistles.

The whistle might fall out of the fatigued dancer's mouth as he spins erratically forward and backward. The spectators rise to their feet; more people try to jam into the lodge, and those who cannot get in try to peek through the brush around the periphery. Dust rises from the feet of the dancer and from the shuffling of the spectators. Often the dancer plummets backward into the stalls of other dancers, but his counterparts catch the falling dancer with sheets, which they hold up as nets between the stalls, and send him back to "fight Buffalo."

Shoshones and Utes believe that the buffalo snorts fire out of his nostrils, that his eyes roll, and that he becomes alive, just like an enraged bull in a bull ring. He challenges those who would accept his power to come and get it. If a person goes down and is knocked unconscious but does not receive a vision, it takes great courage to face Buffalo again. It is believed that, when a person receives his vision, he is "knocked down" as if he were hit by a thunderbolt from above, and it is a foregone conclusion that the dancer will not only dance again but that his dancing will be effortless. Indeed, the Indians pantomime the procedure in which the vision is received by smacking their fists into their hands as if they were striking straight down from the shoulder to the waist. The dancer's body should be so upended that it is raised parallel, four feet or so above the ground. The dancer should then land on the back of his neck and shoulders.

If the dancer has been so hit, he should remain unconscious for three or four hours without budging.[6] This is how the spectators "know" that the dancer is having his

---

5. *Puwarat* in Ute and *pohagandi* in Shoshone means that a person is a possessor of supernatural power. Utes and Shoshones freely translate these words to "doctor" in English. The anthropological term *shaman* is used throughout this book to represent *puwarat* and *pohagandi*.

6. A one- or two-hour vision sleep seems to be sufficient for the Fort Hall and Wind River Shoshones.

vision. During the vision experience the recipient may learn new songs, new curing techniques, and a new dance step. The recipient also hobnobs, dines, and, most especially, drinks water with the spirits. The recipient's body lies unconscious in the corral all the while. As the vision is experienced, the recipient is shamanized by a powerful dancer, usually a chief. Following the shamanizing, yet while the recipient is unconscious, his dancer cohorts cover him with a sheet and move him back to his stall, placing him in it feet first so that his head is closest to the pole. The dancing then resumes. During the vision the recipient's spirit is thought to leave the body. A vision is distinct from a dream because the recipient remembers all that happened to him and all the instructions he received. There is no such specific memory connected with dreaming. The body goes stone cold as it is filled with cool water. The dancers who move the vision recipient back to his stall attest to the recipient's cold body, which is filled with *puwa* or *poha* (power). During his vision the recipient may talk to one or more spirits, perhaps Buffalo, perhaps "That Man." He will then be instructed by the spirit(s) about the extent and meaning of his power and the way in which it is to be controlled, about new or special dance steps, perhaps even about new interpretations of aspects of the dance.

The recipient often shares parts of his experience with fellow dancers by telling them some of the things he saw, or did, or learned. In the same fashion, parts of the vision recipients' experiences are often shared with the Sun dance chiefs and with members of one's own family. If the recipient is a dancer of some stature, he may have received powers to sponsor a dance, although explicit instructions to do so would come at a later date, usually during the winter months. If the instructions included new interpretations of the dance, they would be accepted by the dancers who learn them from the recipient during those dances he sponsors.

All those assembled, including the dancers, respond to the vision by patting the power that has entered the corral into themselves. This procedure is followed by hushed exchanges about how the dancer was "hit" and what the spectators, the dancers, the singers, and the committeemen, saw and felt at that moment. They "know" what has happened because of the cold sleep the recipient has fallen into, the way he fell into it, and the duration of the sleep. Some spectators who have the proper angle even say they see Buffalo's eyes roll and turn red. Singers are known to have had their throats dry out to the point at which singing was almost unbearably difficult, only to be moistened as the vision occured, thus getting some power because of the help they gave the dancers during the vision quest. When the vision recipient awakes, he dances again, completely refreshed and full of water. He has no hunger either.

A dance that ends in a vision for one or more dancers is ideal, but power is earned at all dances whether anyone acquires a vision or not. All dances serve personal ends of chiefs, dancers, singers, committeemen, and spectators, and the public good. All dances serve the individual and simultaneously the whole. Some dances, however, are considered better than others, and some are not very good at all. Dances have been cut short by a couple of hours because their chiefs have been disturbed that the dancers had not been extending themselves and because the dance had been plagued with rain. When rain interrupts a dance, a powerful shaman with special powers to control the weather usually goes out and attempts to stop the downpour by magical means.[7] At one dance in 1963 no one could stop the rain for more than an hour or so at a time. The chief interpreted that to mean that some spirit, perhaps *sinawaf*, was unhappy with the conduct of some of the participants, that is, of dancers, singers, or others. The factors were sufficient to make the chief terminate the dance early.

SYNTHESES OF OPPOSITES

It is clear that the competing hot-dry and cool-wet forces must be fused in order for an adherent to achieve power, and that power is a requisite for life. This synthesis of the power oppositions is accomplished only through sacrifice and enduring. Indeed, some participants in the power quest such as the center pole, the corral saplings, the willow nest, the willow fans, and the "old people" die so that the current generation of Indians may live. That is, they bestow their power on the living (by cooling), in order to help the living to a successful synthesis of power. The living Indians use the power they acquire for their own ends and to help other Indians. The beings who dissipate their power while helping others, die. Yet through death comes life and a new generation of living things. The oppositions of life and death, like the oppositions of hot-dry and cool-wet, are complementary. Life is only possible if there is death. Power is only possible if power is lost.

Both individual and group ends are satisfied by the Sun dance; yet both ends must be satisfied for either end to be satisfied. The Sun dance religion is participated in by singers, dancers, chiefs, committeemen, and other adherents. Each adherent seeks individual power. Yet the pursuit by each individual is attended by group activity which sanctions the proceedings. In order for individuals to achieve power, the singers help the dancers, the group of dancers help each particular dancer, the committeemen help the chiefs, the chiefs help the committeemen, and so forth. Unless all work together, the individual is unsuccessful as is the group. Furthermore, power is used to benefit the individual, the family, the wider network of kin, and the entire Sun dance community. Power and its pursuit in the Sun dance has meaning only in a collective context. Figure 14 schematizes the synthesis of individual and collective power.

VALIDATION AND PERPETUATION OF IDEOLOGY

Each performance of the Sun dance religion is effective in bringing power for good purposes. This is demonstrated each year as people who had good health before the dance was performed continue to have good health throughout the year. People who have been sick, especially those suffering from "fever," are cured. People who have not been able to cope with life at home and who may have had family quarrels in their crowded, financially-embarrassed households, live peaceably, at least for a while. People who accumulate considerable power have wonderful truths revealed to them in dreams throughout the year. And so forth.

One anecdote that is told on every reservation in order to underline the seriousness

---

7. Thundershowers in the Rocky Mountain area do not usually last very long; so the period between the time the shaman goes through his incantations and the time the rain stops is often very short and tends to confirm the efficacy of his power.

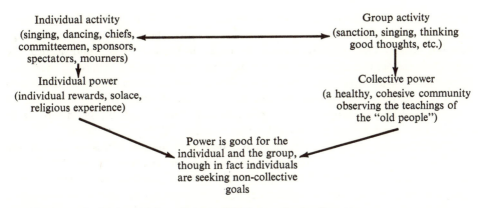

Individual activity
(singing, dancing, chiefs,
committeemen, sponsors,
spectators, mourners)

Group activity
(sanction, singing, thinking
good thoughts, etc.)

Individual power
(individual rewards, solace,
religious experience)

Collective power
(a healthy, cohesive community
observing the teachings of
the "old people")

Power is good for the
individual and the group,
though in fact individuals
are seeking non-collective
goals

FIGURE 14. Activities which makes possible the synthesis of power.

of the dance, the hardships one must endure to complete it, and the character of the persons capable of completing it, is especially interesting. At the Fort Hall Shoshone dance of 1934, Hoebel (1935: 579) reports that a Western Shoshone from Duck Valley, Nevada, participated. On the second day he is said to have bolted from the corral, but was "hauled back by the watchers, proving to their [Fort Hall Shoshones'] satisfaction that the Nevada Shoshones are weaker than they." Although I have never seen anything like this happen, I have collected the same story many times from Utes and Shoshones on all five reservations.

Utes usually say that the person who bolted was a mixed-blood and that he was captured and brought back. It is also said that one white who attempted to dance at Northern Ute bolted from the corral soon after the dance was underway. He made it all the way to Whiterocks Creek, which is about a quarter of a mile from the dance grounds. The Utes let the man go because it was "his life that he was fooling with." On occasion, the names of some recalcitrants have been divulged. It is important in each of these illustrations that the person who bolts is either an Indian from a group considered lower in status than the sponsors of the dance, or a mixed-blood or white who is considered lower in spiritual power, honesty, and personal courage than the Indians. The mixed-blood or white is not considered lower in economic and political power than the Indian, as quite the obverse is true and the Indians are well aware of it.

Variants of the story are told on all reserves, then, to show how some men do not measure up to the requirements of the dance. This is significant because it stresses the unusual qualities of the person who enters the Sun dance religion as a dancer. There are sanctions against bolting, of course, and, in all but the white example, the "watchers" or corral police chase the recalcitrants. Indeed, a group effort is required in order for individuals to achieve power, so each individual must contribute to that effort, and no one should be allowed to spoil it by a selfish act. The fact that whites alone are allowed to act selfishly and to violate the ritual proscriptions suggests that whites are treated differently from other humans. At all contemporary dances the corral police are on the ready, should any Indian (including mixed-bloods) bolt.

Shimkin (1953: 443) reports that Wind River took action against someone running from the corral during the 1937 dance. In 1966 a young Wind River man explained why bolting from the corral was a personally dangerous act. He said that a person (tribe and race unspecified) bolted from the lodge "a few years ago" and the watchers could not get him back. An old shaman predicted that the recalcitrant would get his just retribution. The following winter the dancer in question was found dead in the hills. The personal sanction against bolting seems to be that the angered power, perhaps Buffalo, will bring unspecified harm or even death to the person who cannot and will not meet his challenge after making the initial commitment to do so. Among the Utes the personal sanction is very explicit because dancers are responding to dream instructions which tell them they will wither and die if they do not dance.

Similar stories are told frequently, and their perpetuation serves to validate the supernatural importance of the dance and the dancer. In 1934 Hoebel (1935: 580) reports that several Fort Hall Shoshone dancers "were pointed out, of whom it was said that they were carried into the lodge the year previous because of their crippled condition. They became able to dance on the third day and have been well since." Shimkin (1953: 460, 471) mentions three individuals who, in the late 1930s and earlier, entered the Sun dance to cure their ailments (heart disease, trachoma, "bloat"), and all recovered. The most detailed account Shimkin offers follows the same form as those reported by Hoebel: the person went into the dance very ill, got somewhat better each day of the dance, danced on the third day, and walked out healthy at the end of the dance.

Many such accounts are related, but one of special interest here describes (as does Hoebel's story) how a paralyzed person was carried into the corral, got a little better each day, and walked out on the final day. The details of the incident vary from teller to teller. A Northern Ute explained how a Shoshone was carried into the corral all "gnarled and twisted and laid on his side." Yet at the completion of the dance he was able to walk out of the corral with the help of a cane. On another occasion a Utah Ute pointed toward a Colorado Ute who, he said, possessed special powers for success in gambling. The Colorado Ute had been paralyzed in a mysterious auto accident following some gambling successes and nearly died. He was carried into a Sun dance unable to move, but at the end he walked out only half-paralyzed.

Paralysis, like "fever" and "heart trouble," is attributed to malevolent spirits. The spirits can be acting on their own, or they can be controlled by an *awu puwarat* (in Ute the possessor of power who uses it for evil or bad purposes). The only antidote is *puwa* or *poha* used for good purposes. There is no doubt that the vast majority of all shamanizing is done to cure "fever," and the most frequently told stories about ailing dancers describe them as "paralyzed" or suffering from "heart trouble." Though there is a very high incidence of poor health, disease and accidents on all of the reservations in our study, these diagnoses are made by shamans rather than by white physicians.[8]

On the other hand, many people who seek treatment at the Sun dance have previously been examined by white physicians who have diagnosed them as "incurable," according to Shoshones and Utes. Other cases simply go undiagnosed by white physicians because the sufferer does not go to them for help at all. The sufferer goes to the Sun dance, as dancer, singer, or person to be shamanized, and is cured, if only temporarily, by power. This is done either through power acquisition or through a

8. This is not meant to include the cases of "fever" that are induced during the dance as men "dry out." There are many cases of "fever" of this type, and they too are diagnosed by Indian shamans.

shaman who controls power and bestows it on his client. Each cure validates the dance and perpetuates the belief in its efficacy.

In 1966 a sick and intoxicated man entered a dance.[9] He could barely navigate on his own. As the dance progressed, he grew worse, and by the third day he was experiencing delirium tremens. His fellow dancers were visibly angry, as were the singers and spectators. There was an attempt to comfort him, but little could be done. No one tried to shamanize him, because he had entered the corral drunk and debauched. Indeed, he had behaved against the good advice of the Sun dance chiefs and Sun dance proscription. His behavior threatened the success of each individual and the group.

It is well understood that a dancer should not take alcohol. If one does, he is defeating his own purpose, for alcohol is an evil (perpetrated by whites and indulged in by most Utes and Shoshones) whose effects will not be cured easily by participating in the dance. In fact, "drying-out" will exacerbate the problem because things get a lot worse before they get better as a man dries out. In these cases the cause of the trouble is pinpointed on a definite substance made by whites. The person foolish enough to take too much alcohol (some say "any") must suffer the consequences.

It is of more than passing interest to point out that "fever," "heart trouble," even "paralysis" and delirium tremens are frequent and chronic ailments. Although each type of ailment (excluding the last) undoubtedly includes many quite different organic problems and would not be classified into such broad categories by white physicians, these ailments have a long history on the reservations from the Indian viewpoint. Indeed, their histories are as long as reservation life. They became prominent problems in the 1880s and have been reported frequently since, as have many other diseases diagnosed by white physicians (see part 2 above). These maladies are strong indicators of both the privation and the dysphoria experienced by so many reservation dwellers.

The ailments are real, though the etiologies of all but delirium tremens are probably as often functional as organic. The diagnoses and the cures of all but delirium tremens are Indian. The curative nature of the dance and the focus on not easily diagnosed health problems is of special interest.[10]

BROAD VERSUS NARROW INDIVIDUALISM, AND THE CONFLICT BETWEEN GOOD AND BAD USES OF POWER

Power for the individual's well-being, for healing, and for the community good is attained through a coalescence of individual and group efforts. Once power in inordinate quantities is attained by an individual, he must use it to further the ends of the group that gave sanction and support during the power acquisition process. The community also provides sanction for the *puwarat* or *pohagandi* in future uses of his power.

On the other hand, power that serves narrow individual ends can be invested in

9. The location of this dance is intentionally withheld here.

10. Although no systematic analyses have been made of the predominantly Mormon, white communities around each reservation, the communities in eastern Utah, southwestern Colorado, southeastern Idaho, and western Wyoming do not have high incidences of alcoholism, "fever," or "paralysis." The National Health Survey conducted by the Public Health Service (1963–65) is relevant to this point, but the data are for standard Metropolitan Statistical Areas rather than rural counties.

some individuals, and this power competes with power that serves wider ends. Indeed, Utes and Shoshones sanction the latter and attempt to restrain the former. For instance, the man adept at gambling who later became paralyzed was using power for narrow individual ends. His gambling success was not merely the result of expertise or luck, but was the result of his power (*awu puwarat*). When he became paralyzed, perhaps through the effects of someone else's bad power which had been invoked because of a gambling game, the only cure for the paralysis was good power. In this and many similar cases, power from the Sun dance was used to effect cures.

Figure 15 represents the opposition between power invested in an individual and used for narrow individual ends (bad), and individual power used for wider ends (good). When good power from the Sun dance remedies some of the harm that has been done by bad power, the Sun dance is validated.

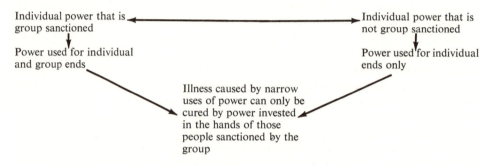

FIGURE 15. Opposition between two kinds of individual power.

Let us take this one step further and show how the classification of ailments and their cures reject hedonic individualism. Whereas "paralysis" is associated with power which has been used to further the advantages of one person at the expense of others (a bad end), delirium tremens is associated with the evil of alcohol. When a person suffers from delirium tremens it is because he has indulged himself. The sick person has rejected collective responsibilities, such as sobriety and obligations to kin, in favor of gaining personal pleasures. If there is no intention to injure, neither is there an intention to help when one turns to alcohol. Yet the alcoholic's irresponsible behavior, which consumes money and withdraws the sufferer from the kinship network labor pool, threatens that person's kin and wider network of friends. It also draws power from the sick man's body as he copes with the evil that is alcohol.

The loss of power is evidenced by delirium tremens; the cause is the evil of alcohol. A person suffering from delirium tremens can be cured through the Sun dance religion. Here, then, the contradiction is between the collective Indian ethic and hedonic individualism. If hedonic individualism is pursued unabated, it will result in death. In the process the kin, friends, and wider Indian community on which the hedonist relies for support are also threatened.

In all of our examples, power used for good purposes can cure, and, to be invoked, that power must have collective sanction. Collective sanction, of course, rejects narrow individualism. Figure 16 represents the conflict between narrow individualism and Indian collectivism. Remedies for sickness are the applications of group-sanc-

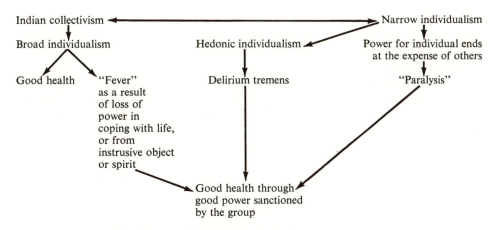

FIGURE 16. Collectivism versus narrow individualism, and remedies to sickness.

tioned power, and, when a cure is effected in the Sun dance corral or at a later date by a person who has acquired power through the Sun dance, the religion is validated.

More Evidence to Validate the Religion

Curing is an important aspect of any dance, but it is by no means the only end for which the dance is performed or the only manner in which it is validated. Many other ritual objects and unusual happenings are preserved or talked about as evidence for the marvelous nature of the dance.

Utes and Shoshones talk about the Arapahos, who have a wooden bowl and ladle for the sacred water ritual at the termination of the Sun dance. Once, it is said, all the dancers and all the spectators had a drink, but the water never went down. The water story has biblical analogues, but among Utes and Shoshones it has a double meaning because water is power itself as well as a gift from power. The water phenomenon is accepted as a validation of the dance, and the story is often told.

A Ute vision recipient who possessed considerable power happened upon some footprints in the hills near a Sun dance grounds one spring. A sheet was placed over the footprints, and the entire prints were absorbed into the sheet. It is said that no specialist, no scientist, indeed no one was able to wash the footprints from the sheet. It is averred that they are the footprints of Jesus, who walked near the dance grounds. The sheet is displayed often at the termination of one of the Sun dances. The story has many non-Indian analogues. One such among the Mormons is that no one has ever been able to scrub the blood of their prophet, Joseph Smith, out of the floor of the Carthage, Illinois, jail. The Ute symbol validates the dance and shows that men of great power, especially vision recipients, are awarded public markers of power, such as control of the weather or ownership of sacred objects.

The Development of Myth

Let us now look at an event that occurred at the first dance of the cycle in 1966—on which occasion a group of about 150 whites (the "Bizarros" mentioned in chapter 6) were camping on the dance grounds. One near-sighted, long-haired fellow in the group, dressed in a basketball referee's shirt, a pair of white duck pants and an inexpensive felt cowboy hat with red piping, chopped wood for the fire tender. By the third night he was carrying wood into the corral. Spectators commented that this was odd and rather inappropriate, but if the fire tender would do nothing about it there was nothing they could do either.

The general reaction of the Indians to the white group was one of cool hostility which became verbally focused on this particular man, yet not to his face. When the dance was over and the spectators lined up to take a drink of the sacred water, the man also lined up to get a drink. When it was his turn to drink the water, the chief appeared rather perplexed. He spoke to the gate keeper and then gave the "Bizarro" the cup.

Much to the surprise and disgust (I think) of everyone, the fellow offered nonsense-syllable prayers to the center pole and to the cardinal directions.[11] He rolled the cup in the dirt at the base of the center pole, took a drink, and carried on for about ten minutes. The water chief, who seemed to be showing more and more anxiety, stopped the young man. Expressing considerable embarrassment, the water chief cleaned and prayed over the cup, and then passed it on to the next person in line.

Throughout the rest of the afternoon and evening several conversations focused on trying to figure out what the "Bizarro" was up to, and why he would want to belittle Indian beliefs.

At the Northern Ute dance eight weeks later a middle-aged man who had not attended the first dance in the cycle but who knew a mutual friend who had attended, gave me a secondhand version of the incident I had witnessed. He said that a "blind" white man had gone to the dance and chopped wood for the fire tender. After chopping wood for two days and offering a prayer over the sacred water, the fellow was cured: he regained his sight. There was no mention of displeasure with the fellow or of his sacrilege. There were no questions raised about his motives, or about the response of the water chief and gate keeper and the others waiting for a drink. What had happened was that in a brief eight weeks the event had been transformed, at least among a few Northern Utes, into a miraculous cure of a white man's blindness. The story conformed to the stylized format of the progressive cure which is effected throughout successive days of Sun dance participation.

SOME DIFFERENCES IN IDEOLOGY

Ideological differences are restricted primarily to a few practices that attend rituals, rather than to ritual beliefs, acts, and observances. Though ideological differences are few, it is nevertheless common to hear Sun dance hosts, dancers and nondancers alike, say that their home dance is the best or is the most appropriate dance in terms of how the ritual ought to be performed. The information to support these claims is freely given, and the charges of the inferiority of other dances center on two broad topics: (1) incorrect or proscribed practices, and (2) imperfectly effected practices. The first represent legitimate ideological differences between Sun dance communities. The second are merely criticisms of performance.

11. It is doubtful that the nonsense syllables issued by this man represented the ecstatic prayers classified as speaking in tongues, or glossolalia. The utterances seem to have been strings of intended nonsense syllables.

We begin by assessing the practices that are accepted on some reservations and proscribed on others. Dancers and nondancers travel from dance to dance throughout their lives and acquire firsthand knowledge of all of the rituals, and all of the chiefs, in the Sun dance cycle. They dance in the rituals on other reserves, sing, lend encouragement to the dancers, and so forth. As a consequence, there is some truth to the stereotypes held by the members of one reservation community about the rituals sponsored at other communities. The differences that are focused on and criticized are not those that stem from the idiosyncratic direction of a chief or the practices of a particular dancer.

The major disagreements can be roughly rank-ordered. The least contested disagreements are over fraternization and gambling. Each takes place outside of the dance corral and accompanies the dance, though not as part of the ritual. For instance, Shoshone dances are characterized by considerable fraternizing between dancers, their families, and their friends, especially during rest periods between morning and night dance sessions, but also when dancers leave the corral to relieve themselves.

The Utes proscribe this fraternization and do not engage in it at their own dances or when they are dancing in rituals sponsored by the Shoshones. Utes also preach that the practice is wrong. Yet only the Southern Utes make an effort to stop the Shoshones from fraternizing with friends and relatives during the course of Ute dances.[12] The Utes contend that dancers should concentrate on "drying out," or working for a religious experience so that benefits will accrue to all. Fraternizing and gossiping with friends and family will break the concentration required, according to this view.

Shoshones, on the other hand, argue that the practice is appropriate and actually helps the dancer by giving him encouragement. Utes and Shoshones are at an impasse on this issue; so they merely criticize the practices of one another. Both refer to traditional practices to bolster their position.

On what seems to be about the same level of criticism, the Shoshones rebuke the Utes for allowing gambling on the Sun dance grounds before the dance is terminated. Gambling begins at the Ute dances on the second day and is engaged in between the end of the day dance sessions and commencement of the night dance sessions. The Shoshones argue that gambling should not begin until the dance is over because power for the wrong purposes will be called into the Sun dance area. In turn, power called for the wrong purposes will have an adverse influence on the dance. The Utes argue that the dance will be influenced only if the gambling is conducted simultaneously with a dance session. Corral police and members of the Sun dance committee insure that the two do not overlap.

It is interesting that Shoshones will gamble at Ute dances before the dance terminates, whereas Utes, following their own custom even when away from home, do not fraternize with friends and family at Shoshone dances. Shoshones explain that gambling before the dance is over is incorrect, but that they can engage in this ritual violation at the Ute dances because "that's the way they do it down there." This answer is consonant with Sun dance ideology, even though it appears to be contra-

12. There were no Shoshone dancers at the Southern Ute dance of 1966, but they dance there from time to time and are always invited to attend.

dictory. The ideology is relatively flexible and indeterminate. Adherents often appeal to what has transpired in the past or to traditional practices (usually attributed to the "old people"), in want of an explicit body of written rules. Appeals to traditional practices of the "old people" do not often clear the air because each reservation has its own dance and its own "old people." Furthermore, appeals to highly revered, living Sun dance adherents do not clear the air either, because each participant, dancer or not, is an authority of a sort, and no single authority can resolve all of the ideological disputes and give final answers to all questions.

The gambling issue has special meaning, as we saw above, because it raises the specter of power used for personal gain at the expense of others. Poker, in particular, is such a game, and it is not played on any reservation until the dance is over. At the Colorado Ute reservations, poker is not played at all. The major gambling game (hand-and-stick) played at Sun dances is collective, pitting teams against each other. Although power is required to win at this game, a camaraderie is generated and narrow individual ends are not served. Gambling activity is more fully described in chapter 11 below.

A more important ideological difference between the points of view of the Utes and the Shoshones hinges on whether photographs can be taken at a dance. The Shoshones allow photographs to be taken of the dancers in the corral and of the corral itself. The Utes do not generally allow photographs to be taken. The reason for this proscription is not clear to me. On the other hand, Utes purchase a very popular postcard which carries a photograph of a Wind River dance in progress. These cards are available in the white-owned drugstores in Lander, Wyoming. Furthermore, the Utes allow Shoshone dancers and their families to take photographs outside of the Ute Sun dance corrals, which is a partial violation of their own rules. On several occasions I have asked Utes to explain why they allow Shoshones to take photos outside the corral when the Utes feel so strongly that photos should not be taken at all. The answer is interesting. First, Utes say one cannot take photographs of the dance proper because the dance is neither a carnival nor a show, and photographs will interfere with the power quests of the participants. Second, they do not have a clear-cut rule about allowing Shoshones to take photographs outside the corral, though whites are not allowed to take photographs anywhere. Third, only the "old people" would ultimately know if taking pictures was wrong.

Again the answer is consistent with Ute ideology as I now understand it. The "truth" is both available and unavailable at the same time. Whereas the "old people" know whether or not photos can be taken, living Utes do not know why Shoshones allow photos to be taken. Thus Shoshone "old people" might have received a revelation to allow photos to be taken which is also known to Ute "old people," but this revelation has not yet been revealed to living Utes. There is no doubt in Ute ideology about the prerogatives of whites on this issue, however.

Cameras have been available since the interreservation Sun dance community was formed between 1890 and 1906. Over the long course of that history, only whites have owned cameras. These devices were out of the financial reach of most Shoshone and Utes until the 1940s for the former and the 1950s for the latter. Moreover, in the 1890s the Sun dance was banned on the Wind River and the Northern Ute reservations. At this time the Utes, in particular, worked to keep their dance out of the view of whites, and the Shoshones disguised their dance with other names and attributed nonreligious meanings to them when queried about its purpose (see chapters 2 and 3).

Cameras surely put the Sun dance within the view of whites, and it is probable that a proscription against cameras and photographs stems from this early time when the Indians attempted to prevent whites from snooping. The Shoshones did not develop the proscription, and when cameras became available to them, especially after their claims judgment of the late 1930s, they began taking photographs at their own dances, and, somewhat later, at Ute Sun dances, although not inside the corrals. When the Ute claims judgment was awarded in the early 1950s and Utes began acquiring cameras, they continued to prohibit their use at Sun dances.

The availability of white-invented technological implements has ramifications for other parts of the ritual. For instance, none of the groups allows use of anything but a steel ax in felling the tree to be used as the center pole. They allow chain saws to be used on the corral posts, however. All of the groups allow the center pole to be moved on a truck, rather than a wagon, and so forth. Another example of the selective proscription of technological devices, particularly snooping devices, is the Ute prohibition of the use of tape recorders at a Sun dance. As with cameras, however, Utes use them in their homes and for nonreligious ends. The Shoshones, on the other hand, allow tape recorders to be used at their own dances.

I have only seen three recorders in use: one was operated by a white, one by a Shoshone, and one by a Ute who was singing at the Wind River dance. The Ute was quite surprised to see permission granted by the gate keeper for use of the other two recorders. He immediately went to his camp, fetched his own machine, and recorded the Ute singing team during part of their stint.

Electronic recording devices seem antithetical to the pursuit of power, though no one is able to say exactly why. Utes have not yet allowed Shoshones to record the singing at Ute dances. It is my prediction that if recordings are ever made of Ute dances, they will be made first by Shoshones.

The ideologies associated with fraternizing and gambling outside the corral and with the use of information-collecting technological devices inside the corral are at variance on the Ute and Shoshone reserves. We have seen, however, that the practices are changing on the Ute and Shoshone reservations, with Utes accommodating to the less restrictive practices of the Shoshones in regard to photographs, recordings, and fraternization, and the Shoshones accommodating to the less restrictive practices of Utes in regard to gambling, especially participation in collective gambling games.

Accommodation has not taken place, however, in the case of certain differences. For instance, Shoshones allow dancers to use wet towels in their morning toilets, and to receive them as gifts throughout the course of the dance. Shoshones can even send their friends and relatives out to soak towels for them. When they get them back they suck them. This is absolutely forbidden on Ute reservations for both Utes and Shoshones. On Shoshone reservations Utes do not use wet towels either. In fact, Utes have publicly rebuked the Shoshones for the practice. The Utes argue that a person enters the dance to "dry out" and to get his "drink" from *puwa*, or power. Drinking water during the dance is, in Ute ideology, a most critical violation of this idea, and will damage a dance so that all dancers may suffer and none will receive power. Shoshones argue that sucking towels is not the same as drinking and that it is not a violation to suck a towel. They are at an impasse over this point.

The Colorado Utes stand together against the other three groups over the features of the dance corral. The Colorado Utes argue that the proper lodge has no roof rafters and has no branches and leaves left on the top of the center pole. The proper corral allows for no shade from roof features, so that the sun's rays will have direct access to the dancers, singers, and spectators and dry everyone out. The Northern Utes and Shoshones vary the features of their corrals somewhat from year to year (four to twelve rafters), but all agree that the proper performance of the ritual requires an "east-running" rafter to channel the sun's rays into the corral. The disagreement about corral form does not stop Utes and Shoshones from participating in the several rituals.

On both the towel sucking and roof rafter issues the opposing parties appeal to specific revelations and traditional practices to defend their respective practices. The maintenance of uncompromising positions seems to be more typical of those practices that are closest to the acts, objects, and observances of the ritual proper. The more compromising stances, with appeal merely to traditional practices of the "old people" rather than to specific revelations for validation, have to do with more peripheral practices.

It should be stressed that individual variation is expected of Sun dance participants and is a result of revelations in the religious experience. It seems clear to me, however, that there are very few ideological differences over Sun dance acts, observances, or objects.

Criticisms of the quality of the performance at certain rituals are tangential to ideology, and are directed by participants both to their own dances and to those of other reservations. For instance, it is generally agreed that a ritual suffers if there are too few dancers and the singing is weak. The ideology behind this is that singing is critical in "calling out" the power, and the dancers have to work inordinately hard to gain power as a result of the low quality of the singing.

Another criticism often made is of the practice of dancing with women at the Fort Hall dance. Men do not say that it is wrong, or that there should be a sanction against women dancers. It is recognized that women have the right to dance and that the ideology cannot be challenged because it stems from dream instructions, the ultimate source of which is power. Yet many men do not enjoy dancing with women, and many have said that they have been goaded into competing with women during Sun dances rather than carrying out their own strategy in the quest for power.

Ute men have referred to advice given over fifty years ago by the influential Southern Ute leader and Sun dancer, Buckskin Charley, and other "old men" who cautioned against dancing with women. These influential men advised the younger people that although women had the right to dance, men should not follow or compete with them. Each dancer knows why he's "in there" and what he has to do. Nobody has to tell him and he certainly should not let women tell him (either by precept or by example). In Sun dance ideology, any dancer runs the risk of *violating* his own dream instructions if he is provoked to compete with a woman.

The attainment of power through individual and collective effort, through individual and joint suffering, should not be minimized. Each living thing sacrifices its power—the trees, the bushes, the earth, the flames of the fire, the singers, the dancers, the committeemen, the spectators—so that others may live. The synthesis of death with life, the passing of power from one form (the dying) to an opposite form (the living) is made complete in the Sun dance.

The earthly recipients of power, particularly the dancers who receive power in huge doses, accept as well the responsibility of power. Not only is sobriety important to the recipient, but equally important is the obligation to use the power that has been earned to help others and to maintain the public trust. Thus individual and communitarian ends are jointly served.

The Sun dance religion and the religious experiences it affords is validated when the power that is gained is proved efficacious; the singer's throat is moistened and soothed, the shamans cure the sick, the ailing dancers recover, the rain is stopped by a powerful shaman, and wonderful objects with deep significance are received that cannot be explained by "white" knowledge.

IV

THE RELIGION AND THE CONTEXT: REDEMPTION

8 Toward an Explanation of the Sun Dance Religion

It is now appropriate to tie together the two strings with which we have worked—context and religion. The hypothesis advanced here to explain the persistence of the Sun dance religion (the why and how possibly explanations referred to in the introductory remarks) will be supported and analyzed throughout the remainder of the book.

THE BRIDGE BETWEEN RESERVATION LIFE AND SUN DANCE IDEOLOGY

In parts 1 and 2 we analyzed how and why the Shoshones and Utes came to occupy neocolonial niches in the metropolis-satellite political economy. In brief, these people have been the victims of a process of expropriation, exploitation, domination, and dole, promoted primarily by the metropolis, which used the military and the BIA as instruments, and secondarily by local small-scale entrepreneurs such as farmers, stockmen, and shopkeepers.

Since the reservation period began, the Shoshones and Utes have been economically, politically, and socially dominated by whites on national, state, and local levels. Throughout the period of this domination the Indians have been beckoned in several contradictory directions. The dominant whites have encouraged the Indians to organize as corporate entities, while expropriating Indian resources, exploiting their resources and labor, and denying them political and economic autonomy. Indian corporate collectivism has been encouraged along unfeasible lines (particularly agri-business) while the satellite sectors of the economy have shriveled. Thus, Indians have not created successful corporations, even though they have tried.

At the same time that the dominant whites have encouraged corporate collectivism among Utes and Shoshones, they have urged them to practice competitive Protestant-ethic individualism. Currently Indians are encouraged to sever their ties with family, wider networks of kin, friends, and the Indian community, and to pursue narrow individual and narrow family ends. Because the satellite economies are withering, jobs within the satellites are few, and those that are available generally go to local whites. If Indians are to succeed in a narrow individual sense, they must move to an urban area. Yet because Indians have few skills, meager educations, and little knowledge of urban life, they acquire only low-paying jobs, reside in urban slums, and have few people with whom to socialize. Indians often begin drinking heavily and lose their jobs, or return to the reservation for support and friendship, or some even commit suicide. Thus, those Indians who are beckoned by Protestant-ethic individualism are seldom successful when they try to live by that ethic. While they are tempted by crumbs of wealth, they must sever their reservation ties and deny their obligations to kin and friends in order to keep those crumbs to themselves. Yet in the process of trying to make it in the city, the Indian merely trades rural poverty among kin and friends for an ignominious life in urban poverty sans kin. All the while the urbanite is being beckoned back to the reservation.

So Indians are steered toward corporate collectivism *and* Protestant-ethic individualism by the dominant whites; yet they cannot successfully attain either. Partly because Utes and Shoshones cannot attain corporate or narrow individual success, they are drawn toward Indian collectivism. They are asked to observe obligations and responsibilities to family, to wider networks of kin, and to the Indian community. They are asked to forsake narrow individualism and to maintain Indian integrity by following the cooperative precepts of revered Indians. We have seen that Shoshones and Utes have done precisely that; that is, they have pooled their meager and fluctuating resources, their skills, and their labor in order to cope. But this collectivism, which makes for a somewhat equitable distribution of resources, is conducted amidst great privation and disease. People are crowded together, and one household member's business becomes the business of all. Friction, even fights, ensue, and the collective ethic is constantly threatened.

One threat posed to Indian collectivism is hedonic individualism. When collective life is intolerable, a person may wish temporarily to escape his obligations to others. He may choose to spend money on a meal for himself, when that money should be spent on food for everyone. Or he may turn to alcohol, and, if he does, the escape from temporary obligations may become permanent. The alcoholic could end up dead, or as a patient with delirium tremens in some hospital where his skills and labor can no longer help the Indians at home. The Indian collective ethic cautions against hedonic individualism—indeed, against all forms of narrow individualism. It is only the Indian collective ethic which has in any way coped successfully with recurrent economic deprivation for most Utes and Shoshones residing in the reservation context.

Figure 17 diagrams the oppositions that have obtained among the normative ethics preached by whites and Indians since the reservation period. Only Indian collectivism has allowed Indians to cope in their neocolonial, satellite niches.

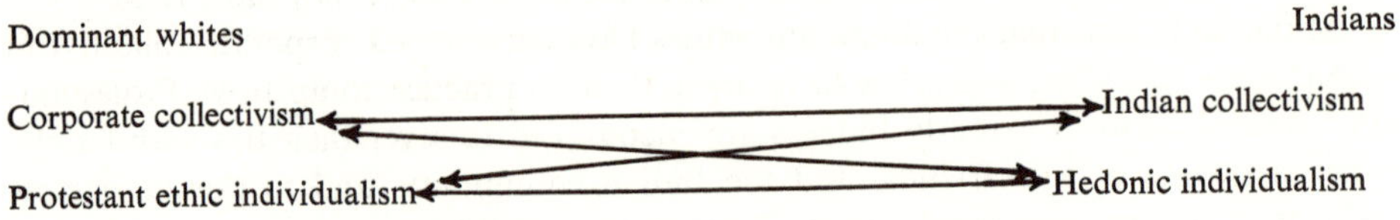

Dominant whites   Indians

Corporate collectivism ←————————————————→ Indian collectivism

Protestant ethic individualism ←————————————————→ Hedonic individualism

FIGURE 17. Oppositions among white ethics for Indians and Indian ethics for Indians.

DOMINATION AND POWERLESSNESS

We have laid bare the contradictory directions in which Indians are pulled and pushed. There are further contradictions between the practice and the teachings of the dominant whites that go unresolved, but not unnoticed, by Indians.

Shoshones and Utes exercise only a modest amount of control over their own lives. Since about 1880 the Bureau of Indian Affairs has served as liaison to the Indians for the federal government. The BIA has also occupied an important position in the chain of dominant authorities over Indian affairs with the power to effect and override Indian decisions—robbing Indians of real power and autonomy. Only the Secretary of the Interior and the House Committee on Interior and Insular Affairs have been dominant over the BIA.

The BIA is the arm of the federal welfare bureaucracy that is commissioned to administer Indian affairs. The BIA envisages its role as dispensing federal dole to Indians and managing the affairs that Indians are not able to manage themselves. There is a contradiction here between the obligations of the federal government by treaty rights toward Utes and Shoshones, and the practice of federal officials and BIA officials who treat Indians as welfare recipients.

A further contradiction follows: the federal government has repeatedly encouraged Indians to leave the welfare rolls, and the BIA in particular has pushed Indians toward the city and pulled Indians toward the ethic of narrow, Protestant individualism. The BIA has rebuked Indians for living on welfare dole and has counseled them to stop doing so. Yet the BIA exists because the federal government has treaty obligations to Indians, and BIA officials live off federal dole, in a manner of speaking, even as they counsel Indians to do otherwise.

There is still a further paradox in Indian-BIA relations. As dominated populations subject to federal whim, Utes and Shoshones are ambivalent in their relations toward the BIA. That is, Indians cannot live with the BIA, and they cannot live without the BIA. As liaison to the federal government with considerable power over Indian lives, the BIA serves as the buffer between something (federal "favors") and nothing (termination of federal-Indian relations). In turn, of course, the BIA needs the Indians, and the Indians must be maintained in a dominated state in order to justify the existence of the BIA. The paradox is not resolved. While acting as if they want Indians to sever their kinship ties and leave the reservations, the officials also want Indians to remain on the reservations and to receive federal supervision.

When we turn our attention to the duly constituted and chartered tribal governments, we see that the federal government has offered Indians local autonomy with one hand and taken most of it away with the other. As a partial consequence, it is difficult to achieve status in the Indian communities by serving as elected or appointed officials in the tribal governments because (1) tribal governments operate under the aegis of the federal government, (2) tribal acts are confused with federal acts, and (3) meager tribal resources are seldom allocated with respect to the desires of the populace.

Factional disputes flicker on and off over tribal government affairs, and verbal abuse stemming from these disputes is often directed at tribal officials. In turn, tribal officials either resign from their positions (often becoming critics of the tribal governments themselves), or stay on in their jobs and direct their own verbal counterattacks to those people who have criticized them. Although this is not a common practice, when tribal officials respond to criticisms by fighting back, they run the risk of being further associated with the dominant authorities such as the BIA or white advisers contracted by the tribe, whose advice and its implementation may have given rise to the dispute originally. The powerlessness of the Indians who do not hold positions in tribal government is a constant source of deprivation. The tribal officials who remain in office in spite of criticisms are usually compromised by the BIA and white advisers; so they cannot look to the Indian community for prestige.

A critical point is that Utes and Shoshones are not always aware of the source of the problems that lead to their factional disputes. When per capita payments are terminated or nepotism is practiced, blame is cast directly on tribal officials—the agents of the actions—not on the political economy that has subjected Indians to squalor and powerlessness. Whereas the Indian wants power and autonomy in his tribal government and over his own affairs, as a participant in federally-sanctioned Indian governments he gets neither; yet the excesses of those involved in decision-making capacities in tribal governments often irritate the powerless.

Factional issues can be catalyzed and galvanized in several ways by several agents. First, internal discontent can occur among Indians over joint tribal-federal allocation of group resources, or over the actions of tribal courts such as in child custody cases wherein children are taken from their parents. Second, disputes can follow from BIA actions such as denial of access to Individual Indian Monies, or refusal to follow the wishes of allottees or heirs to terminate a lease held by a white entrepreneur. Third, disputes can be triggered by outside sources such as the retired general of the United States Army, who counseled the True Utes at Northern Ute in 1960, or welfare rights groups like the one instrumental in getting Northern Ute welfare recipients to challenge the welfare commission of the State of Utah in 1968. No matter how factional issues arise, the dominated and powerless Shoshones and Utes respond to symptoms of deeper problems, and the pervasive factionalism itself tests the fabric of collective Indian life.

STATUS AND ESTEEM

Like other Indians of the United States, not only are Utes and Shoshones the subjects of federal powers which are not exercised over other citizens of the United States, but they also live in contexts in which the small-scale entrepreneurs who control the local polities, economies, education systems, and religions deny status to Indians partly just because they *are* subject to special federal domination. Indeed, the very entrepreneurs (or their first- and second-generation progeny) who expropriated Indian resources under federal supervision and who continue to exploit Indian resources and labor, heap opprobrium on their victims for not severing their ties with the federal government.

Local whites criticize Indian drinking as immoral, Indian housing and clothing as slovenly, Indian family life and sexuality as savage and immoral, Indian intelligence as low, Indian work motivation as nonexistent, and Indian behavior as childish, or deceitful, or both. Local whites are unhappy that Indians receive special financial privileges from the federal government which, the local whites aver, are paid for out of taxes exacted from whites. The whites argue that federal and state coddling makes Indians more dependent, and the more dependent the Indians become, the more of a drain they create on the resources of the local whites.

The point is that local whites, in judging the behavior of whites and Indians in the greater reservation areas, deny approval to Indians. In analyzing why this is so, we have learned that the satellite economies are shriveling. Whites are being pushed from rural areas as a consequence. In order for local whites to survive in the rural and reservation areas, they give jobs to their kin, sell goods to Indian consumers, exploit Indian resources under special tax privileges applicable to Indian-owned land, and, as occasions arise, exploit Indian labor. The federal dollars that make their way to BIA employees and Indian families are spent in white-owned shops. Thus, in order for local whites to cope, their surplus labor force and population must be drained off, they must exploit Indian and Indian-related resources, and most of the remunerative jobs that are in white control must be denied to Indians. Some temporary and remunerative jobs are available for Indians around Fort Hall. The dominant practice in the exploitation of Indian labor, however, is nonremunerative, such as the payment by local ranchers and farmers of fines levied against Indians in turn for labor services to be performed by the Indians as the whites' needs arise, or the blatant forced labor of men convicted on misdemeanor charges in local white towns. Indians are exploited and dominated by local whites in their own struggle to cope with the withering satellites. In turn, the local whites rebuke Indians and deny status to them because Indians are not productive, Christian, and white.

THE ECONOMIC RESOLUTION: INDIAN COLLECTIVISM

Power, autonomy, status, and esteem are denied by the dominant whites to Utes and Shoshones within the neocolonial niches they occupy in the shriveling satellites. Indian collectivism has worked to allocate meager resources and to pool and share Indian labor and skills. Yet Indian collectivism is constantly challenged (1) by the appeal of narrow individualism (whether hedonic or not), and (2) by the problems that stem from crowding and privation. Power, autonomy, status, and esteem do not accrue to the Indian simply because the collective ethic is observed. It is argued here that a measure of power, of autonomy, of status, and of esteem can be achieved by individuals within the beautiful Sun dance religion, and that these achievements are possible only because the religion is simultaneously communitarian and individual, public and private, spiritual and mundane, and Indian rather than white.

RELIGION AS COMMUNITY AND INDIVIDUAL EFFORT

Let us recapitulate for religion as we have for context. We have seen that power can be earned when the competition between opposing forces is resolved, and, although power is achieved by individuals, it can be achieved only within the group context. Indeed, the power that is earned is sanctioned by the group, and it is expected that individual power will be used for broad ends—for family, the wider network of kin, friends and community.

The communitarian ideology of the dance complements the collective Indian ethic. Both preach that Indians must work together in order to achieve. Furthermore, the collective Indian ethic is religiously sanctioned and approved by the entire community when it is preached during the performance of the dance. At these times shamans exhort adherents to think good thoughts and to sacrifice so that the society will be whole in time (satisfying the expectations of the "old people" and providing for the birth of future generations) and in space (the entire Sun dance community is drawn together to the exclusion of others for health and happiness).

The broad individualism that is fostered by the dance, on the other hand, allows a person to achieve religious satisfaction and a feeling of personal success while setting off each participant from the others. Successful dance participation and the acquisition of power also entails a personal code for behavior that each recipient should observe. In the following chapters we will learn how the Sun dance participants, especially the dancers, have their personalities transformed through participation in the dance and how they observe their newly acquired responsibilities and obligations outside of the Sun dance context, but within the Indian community.

REDEMPTION, RELIGION, AND CONTEXT

An explanation of how and why the Sun dance religion arose among Shoshones and Utes requires more than explication of the Sun dance ideology and the neo-colonial context in which it persists. We shall show how participation in the dance not only satisfies the quest for religious experience, but how the individual who has a religious experience also has his personality transformed. We shall see how the Sun dance community provides the context in which this person can achieve status, esteem, some power, and autonomy. These are the very things which are denied to Shoshones and Utes in their neocolonial context.

The religious experience entails the transformation of the personality in the here and now. The experience and the performance of the ritual allow Utes and Shoshones to have beauty in their lives and to maintain a sense of community and pride in the community. It is the personality transformation, with its religious and mundane aspects—or all that the religious experience entails, that we shall refer to as *redemption*. Redemption is critical to Ute and Shoshone life now, as it has been in the reservation past, because the redeemed are instructed to reject hedonism and other forms of narrow individualism. The redeemed are expected to keep "good hearts," to "help out" family, kin, friends, and the Indian community, and to be exemplars of how Indian life ought to be lived all of the time. These are instructions for lifelong commitments. The Indian community sanctions, lauds, and approves the behavior of the redeemed, and encourages all other Indians to behave likewise. We will show how those adherents who falter along the arduous path are admonished to straighten up and behave properly for the good of all. We will also show how within the Sun dance context the Indian community separates itself from the whites, how it castigates white ways, and how it challenges all of its members to sacrifice and to be generous for the good of all.

We will begin the final part of our analysis of Ute and Shoshone life and the role of the Sun dance religion in it by focusing on chiefs, initiates, and redemption. We take up the analysis of the Sun dance as a redemptive movement here because we can clearly see the interplay between religion, the context in which it is embedded, and the call for redemption. The following analysis of chiefs and initiates explains how people become drawn into dancing—the efficient actors and their efficient cause.

CHIEFS, INITIATES, AND REDEMPTION

CHIEFS

There is no doubt about the considerable influence chiefs exert over the dances that they sponsor, and there is no doubt that the individuality of each chief separates chiefs from one another, and separates them as a group from the Shoshone-Ute community at large. Yet it is the community that allows each chief to be recognized as distinctive.

Sun dance chiefs on all five reservations are distinguished from other Sun dance adherents in two important ways: they are considered to have vast amounts of power; and they receive special dream instructions to direct dances. One man may dance for four or five decades without himself directing a dance, whereas another may receive dream instructions to direct a ritual after performing in as few as eight or ten dances spread over four or five years.

At each of the Colorado Ute reservations there is only one prominent chief, although other men have acted as chiefs at dances since 1960. The dominant spiritual leader on one of the Colorado Ute reserves is middle-aged and has been an active Sun dancer since the late 1940s. Before his participation in the Sun dance religion he was a heavy drinker. He received dreams, interpreted by another shaman, which instructed him to participate in the Sun dance. Part of those instructions warned him to abstain from alcohol, which he did when he took up the dance. A short time later he also took up peyote. But as his knowledge of the dance increased and as his shamanistic services were requested more and more during Sun dances, he gave up peyote. Whereas some men and women receive dream instructions to acquire power through peyote, and others to acquire power through the Sun dance and peyote, this man's instructions were that the two together were not appropriate for him and that if he continued as an active participant in both religions the joint effect could be counterproductive.

After he had received his dreams to direct dances, and as he began to act on them, the chief gradually began interpreting the dance in accordance with his dreams. He does not reveal all of his knowledge nor all of his instructions, but he does reveal some information to everyone in the corral, still more information to the dancers who join him, and more information yet to his cohorts on the Sun dance committee. This leader strongly counsels against drinking, suggests that peyote and the Sun dance do not mix, has reinstituted many Sun dance practices that have fallen into disuse elsewhere,[1] and has initiated several new practices including eight special sunrise songs, the ubiquitous use of willows, a stone pipe ceremony, and the shamanizing of each dancer at the end of each day and night dance session. Moreover, this chief keeps very tight supervision over the dance. When the singing lags, he orders men to sing and demands the participation of everyone in the corral.

The fame of this man precedes him, and he is highly respected on all of the reservations in the Sun dance cycle. He is called on to administer final blessings whenever he attends dances sponsored on other reserves, and throughout the year there is discussion about his abilities.

The most prominent chief on the other Colorado Ute reservation probably has the best reputation in the entire Sun dance community for being able to cure "fever." The dances he directs are well controlled, and the dancers are very vigorous participants. He leads the singing at sunrise, gives separate blessings to each dancer at least once during the dance, and encourages the dancers to work hard in the pursuit of

1. For example, he takes a sweatbath before the dance begins, and only one other Ute chief does so. He also maintains a very brief version of the Sun dance parade.

power. He does not select assistant chiefs, but if another man has dream instructions to direct a dance the same year that the dominant chief has his dream, the chief of lesser influence serves as the assistant chief and does not make the major decisions. When this prominent Ute chief dances away from home, his services are constantly requested to cure invalids and other dancers suffering from "fever." When he is attending but not dancing at a ritual, his services are highly prized in the hand-and-stick games which attend the rituals as extracurricular activities, because he is said to have great powers to hide the marked and unmarked sticks used in this group gambling game.

There are more active Northern Ute chiefs than chiefs on any other reservation in the Sun dance cycle. Eight men have sponsored dances in recent years, and it is not uncommon for as many as three men to announce that they will direct one or the other dance sponsored at Northern Ute each year. When more than one man announces his instructions to direct a dance, the one acknowledged by the other would-be sponsors to have the greatest power or to run the best dance is selected to serve as head chief. The two currently most prominent chiefs at Northern Ute are middle-aged, highly revered as shamans, and very different from one another in the way each runs the dance. One man keeps very tight controls on the dancers, orders singers to sing, demands the concerted attention of spectators, uses the flag ritual, and adds many touches in ritual paraphernalia and performance not used by the other Northern Ute chiefs.

During one Northern Ute dance in 1963 this chief was bothered by two indicators of the violation of ritual proscriptions. First, there was considerable rain throughout the days of the dance and, second, he had to evict a menstruant from the corral.[2] He interpreted both the rain and the menstruant as bad omens, suggesting to him that the dance was not going well and that power and its emissaries were displeased. He terminated the dance a few hours early.

The other chief exercises much less overt control. He is greatly respected, but he does not direct dancers, order singers about, or do much more than signal when the dance sessions should begin and end. Nevertheless, he is a famous shaman, receives handsome gifts for his services from invalids and fellow dancers, and is popular on every reservation in the Sun dance community.

The currently most prominent male chief among the Fort Hall Shoshones (Bannock Creek) became a chief after receiving dream instructions to sponsor a dance and subsequently serving a long apprenticeship to an old chief. When the old man died, the younger man announced his intention to direct the dance—as the local community expected.

The Bannock Creek dance is run in a loose and simple fashion. The male chief does not solely direct the dance; a head woman chief also serves, and in recent years this position has been filled by a woman from Duck Valley (Western Shoshone from Owyhee, Nevada). Few instructions are given to dancers, singers, or anyone else at the Bannock Creek dances, and the female chief usually dominates the proceedings. Along with her female assistant chief, the dominant woman shamanizes all of the dancers, whereas the male chief seldom participates in the act except as a recipient of

2. Sun dancers claim that they can smell a menstruant and it makes them sick. There is a proscription against menstruating women entering the corral because the menstrual flow carries evil spirits.

the treatment. The women also lead most of the dancing. Furthermore, the Fort Hall chiefs have transferred all the responsibility for singing to the singers.

An important point about all the Shoshone dances is that head chiefs invite assistant chiefs from other reservations to help them perform good dances. This practice serves communitarian and individual goals by drawing together participants from several reservations in the Sun dance community and stressing their communality, and also by recognizing the special powers and expertise of participants from other reservations. The practice also draws dancers from foreign reservations who prefer to dance with the assistant chief. At Fort Hall the female chief also invites another woman to help her. Ute chiefs invite men from other reservations to dance and sing, but not to serve as co-chiefs or assistant chiefs.

It is my impression from speaking with dancers and spectators at both of the Shoshone reservations that the Shoshone chiefs are somewhat more highly revered on other reservations than they are at home. Perhaps this suggests only that at home most people are known to a fault. Whatever the case may be, there is no doubt that many Fort Hall Shoshones, from teen-agers to people in their sixties, mentioned that the current Bannock Creek chief had great understanding of the dance and that he was the man best qualified to direct it.

At Wind River Shoshone there are three active chiefs. One is middle-aged, one is in his sixties, and one is in his eighties. The oldest has been directing dances for over three decades, and he initially began dancing and sponsoring dances because of dreams that gave him specific instructions about how to overcome his general "ill" health. This man directed the major Wind River dances of 1965 and 1966, both of which called for community peace and the cessation of the Viet Nam war. He attended the Bannock Creek Fort Hall dance and the major dance at Northern Ute in 1966 as well. At all dances this chief's opinions were solicited and his services in administering final blessings were requested. At home he was called on many times to give family blessings and to shamanize invalids. His reputation at Wind River seems to be greater than that of the younger chiefs, and it also seems to be higher than that of his Bannock Creek counterparts at Fort Hall.

In terms of the amount of control exercised, the 1966 dance directed by the Wind River chief stands about midway between the most rigidly supervised Ute dances and the least rigidly supervised Bannock Creek rituals. For example, one morning during the 1966 dance the singers were slow to arrive. The Wind River chief would not allow the dancers to sing the morning flag song in order to get the session going. He said the song should be sung by the singers, and that ended the discussion. During the sunrise ceremonies the same chief sang the four sunrise songs, and at the commencement of the dance he sang the special opening songs. He also gave a group blessing to all of the dancers, thus expressing a special relationship between chief and dancers. On the other hand, the Wind River chief did not salt the ritual with special prayers, nor did he issue frequent instructions to singers, dancers, and other adherents in the corral.

In 1967, the Wind River chief (a different one from the 1966 chief) invited a Crow Indian to serve as his co-chief. The Wind River man had introduced the modern Sun dance to the Crow Indians several years earlier, and at the 1967 dance many Crow Indians participated (whereas few Crows had participated in Wind River dances directed by other chiefs). Furthermore, Crow tobacco rituals were added to the ceremony. With the influx of Crow dancers, over sixty men danced, so that an extension had to be built onto the corral to accommodate the singers. The influence of each chief in setting the tenor of the dance, and drawing adherents from other reservations should not be underemphasized.

In 1966 the co-chief at Wind River had been a mixed-blood from Northern Ute (his wife and children are on the fullblood roll, but he is not). Although he is generally recognized by Ute fullbloods as having the ability to control the weather, he is not influential in the Northern Ute dance, seldom dances there, and is seldom called upon to confer final blessings on participants. In recent years he has restricted most of his dancing to the Wind River and Ute Mountain rituals. At these dances his services are appreciated, and at Wind River he is frequently chosen to administer family blessings and to shamanize "fever"-ridden dancers. His prayers, instructions to dancers, and the revelation of his own special knowledge about the dance added variation to the performance and contributed to the differences between the Wind River dance and other dances in 1966. But his presence at the Wind River ritual did not draw an unusual influx of Northern Ute fullbloods.

Each of the Shoshones and Ute Sun dance chiefs alter their dances somewhat from year to year. The same chief may use a stuffed bison head on the center pole one year and an eagle the next, or a doll one year and not the next. Some chiefs strip the center poles of their bark one year and not the next. The chiefs are, of course, aware of one another's practices, but do not appear to try to imitate one another. The variation among them is caused by different dream instructions. The innovations that are made serve as evidence that the chiefs are indeed special and that they continue to receive new powers from spirits that appear to them in their dreams. It is necessary for a spiritual leader to continue to distinguish himself from other adherents in order to demonstrate that he is a powerful person. Because he is powerful, his advice and help is sought throughout the year.

INITIATES

The chiefs are active all year long in the affairs of the reservation community. They administer to the sick, provide counsel to those who seek it, and, on the Ute reservations, interpret the dreams of prospective Sun dance initiates. On the Shoshone reservations a prospective dancer may be encouraged to enter the Sun dance, but he or she need not receive specific dream instructions to do so.

Whether Ute or Shoshone, Sun dance novices usually enter the dance for the first time between the ages of fifteen and about twenty-five, although there is a present tendency for dancers to be initiated in their teens. Men are initiated several years younger than are women.

Among the Utes a boy about fourteen years old might begin dreaming that he is seeing the "ghosts" or "shadows" of deceased relatives ("old people" or *nusakac*). Dream spirits are also seen in the form of animals such as buffalo, eagle, or bear. At first, recipients divulge very few of the details of these dreams. They might, however, relate some of the experience to a brother, a cousin, or some other close relative of about their own age in the household.

The recipient withholds the information because he is frightened. He usually awakes from the dream wringing wet with the symptoms of "fever." When the same dream recurs as well as the symptoms of "fever," this is a "call" or sign that the recipient must seek power. If a recipient ignores the dreams, or ignores the fact that he is "getting power," it is thought that he will get sick and die.

When dreams recur, the youthful recipient is directed by some member of his family to go to a shaman and have his dream interpreted. Upon doing so he will probably be instructed to dance in the Sun dance, to become an active peyotist, or merely to serve an apprenticeship to the shaman whose counsel he has sought. All of the means which the Utes recognize as legitimate ways to acquire power require the intercession of a shaman at some point. Moreover, the acquisition of the shaman status requires an apprenticeship. Sun dance chiefs are special shamans who have acquired power through the dance and who have either studied under other chiefs or have participated in many dances and observed many chiefs. This aspect of their training is critical, it seems, to gain the public trust. Not all dancers become chiefs.

A boy who has been told to dance in the Sun dance, whether by a Sun dance chief or by some other shaman, will begin getting counsel from a Sun dance chief. The prospective initiate is taught what is expected of him and what will happen to him if he does not observe certain rules. For instance, there is a supernatural sanction that a person will "wither up and die" within a period of three months following the next Sun dance if he does not participate. This is the same amount of time that the center pole is supposed to maintain its water. So the prospective initiate is told that he will lose his water when the pole loses its water if he does not dance.

The chief will also counsel the youth about how to prepare for the dance. He instructs the youth to eat dried meat and crackers and little else for a few weeks before the dance begins. The initiate is also told to meditate about the buffalo and about the reason for which he was called to the dance. Often the meditation sessions are conducted with the chief and other meditators. The counsel offered when each meditation session is complete makes it clear that the prospective initiate is young and strong and that the dance will be easy for him, perhaps too easy; so he must dance with caution and under control lest fatigue overtake him suddenly and without warning, causing him to be "knocked down." Being "knocked down" is a sign that the person has been foolish and has angered Buffalo. He is reminded that he should dance twelve dances, that he will not receive his vision until the twelfth, and that he might not receive a vision at all. He is reminded that each dance will become more difficult than the last. Some men are instructed to dance only four dances, but all are told to stop dancing on an even number of performances.

The prospective initiate is counseled on many other topics, including some that define how life "ought to be," and how he should practice his life. He is told to honor his family and kin. He is told to respect the "old people" and the sick and to do all he can to make the ailing Indians healthy. The initiate is told to marry an Indian woman, not a white or a Mexican American, and to maintain the integrity of Indian life in other ways.

These instructions are not simply guidelines that, when not followed, leave things unchanged. The prospective initiate is told that he will leave the dance a different man from the one he was when he entered. He will acquire power, and with power go many responsibilities to handle it properly. For instance, he is told that the acquisition of power will make him extremely virile, supernaturally so. Therefore, he is instructed to suppress his hedonic impulses and told not to cohabit with women unless he is willing to marry them and take care of the children that will surely come from the union. This alteration in his person, and the stress on maintaining the Indian family, means that he should be cautious, find an Indian woman, and enter the relationship with an awareness of the consequences.

He is told that his new powers entail special responsibilities to live amicably at home. He must be a man of good heart who meditates about the good life and who practices the good life with family, the wider network of kin and friends, and the greater Indian community. A person is counseled not to drink because alcohol is evil and causes evil acts such as fights between kin. Indeed, drinking can end in the death of a weaker man. The person who begins drinking and starts disrupting the lives of his neighbors, kin, and friends is not a person of good heart. Moreover, drinking can lead to cohabitation at the wrong time and with the wrong person. Alcohol can demoralize a person and dissipate his power, power that is needed for his well-being and for the well-being of others. In short, the prospective initiate is counseled about why he must seek power, how he must seek power, what will happen to him after he begins the procedure (through the Sun dance religion), and what his responsibilities are in controlling his power.

REDEMPTION

Redemption is achieved by the Sun dance initiates through the transformation of his or her personality. The initiate becomes virile, helpful, responsible, and knowledgeable. Although he becomes all of these things, he also knows that he must continue the quest so that he will gain more power and more knowledge. This is a long and arduous journey and it requires fortitude. A man's (or a woman's) fortitude is challenged by the context in which he lives. The white society that dominates his life is castigated, as are the ways of many Indians—those who drink, fight, or do not maintain their households. The irresponsible Indians are considered redeemable and their redemption is encouraged, whereas the whites are not. Indeed, it is the whites in general, rather than irresponsible Indians in particular, at whom the Sun dance leaders direct most of their scorn. Initiates learn that they are acquiring knowledge and power that whites do not have. In learning how to cope with day-to-day life they also learn that the harder *they* work, the better off *all* Indians will be.

The Responsibilities of the Redeemed

The young people, especially, are resistant to the dreams they receive before they are initiated to the dance because they understand the price they will have to pay in suffering to acquire power. They also understand the responsibilities they must shoulder after they acquire power, and the consequences that will befall them if they do not heed their dream instructions. Older men, particularly those who are heavy drinkers, realize that when they enter the dance they should give up drinking, and they are not sure whether they can do so. This forces men to contemplate their actions at considerable length and in great depth. They have great faith in the efficacy of the dance to improve their lives, but they also know that their lives can get considerably worse if they enter the dance, yet flout some of its loose proscriptions by continuing to drink.

Many men cannot successfully cope with their problems even after they have started participating in the dance. The road to redemption is a long and arduous one, though the Sun dance religion provides support for the stumbling adherent. But the obstacles that litter the Sun dancer's path are many. We will analyze these in the following chapter on post-initiate dancers, their intentions and reasons for dancing, their ages, and their interreservation participation. The following analysis addresses itself to the question of how those obstacles are conquered.

9   *The Dancers*

Here, then, we shall explore the sacred and secular meaning of redemption and the factors that urge Shoshones and Utes both to seek redemption and to maintain themselves after achieving it. Because the obstacles in the paths of the redeemed are many —unemployment, crowding, discrimination, alcohol, etc.—redemption is not a simple condition to maintain.

In the following analysis it is convenient to separate the explanation of the sacred ends from the explanation of the secular ends of dancer participation, although the two are contingent upon each other. In analyzing the sacred goals of dancer participation, we shall appeal to *intention* explanations. By an "intention" we presuppose that an action is done by design, and that the action is a means toward a goal, aim or purpose. In regard to the Sun dance, dancers have conscious goals, explicitly verbalized, that they hope to attain by entering the dance. They are following religious prescriptions and proscriptions to observe the faith and to seek power, and they intend to use the power they acquire to bring good health to themselves, to bring about the good health of ailing kin and relatives, to bring about the happiness of mourners, to pacify the spirits of the deceased (who do not always behave in a kind fashion), to bring about the well-being of the *entire* Sun dance community, and, in some cases, to acquire the special powers and skills of a shaman.

The intentions of dancers are based on their dreams and their interpretations, but neither intentions nor dreams sufficiently explain dancer participation. What they do explain are the sacred ends which dancers pursue—including faith healing and the moral-spiritual transformation of the participant. In order to gain a fuller understanding of dancer participation we must also explain the secular ends sought through dancing. We call these secular ends "reasons," for they relate to actions that are conscious responses to situations or events but are not accounted for by a fully explicated and verbalized design. On the other hand, the intentions of Shoshones and Ute dancers are fully explicated and verbalized and are accounted for by a design replete with ritual prescriptions, proscriptions, and accompanying sanctions. The secular reasons for which Shoshones and Utes dance stem from the fact that they are discriminated against by local whites who deny status and, consequently, esteem to the Indians. Whites discriminate against Indians in their employment practices, whites disapprove of Indian morality and belittle Indian intelligence, Indian integrity, and Indian industriousness. The secular reasons (as opposed to the sacred intentions) for which people dance are to gain personal status and esteem *within* the Indian community.

It is important to offer an explanation as to why a person will verbalize his sacred intentions for dancing, but why the secular reasons for dancing are not so well defined and fully verbalized. Indeed, why is it that the reasons for dancing must be inferred from comments made by dancers, chiefs, committeemen, singers, spectators, and so forth, on secular subjects, and from the non-verbal behavior between members of the Sun dance community?

From our analyses in the preceding chapters the explanations for the difference between sacred and secular explanations for dancing is offered. Although dancers gain prestige and status from dancing and suffering, narrow personal ends are eschewed by the Sun dance community. The braggadocio is not admired and does not gain prestige and status. Prestige and status can be achieved only in the group context and only by suffering and giving for the good, and the life, of others. So personal success is contingent upon maintaining decorum and dignity. Anything else is a threat to the tenuous social, political, and economic fabric of the reservations. Dancers earn status and, consequently, esteem by dancing, but not by talking about how grand or important they are or will become.

The status and esteem that is earned has individual and collective effects. The individual dancer can cope at home, enjoying his new status, and he can better cope with the discrimination he receives daily from local whites. The redeemed is, after all, the possessor of power and spiritual truths unknown and unpossessed by whites, and the redeemed is supported by the Indian community from whom he or she receives approval. The Indian community sinks or swims, on the other hand, according to the behavior of its members. So the community can have pride in itself—let us call it general esteem—if the adherents observe the collective ethic and remain people of good heart. It is bad form for a dancer to exploit his personal advantage (sacred knowledge and power), or to talk about how swell he is, or to abuse his power and status by acting irresponsibly (drinking heavily, for example). Personal advantage in the nature of power, status, and esteem accrues to the Shoshone or Ute dancer. The Sun dance community is not only conscious of these benefits, but has a vested interest in maintaining them.

The interplay between the intentions Utes and Shoshones express for dancing, their reasons for dancing, and the economic, social and political conditions in which these people live can be seen in the following example, which will help define the rather wide boundaries of the subject pursued here. At a Ute dance in the early 1960s a white man in the employ of one of the Colorado Ute tribes danced and collapsed. He broke all the guidelines by going as hard as he could for a vision in this, his first dance. When he collapsed, the Indians in attendance were quite perturbed. Many openly showed their anger. Aside from his impudence in attempting to acquire a vision of his first dance, the white dancer had no way in which he could *use* his power. He was not considered a member of the Indian community but was a member of the dominant white society and thus an agent of Indian problems. No one would seek him out in order to be doctored by him. No one would seek his advice, etc. The question they asked of me and each other was "What is he going to do with it [his power]?"

RECRUITMENT

The annual recruitment process to get established dancers to join the various dances is considerably different from the manner in which the novice is initiated to the dance. After the initial counseling sessions the established dancer need not continue to seek counsel from shamans before each subsequent dance in which he performs; as often as not the Sun dance chiefs do not know how many men are going to enter the dance corral to dance with them. It is customary, however, for men and women who intend to dance at their home reservation to make their intentions known to the chief well beforehand. Often these same men and women will join with chiefs throughout the year for meditation sessions. If visitors are going to dance, they usually make their intentions known to the chief a day or two before the dance commences.

The chiefs will solicit the aid of friends and close relatives to help make their dance a good one. In turn, their friends will encourage their own relatives to help make it a successful dance. Yet dancing is a personal thing, Utes and Shoshones do not badger anyone to perform. Men and women ostensibly dance to satisfy the ritual prescriptions learned in their dreams and interpreted by shamans.

SACRED INTENTIONS FOR DANCING

The key intention for dancing, of course, is the acquisition of supernatural power (*puwa* or *poha*). A person is instructed by his dream experiences and by the shaman who interprets the dreams to observe the call to seek power lest he wither and die. The call is not for a narrow end, and is not simply for the recipient of the dreams. With the charge to acquire power goes the responsibility to seek power for "everyone." Furthermore, the religious nature of the Sun dance, the complex beauty of the ideology, and the deep satisfaction of the religious experience (the acquisition of power and all it entails) are great factors influencing dancers to participate, regardless of the ritual prescriptions and proscriptions.

COMMUNITY HEALTH AND HAPPINESS

When Shoshone or Ute dancers say "for the good of everyone," they mean for the good of those people in their families, their tribes, and in the Sun dance community. The reference is to Indians, not mixed-bloods and surely not whites.[1] In "the good of everyone" several things are understood. The dancer seeks power to insure health and happiness. Dancers hope that everyone will be healthy, and this means, among other things, that everyone will have sufficient spiritual food (power), food, and shelter throughout the year, that household members will not quarrel and injure one another, that Indians will not drink and become ill, thus becoming burdens to their kinsmen and friends. Indeed, dancers fast during the dance so that they will be rewarded with spiritual food (power) at the end of the dance, and so that spiritual food (power) will be bestowed on the people in the Sun dance community. The community members encourage and support the dancers in their ordeal, and provide a feast at the termination to signify thanksgiving.

Happiness, too, is sought for the community. Factional strife is rebuked as is disruption in the home. Dancers emphasize that Indian morality, that is, "doing what is right," "remembering what the 'old people' did," or "following the counsel

1. Percentage of Indian blood seems to be a relevant consideration only among Northern and Ute Mountain Utes where mixed-bloods, that is, people with less than 50 percent Indian blood, are generally treated with disdain. There are obvious exceptions on both reserves, however.

of the 'old people,' " and a renewed emphasis on the importance of their kinship obligations will bind the community together. Again, the community is not simply the reservation, but people from all reservations involved in joint participation in the dances. The white man is not a part of this community. Far from experiencing its deprivations, he has caused them, and the Shoshones and Utes know this well.

HEALTH AND HAPPINESS OF INVALIDS AND MOURNERS

If the dancer expresses collective concern and if he seeks power for the collective good, he also seeks power in order to aid the infirm and the suffering. Every dancer says that he is going to dance, or has danced, *for* someone. The various persons danced for by each dancer can be physically ailing relatives, and often are, or merely widows, widowers, or other persons who have recently lost close relatives through death and are experiencing mental anguish. Whether the suffering is physical, mental, or both, power is sought to cure the invalid or to convince the ghost of the deceased that genuine grief is felt on his behalf. In turn, family and interpersonal bonds are strengthened through sacrifice, and the dancer receives respect and admiration for his selflessness. This "selfless" behavior often leads to a position of respect within the community (an important *reason* for dancing).

PERSONAL HEALTH AND SHAMANISTIC SKILLS

Among the intentions of dancers participating in Sun dances is to cure themselves of some malady or merely to insure good health in the future. In 1966 alone, over a dozen men and women suffering from "heart trouble" and "fever" entered and danced in the various rituals.

The good health sought by many dancers is often linked to moral convictions and guilt. Although Sun dancers, generally, are admonished to stay away from alcohol, we have pointed out that some drink rather heavily and even enter the dances quite drunk. Those people, who have stumbled along the path to redemption, enter the dance to purge themselves of their wrongful ways as well as to give themselves better health. The two are inseparable, as is attested to by the orations given at Sun dances by chiefs, committee members, and prestigious spectators.

Another intention of dancers is to acquire power to become a shaman capable of curing others. Some dancers (including all of the chiefs) receive dream instructions to pursue a shaman's skills and role. These instructions set some men and women off from others, and lay heavy community obligations and responsibilities on their shoulders (as counselors, healers, and people of good will).

The sacred intentions of dancing, then, emphasize the uses to which power is put and allow individuals to distinguish themselves in a sacred fashion. The good of the entire Sun dance community, help for ailing or mentally anguished friends and relatives, and native curing skills are sacred goals of Sun dance participation that sharply sets off the Indian from the white community. The conscious focus on individuals, family, and the wider Indian community stresses broad individualism within the collective Indian ethic.

SECULAR REASONS FOR DANCING

As early as 1937, Shimkin (1953: 71) suggested that men participated in the Sun dance to achieve prestige, and that the Sun dance provided one of the few avenues to prestige open to them. Others, including Opler (1941) on the Southern Ute, Jones (1955) on the Northern Ute, and Dorn (1966: 59–60) on the Fort Hall Shoshones, have suggested that dancers participate to revitalize the past and validate and perpetuate the integrity of their cultures.

These explanations focus on secular subjects, on prestige, on identity, on restoration and maintenance of cultural integrity. There is no doubt that secular considerations are important reasons for which Utes and Shoshones participate as Sun dancers. Through dancing a person can have his personality transformed, he can acquire status, and he can generate pride in his behavior (self-esteem) and pride in the behavior of the community of adherents. Furthermore, in observing his or her own responsibilities to the community, the dancer is in the position to encourage everyone—verbally and by precept—to observe their communitarian responsibilities. Dancers and nondancers alike have affirmed that dancers earn high status (including prestige) and esteem within the Sun dance community by participating as dancers in the religion and by observing the collective ethic (being generous, sober, responsible, of good heart, etc.). Furthermore, high status and approval by the Indian community generates self-esteem—pride in proper Indian behavior that the adherent knows to be moral rather than immoral (as whites contend). Ultimately self-esteem, power, and community recognition that allows and supports that esteem, provide the redeemed with insulation against white criticisms.

Shosones and Utes constantly extol the skills and powers of various Sun dancers, or assert that some men and women know the accurate history of Shoshone culture or Ute culture—as opposed to the histories of these cultures that have been set forth by white men. They also extol the Sun dance adherents who make the collective ethic an actuality by adopting children, taking care of the elderly and the sick, and sharing their labor and resources with others. They laud the orators who, during the Sun dances, define the meaning of Indian morality and the evils of whites' ways.

STATUS DEPRIVATION AND LOW SELF-ESTEEM

The dominant white society determines the social status hierarchy around the reservations, just as it does in the cities. On the whole, Indians are accorded the lowest possible status relative to whites, and the burden of low status and disapproval weighs heavy. We have pointed out that approval cannot be won short of severing ties with the Indian community, and that because of the nature of the economy and the quality of Indian education, status and approval can seldom be won even if Indian ties are severed and the individualist Protestant ethic is observed. The more probable result of severing ties with the Indian community is alienation of friends and relatives whose lives are jeopardized by the action. The result is to lose status among Indians without gaining status among whites.

Shoshones and Utes recognize early in their lives that whites accord very low status to Indians, evidenced as disapproval and disrespect for Indians. It is not a coincidence that many young men and women drop out of school around the eighth or ninth grade and begin severing their ties with whites, nor is it a coincidence that young men between the ages of sixteen and thirty are especially underskilled and underemployed. With neither educations nor jobs, they have little possibility of winning white approval. Indeed, the whites focus on these deficiencies, among others, to deny approval and status to Indians. So Shoshones and Utes partly sever their ties with whites because of disapproval and disrespect, and, by so doing, merely earn more disapproval and disrespect.

Shoshones and Utes remain very much in touch with white society, however. Young Shoshone and Ute men are seldom able to provide for a family, yet they know of local whites their own ages who can do so. These young Indian men have attended public schools often with the same whites. They have also watched television shows depicting middle-class American life, attended movies depicting the middle-class life style, and many have served in the armed forces. Indeed, Shoshones and Utes have scores of direct and sustained contacts with whites in the employ of the BIA, in the employ of the tribe, in the employ of various religious organizations, as well as contacts with local shopkeepers, ranchers, farmers, and law enforcement personnel. In these experiences the Indians have developed legitimate expectations about the quality of their own lives and the status accorded to whites but not to themselves.

Utes and Shoshones often have low self-esteem because they are accorded low status and disrespect by whites. For instance, Indians seldom challenge local white policemen or judges who incarcerate them because they know that the whites will not believe their arguments. If Indians challenge BIA officials, they know the bureaucratic response will probably be paternalistic. If the Indian escapes from his own responsibilities at home or in the Indian community, disrespect will be accorded to him there. Participation in the Sun dance, which allows the conscientious adherent openly and intentionally to seek power, to help the ailing, to contribute to the good of the community, and to be accorded status in a moral Indian community, also develops in the dancer a feeling of self-esteem, a feeling of respect in himself and pride in his behavior. The adherent's behavior is admired and approved by other Indians because it exemplifies the broad individualism that is consonant with the collective Indian ethic.

A partial solution to the status deprivation Shoshones and Utes experience from the white community is to gain status within the Indian community, even if Indians cannot acquire employment or possessions.

Status and esteem considerations appear to have contributed to the persistence of the modern Sun dance as a redemptive movement, and to initiation and participation of the younger generation along with the older generation in the movement.

INDIAN VERSUS WHITE COMMUNITY

Whereas a few Utes and Shoshones seek status in the white community by doing the bidding of whites and observing the Protestant ethic, most gain status and acquire some self-esteem in the Sun dance community. Participation does not, of course, give status and esteem in the white community, as some Utes and Shoshones have perceived.

To carry this a little further: I have learned—over the past ten years of close association with Utes employed by the tribe or the BIA or unemployed, of some association with Shoshones employed by the tribe or the BIA or unemployed, and of extensive and close association with whites both on and near Shoshone and Ute reservations—that Indians *always* possess considerably more knowledge and understanding of whites than vice versa (see chapter 5). Moreover, whites seldom have more than the most rudimentary knowledge of the dance or its participants. Very few whites attend Sun dances. If they do so, it is usually out of curiosity, or a desire to be entertained.[2] The usual response of whites near all of the reservations when queried about the Sun dance goes something like this: "The old bucks still do a little dancing, and a few young bucks dance for a thrill, but there isn't much left but a show." A few whites, especially missionaries, are incredulous that the Indians can believe in what they are doing.

If whites neither understand the dance nor know the participants, it seems rather obvious that the Sun dance participant, while gaining status at home, probably only reinforces the low opinions whites have about him.

As we saw in chapter 2, Indians believe that the dance was given to Indians for Indians by Buffalo, a repository of power as well as a channel through which power is directed. It is not a white religion. Utes and Shoshones also know, of course, that the Wind River Shoshones donated the ritual to the other members of the community. And several Wind River Shoshone shamans reworked the ritual so as to give religious meaning to *Indian* lives and to help solve Indian problems. This was done at a time when the Shoshones had lost faith in the transformative promise of the Ghost dance religion.

The "Indianness" of the ritual is stressed here because Utes and Shoshones agree that the dance is performed for collective and specific Indian purposes. The intention is to acquire power and the power is to be used for several ends. Power brings good health, and so forth. These ends are not contradictory but rather complementary aspects of the Sun dance ideology, which focuses on both the acquisition and the use of power, on both the individual and the community.

The white is regarded as an interloper. It is not clear to Indians just what whites would do with power if they were able to acquire it. Who would turn to whites for advice, or for a cure, or for help in assuaging the wrath of a malevolent spirit? Orations at dances stress Indian integrity, the acquisition of power for Indian ends, and the need to respect and observe the practices of the "old people." Thus the focus is on Indian life, not white. It is a conscious, explicit, verbalized focus.

PARTICIPATION OF DANCERS THROUGHOUT THE SUN DANCE COMMUNITY

The 194 male and female dancers at the five dances in 1966 more often danced at their home reservations (54 percent or 105 dancers) than as guests at other reservations (46 percent or 89 dancers). Although dancers are more apt to dance at home than away, these figures alone suggest an intense interreservation participation at Sun dances.

We have noted that Sun dance chiefs send special invitations to chiefs and renowned dancers from reservations other than their own to influence them to join the host in conducting a good dance. Chiefs or the Sun dance committees have flyers printed or

2. Over the years I have seen only one "white" singer, and he also dances occasionally. But he was raised by Southern Paiutes, speaks Southern Paiute, and has been married to Paiute women. On occasions other whites have danced—anthropologists, a white married into one of the tribes, a member of a psychedelic cult, a tribal employee, an Episcopalian minister, etc.—but this is very rare and not generally encouraged by the Indians. (The castigation of whites and white attendance at Sun dances will be more fully discussed in chapters 10 and 11.)

mimeographed to announce each dance, and these are circulated throughout the Sun dance community. The flyers serve notice to many who do not receive special invitations of the scheduled dates for the Sun dances. Dancers can make their plans accordingly.

SOME REASONS FOR PARTICIPATION AWAY FROM HOME

Host dancers outnumber visiting dancers, and the host Indians seem to prefer it that way. It allows them to have pride in their dance and dancers and to assert their numerical, if not moral and cultural, superiority over the other sponsoring reserves. Nevertheless, visitors are sought, and invitations are extended to prospective visitors in many ways. Dancers who journey from other reserves draw relatives and friends with them, and all lend legitimacy and contribute to the activities of the dance. Visitors serve to admire the elegance and to recognize the virtue of each dance, and to accord each reservation community the respect it seeks.

Dancers are solicited to attend the various Sun dances at the several Ute Bear dances held each spring and attended by Utes, Southern Paiutes, a few Shoshones, and some other Indians linked by marriage and friendship to the hosts. Camaraderie or even courtships engendered between members of different reserves at these times influence men to travel and dance at Sun dances sponsored on other reservations. Joint participation at peyote meetings or basketball tournaments on the various reservations widen the contacts of many men and women and serve to draw them into a community. If they desire to dance, they often perform where friendly contacts have been previously made.

Contacts made in one generation often lead to interreserve marriages, thus linking children through kinship to two or more reservation groups. This is true not only of internal tribal relations but, to a lesser extent, of relations between Shoshone and Utes. Circumstances such as flight from the law or from boredom and economic privation sometimes prompt dancers to visit relatives and dance away from home.

Another reason for dancing away from home, expressed by many dancers, particularly those in their fifties, sixties, and seventies, is to help one's friends sponsor a good dance. The expressed interest of these older people is toward the host chief, the ritual itself, and the dance community. Older visitors often insure a good dance because they nearly always travel in pairs whose members are vowed to dance together, thus adding visibly to the numbers of dancers and giving the dance an interreserve flavor. Because of their age and team dancing, the older people command great respect in the communities they visit. They are invariably assumed to have considerable power and are frequently sought out to administer blessings during and after the dance. The blessings are, in part, motivated by economics, since the most prestigious shamans who are called on to do the shamanizing receive remuneration for it. The modest amounts of cash and goods reaped by a few men and women are incidental to the considerable prestige that is accorded to some of them.

What is interesting is that prestige (as evidenced by the respect these shamans receive and the stories people tell about the miraculous cures or changes of weather they have effected) is more often accrued by older visitors than by local people. This does not go unnoticed by younger people. It is true that younger people are seldom employed and, partly as an effect of this, have time to move from dance to dance.

But because they are not employed and do not have ready access to means which will win them status as providers or as influential members of the family, they seek status away from their reservations.

Unemployment and other deprivations are often associated with drinking, which generates no respect in the Indian community, though most people do drink. After getting drunk, a young man might, for instance, have an automobile accident or beat a woman, and then leave the reservation, pursued by tribal or local police. By moving in with relatives on another reservation he can often avoid the law and, by dancing or by helping out in the household, gain some status and some self-esteem as he wins the respect of others.

During the summer of 1966 some young Indian men were avoiding state and tribal police in Utah by residing on a Ute reserve in Colorado. In Utah a Colorado Indian was avoiding police in his home state. In each instance the men were staying with kin or in-laws and contributing their skills and labor to their new households. Each of these men danced at the dances sponsored on the reserves they were visiting. The religious excitement they experienced and the social successes they registered in their new households from dancing and helping out prompted them to participate in other dances in the Sun dance cycle. All the men joined the summer dance circuit, and eventually all were apprehended in their home states. The desire to participate became greater than their fear of apprehension by legal forces that were alien and repressive intrusions in their lives. Two men traveling north from Colorado on their way to the Wind River Shoshone dance, slipped into Utah during the middle of the night in order to stop at their homes as well as to avoid the police while stopping. They got in and out of Utah on the way to Wyoming, but when they tried to do the same thing on the return trip they were caught and sent to jail—one in a local white town and the other in Salt Lake City pending a federal charge.

It has been demonstrated that the Indians in this study are, for the most part, excluded from any participation in the legal system of the country except to pay fines and serve sentences. They often try to work around the system, are hostile toward it, and flee from it. When caught, they will serve their time. Although Shoshones and Utes can lose the approval of their counterparts when they fail to provide for their families, or commit ugly crimes against other Indians while drunk, there is no loss of status or prestige for avoiding the "law."

Many young Utes have done most of their dancing away from home, especially at Ute reservations other than their own or at the Wind River dance (although they have not necessarily fled to other reserves because they were sought by the law). Although it cannot be demonstrated empirically, it is my impression that many of these boys enjoy greater prestige and feel fewer pressures to dance every minute of every dance set when dancing away from home. Often it is only when these young men have proved themselves away from home, developing some confidence that they can meet the dance's challenge without faltering or collapsing, that they begin to dance at home.

There are of course some who have their first dancing experience at home. Still others dance away from home but never dance at home. In the last case men often cannot convince their acquaintances at home that they should receive their respect, regardless of their dance performances. Some of these men have said that they dance away from home because they have been instructed to do so in their dreams, while others, especially some Utes, are convinced that dances other than those sponsored at home are better for them. These explanations are often questioned by Utes and Shoshones, though there is little doubt that some men always dance away from home for the reasons they cite. Some Northern Ute men in particular claim that they get their power at Wind River; others have said they get theirs at Southern or Ute Mountain Ute. Women, of course, say Fort Hall. Southern Utes have told me that they "dance better" at Northern Ute. All of these men are respected at home, and their choices to dance away from home are not challenged. It is not true, however, that all dancers who choose to dance away from home (especially a few mixed-blood dancers from Northern Ute) do so unchallenged by public opinion.

WOMEN DANCERS AT FORT HALL

Women are allowed to dance only at Fort Hall, and Shoshone and Ute men do not encourage women to dance even at Fort Hall. Sons and husbands are known to discourage their mothers and wives from dancing; brothers are known to discourage their sisters from dancing. Some men refuse to dance with women, claiming that the women press them into competition, thus destroying their concentration. Other men dance with women, but work hard not to be distracted by the female dancers, who often display incredible stamina.

There is no simple explanation why men discourage women from dancing. If a woman receives recurrent dream instructions to dance, she dances. She must be discouraged before the dream recurs several times, and her family will often discourage her early in the course of her dreaming. If the woman dances, her kin will discourage her from dancing in, say 1967; they tell her that she can always dance another year. The hope is that she will postpone her dancing indefinitely.

There is also no obvious explanation why some men will not dance with women, and why, of the men who do dance with them, some compete with women and others try to ignore the pace that the women set. Some men, usually elderly, refuse to be goaded to dance competitively with women—they merely pursue power amicably with them. But most young men who dance with women compete for all they're worth. They accept the challenge in hopes of withstanding the dry and hot power and outdancing the women. It is critical to note that very few young women dance; so the young men actually compete with women several years older than themselves. There is always one group of men, generally middle-aged, who refuse to dance with women. When they do dance with women, no matter for what reason, the men are goaded to dance harder.

Women are ritually proscribed from dancing on the reservations other than Fort Hall. On the other hand, female participation as singers, attendants to the male dancers' morning toilets, preparers of feasts, givers of gifts, and so forth, is greatly encouraged on all reservations.

Let us propose a possible explanation for the manner in which women dance and the manner in which Shoshone and Ute men respond to them. Perhaps because women are denied the right to dance everywhere but at Fort Hall, even though women receive dream instructions to dance, they resent their exclusion from other dances. When these women participate at Fort Hall, they are encouraged to dance vigorously for two reasons: (1) to leave no question in anyone's mind that they can withstand hot and dry jolts of power, and (2) to tease, if not punish, men for their male chauvinism.

The refusal of many men in their middle years to dance with women, the practice of younger men to compete with women, and the general practice of Shoshone and Ute males to discourage women from dancing may stem from the nature of the roles women must assume vis-à-vis men in the reservation context. Women frequently manage the household budgets and serve as economic providers (a male responsibility) for their fathers, their sons, their brothers, perhaps even for their husbands. Yet the same women are also mothers of the children of dancers, sex partners of dancers, and mothers of dancers. There is already a conflict between these two roles, and it is intensified when women dance, vigorously and with stamina, and outdo men. An important avenue through which men can excel is also an avenue through which women can surpass men. Thwarted by the economy, white polity and society, men want something of value for their own esteem. They want support from women in this endeavor, not competition from them.

It is possible that some young men—men who are neither husbands, nor fathers, nor lovers of the female dancers—will compete in order to show their own stamina. Some elderly men—that is, husbands and grandfathers, who are accorded respect because of their age—are willing to dance with women possibly because, with some equanimity, they are able to focus clearly on their religious goals and not on the conflicts in the female roles.

Women are desperately needed for the performance of all Sun dance rituals, but in capacities other than dancing. Recognizing this need, men actively encourage the participation and support of women. Recognizing the power women possess, men listen attentively to the orations of female shamans, and male dancers seek women to administer final blessings to them at the end of the dances.

INTERRESERVATION DANCER PARTICIPATION

The tabulations in table 44 makes it clear that Indians who are not Utes or Wind River or Fort Hall Shoshones participate in the dances sponsored by the five groups in our analysis. It is also clear that the dances at the Fort Hall and Northern Ute reserves draw more dancers from more locales than do the dances at the other reserves. Fort Hall draws dancers from north and west of their reservation who do not dance at Northern Ute, in part because of affinal ties between Fort Hall Shoshones and Western Shoshones and Cree, and in part because the Fort Hall dance allows women to participate as singers *and* as dancers. Indeed, females from Fort Hall make up only about one-third of the female dancers, whereas on all reservations the host males make up one-half or more of the male dancers.

The hub position occupied by the Northern Ute dance is clear. Whereas the Northern Utes participate in all dances in the Ute and Shoshone Sun dance community (some Northern Utes have even danced with the Cree and the Crow in Montana from time to time), and dancers from all host reservations participate in the

TABLE 44

TRIBAL AFFILIATION OF DANCERS, FIVE SUN DANCES, SUMMER 1966

Tribal Affiliation	Reservations					
	So. Ute 2–5 July	W.R. Sho. 8–11 July	F.H. Sho. 26–30 July		No. Ute 5–9 Aug.	Ute Mtn. Ute 11–15 Aug.
			Males	Females		
Southern Ute	9	0	0	0	2	3
Ute Mtn. Ute	5	0	2	16	4	13
Northern Ute:						
Uintah–White River	3	7	2	5	18	4
Uncompaghre	0	0	0	0	16	0
Wind River Shoshone	0	27	6	3	6	0
Fort Hall Shoshone	0	5	13	9	6	0
Western Shoshone	0	0	2	4	0	0
Cree	0	0	2	0	0	0
Crow	0	0	0	3	0	0
No. Ute Mixed-bloods	0	0	0	0	9	0
White[a]	1	2	0	0	1	0
Totals	18	41	27	26	62	20

a. At Southern Ute a white, former employee of the Ute Mountain tribe, participated. At Wind River a white man from the psychedelic community at Washo Nevada participated, as did a white anthropology student from the Midwest. At Northern Ute a white adopted into the Southern Paiutes participated.

TABLE 45

A SCALE OF DANCER PARTICIPATION AT FIVE SUN DANCES, SUMMER 1966

Location of Dances	Tribal Affiliation of Dancers				
	So. Ute	Ute Mtn. Ute	No. Ute	W.R. Sho.	F.H. Sho.
Wind River Shoshone	−	−	+	+	+
Fort Hall Shoshone	−	+	+	+	+
Northern Ute	+	+	+	+	+
Ute Mountain Ute	+	+	+	−	−
Southern Ute	+	+	+	−	−

Northern Ute dance, this is not true for any other reservation's dancers and dance. Fort Hall Shoshone has the second greatest variety of visitors participating at their dance, while the Ute Mountain Utes are the second most traveled dancers. Southern Ute on the extreme southeast of the Sun dance community, and Wind River on the extreme northeast, have the smallest variety of dancers from other areas and also dance at the fewest dances away from home (at least in the Sun dance community as it has been defined here). In the late 1930s, Wind River Shoshones performed at Crow Sun dances (Shimkin 1953: 470). In 1967, many Crow performed at the Wind River dance, and some Wind Rivers still dance with the Crow in Montana. It is possible that Wind River dancers perform at other dances, such as the Cree, besides those mentioned here.

Our data for 1966 show that the Northern Utes occupy a crossroads, which is the terminal point for Southern Ute dancers from the south and both the Idaho and Wyoming Shoshones from the north.

TABLE 46

Refined Rate, Sun Dancers per One Hundred of Five Tribal Populations,
Aged Sixteen and Over, Summer 1966

Tribal Affiliation of Dancers	Dancer Rate							
	So. Ute 2–5 July	W.R. Sho. 8–11 July	F.H. Sho. 26–30 July		No. Ute 5–9 Aug.	Ute Mtn. 11–15 Aug.	Male Ref. Rate Tot.	Male & Female Ref. Rate Tots.
			Male	Female				
Southern Ute	5.0	0.0	0.0	0.0	1.1	1.7	7.8	3.8
Ute Mountain Ute	2.0	0.0	0.8	0.8	1.6	5.3	9.7	3.7
Northern Ute	0.7	1.7	0.5	1.1	8.0	1.0	12.0	4.6
Wind River Shoshone	0.0	4.9	1.1	0.5	1.1	0.0	7.1	3.8
Fort Hall Shoshone	0.0	0.6	1.5	1.0	0.7	0.0	2.7	1.8

Refined rates are calculated as follows: [(No. of dancers, male and female) ÷ (Tribal pop., male and female, 16 yrs. +)] × 100. Each tribe is normed on its own base so that large tribes (e.g., Fort Hall Shoshone males 16 and over = 886) and smaller tribes (e.g., Southern Ute males 16 and over = 180) can be compared. The age group totals (i.e., males and females 16 years of age and over) as of summer 1966 are as follows:

	Males	Females
Southern Ute	180	188
Ute Mountain Ute	247	258
Northern Ute	416	440
Wind River Shoshone	547	557
Fort Hall Shoshone	886	923

TABLE 47

Standardization of Four Male Populations on Northern Ute
Male Sun Dancer Rate, 1966

Tribe	Male Pop. 16 Yrs. and Over	No. Ute Male Dancer Rate	Dancers Expected	Dancers Observed	Percentage Difference between Expected and Observed
Southern Ute	180	12	22	14	−37
Ute Mountain Ute	247	12	30	24	−20
Wind River Shoshone	547	12	66	39	−41
Fort Hall Shoshone	886	12	106	24	−78

Refined rate for Northern Ute is (416 expected dancers ÷ 50 observed dancers) × 100 = 12 or 12 male dancers per 100 enrolled Northern Ute males sixteen years of age or older.

Tables 46 and 47 make it possible to compare the Sun dance participation of people from large and small tribes by controlling for the distortion created by population size. These data show that at five Sun dances in 1966, Northern and Ute Mountain Utes participated at a greater rate than the other populations in the study.[3] The rates are very high when we consider that twelve out of every hundred Northern Ute males sixteen years of age or older danced in 1966. The relatively high rates for the Northern and Ute Mountain Utes make sense in that those populations are closely linked by kinship and tradition, and because they are, perhaps, more alienated from, and hostile toward, the dominant white society than the other groups in this study.

3. The rates are calculated for five dances only. They do not account for the participation of the fifty or so men at the first Northern Ute and the second Wind River Shoshone dances of 1966; nor do they account for dancers on the five reservations who were inactive, that is, did not dance, in 1966, but who intended to dance at a future date.

Participation breeds more participation. Furthermore, interreservation participation is constantly preached by elderly Indians, especially shamans, as they extol the collective Indian ethic. The Northern Utes receive the greatest stimulation to participate at the dances of others because of visitor participation at their own dances. This, in turn, creates informal obligations (desires may be a better term) to reciprocate.

Male dancers from all the reservations except Fort Hall participated at relatively high rates in 1966. As was pointed out in part 2, after 1900 the Fort Hall Shoshones and Bannocks, except for the group from Lemhi, never seemed to respond to their oppression with quite the intensity that their Wind River and Ute congeners did. Their population reached nadir sooner and increased at a steadier rate than the other groups, even though their general conditions have been on the whole worse than those of the other Shoshones and Utes. On the other hand, the Fort Hall people have not experienced the many ups and downs in their economy, especially in unearned income, that the other groups have experienced, and perhaps do not, therefore, have the same high expectations. This seemingly passive post-1900 "adaptability" of the Fort Hall people to their oppressive conditions might partially account for the relatively meager number of Fort Hall dancers in 1966. Indeed, their participation is 78 percent less than what we would expect if they participated at the same rate as the Northern Ute. It would take about sixty Fort Hall Shoshone male dancers at the Fort Hall dance and twenty-five Fort Hall dancers at both the Northern Ute and Wind River dances to achieve a rate equal to the Northern Utes'.

Factors other than passivity are involved, however. For one, the Sun dance corrals on all reservations are only large enough to accommodate about a hundred dancers if there is to be any room at all for singers and spectators. There must, of course, be room for singers and spectators because they are critical to the proper performance of the ritual. (In 1967 at Wind River an extension had to be added to the corral owing to an influx of dancers and the subsequent need to accommodate singers.) When we remember that women dance at Bannock Creek, we can see that it is highly unlikely that sixty male Shoshones would enter the dance at all; the crowding would make it impossible, few if any visitors would dance if they expected excessive crowding each year; and—perhaps most important—Shoshone men would be enticed into testing their stamina and competing with Shoshone women throughout the course of the dance, thus performing in a fashion that is not consonant with the Sun dance ideology.

A second reason why the Fort Hall Shoshone rate is low is that the "Eagle" and "Buffalo" lodge Sun dances associated with the Lemhi Shoshones and Bannocks were not performed in 1966. For reasons unknown to me, these two versions of the dance have been sponsored only sporadically over the past ten years. Women cannot dance in these rituals, and so greater male participation is possible when they are staged.

AGE DISTRIBUTION OF SUN DANCERS

Young and old alike participate in the modern versions of all five Sun dances (see table 48). The range of ages, from the late teens to the mid-eighties, and the relatively youthful median ages, circa 30 for hosts and 27 for visitors, demonstrates not only the wide age range to which the dance appeals, but suggests the viability of the Sun dance religion as well.

As is expected from the absolute figures, the greatest variation in host male dancers'

TABLE 48

RANGES, MEDIANS, AVERAGE DEVIATIONS, AND COEFFICIENTS OF RELATIVE
VARIATION IN AGES OF SUN DANCERS, HOSTS, AND VISITORS AT
FIVE SUN DANCES, SUMMER 1966

Hosts and Visitors: Central Tendency and Variation of Ages	Reservations					
	So. Ute 2–5 July	W.R. Sho. 8–11 July	F.H. Sho. 26–30 July		No. Ute 5–9 Aug.	Ute Mtn. 11–15 Aug.
			Males	Females		
Hosts Total	9	27	13	9	34	13
Range	18–58	16–85	17–70	19–60	16–70	18–75
Median	30	29	33	33	28	46
AD_{Md}	11.3	12.1	7.6	10	11.7	15.9
CRV_{Md}	37%	42%	23%	30%	42%	34%
Visitors Total	9	14	14	17	28	7
Range	18–55	17–59	19–50	20–65	19–60	22–55
Median	27	23	22	47	28	33
AD_{Md}	9.7	9.2	7.6	13.2	10.8	10
CRV_{Md}	35%	40%	34%	28%	38%	30%

AD_{Md} = average deviation calculated from the median. CRV_{Md} = coefficient of relative variation or the percentage of variation measured from the median base.

ages occurs among the Wind River Shoshones and the Northern Utes. These groups also have the greatest number of active participants, even though their population bases are smaller than Fort Hall's, which has the least relative variation in the ages of the host dancers. The Southern and Ute Mountain Utes take an intermediate position. It is interesting that the ages of the host dancers range from the late teens to the early or mid-seventies (at least) for all but Southern Ute. Nevertheless, even though no aged men participated in 1966 at Ignacio, I attended dances there in 1961 and 1963 when men well into their eighties performed.

As interesting as the wide range of ages of the host participants is the low median age for host dancers. On the whole about 50 percent of all host dancers are between the ages of 16 and 30, whereas the remaining 50 percent are between 31 to 75. Among the Ute Mountain Utes there is a rather extreme distribution: six dancers are under 30 years of age and the remaining seven are 46 or older. This is an interesting phenomenon, which, in a less extreme fashion, occurs among all of the dancer populations.

Table 49 demonstrates the age frequency distributions of the host male populations and the percentage of dancers from each age interval expected to dance, other things being equal. We see that only 10 percent of the dancers are between the ages of 31 and 46, whereas we expect 28 percent of all dancers to be from this age group. Thus, 40 percent of all dancers are 46 years old or older, and the "young middle-age" group seems to be underrepresented. Among visiting dancers, only 8 percent are between the ages of 31 and 46, whereas we expect 28 percent to be from this age group. Among visitors generally, however, there are more young dancers than old, and the median ages in most instances are markedly lower than the median ages of the host groups.

When Shimkin (1953: 466) observed the Wind River Shoshone dances of 1937 and 1938, he noted that almost no men in their thirties danced. He attempted to explain this phenomenon in part by showing that fathers and sons, brothers, and cross-cousins danced together. He implied that men thirty years of age would be too

TABLE 49

Ages	Tribes						Standardization		
	No. Ute	So. Ute	Ute Mtn. Ute	F.H. Sho.	W.R. Sho.	Total	% of Total Expec.	% of Dancers Observed	Difference between Expec. & Observed
16–30	169	75	197	417	252	1,020.	45	50	+ 5%
31–45	122	49	82	237	147	637	28	10	−18%
46+	125	56	58	232	148	619	27	40	+13%
Totals						2,276	100	100	

young to have sons old enough to participate with them, and, in turn, their own fathers might be too old to dance with them or they might even be deceased.

Kinship relations are still very important in the composition of the dancers. Brothers, sisters, cousins, fathers and sons, mothers and daughters will pledge to support one another at the various dances. This is evident at Southern Ute, where a few families are especially instrumental in staging the dances and performing in them (see Stewart 1960b: 2–3, 1962: 30–32; Southern Ute Council Minutes, 31 August, 1961; Clifton 1961: 1). This is also true at Ute Mountain Ute, Northern Ute, and Wind River Shoshone, where relatives dance together both at home and away, and at Fort Hall Shoshone where female relatives (Western Shoshone as well as Fort Hall Shoshone) are important in staging and performing the dance.

It is my impression, nevertheless, that a paucity of kinship ties with potential dancers does not explain the meager participation of men between the ages of thirty and forty-six. Men in this age group have brothers, sons, cousins, uncles, nephews, fathers, etc., with whom they could dance. A more acceptable reason is that they dance less often than their older and younger cohorts because of economic factors. Men between the ages of thirty and forty-six are more apt to be employed, especially part-time employed, during the summer than are older and younger men. We will explore this idea further on.

NORTHERN UTE DANCERS

A more complete analysis of Northern Ute dancers will be made for three reasons: (1) the Northern Ute dance is the hub of the Sun dance circuit and both receives and donates more dancers than any other reserve in the community; (2) I have more information on Northern Ute dancers than on the dancers from the other reservations; and (3) we can interpret the Northern Ute case in more depth than the other reserves because we have gone into more detail about Northern Ute politics, economics and relations with whites than we have for the other groups (see chapter 5).

AGE DISTRIBUTIONS OF ACTIVE DANCERS

Tables 50 and 51 show the age distribution of fifty-four Northern Ute males who have danced either at Whiterocks or elsewhere from 1963 through 1966. Many others who have danced in earlier years but now participate in the dance only as singers, committeemen, or the like or who have escaped my attention, are not, of course,

TABLE 50

FREQUENCY DISTRIBUTION, ACTIVE NORTHERN UTE MALE SUN DANCERS BY AGE,
UINTAH AND OURAY RESERVATION, UTAH, 1966 (N=54)

Age	Frequency		Age	Frequency
16–20	9		51–55	1
21–25	17		56–60	2
26–30	10		61–65	3
31–35	2		66–70	3
36–40	3		71–75	1
41–45	1		76–80	0
46–50	1		81–85	1

TABLE 51

ACTIVE MALE SUN DANCERS FROM THE UINTAH AND OURAY RESERVATION, UTAH, 1966

	Total Dancers	Uintah Band	White River Band	Uncompaghre Band
N	54	30	7	17
Range in ages	16–85	16–85	17–42	17–70
Mean age	33.7	36	28	31.7
Median age	26	25	26	27
AD_{md}	12.33	15.1	5.42	10.11
CRV_{md}	47%	60%	21%	37%

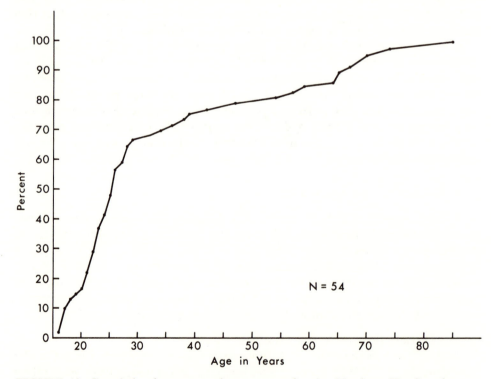

FIGURE 18. Cumulative frequency polygon: ages of active Northern Ute Sun dancers, Uintah and Ouray reservation, Utah, 1966.

included in the table. It is highly probable, nevertheless, that the age distribution demonstrated here is representative of the majority of active Ute Sun dancers.

The youthfulness of the dancers is apparent. Whereas the oldest active dancer is 85, a full 50 percent are between the ages of 16 and 26. The percentage distribution is demonstrated in the ogive curve in figure 18. One clearly cannot argue that the dance has no vitality, or that it is being performed solely by a few aged traditionalists. As for vitality, male dancer participation has been considerable—13 per 100 men 16 years of age and over during the four-year period 1963–66. And as for the recruitment of youths to the dance, young men are disproportionately represented in the dance in relation to the age profile of the total Northern Ute populations and the dancer population.

Table 52 demonstrates the relative age participation. We can see, for instance, that whereas the 21–30 age group contributes 50 percent of the dancer population, the same age group constitutes only 25 percent of the male Northern Ute population over 16. The difference is 25 percent *greater* than expected. The 31–40 year age group, on the other hand, contributes 9 percent of the active dancers and constitutes 20 percent of the adult male population. The observed frequency for this age group is 11 percent *less* than expected. From ages 41 to 50 the proportional representation is still well below the expected. The negative discrepancy is not significant for the 51–60-year age interval, and the men over 61 are represented about proportional to their total in the population. The modest upturn in the 61–70 age group, which contributes 10 percent of the active dancers but constitutes only 7 percent of the adult male population, roughly parallels the lowest end of the distribution; the aged and teenagers dance at rates proportional to their representation in the population. The participation of the 21–60 age group requires explanation because of the over- and underrepresentation that obtains within it.

TABLE 52

RELATIVE PARTICIPATION OF NORTHERN UTE MALES SIXTEEN AND OVER
IN THE MODERN SUN DANCE, 1966

Ages	Standardization			
	Frequency	Percentage of Dancers Expected	Percentage of Dancers Observed	Difference
16–20	72	17	17	0
21–30	105	25	50	+25
31–40	83	20	9	−11
41–50	57	14	4	−10
51–60	43	11	6	− 5
61–70	30	7	10	+ 3
71+	26	6	4	− 2
	416	100	100	

EMPLOYMENT AND ACTIVE DANCERS

The detailed data on Ute employment by age and skills in chapter 5 make it quite clear that Utes have never enjoyed much employment, and we can add here that over the past decade or so proportionately more men in the youthful and aged categories are available to dance because they do not have to lay off work to do so. Fewer men in the 31–60 age group, especially, are able to dance because they cannot afford to leave their jobs—whether temporary or full time. To dance at home, a man must lay off at least the day before the dance begins and prepare to enter the grueling ritual. The dance, when performed in the shorter form, consumes three nights and four days. It is followed by a night of rest and the traditional feast. In order to dance away from home a man must be prepared to spend nine or ten days away from work, counting travel.

Because the youthful population is about as large as the middle group and is larger than the old-age group, because middle-aged men are more apt to be employed, and employment is most apt to occur in the summer, and because cash earnings are extremely scarce and desirable, more younger and old-aged men dance both at home and away than middle-aged men. Middle-aged men who are permanently employed, however, can be and often are granted leaves from their tribal or BIA employers to dance in their home dances, but very often they cannot afford the time to dance away from home. However, they attend their home dances each night and all day on Saturday and Sunday. They usually sing or make offerings to the dancers at these times. The permanently employed may even have saved a few dollars, perhaps enough to allow them to drive to a neighboring dance for at least a full Saturday and part of a Sunday.

The employed Utes, even the few tribal elites, contribute to the welfare of their households, which, along with the nuclear family of procreation, usually include representatives from two other generations of lineal kin if not several collateral relatives and affines (see chapters 4 and 5). The employed man or woman's father or grandfather might request that his grandchildren—that is, the children of the income-earning family head—drive him to a Sun dance sponsored away from home. The people who eventually make the trip may not be dancers, but they have the time and the desire to attend. The family income earner—who usually furnishes the car for the trip—either pays the modest expenses of family groups on trips like these, or makes up the cash difference that is not covered by the elderly person's welfare, IIM funds, or gifts of food and cash received at the Sun dance. Thus, the income earner who cannot attend or participate in the dance is intimately involved with the dance nonetheless.

In sum, a *partial* answer to the question of why men between the ages of 30 and 46 dance less often than younger and older men, at least in the Northern Ute case, lies in economic rather than kinship factors.

Intrareservation Dancer Participation

Economic and tribal political factors also influence intrareservation participation. Table 51 subclassifies the active Northern Ute dancers by reservation band affiliation. The Uintahs and White Rivers are momentarily separated here for analytic purposes. The Uintah band has more participants as well as a wider age range of participants than the other two bands. These differences are of more than passing interest, because 50 percent of all dancers from each band are less than 27 years old. Whereas the Uintah dancers have the youngest median age (25), they also have the oldest mean age (36). Uintahs not only are youthful dancers but they continue to dance later in their lives than dancers from the other bands.

The Uintah and Uncompaghre populations are about equal in size; yet nearly twice as many Uintahs were active dancers during the 1963–66 period than Uncompaghres. Moreover, the joint Uintah–White River population comprises roughly 61 percent of the tribal total, yet contributes 69 percent of the active dancers. The Uncompaghres, with 39 percent of the tribal population, contribute only 31 percent of the active dancers. The differences in the amount of dancer participation between Uncompaghres and Uintah–White Rivers should not be confused with differences in attendance and support of the dance. Uncompaghres dance less but participate at the same high rates as the other Northern Utes. The Uncompaghre dancer rate, which is lower than the other groups, seems linked to their greater employment and political influence. This was particularly noticeable in the 1950s and the early 1960s, when an Uncompaghre—college graduate, progressive, Catholic—gained de facto control of the tribal corporate body (see chapter 5, pp. 151–55).

Just as the discrepancy between legitimate expectations for political influence and economic solvency and the actual conditions for all Utes has increased since 1950, as compared to whites, so has this process gone on within the reservation. The actual differences between Uncompaghres and Uintah–White Rivers is relatively large, and the legitimate expectations of the latter have increased as the differences have increased. More Uintahs, perhaps the White Rivers less so, have turned to, and persisted in, dancing the Sun dance than have their Uncompaghre counterparts. It is important to recall that the True Ute uprising was primarily a Uintah–White River undertaking and that some of the leaders of this uprising were Sun dance chiefs.

Female Participation

Among the Northern Utes, as among the Colorado Utes and Wind River Shoshones, very few women dance. Six active Northern Ute female dancers are known to me. There are several others who have danced in the past and who danced in 1967, but who did not do so from 1963 to 1966. The youngest female dancer in my survey is thirty-three and the oldest is sixty-five. The explanation the Utes offer for the paucity of women dancers is that very few women receive recurrent dreams instructing them to dance. Those who do, are practically always instructed to become shamans also. The conflicts posed by female participation have been assessed above. It is important to note here that women can and do become shamans in ways other than dancing—more often by serving apprenticeships to established shamans or through peyotism. These are the routes that men prefer the women to take.

Mixed-Blood Participants

Mixed-bloods, that is, people with less than 50 percent Northern Ute blood who have been legally separated from the tribe since 1954, are allowed to participate in the dance. In the 1963–66 period, ten mixed-blood men between the ages of 19 and 57 danced at one or another Ute or Shoshone Sun dance. Nine of the ten men are under 30 years of age, and the median age for these dancers is 22, four years less than the total Northern Ute male Sun dancer median.

The bitter fight between fullbloods and mixed-bloods over tribal politics, particularly over the expenditure of tribal funds during the 1930s and 1940s, which was intensified by the first land claims judgment in 1950 and culminated in the political split of 1954, left many of the older generations on both sides at odds with one another. As a partial consequence, the only active mixed-blood dancer over 30 years of age does not dance at Northern Ute dances, although he attends them. His fullblood sons (his wife is a fullblood) and their mixed-blood friends dance at Northern Ute, however.

There has been a rapprochement between many young fullbloods and mixed-bloods, and the latter join in the dances with self-assurance. But they are not encouraged to dance by all fullbloods, nor do the spectators pamper them and cater to their needs as they do for the fullblood dancers.

10   *Participation of Nondancers in the Ritual*

There is no doubt that the Sun dance ritual is actively participated in by nondancers except for the few Anglos and Mexicans who attend. Indeed, the dance is as much performed for and by nondancers as for and by dancers. Although dancers seek personal power, they also dance for the general welfare of the community, and it is the community that watches and encourages them. In the process dancers are accorded status and prestige (generating some self-esteem as a result) from those people who encourage them. In turn, those who support and encourage the dancers also gain some status and prestige (again generating some self-esteem) from one another and from the dancers.

In 1966 spectators at all five dances repeatedly said that the ritual was performed for the community's welfare. No one said it exactly this way, but that is not important. What is important is that the communitarian ends of the religion and the Indian collective ethic were stressed. Usually the Shoshones and Utes said something like the following: "The Sun dance is for the good of everybody"; or "The Sun dance makes it so that the Indian people will be happy"; or "It is done so that everybody will have what they need, good health and things like that." Just as the dancers perform so that all nondancers, all invalids, the entire Indian community will be well and happy, so do nondancers visit the corral, sing, make offerings to the dancers, help in the construction of the corral, etc., in order to help all the dancers acquire the power they seek, and to make the community whole and healthy. Furthermore, just as dancers pursue individual ends such as to make themselves well and healthy, to help specific ailing relatives, to pacify specific bereaved Indians, and to propitiate specific descendents, so do nondancers pursue the same broad individual ends. The nondancer earns power for himself and others if he lends strong support and encouragement, if he nourishes the dancers in their quests for power.

Spectators, like dancers, have other reasons for attending the Sun dance and participating in the religion. The singer with a good strong voice, the shaman who lauds Indian morality and the integrity of Indian kinship while castigating the evils of white society, and the woman who makes lavish offerings of cool willows, cigarettes, and other gifts, to name a few types of nondancer participants, gain status and prestige in the Indian community and earn a measure of self-esteem as an effect of high status and prestige within the Indian community.

The many reasons and intentions for attending the dance that are not oriented towards religious, health, or status ends will be discussed in the following chapter on the interreservation Sun dance community and the extrareligious and ritual features that attend the dances.

FORMS OF NONDANCER PARTICIPATION

Utes and Shoshones think about the Sun dance throughout the year. Preparation for the dances begins in the winter and continues until each dance begins. Men and women jointly participate in most of the preparation, although with some differences in their roles.

SINGING

In the previous winter, as early as Thanksgiving on the Ute reserves and closer to February on the Shoshone reserves, men and women assemble at the homes of respected chiefs, members of the Sun dance committees, or simply good singers, and practice the Sun dance songs they will sing during the forthcoming cycle. The sessions during the winter months occur no more than once a week, but, about the time of the Ute Bear dances in May, sessions on all reservations increase in frequency as well as in number of participants.

Singing the complex rhythms and often tongue-twisting canonical lines requires considerable practice, and great emphasis is placed on the role of the music in the dance. Good singing, it is believed, "calls out" the power—makes "it" take notice that singers join with dancers in the quest for power and that singers, like dancers, have respect for power. Poor singers, as a matter of fact, often practice Sun dance songs at home, out of earshot of their critical kin and neighbors. When they feel they have mastered a few songs, they will join a practice session around the drum. Their stern friends will rap them on the hand with a drum stick or openly ridicule them when a song is completed if they have sung badly and have been a drag on the team. Some people, on the basis of three or four embarrassing experiences at these sessions, refuse to practice any more.

The male singers form teams of ten to twenty members to develop coordination. The men lead the singing; they are the only ones to sit around the drum. The teams on the Northern Ute and the Shoshone reserves are organized, by and large, on the basis of their intrareservation communities. At Northern Ute, for instance, singers from Whiterocks and Indian Bench will get together, as will groups from Randlett, from Ouray, and from other local communities (see chapter 5). When the Northern Ute dances are held, male teams from the various communities, or even band factions (Uncompaghres sing together, Uintahs and White Rivers sing together) are prepared to perform. At other reservations, depending on how many visit from Northern Ute, singers from the several Northern Ute communities (cross-cutting the band factions) will either join together or maintain their distinct teams. If Northern Ute singers join singers from other reservations, it is more often with Utes (Southern or Ute Mountain) than with Shoshones. Shoshones, too, are more apt to join with other Shoshones than with Utes. Any combination of singers, however, can and does occur. Usually only the home reserve teams are composed solely of local singers. Linguistically and culturally the Ute groups are closer to one another than to the Shoshones, and vice versa. Furthermore, each reserve has its own singing style replete with a few songs recognized as its own. For these reasons, Indians prefer to sing with members from their own reservation or, at least, with close linguistic kin. The ritual importance of good singing should not be underestimated.

Special songs are sung at the sunrise service, during the day sessions, and during evening sessions. The singing teams from the various communities and reservations prearrange the approximate times that they will relieve one another. At these change periods the incoming team sometimes creates a delay. If a team does not have a sufficient number of singers in the corral to take over, spectators are recruited either to fill out the depleted team or to organize a makeshift team. Although this is a traditional practice, the singers seem to enjoy being late to relieve the overworked team, and it also seems that the overworked team enjoys singing longer than the agreed-upon period.

Singers may perform for as long as two hours, become fatigued, look for replacements, call for help, and, if help does not come, keep right on singing. They feel that if they endure a little longer, they too will be contributing to the success of the dance, and the spirits and the dancers, not to mention the spectators, will appreciate their heroic efforts—and they are spartan indeed. When they quit, the committee officials begin to call the names of good singers. If those who are called do not respond immediately, they are admonished in Ute or Shoshone to help out. They are told, "Come on and sing, help these boys out, help all of us get the power. Come on, they're going now, they're going." If the lull is longer than five or six minutes, the Sun dance chief will walk to the center pole and demand that men sing. He might say, "This is for all of us. Get out here, sing for us, sing for all of us." Slowly the men gather around the drum and begin to sing.

During the morning and afternoon, women pour into the corral to aid the dancers with their singing. Some are moved to sing because of sadness, and they cry out for dead husbands or relatives who once danced and who might, they believe, be lurking around the corral. The good intentions of the bereaved toward the deceased is registered in this act. Others sing to lend encouragement to the dancers and to help them acquire power. While the women sit and sing, they constantly wave handfuls of willows to the rhythm of the drum. Women use willows to fan themselves, but, most important from the Ute point of view, they use willows to attract power to themselves and to the dancers. Just as the willows in the crotch of the center pole give water to the pole and to Buffalo or whatever else may be attached in its stead, so the women think that their willows will bring them power to sing well, power so that their throats will stay moist, cool-wet power so that they can endure the hot-dry power and encourage the dancers, and power for their own good health and happiness.

CORRAL CONSTRUCTION

We know that, at each reserve, nondancers join with dancers under the auspices of the chief and his committee to erect the Sun dance lodge. Women participate only at Fort Hall. Men dig the holes for the center pole and the twelve side posts following the instructions of the chief. The work goes fast and is salted with good humor as well as prayers. Nondancers make a special effort to have the corral finished several hours before the dance is scheduled to begin, so that the chief and his dancers will be able to rest.

On rocky ground, as at Wind River, the work is extremely arduous, and the help given by nondancers is well appreciated. At one of the dances in 1966 a chief made an error in his calculation of the circumference of the corral. As a consequence, twenty-four rather than twelve post holes were dug, and at the conclusion most of the helpers walked away with blistered and bloodied hands. It is my impression from the comments of the helpers (I helped erect the corral) that their own contribution was more significant as a result of their double work.

GIFTS AND SUPPORT OF THE DANCERS

Women will often make garments for their sons, husbands, brothers, or close friends to wear in the dance. Sometimes these articles come as a surprise just before a man or woman enters a dance. At other times such items are requested by the prospective dancers. Either way, women spend many hours making beaded pendants, sequined aprons, and other apparel for the dancers. If the woman can afford it, she will buy the materials herself, and if she cannot, her close relatives, even the prospective dancer, will help pay for the materials.

These acts of giving, especially when the gift is used in the performance of the dance, link the giver to the performance and "help" the dancer in his quest. They can also be tokens of thanks if the dancer is praying for the health of the donor or someone close to the donor.

Gifts are given at other times. For instance, throughout the rest periods of each day's dancing sessions, men and women carry neatly bundled packages of willows, cool grass, and cottonwood poplar leaves into the lodge. They approach the center pole but do not enter the dance area. They call out the name of a favorite dancer, who may be a relative or merely a well-liked shaman, and give him the package. The dancer unties the bundle and holds the greens to his chest and body, ritually and literally cooling himself. If a dancer is especially popular, he will receive many such offerings, enough in fact to make a bed of them and pass others on to his less popular cohorts.

Dancers also receive cigarettes, particularly mentholated cigarettes, from the spectators. Dancers call them "Sun dance" cigarettes. The name is appropriate because, as the Indians say, these hot cigarettes are cooling and soothing.

The gift of cigarettes does not require a great expenditure of effort on the part of the donor, but it does require an expenditure of cash, which is scarce on reservations. The willows and grass, on the other hand, require some work to collect and prepare. Families will walk or drive to a nearby stream (at Fort Hall the distance is several miles) and cut branches from willows and poplars. It is thought that stream-fed vegetation is cooler and wetter; so it is preferred. Willow, of course, has ritual significance as the channel for power, and this enhances its desirability, but all green things have life, hence cool-wet power. These bundles, when tied, often decorated with flowers, are presented with some fanfare. The donors are usually dressed up in their best clothes and are obviously making an all-out effort to look good.

As the dance progresses, Utes, but not necessarily Shoshones, watch the musicians to make sure that they are properly accompanying the dancing. They keep a close watch on the dancers, and if someone is in the middle of the sacred dance area when the music stops, they will rebuke the singers and admonish them to keep singing or to watch the dancers. Elderly people (especially members of the Sun dance committees, ex-dancers, or dancers who are not currently participating) watch and even admonish the dancers to make sure they do not rest (liberally interpreted by the "watchers") when they should be dancing. In return, dancers will often begin dancing again, but they are just as often provoked to respond negatively, telling their overzealous advisors to "get in here and show us how." This usually brings a good laugh. Aside from the levity these admonitions can create, the exchanges between non-dancers and dancers, and non-dancers and singers show that many people who are neither dancers nor singers consider themselves integral to the ritual.

Aside from the admonitions and the banter, there is a more tender concern for the ritual and the dancers that is expressed throughout the dance. The spectators are always concerned about the novice dancers. Moreover, even Shoshones and Utes who have not attended a dance session will always ask those who have whether "everybody made it." The question means, Did any dancer collapse who should not have collapsed? In chapter 7 we saw that the incautious dancer can be "knocked down" for the wrong reasons. It is highly doubtful that any Shoshone or Ute *wants* a novice or an overenergetic dancer, even a dancer who has broken the rules of conduct he is expected to observe and enters the dance drunk, to be "knocked down" by an angered power. When a dancer who should not fall down does so, the spectators are alarmed and wish him well. The threat which is posed by the hot-dry force for the individual is also posed for the members of the community. It shows that those who do not observe the ritual prescriptions and proscriptions, who do not act with measured restraint, can pose problems for all. If the dancer is someone working his way out of an alcoholic hangover, the spectators tell one another, "That's what happens to a person who flouts the rules that the 'old people' have taught. He is making it bad for everyone." There is, then, a general solicitude for the health and welfare of each dancer, especially the young ones, for the nondancers want a good dance for *everyone*. Dances have been "spoiled" through rain, or because no one receives a vision when novices or drunks or adherents with delirium tremens have broken too many proscriptions.

The spectators make their concerns for the ritual and the purposes of all concerned known from the first night. They need not participate in the singing or the lodge construction, or even in making gifts to the dancers. Their presence alone is sufficient to help the cause. For instance, the first night at each dance is an important time to show the dancers that they are supported. We have seen that on the first nights of the 1966 dances 700 persons were on the grounds at Southern Ute, 1,300 at Northern Ute, etc. When the dancers enter the corral, as many as 350 spectators crowd in and around the corral, from 100 at Southern Ute to 350 at Northern Ute. The sponsors and relatives bring the dancers' bed rolls and suit cases into the lodge, and, as the excitement subsides somewhat, the dance begins.

Throughout the night and during the subsequent dance sessions the average spectator, along with the corral police, keep guard so that dogs do not enter the dance corral, children do not bring soda pop, food, or gum into the corral, people do not enter the sacred dance area with their shoes on, drunks do not enter the corral and disrupt the proceedings, and so forth.

Dogs are not brought to the Sun dance grounds because they can be disruptive. Moreover, an unknown dog is feared, at least by the Utes, because dogs are suspected of being *pakuwic*, or Navajo werewolves. They can bring disease and death according to Utes. Soda pop, food, and gum are kept out of sight of the dancers so that they will not crave them. Dancers will shout at children or whites if they wander in with food and drink, but adult Indian spectators try to keep these things out of the corral so that dancers will not have to shout, and it is very rare for anyone to take food or drink near the corral. Dancers claim that they can smell food from every camp fire on the grounds, especially during the mornings. They also claim that they can smell menstruating women.

During the course of a dance the dancers will tease one another about the foods they smell, "Hey——, that fried bread (*uvana*) and bacon (*kacini*) would really taste good now. I'll bet you really want some." They also tease one another about their last drink of water or last meal. This teasing is acceptable so long as those involved are dancers, but no dancer wants to be taunted by an inconsiderate spectator. As a matter of fact, with a little prodding all Utes and Shoshones will talk about the in-humanity of the Cree dances, where spectators bring lunches into the corral to taunt the dancers. Shoshones and Utes think that this action is in keeping with the Cree dance generally. They scoff at the Cree for dancing in place (they do not leave their stalls) and for drinking water during the course of the dance. (I cannot confirm these accounts as I have not attended a Cree dance.)

Spectators and tribal police also patrol the dance corral in the early morning. At some dances, especially four-day dances, the singers also retire when dancers become fatigued, and all bed down for the night. Packs of children are frequently roaming the camp grounds at these wee hours (see the following chapter) and tend to gather around the drum. They soon begin beating the drum and singing. When this is carried too far—the adults will tolerate some of this "practice"—a few men and women will chase the children away from the drum so that the dancers can rest. On the second and third nights of the dance, the problem does not arise because the singing and drum-ming by the adult singing teams usually continues through the night.

In the early mornings following the sunrise ceremonies, dancers rest outside the dance corral. At these times, as we have seen, several groups of two or three women—variously a dancer's mother, sisters, wife, or some other relatives or friends—will carry wet wash cloths, tooth brushes, other toiletries, and changes of ritual apparel and attend to the needs of the dancers. Every dancer is attended by some women. Dancers from a distant reserve may receive as much attention as those from the sponsoring reserve, because visiting dancers usually have kin or affines residing on the reservation they visit, though sometime they are attended by women who have traveled from their own reserve. The local women are pleased to provide this kindness and to make this contribution to the success of the ritual, and they make a special point of being at the corral immediately after the sunrise ceremony.

On the second morning of each dance, sandwiched between the sunrise ceremony and the next dancing session, the dancers' friends or sponsors bring in the small trees that they have cut early that morning of the previous evening. The men will strip the bark and limbs from the saplings and paint them up to about five feet from the ground. Stalls are made from the saplings for each dancer (or pair of dancers), and then the men shovel and rake the dance paths to the center pole free of rocks and ruts. If a dancer from a foreign reserve has no one to provide these services, someone from the host reservation, perhaps a member of the Sun dance committee, will do it for him. Each of the services and gifts makes the spectator who provides them an active participant in the ritual.

ORATIONS AND CASTIGATIONS

Singers, former Sun dance chiefs, renowned shamans, indeed, any of a number of prominent Utes and Shoshones make orations to the dancers and to everyone else in the corral throughout the course of each dance. Most of the orations are given during the afternoon dancing sessions, though they are sometimes given at night sessions, and, on the whole, more orations occur on the last day than on the first day or second day of the dance.

The speeches offered by nondancers serve an important end. The messages vary somewhat, but essentially they call for (1) increased and more spirited singing, (2) increased and more spirited dancing, and (3) more thinking about the *purpose* and *meaning* of the dance, which includes castigation of white society and revering Indian ways. There is no doubt that the speech makers intend to focus the attention of all participants and spectators on their common purpose of acquiring power to insure a healthy, moral community. They exhort everyone to work a little harder so that their expectations will be met.

During the afternoon sessions a respected singer might stand up at the drum; or the gate keeper, fire tender, or some respected shaman might walk up to the east side of the center pole and tell the dancers that they must not loaf but must be vigorous in their pursuit of power. They must challenge Buffalo, or the eagle, or the center pole itself if no other symbolic "power channel" is fastened to it, in order to show the power that the dancers respect but do not fear. This must be done not only for the dancers but for the good of all. "After all," the orators say, "that's what you're in there for."

If dancers are remiss or show little respect for power, the repercussions will be felt throughout the Indian community. For instance, at one dance in 1966 a venerated Ute leader told the dancers that their "half-hearted" dancing had angered the power and caused it to create bad weather (cool air with overcast skies). The threat of rain was present, and rain literally allows men to quench their thirst before they are "dried out," thus keeping them from their goal of acquiring power and helping themselves and the community. It is stressed that the community needs help, and this can be had only if spiritual water is earned. Rain following the dance, however, is interpreted as the contribution of a successful dance to all living things, but especially to the living things that sacrificed themselves for the success of the dance.

It is not only dancers who are implored to dance. Singers, too, are the targets of speeches that explain why they must sing better and louder so that the power will hear and recognize the sincerity of all concerned—dancers, singers, Sun dance committee, and spectators. Orations of this nature do not have to be given very often, except at dances where the singing teams are small, few, and overworked. The orations prod singers into action, and they will often continue to sing during a speech. When this happens, the singing is very loud and spirited. This encourages dancers to dance more vigorously, and inspires other would-be orators to queue up and wait their turn to orate. These highly infectious speeches are usually given on the third day, although every session includes at least one speech.

Distinction between Whites and Indians

The speeches (particularly at Ute dances) stress Indian morality, the necessity of maintaining the integrity of Indian kinship, the obligations of Indians to each other, and the basic immorality of white ways. Indians are urged to remember the teachings of the "old people" who took care of the very young, and the youthful who take care of the very old. They are reminded that the "old people" resolved community problems amicably and drew the bands together to discuss their problems. In these appeals to the wisdom and moral correctness of the "Indian way" (which is constantly referred to but rarely spelled out in great detail), listeners are reminded of the better days in the past—days which can be realized again in the future if, and only if, the teachings of the "old people" are followed. The call to return to the "Indian way" takes on significance when its promise is contrasted to the degraded life that has been foisted upon Indians by whites. In castigating whites for their insensitivity to Indian ways, for the introduction of alcohol, and for their "bad hearts," the Indian orators focus on the source of many Indian problems. They call on Utes and Shoshones to redeem themselves and to help the Indian community by avoiding the evils of white ways. Yet these speech makers also recognize the awesome power possessed by whites, emphasizing that what is good for whites is not necessarily good for Indians.

The speeches often call for keeping the family together as a domestic, co-residential unit, and sharing with the wider network of kin and friends (whites stress the nuclear family); following the advice of the old and wise leaders (whites emphasize legal-rational leaders or religious doctrines, etc., rather than the teachings of venerated elders); remembering that power comes to him who thirsts and sacrifices (whites consume and indulge rather than sacrificing or thirsting); and for keeping in contact with Indian brothers from other reservations who have attended the ritual with the intention of supporting them in return. Indians are admonished to marry Indians and to maintain the integrity of Indian blood; yet at one reservation in 1966 a man requested that everyone assembled accept a Negro child who had been adopted by a member of the tribe. The collective Indian ethic was being invoked in this extreme case, but here the distinction was between white and nonwhite rather than Indian and non-Indian. Whatever the case, charitableness toward the individual and the needy is stressed, for through it comes strength.

Orations of the sort just described are usually much longer than those that are directed only at dancers or only at singers. They are often given after the person who wants to make a speech has called for a lull in the activities and this has been approved by the Sun dance chief. The orations are always given in Ute or Shoshone languages, and sometimes bits of them are translated into English (the "white" language) by the gate keeper, the fire tender or some other dance functionary. This is a simple service to those Utes who do not speak Shoshone, for example, or visiting Kiowa, Cheyenne, Crow, etc., who do not speak Ute. (See chapter 11 on interreserve participation.)

One need not be from the host reservation in order to give a speech. An old Ute Mountain Ute leader and a Northern Ute female Sun dancer gave speeches at every dance in 1966, and Shoshones spoke at their own and others' dances. The evidence is solid for interreservation participation. Goals are explicated at each dance, and the explications are almost identical from dance to dance. There is, again, reason to believe that speeches made by aliens are somewhat better received than those made by locals. (That is not true for the Ute Mountain leader mentioned earlier.) This prestige phenomenon is similar to that among the dancers, where many are considered more important and powerful, even more authoritative, away from home.

Table 53 gives an idea of the types of speeches that were made during the 1966 dances. Some speeches stress the power quest, some stress broad individualism, some

TABLE 53

Sun Dance Orations, Five Ute Sun Dances, 1966

Days of Dance	Speeches Made by	Subject of Speeches
First (11:00 A.M.–4:00 P.M.)		
Southern Ute	Influential Ute Mountain leader, singer, gatekeeper, shamans	Exhort men to dance and singers to sing
Ute Mountain Ute	Influential local leaders, gatekeeper, shamans	Exhort men to dance and singers to sing
Northern Ute	Influential local leaders, gatekeeper, shamans	Exhort men to dance and singers to sing. Also exhort dancers to challenge bison.
Fort Hall	Local shamans, gatekeeper	Exhort men to dance and women spectators to sing, not watch
Wind River	Local shamans, gatekeeper	Exhort men to dance
Second (11:00 A.M.–4:00 P.M.)		
Southern Ute	Local leaders, three influential Ute Mountain Ute shamans	Exhort men to dance, singers to sing. Attribute cold and wet weather to half-hearted interest in dance
Ute Mountain Ute	Local leaders, gatekeeper	Exhort men to dance
Northern Ute	Influential local singer, gatekeeper, firetender	Exhort men to dance
Fort Hall	Local crier chief, committeemen, Ute Mtn. leader	Exhort men and women to dance
Wind River	Local gatekeeper, No. Ute shaman	Exhort men to dance
Third or last (10:00 A.M.–Termination)		
Southern Ute	Local gatekeeper, firetender, shamans; Ute Mtn. shamans; No. Ute male and female shamans	Exhort men to dance and singers to sing. Speeches on Indian kinship, integrity and morality. Rail against white ways and Indian defilement of Indian ways
Ute Mountain Ute	Influential local leaders, committeemen, two So. Ute religious leaders, two No. Ute females and one No. Ute male shaman	"
Northern Ute	Local gatekeeper, firetender, ex-chiefs, influential leaders, female shamans; So. Ute, Ute Mtn Ute and Wind River Shoshone religious leaders	" Especially stressed remembering the virtue of the Indian family life and the need for group solidarity
Fort Hall	Gatekeeper, firetender, other committeemen; No. Ute male and female shamans, Fort Hall shamans, Ute Mtn Ute religious leader	" Less emphasis on Indian integrity and white immorality than at Ute dances
Wind River	None	Gave way to family shamanizing

stress the collective Indian ethic, and some combine these subjects. Whereas Ute Mountain Ute, Fort Hall Shoshone, and Northern Ute oration patterns were very similar to one another, orations at Wind River ceased on the third day while shaman-izing of families and parts of families took the spotlight. At Southern Ute there was a more general exhortation for singers to come forth and sing—because there were fewer singers—than at any other dance. The lack of speeches at Wind River on the last day of the dance complements the peaking of spectator interest and general dance activity that occurs on the previous day. In table 53 "religious leaders" and "shamans" refer to the same roles and are used interchangeably, whereas "committeemen" in-clude gate keeper, fire tender, crier, etc.

SHAMANIZING

From the first day on at the 1966 Wind River dance, nondancers were shamanized by the local dance chief and his guest chief from Northern Ute, as well as by other leading dancers—many of them from alien reservations. The shamanizing of non-dancers seems to have a somewhat more prominent role at Wind River than at the other dances, where it does not begin until the penultimate day. Shamanizing on the final day of the Wind River dance leaves no time for orations.

Those who are shamanized are usually well scrubbed and impeccably dressed. They have made extra efforts to look good for the sake of their spectator friends and rela-tives, for the Sun dancers, for their self-esteem, and in order to show respect to the power whose help is sought. Some ailing people enter on crutches, some are carried in on chairs, some are carried in on litters, and the blind are led in.

The person seeking help presents himself or herself to the gate keeper (or to some other committeeman.) The first person in whose care the sufferer is put serves as the first diagnostician, inquiring about the nature of the illness and ascertaining whose shamanistic services are desired. The client is then taken to the center pole as the dance set ends, and the committeeman relays his preliminary diagnosis to the dancer who has been requested to effect a cure. At this time all of the dancers are expected to help the shaman whose services have been requested. They stand in the front of their stalls, and as the singers play and sing they blow their whistles. This helps the Indian doctor channel his power to the invalid or, as at Wind River, to the invalid as well as the invalid's kin, who enter the corral with the sufferer. During the treat-ments the spectators in the corral speculate about the kinds of illnesses being ad-ministered to, and say "good" words as they watch the ritual incantations.

It is the special powers of the dancers, as opposed to the skills of white physicians, which adds an important dimension of meaning to the dance and helps validate and perpetuate the ritual. We have made it clear that a basic intention of dancers and spectators is to receive supernatural power which will cure the ailing and allow a functionary to effect cures. Stories about how dancers have effected cures unattainable by white doctors, much to the latters' puzzlement, are legion at Sun dance time. Many Utes and Shoshones are ill periodically and remain ill after visiting Public Health Service doctors and other white physicians. After undergoing Sun dance treat-ments, however, they get better. The etiologies of their problems are not always clear (see chapter 7), but there is little reason to doubt that the cures are effected by faith in the shaman's power, in the presence of power at the dance, and in the good will of the nondancers, who expect cures to be forthcoming for the invalids. The superiority of Indian power over white power to solve Indian problems is a very important aspect of Sun dance belief, and the effects of Indian power have wide repercussions in validating the religion. The power demonstrates that Indians *can* solve their ultimate problems (the problems of sickness, of life and death, of Indian community welfare), even to the amazement of whites.

The medico-religious intention for performing the dance requires invalids. Invalids, as we learned in chapter 4, are not scarce on the Ute and Shoshone reserves. Yet not all invalids get counted in the public health statistics. Aside from those who do not go to agency doctors for diagnosis and treatment, it is my impression that as many Shoshones and Utes are suffering from functionally (psychologically) induced ailments as from organically induced ones (see chapter 7). There are, for instance, many more sufferers from, and many more cures for, "fever" than from anything else. This general malaise is symptomatic of a deprived, depressed, and oppressed people.

Shamanizing for general spiritual aid on behalf of families and segments of families far outstrips all other forms of shamanizing at Wind River and has done so for several years. Only at Wind River, however, has this group-oriented shamanizing of nondancers really caught hold.

Final Blessings at Dance's End: Individual and Group Requests

Venerated shamans (male or female) are chosen at the termination of each dance to offer blessings to the dancers who have just completed the dance. The shamans who are chosen by the dancers can be fellow dancers or they can be someone outside the dancing area. Often they are not persons from the home reserve. This is another significant way in which nondancers participate in the Sun dance and the collective interreserve bonds are marked. The final blessings which the dancers receive are considered vital. A powerful and renowned shaman is called on to "cement in" the dancer's new power so that the dancer can leave the dance corral without fear of losing control of that power. It takes a wise hand to prepare the dancer for this control. After the final blessing is administered, the client pays the shaman for the services rendered.

At the Ute and Fort Hall Shoshone dances, sometimes immediately before the last dance song but always continuing after it, each dancer chooses a shaman to administer his final blessing. The treatment the client receives is rather similar to the general fanning treatment for "fever." Shamans often sprinkle some dirt from the center pole on an eagle wing fan and then press the contents on the dancer's head. They then hold the fan firmly on the dancer's head with their other hand and pull the fan out under considerable pressure. Final blessings from shamans may take as long as ten minutes, at the end of which time each shaman is given a "gift" (payment) for his services.[1] The "gift" given by most Ute dancers is, in order of popularity, a Navajo blanket, Navajo jewelry, Ute headwork, doeskins, yard goods, or money. The emphasis on "Indian" goods is apparent. At Fort Hall, the dancers most often offer cash in small amounts (payments are seldom over five dollars) or buckskins.

At Wind River in 1966 only four men (other than some Northern Utes), requested and received individual final blessings, and each paid in cash. Another minor difference

1. The payment or prestation problem is discussed in the following chapter.

at Wind River was the fact that a Northern Ute mixed-blood administered all of the individual blessings. Wind River was also aberrant in that women were not chosen to give final blessings.

It is interesting that, at Fort Hall, women dancers chose male shamans and male dancers often chose female shamans to administer the final blessings. At Northern Ute two local women, a local man, a Ute Mountain Ute religious and political leader, and a Wind River religious leader were called upon to give blessings. The dancers at Ute Mountain Ute selected a local man and woman as well as a Northern Ute dance chief to administer their final blessings. At Southern Ute eight shamans were called on to administer final blessings to the eighteen dancers. The dancer/shaman ratio was lower here than anywhere else. Of the nondancer shamans, two were locals, one was a Northern Ute who was popular at the other Ute dances as well as at Fort Hall, and one was a Ute Mountain Ute religious and political leader who was in demand everywhere. The last two men gave the most blessings. At Fort Hall the Ute Mountain Ute leader was again called upon, as was the Southern Ute Sun dance chief and the major Wind River Sun dance chief. The bulk of the shamanizing, except for these three most popular men, was carried out by powerful dancers.

The Wind River dance stands out here too. According to Voget (1953: 495), in 1947 the final blessings that used to be given just before termination of the dance were given to groups of men throughout the afternoon. No final individual blessings were given in that year. At present we know that only a few individual blessings are given. The current group shamanizing at Wind River, though stressed to the near exclusion of individual blessings, is not much different from the group shamanizing that occurs throughout many Southern Ute and Northern Ute dances. The number of times the dancers are shamanized as a group in the course of a Northern or Southern Ute dance varies with the dance chief and perhaps with his own dream about the particular dance in question. Often the dancers are administered to at the end of each afternoon's dancing session and at each sunrise ceremony by one Southern Ute and one Northern Ute chief. This is each chief's prerogative and, to my knowledge, not requested by the dancers.

At Wind River in 1966 the Northern Ute mixed-blood (guest chief) offered, on his own volition, several group blessings in the course of the ritual to all dancers (consonant with the practices of the Ute chiefs mentioned above). On the last day, on the other hand, he was *requested* to bless a group of ten dancers at one point in the late afternoon. A Wind River Shoshone dancer, although not the chief, was requested to bless twenty dancers just before the termination of the dance. Although the final blessing ritual has been modified at Wind River to emphasize groups (the collective ethic) rather than individuals, there is evidence of some straining toward individual recognition at Wind River, since some men still request individual blessings. As long as visitors from other Shoshone and Ute reservations attend the Wind River dances, it is probable that the individual blessings will continue.

SACRED WATER RITUAL

The sacred water ritual follows the termination of the blessings and dancing. The water chiefs of the Sun dance committees fill two ten-gallon containers with water and white clay. They take them to the dance, where they are prayed over by the water chief or the gate keeper. The first drink of water is offered either to the center pole or to the person who said the prayer (see chapter 6). After the dancers have taken their drinks and filed out of the lodge, the spectators queue up in front of the center pole to get a taste of the bitter drink. The bitterness reminds them that those who thirst shall be blessed. Nondancers will stay near the corral as long as it takes to get a drink of the water—sometimes forty minutes to an hour.

Table 54 tabulates the general similarities and differences in the nondancer participation at each dance. The evidence shows that the nondancers on each reserve participate in about the same way in corral construction, offering gifts and encouragement to the dancers, preparing the dancers' stalls, and partaking of the ritual water. Differences occur in shamanizing, in the way final blessings are administered to dancers, and in the attention that nondancers pay to the proper conduct of the ritual.

TABLE 54

PARTICIPATION OF NONDANCERS AT FIVE SUN DANCES, 1966

Forms of Nondancer Participation	So. Ute	Ute Mtn.	No. Ute	Ft. Hall	Wind Riv.
Keep watchful eye on proceedings and shout instructions if dancers or singers violate proscriptions	+	+	+	−	−
Invalids pay for shamanizing in "Indian" goods rather than cash	+	+	+	−	−
Prominent in administering final blessings to dancers	+	+	+	+	−
Invalids shamanized by dancers	+	+	+	+	+
Help in the ritual construction of the corral	+	+	+	+	+
Offer gifts and encouragement to the dancers	+	+	+	+	+
Prepare dancers' stalls in the dance corral	+	+	+	+	+
Partake of the sacred water	+	+	+	+	+
Singing and drumming	+	+	+	+	+
Committee controls fire, gate, water, etc.	+	+	+	+	+
Orations to instruct and admonish dancers, singers and spectators	+	+	+	+	+
Orations to explain meaning and goals of dance, emphasize Indian integrity, kinship, morality, castigate whites	+	+	+	+	+
Shamans paid primarily in cash for giving final blessings to dancers	−	−	−	+	+
Families and family segments shamanized by dancers	−	−	−	−	+
Types		1		2	3

The Interreservation Sun Dance Community

The Shoshone-Ute interreservation Sun dance community has been maintained for about seventy years. It is this Indian community that Shoshone and Ute elders extol as the ultimate group of people to whom Indians are obligated and within which each person should work and sacrifice in order to maintain general well-being. Whereas interreserve cooperation and sharing at the tribal level is actually minimal in that each reserve is a separate corporate body pursuing its own ends, there is considerable sharing, visiting, and cooperation among Shoshone and Ute individuals and families. Furthermore, intermarriages and joint participation at rituals, basketball tournaments, and other recreation activities serve to bring people from several reserves together. These occasions also provide forums in which the collective ethic (which should direct Indian life) is preached.

Through participation in the interreserve community, the circle of Indian friends and adherents is widened, and support and approval are won from more quarters than one's home reserve (or maintained in areas beyond one's home reserve). By attending and helping with one another's dances, high status and prestige can be achieved by individuals, and, as an effect, self-esteem and esteem in the interreservation community can be maintained. Blending the religious and the social, Shoshones and Utes say philosophically that Sun dances are held, not only for the acquisition of power and the good health of all, but for the good will they engender and the Indian identity they support and nourish. A middle-aged Northern Ute man at one of the dances in 1963 said: "We sing for the good of the dancers and to remember dead relatives. What would the people do if they didn't have this dance? How would they get together? I thought about this the other night. I hope it isn't forgotten in the future. It is good for the people. We see old friends and have our own religion."

Recently when Fort Hall, Wind River, and Western Shoshones, the three Ute groups, Southern Paiutes, and Gosiutes have convened at the various dances, Indians from each group have said that Indians (that is, those speaking "Shoshonean," treated in this study) were one people before the whites came and separated them. At Sun dances in the early 1960s this opinion was expressed time and again, both in orations in the Sun dance corrals and at political organization meetings that followed the dances at Northern Ute (see chapter 5). It is quite clear that the Indians understood they were joining at Sun dances to underscore their similarity and common plight, to help dancers from all reserves get their power, and to help one another stage successful dances. As an effect, they also achieved status and prestige in the interreservation community, and, as further effects, they generated self-esteem. Status deprivation for Shoshones and Utes, as we know, is a product of white-Indian relations, wherein the dominant whites have denied high status to Indians.

Every member of every reservation community does not hold the same opinion of the Sun dance religion. Furthermore, all Utes and Shoshones are not adherents of the dance. Although the great majority do support the dance and believe in its efficacy, some tribal members on all reserves disagree about such things as the propriety of the Sun dance leaders. These disagreements are not about the *religious* behavior of the Sun dance leaders. They are examples of the endemic factionalism associated with tribal governments in these deprived communities, rather than disagreements about the meaning or desirability of the religion.

Let me give two examples of disagreements that have occurred in the past decade on separate reservations. In the early 1960s, one tribal council got locked in debate over whether it should allocate funds for a dance. Several members of the council argued that the funds they had provided for a recent dance had been misused. The council members who were critical about the alleged misuse of tribal funds asserted that a Sun dance leader had been given tribal money to provide food and assistance for visitors from other reservations. There was some disagreement whether some of the visitors ever received the assistance. The manager of the council at the time railed against the Sun dance committee and called it a "private club" that operated the dance to no benefit for the tribe. The manager did not say that the Sun dance did not benefit the tribe. A schism then occurred between the Sun dance leadership faction and another tribal faction represented by the then manager of the council. When the manager called the Sun dance an operation of a private club, and asserted that the private club did not benefit the tribe, the other members of the council rallied to fund the dance. The appropriation passed by majority vote, although some council members registered mild reservations about the use of some of the funds entrusted to the Sun dance committee to help visitors.

The arguments presented by the council members in support of the appropriation of funds for the dance are important to show how secular factionalism can be smoothed out by sacred considerations. One committeewoman said she would go along with this financial request because she had some relatives who needed help from above, and that she needed help herself. Another committeewoman said that she did not feel something sacred should be violated and that what was needed most was faith. A third committeewoman, who raised the issue in the first place and whose husband was an active dancer, said that she wanted an accounting of the funds and was not questioning the beliefs. (This woman abstained from the voting.) All of the committee members agreed that no one should participate in a Sun dance just to get something, that is, financial remuneration out of the dance.

The second example is from the Northern Ute reservation. It, too, is an altercation over funds and the relationship between the Sun dance committee and, indirectly, the tribal business committee. On this reserve, however, the tribe does not contribute toward the expenses of the visitors, except at the termination feast. Rather, the Sun dance chief lets bids on the food concession for the dance. The high bidder (circa $200 to $500) pays off the bid by giving the amount in food to the visitors. This cuts off most of the profit a concessionaire would realize during the dance, but assures food for everyone who attends the dance, and the Sun dance committee does not have to hassle with the tribe for funds to take care of the visitors. It is perhaps not necessary to add that the concessionaire is nearly always a Ute. He gets his initial goods on short-term credit and then pays back the local supplier as he reorders each day of the dance.

Almost everyone at Northern Ute is highly supportive of the dance, and the dance committees themselves vary from dance to dance and year to year. Nevertheless, in 1960 the white tribal recreation director and her mixed-blood assistant attempted to usurp the Sun dance committee's job of preparing the traditional dance feast. The tribe had been providing funds for the feast for about a decade. As it turned out, both the Sun dance committee and the recreation director separately ordered food for the dance. The tribe was forced to pay two bills, and there was a mild altercation between the dominant Uncompahgre business committeeman, who showed some contempt for the dance and encouraged the recreation director to prepare for the feast, and the Sun dance chiefs. To add insult to injury, this event occurred soon after the True Ute rebellion.

Although there is a minor amount of intrareservation quibbling over the politics and funding of Sun dances, it is far outweighed by the intra- and interreservation harmony that attends the dances. Group interest in the dance as well as participation in it is great. Utes, Shoshones, and others are drawn together for religious and social purposes. As deprived Americans whose legitimate expectations for status and self-esteem are not satisfied in the dominant culture, they can satisfy some of their expectations by participating in the pan-Shoshone-Ute community that they have created in the past several decades. Status is won, respect is accorded, behavior is lauded as moral, and the participants reap religious experiences through suffering and giving.

In stressing the integrity of the Indian way of life and the ritual means by which it can be maintained, Shoshones and Utes have perpetuated a common identity and tradition. The collective ethic and individual ends of the dance expressly provide goals and purposes and the means to achieve them. Respected leaders admonish those in attendance to change their ways and remember what it means to thirst (self-sacrifice), for rewards will be given to him who thirsts. A most articulate forty-eight-year-old Northern Ute man summed it up this way:

Sun dance [*tavukai*, "thirst dance"] is given for the good of all the people. All the people know that. The old man told us that. The men who go in there and get thirsty, they get the power, and they cure the sick people with it. Sun dance time is also a time for fun, or recreation as you might call it. It doesn't mean what it did in the old days, but we enjoy it. We dance [round dances] and gamble, and get together [fraternize, cohabit]. The dancers go in there for everybody.

ATTENDANCE AT THE DANCES

There is no question that more people from more reservations get together for longer periods at the Sun dances than at any other Shoshone- or Ute-sponsored event. The dances are eagerly anticipated and are subjects of discussion at interreservation basketball tournaments, peyote meetings, and informal visiting throughout the year. The interest begins to build more and more during the Bear dances that are sponsored by the three Ute reservations during May and early June. Utes, a few Shoshones,

Southern Paiutes, and other Indians from adjacent tribes attend the various Ute Bear dances and learn about the plans for the coming Sun dance cycle. Except at Ute Mountain Ute, Bear dance attendance is not nearly so great as at the Sun dances, and nowhere is the activity nearly so intense and prolonged as at the Sun dances.

As the Sun dance cycle progresses each year, those who attend each dance are stimulated to attend the next one on the calendar. If they can afford to do so, they will visit the following dance. At the termination of each dance, people in nearly every lodge on the camp grounds can be heard singing Sun dance songs as they prepare to break camp and head for home, or a relative's home, or even to the next dance if it is to commence in three days' time as is the case once in a while. Usually there is a week and a half between dances.

Many people would like to dance at neighboring reservations but cannot, either because they are financially embarrassed or because of the economic hardship it would impose if they left their seasonal or full-time jobs for the five- or six-day jaunt. More often than not, most Ute and Shoshone families must remain at home and be content with participating at their own dance. But a person who cannot afford to visit another reservation one year, might well do so the following year.

The dancers normally go into the Sun dance corral on Friday night and come out on Monday afternoon. Weekends are chosen so that those who are employed can spend a couple of days, generally from Saturday morning to Sunday night, at each dance without missing work. For a day or so prior to the commencement of each dance, the preponderance of youth, middle-aged women, and elderly men and women is noticeable. It is a common practice for old men to ask their grandchildren to drive them to a dance on a distant reservation and for the youths to comply. The youths seldom have work to keep them at home, and they have respect for the aged, especially their grandparents. So when they are asked to accompany the older people on the trip, they are more than willing to do so.

A family will travel to the dance if it has a little cash and a car or truck that will make the trip. If the family has a wage earner, his funds are used to finance part of the affair, even if he does not make the trip himself. Relatives and friends at the sponsoring reservation, even the tribal councils and concessionaires at the Utes dances, help out by providing food. If requested they also provide lodging, either in their homes or in the lodges at the camp grounds. In turn, those who give help will be repaid in kind when they visit their guests' home reservations.

The visitors' presence and ritual activity adds to the success of the dance and is appreciated by the sponsors. Invitations to return the favor are always extended before people return home, but it will be remembered that invitations are extended *before* each dance also. The Shoshone-Ute Sun dance community is linked through hundreds of kinship and friendship reciprocity ties and a common ideology to help the other group sponsor a good dance.

Figure 19 is a schematic representation of the distances between reservations. The natural center position of Northern Ute is made clear in this scheme. Table 55 represents those people who camped at the Sun dance grounds or, if they did not camp there, regularly attended the dances. Occasional visitors, such as missionaries, tourists, and local whites, are not included. The greatest number of white visitors was at Wind River, where about 250 dropped in during the course of the dance. Many were

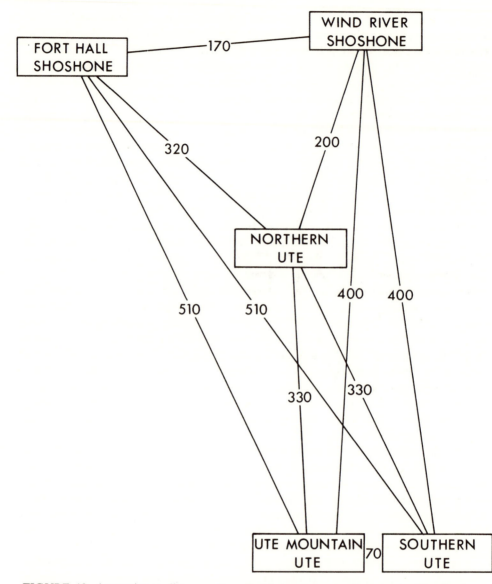

FIGURE 19. Approximate distances (in miles) between reservations in the Ute-Shoshone Sun dance community.

on their way to or from Yellowstone Park and had learned of the dance in the white towns of Lander and Riverton, Wyoming. The greatest number of white spectators at any one time on any reservation was less than fifty.

White attendance at Sun dances is encouraged by a few tribal employees at Southern Ute, Northern Ute, and Wind River Shoshone, and by the chambers of commerce

TABLE 55

Overall Indian[a] Attendance at Sun Dances, Five Reservations, Summer, 1966[b]

Indians in Attendance	Reservations				
	So. Ute 2–5 July	W.R. Sho. 8–11 July	F.H. Sho. 26–30 July	No. Ute 5–9 Aug.	Ute Mtn. 11–15 Aug.
Northern Ute:					
Uintah–White River	60	70	120	850	80
Uncompaghre	40	30	0	550	30
Ute Mountain Ute	300	50	76	150	920
Southern Ute	400	25	4	75	180
Wind River Shoshone	0	1,500	200	100	0
Fort Hall Shoshone	0	160	1,700	75	12
Jicarilla Apache	10	0	0	20	20
Navajo	10	0	0	10	25
Southern Paiute	0	0	0	45	15
Western Shoshone	0	0	120	10	0
Arapaho	0	50	0	10	0
Gosiute	0	0	45	15	0
Taos Pueblo	16	0	0	0	0
Warm Springs	5	0	0	0	0
Cree	0	0	20	0	0
Crow	0	0	10	0	0
Blackfeet	0	0	.....	0	0
Whites	190	16	2	0	0
Total (rounded)	1,030	1,900	2,300	1,910	1,280

a. Two exceptions are noted. (1) Whites who have married into the host tribe and who established camps at the dance grounds are included in the totals. About 40 Mexican-Americans and other whites fit this description and are included in the "white" total (along with the psychedelic cultists) at Southern Ute. Two whites fit this description at Fort Hall Shoshone. Eight whites fit this description at Wind River. (2) Several whites belonging to a psychedelic cult pitched camp and attended dances at Southern Ute and Wind River Shoshone: 150 attended the former and 8 attended the latter.

b. Occasional visitors (tourists and local passers-by) are not included in these totals. These data represent campers or regular Indian attenders who have not established camps but who live close enough to the dance grounds to visit each day and night, yet sleep at home.

in some of the local towns around the reservations. The chambers seem happy about "their Indians" during the Sun dance, for they constantly invite tourists to "spend the night in Lander, Wyoming, and see the Sun dance."

At the Sun dance grounds themselves, however, Indians are hostile, or indifferent, to whites. White attendance is discouraged at Ute Mountain Ute. The Fort Hall Shoshones seem indifferent. The Northern Utes show their hostility by charging admission fees to whites and to no one else. In 1966 the price was one dollar per car. The Sun dance committee may have grossed fifty dollars from the admissions, which they used for non-reimbursed expenditures for running the dance (most of it went to feed the Indian visitors). In 1959 the Southern Utes charged admission fees to whites and then gave the money to the visiting Indians. The Ute Mountain Utes charged admission fees to whites in 1961, but in 1966 there were neither whites nor admission fees at the Ute Mountain Ute dance. The Ute Mountain Utes are openly hostile to whites.

In spite of the general hostility or indifference to whites, a common theme of some anthropologists is that the modern Shoshone and Ute Sun dances are mere commercialized remnants of the old dances (Voget 1953: 491; Witherspoon 1961). Some, too, have alleged that the dancers are paid for their services out of the admission fees. It is true that in 1965 admission fees at Northern Ute were given to the dancers. Each man received a gift of two or three dollars for his services. This is the only such instance known to me that is remotely supportive of the allegation that Sun dancers are paid. Financial gain is not the reason for which men enter the dance. Indeed, quite the contrary is true. As we have seen, dancers give gifts to visitors for attending and helping with the singing and to shamans for bestowing final blessings on them. The dancer must be prepared to make a relatively large financial outlay if he dances. Ten dollars is a considerable amount of money on any of these reservations, and a dancer often gives that much for his final blessing alone. The sum is usually collected from within his own family so that he can give it at the end of the dance. Rather than a tourist attraction or a ceremony performed for the emolument and remuneration of the dancers, the Sun dance is a religious ritual used to pursue religious and social goals. The time during which a Sun dance is performed allows Utes, Shoshones, and others to meet and fraternize, to establish the sort of community that allows men to overcome, albeit perhaps only temporarily, some of their deprivation.

In most cases the Indians who visit from other reservations camp at the dance grounds. Some camp near the homes of relatives in the host tribe, and others move right in with their relatives or close friends. Between 50 or 60 percent of the membership of each tribe camps at the dances sponsored on their home reservation. Those who do not set up camp, travel to the dance each day, as the figures attest. On several occasions I have traveled through Ute and Shoshone communities during the noon hours of dance sessions. Except for a few dogs, they are unoccupied. At the Wind River Shoshone and Northern Ute reservations, where two dances are sponsored by each group each year, it is my impression that 90 percent or even more of the members of these tribes camp at one or the other of the dances.

Although there is intercommunity and interreservation fraternizing at these dances, Indians who live in the same community or on the same reservation tend to cluster together and build their camps at roughly the same spots each year. As we shall see in several figures below, intrareservation clustering is more marked on some reserves than others. A camp is usually occupied by a kin-related household of from fifteen to twenty persons of all ages. Basic four-pole rectangular shade houses are built and covered with young poplars and aspen; no sides are left open (as in most shade houses). A small, rectangular shade house or a tent is often attached to the larger structure. The women cook in the shade house.

A striking exception to the all-Indian composition of the dance was the 150 whites ("Bizarros") who squatted at the Southern Ute dance. The group claimed to live the "Indian style" life. They also claimed to belong to a growing peyote cult that had dropped out of the mainstream of middle-class American life. Several said that they appreciated the deep religious significance of the Sun dance, and some said they were preparing to dance the following year. One danced at Wind River that same year. It turned out that several in the entourage were college professors and students on a psychedelic outing. These whites had assumed bits of American Indian dress, such as Navajo skirts and blouses or Hopi shirts, which they had integrated with their own favorites, such as football referees' shirts, stretch jeans, paratrooper boots, or Mexican sandals. Initially many Indians were offended at what they interpreted to be a parody of the Indian life style. They were repelled by some particularly dirty families and by a young man who drove around in a new Mercedes-Benz sedan wearing a stove pipe hat. The Indians laughed at some of the antics of the whites, but they were very much distraught over the sacred water incident report in chapter 7.

The Sun dance is obviously the most important event of the year for most Utes and Shoshones. Adults and children alike emphasize neat appearance at the Sun dance, changing into clean clothes at least once and often twice a day even though the average woman's summer wardrobe consists of only three or four cotton dresses (even fewer among Fort Hall Shoshone women). The men change their cotton shirts and levis every day also. Moreover, the men and the women wear whatever "Indian" items they own—beaded mocassins, bags, belts, Navajo or Pueblo jewelry, and Navajo blankets. Those who can afford it wear Pendleton (brand) shirt jackets—often several years old and worn especially for this event—and Chimayo wraps.

Shoshones and Utes are not celebrating their poverty; they are, among other things, explaining away their poverty. The Sun dance is a time when they can pursue religious experiences, enjoy interreservation camaraderie, and prepare themselves for the next long period of relative isolation from friends and community respect. The "Bizarros" cannot "live the Indian style," and the Indians know it.

ATTENDANCE AT SOUTHERN UTE

In 1966 there were about 690 individuals on the Southern Ute tribal membership roster. The majority of the enrollees visited this first Sun dance of the year. Table 55 shows that Ute Mountain Utes were represented nearly as heavily as the hosts. Southern Ute and Ute Mountain Ute agency towns are about seventy miles distant, separated by the LaPlata Mountains and the Mesa Verde, and so one expects a large number of representatives from each group. Nevertheless, on two separate counts there were ten more Ute Mountain Utes camped on the grounds than there were Southern Utes. This is most simply explained by the 60 percent larger Ute Mountain Ute population and the proximity of Ute Mountain Utes to the Southern Ute dance. Most Southern Utes visit the Sun dance corral at some time during each ritual, although many do not camp at the ground. The daily round trip from Towaoc and White Mesa is too far for many Ute Mountain Utes; so they camp.

The Northern Utes were the second most numerous visitors at the Southern Ute dance. There is considerable intermarriage, as well as a common history, to draw Northern Utes to the dance. The rest of the visitors at Southern Ute were from Taos (connected through long trade and, more recently, peyote contacts), Jicarilla Apache (intermarried with Utes and, in historic times, banded with Utes to battle the Comanches, Kiowa, and Navajo, and dealt with jointly by the U.S. government at one time), Navajo (intermarried with the Ute Mountain Utes at Towaoc and White Mesa and tied in through peyotism, also), and a few vacationing Indians from Warm Springs, Oregon. The whites (Mexican-Americans and Anglos) who attended were either linked to the Southern Utes through marriage or they were camped with the "Bizarro" cult.

Kinship and friendship ties for the Southern Utes are most apparent with other Utes. The Shoshone groups, notably, were not represented at this dance; yet some Southern Utes attended each of the Shoshone dances in 1966. Perhaps a combination of factors explains why Shoshones did not attend in 1966. The Southern Ute dance was the first dance of the year and hence did not benefit from the cumulative excitement generated by the entire dance cycle. Moreover, most Fort Hall and Wind River Shoshones have less cash than Utes from the Colorado reservations, and this may have restricted travel.

The other Indian groups represented at the Southern Ute dance are from the Southern Colorado–Northern New Mexico area. Intermarriage and peyotism maintain the links between these people, although no Apaches or Navajos dance. For several decades Kiowas and Cheyennes from Oklahoma have been invited to attend the dance. Although none visited the 1966 dance, they frequently attend and, because they have Sun dance traditions themselves, usually provide some excellent singing. I have never seen Kiowas or Cheyennes dance.

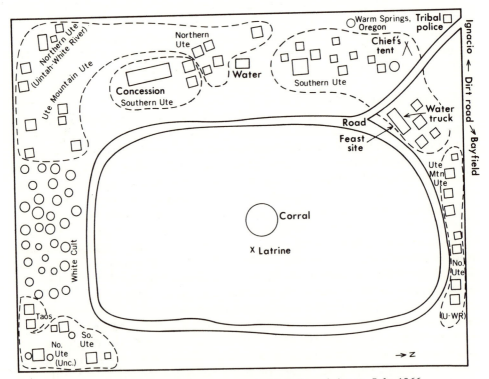

FIGURE 20. Southern Ute Sun dance ground, third day of dance, July 1966.

Figure 20 shows the placement of the camps on the dance grounds as of the third sunrise ceremony. The distribution is not random. Southern Utes cluster together, as do Ute Mountain Utes. Except for the Southern Ute camps at the concession stand, the majority of Ute Mountain Utes and the majority of Southern Utes would have been positioned in two separate areas, roughly divided by the water tank. A group of later Southern Ute and Northern Ute (Uncompaghre) arrivals situated themselves in the southeast corner and complemented the late arrivals from Ute Mountain and Northern Ute (Uintah–White Rivers), who located in the northeast corner. The distribution of the Northern Utes is interesting: Uncompaghres located themselves with Southern Utes, as did those from Taos, and Uintah–White Rivers located themselves with Ute Mountain Utes.

ATTENDANCE AT UTE MOUNTAIN UTE

Ute Mountain Ute had the second smallest attendance of all the 1966 dances (see table 55). Because the Ute Mountain Utes are the most widely traveled dance attenders, it was expected that there would be many more visitors than actually showed up. My expectations went against my better judgment, however, because two dances I visited at Ute Mountain in 1961 and 1963 were sparsely attended by non-Utes. Nevertheless, I expected large crowds because the Ute Mountain Utes had sung at every dance in the cycle in 1966 and had invited the hosts at each dance to attend the Ute Mountain dance. Moreover, the Ute Mountain Utes gave more elegant gifts in greater number to visitors than did the hosts of any other dance.

Northern Utes attended in 1966 in about the same numbers as at the Southern Ute dance, yet in different intrareservation proportions: more Uintah–White Rivers and fewer Uncompaghres showed up. Southern Utes visited also, but in considerably fewer numbers than those from Ute Mountain who had visited the Southern Ute dance six weeks earlier.

A few Shoshones from Fort Hall made the trip, and, as at Southern Ute, several Jicarilla Apaches and Navajos attended the dance. Unlike the Southern Ute dance the Ute Mountain dance drew several Southern Paiutes from southeastern and southwestern Utah. There were no dancers from these groups. On the other hand, the Southern Utes drew a few Taos Indians from the east to their dance, whereas the Ute Mountain Utes did not. The main ties, as measured by attendance at the dances, are Ute Mountain Ute and Southern Ute with one another and each with the Northern Ute.

Figure 21 represents the location of the camps at the Ute Mountain Ute Sun dance grounds in 1960. This is the only dance locale where the camps do not form a 75 percent or complete circle around the corral. The camp area is on a hill above the dance corral and is separated from it by pinyon, juniper, spruce, and bushes. The dance ground is located about 8,500 feet above sea level on Ute Mountain, high above the reservation and remote from people and traffic.

The camps in the corral area in 1966 were occupied by the families of the Sun dance committee and no one else, although the tribal police had a temporary headquarters there. The larger camp area, as at Southern Ute, was segmented into patches of Southern Ute, Ute Mountain Ute, and Northern Ute camps. A few Southern Utes and Uncompaghres from Northern Ute camped together in the northwest corner, whereas Southern Paiutes camped with the Ute Mountain Utes and Payuchis (from White Mesa) across the road to the south. The trees and bushes throughout the campground provided shade and privacy unknown to any other dance.

ATTENDANCE AT NORTHERN UTE

The Northern Utes had 1,600 on the tribal rolls in mid-1966. Most lived on the Uintah and Ouray or adjacent reservations. The Uintahs and White Rivers comprised about 950 of the enrollees, and the Uncompaghres accounted for the other 650. Both were well represented at the 1966 dance. In fact, practically all of the Northern

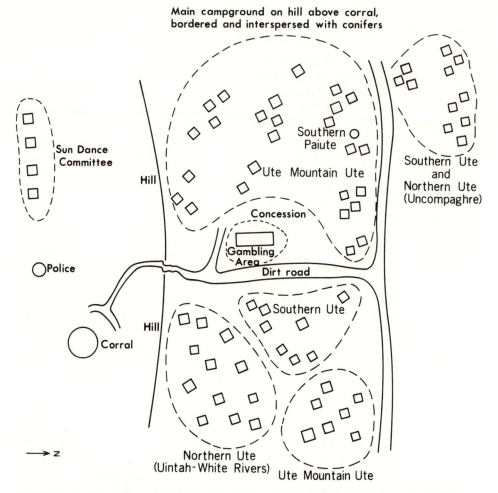

FIGURE 21. Ute Mountain Ute Sun dance ground, third day of dance, August 1966.

Utes either camped at the grounds or spent most of their time there for the duration of the dance.

Although the overall attendance at the Fort Hall Shoshone dance was higher, there was considerably more activity and more people in and around the dance corral more of the time at Northern Ute than at Fort Hall. Indeed, the vitality of the spectators and the sundry activities in which they engaged turned the Northern Ute dance into a beehive of activity.

The relative importance of the Northern Ute dance as the major meeting place for Shoshones and Utes has been discussed above. Attendance figures show that relatively large contingents of Ute Mountain and Southern Utes attended in 1966, as did smaller but still impressive contingents of Fort Hall and Wind River Shoshones. On the basis of attendance alone, the Northern Ute dance is the destiny center of the distribution of Sun dance spectators and participants.

We have already mentioned kin and affinal links between Colorado and Utah Utes. Northern Utes have also intermarried with Shoshones, Gosiutes, Southern Paiutes, and Jicarilla Apaches. The Jicarilla were represented at the 1966 dance, as were the Arapaho (Wyoming) and Navajo (Ute Mountain area). The principal visitors, however, were Fort Hall Shoshones, Wind River Shoshones, Ute Mountain Utes, and Southern Utes.

The campground layout at Northern Ute (figure 22) is somewhat more organized than at any of the other camps. Many visitors locate with their Northern Ute hosts (some camp at the hosts' homes rather than at the Sun dance grounds, however) and many others locate in selected areas that they traditionally occupy on the Sun dance grounds.

Though the figure does not show it, several Fort Hall and Wind River Shoshones in 1966 were dispersed through the Uintah–White River area, as were a few Southern and Ute Mountain Utes.

ATTENDANCE AT WIND RIVER SHOSHONE

There were 1,970 Shoshones enrolled at the Wind River Agency in mid-1966. They shared their reservation with over 2,600 Arapahos. It is interesting that fewer Arapahos than Northern and Ute Mountain Utes attended the first Wind River dance of 1966, suggesting that Shoshone-Arapaho friendliness has not increased much in the past few decades. Indeed, the majority of the visitors were Utes and Fort Hall Shoshones. Cree, Blackfeet, Crow, and Sioux visitors were not in evidence,

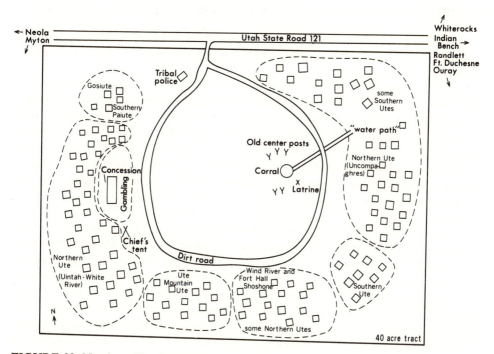

FIGURE 22. Northern Ute Sun dance ground, third day of dance, August 1966.

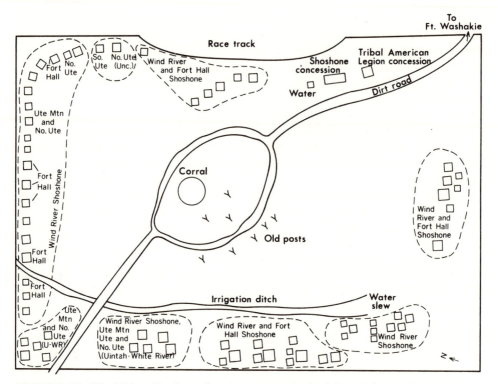

FIGURE 23. Wind River Shoshone Sun dance ground, third day of dance, July 1966.

but all sponsor Sun dances, and Utes and Shoshones are known to have participated at those dances in the past. A large contingent of Crow Indians attended the Wind River dance in 1967, however.

Attendance at the 1966 Wind River dance peaked on Sunday night (third night). The crowd at the termination of the dance, however, whereas one would have expected it to be somewhat smaller, was only half that of the preceding night. This, among other things, gave the dance a flavor that was different from the others. Many attended the dances, but few camped on the grounds, and when large throngs of Wind River Shoshones visited, they did not tarry long. This may have been due in part to the inviting location of the Sun dance grounds, which were adjacent to the Wind River Shoshone community buildings and the Fort Washakie community. This is a relatively "urban" setting for a Sun dance corral.

Figure 23 shows the camp layout at Wind River. The pattern shows that visitors normally establish camps with, or adjacent to, their friends or kin from the host reservation. Sections of predominantly Wind Rivers in 1966 were interrupted by several joint camps of Wind Rivers and Fort Hall Shoshones, Ute Mountain–Northern Ute clusters, or other combinations. Nevertheless, a striking feature was the joint Wind River–Fort Hall Shoshone camps. The two camped with one another more than either did with any other group. This is one simple indicator of the large number of kin, affinal, and friendship ties that have persisted over the past century and which still obtain between these groups.

ATTENDANCE AT FORT HALL SHOSHONE

In 1966 there were 2,800 Shoshones and Bannocks enrolled at Fort Hall. About 2,470 of them lived on the reservation, and about 1,700 of them attended the Bannock Creek dance. Although it was predominantly an Idaho Shoshone affair, visitors were drawn from Montana (Cree) and southern Colorado. (Both Colorado Ute reserves were represented.) The majority of off-reservation visitors came from Wind River, with which there is considerable intermarriage.

Western Shoshones and Gosiutes attended in considerable numbers, and the joint camps these people established with the Fort Hall Shoshones give some idea of the relationships that obtain (see figure 24). Fort Hall drew the largest attendance overall, but there was not so much activity nor many people on the grounds as much of the time as at Northern Ute.

The pattern of camp locations at Fort Hall shows interreservation camps, the dominant feature of the Wind River campground, as well as several patches of camps representing separate reserves. Again, Uintah–White Rivers from Northern Ute and Ute Mountain Utes tended to camp near one another. All Nevada Shoshones and Gosiutes camped with Fort Hall Shoshones.

GIFT GIVING AND THE FEAST: GENERALIZED RECIPROCITY

Gift giving and terminal feasts are features of every Sun dance. No practices attendant to the dance foster interreservation camaraderie and a pan-reservation

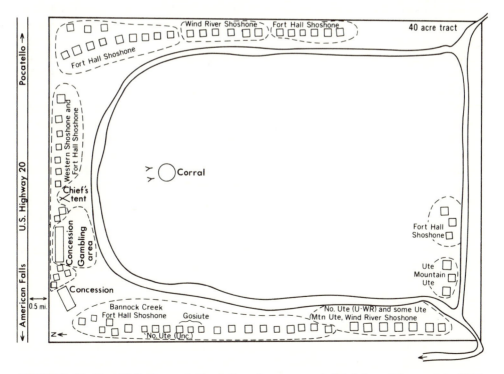

FIGURE 24. Fort Hall–Bannock Creek Sun dance ground, third day of dance, July 1966.

identity more than these. On four of the reservations even the ghosts of the "old people" are given gifts: they are offered silk scarves, tacked to the center pole, in memory of their services and teachings to the Indian community. The ghosts of the "old people" reciprocate by giving health and happiness to the living. More often than not, this means that the ghosts do not return to pester and harass their living kin.

We have seen how a chattel is given, directly or symbolically, by one party in a relationship, and supernatural help is given by the other. The dancer prays and dances so that he can channel his power to help his ailing relatives or friends. The shaman's gift is the healing power he bestows on the invalid or the legitimate power with which he seals in the dancer's newly earned powers. The ghosts' gift is not to harass, and so forth. The reciprocal nature of each interaction is not rigidly prescribed. The person who asks someone to dance on behalf of an ailing relative is not, by so doing, obligated to attend each dance session and to make gifts of willows and cigarettes to cool and comfort the dancer during the heat of the day. But it would be bad form not to help the dancer for two reasons: (1) it is expected that a person care enough for the ailing to make some personal sacrifice so that the sick person will get well; and (2) a person is expected to make gifts to the dancer so that he will be more effective in his power quest. The same is true of the presentation for a shaman's service: one need not pay, especially if one has nothing to give, and there is no set fee in goods, cash, or services. Nevertheless, shamans are given gifts so that their services will be efficacious. Shoshones and Utes believe that some gesture of good faith and good will on the part of the recipient is needed in order to complete the cure or the blessing. Thus the fee, that is, cash, blanket, buckskin, etc., is not established on the market, it is not determined by the kind of service rendered, and it does not ebb and flow with the number of shamans or the number of persons desirous of a shaman's help. A client is free to give whatever he wants for the services, yet it would be bad form not to give anything. All of these reciprocal relationships are embedded in a social and ceremonial context. Indeed, there seems to be comparability in the nature of transactions when a Southern or Northern Ute offers silk scarves or prayers to the ghosts of the deceased and when he offers gifts for a shaman's services.

The foregoing centers on individual transactions. Even the gifts to the "old people" are given with particular "old people" in mind. There is another kind of reciprocity practiced at Sun dances. Since the early 1900s, members of the host reservations have given gifts of goods (including food and money) to dance visitors, for visitors are invited with the understanding that the host reserve will lessen the expense burden of the trip. The recipient often, but not always, has a chance to reciprocate, usually during the same year in which he visits another reservation. A Fort Hall Shoshone may travel to the Northern Ute dance, get food from the Sun dance committee or from a relative during his stay there, and be given a gift of cash and, perhaps, a Navajo blanket at the termination of the dance. The visitor is also treated to a large feast. In turn, a Northern Ute may travel to the Fort Hall Sun dance and receive similar help from relatives, friends or anonymous donors.

The reciprocity is generalized in that the members of the host reservation, in order to demonstrate that they are good hosts, give freely to the visitors. Gifts are made not merely from one relative to another, but from host to visitor. A special form of this gift giving occurs on the last day of the dance, when members of the host group pool individual gifts of cash, blankets, cloth, beadwork, buckskin, and sundry odds and ends. These items are then distributed to the visitors.

This allows considerable latitude for the giver. A person can give little, perhaps a couple of yards of calico, yet expect to receive help in the form of money, food, or other commodities at every reservation he visits during the Sun dance cycle. Not only is no special accounting made of each gift (between donor and recipient), but those who have nothing to give or no way to repay are not expected to give or repay, nor need a gift given be of comparable quality to the gift received. When Kiowas or Cheyennes visit a Ute Sun dance, they are welcomed, fed, and gifted. Utes and Shoshones are pleased to have Indians other than Shoshones and Utes attend, for they make a contribution to the success of the dance by being there, singing and fraternizing. The visitors are accepted as part of the Sun dance community, even though they might no longer sponsor Sun dances on their own reservations—at least not regularly —and have no chance to reciprocate.

RITUALIZED GIFT GIVING

On the last day of each Sun dance in the annual cycle the members of the host group contribute to a common pool of gifts. Two methods of gift distribution are observed. About one hour before the last dance, the Sun dance chief or a ranking member of his committee calls for the collection of the gifts. A couple of sheets or blankets are placed in front of the center pole on the east side and are manned by one or two members of the Sun dance committee.

As the drummers sing and beat the drum, the hosts are encouraged to contribute. Speeches are made by members of the committee as well as by prestigious shamans and tribal leaders asking the hosts to dig deep so that the visitors, who have traveled so far to help, can be helped in return. A common theme in these speeches is a request for cash to help pay the gasoline bills. Another request is for cloth or blankets. Anything is acceptable, however.

The gifts tend to be given anonymously everywhere but at Wind River. Yet men and women are proud of the gifts they contribute and enjoy the brief moment of acclaim they receive from the spectators when they make their contributions. Although the gifts are pooled in a collective effort, the individual contributors are also encouraged by individual recognition and the individual prestige that accrues to the generous giver. Hosts step up to the men collecting the gifts and, sometimes with a flourish, present their offerings, whether it be five dollars in cash, a Navajo rug, a Pendleton shawl, Indian jewelry, or a few yards of cloth. Dancers at Northern Ute always contribute in appreciation of the singing that the visitors have done for them. Every so often, after the first appeal, a leader will ask the hosts to give yet a little more to help the visitors out. Often the hosts are reminded that the dancers have expended themselves for the good of everyone and that gifts should be made in the dancers' honor. These occasions provide further opportunities for the individual contributors to give more gifts and to be distinguished from the anonymous collective enterprise in the process.

At Wind River the dance committee observes an otherwise unusual practice of announcing the name and contribution of each contributor over a portable loudspeaker which has been set up especially for this event. Here the role of the individual contributor is recognized with gusto rather than subtlety. At the Southern Ute and Ute Mountain Ute dances, the two groups are considered one unit when it comes to receiving gifts. Whereas each is host to its own affair, neither is treated as a visitor at the other's reserve. Each reserve will often contribute to the pot at the other's dance. The most prestigious ritualists from each tribe have contributed at every Southern and Ute Mountain Ute dance I have attended.

The contributors at all dances say that they are giving gifts for several reasons. Two explanations that are always offered—the same as those stressed by leaders when they encourage people to contribute—are that the gift is made in honor of the dancers who have "gone thirsty" for the good of everyone, and that contributors want to help the visitors who came from great distances to help make it a successful dance. If pressed, both Shoshones and Utes also admit that the visitors from tribes that sponsor dances themselves are obligated to help them in their turn, when they are visitors at a Sun dance.

The responses of the recipients are often amusing and have many parallels in non-Indian society. Although gifts are supposed to be received graciously and gratefully, at one Ute dance some of the visitors were displeased with the color or style of the material they received or with the item that was offered to them. Often they refused the things they did not want and pointed at the gifts they desired. At a Shoshone dance several Ute women were unhappy with the sparse gifts of material offered to them and were audibly upset. One woman announced that they gave a great deal more at her own dance and she did not appreciate receiving so little in return.

The discrepancy between the gifts among these reservations, particularly at Ute Mountain and Fort Hall, is no accident. Of all the Sun dance sponsors, the Ute Mountain Utes have the greatest amount of available cash, and the Fort Hall Shoshones have the least. Also, since nearly twice as many visitors attended the Fort Hall dance as attended the Ute Mountain dance, the meager Fort Hall gifts, predominantly cotton material, were spread out among more people than were the more elegant Ute Mountain gifts, predominantly cash, Navajo jewelry, and blankets.

The distribution follows two patterns. At Southern and Ute Mountain Ute the gifts are collected during the last hour of the dance. The Southern Utes usually display the miraculous sheet at this time (see chapter 7). When it is unfurled, the local Indians are asked to remember the sacrifice of the dancers and to contribute to the visitors. Goods are collected by the dance committee, usually two to four men. The Ute Mountain Utes do not display the miraculous sheet, but the rest of the distribution practice is the same at Southern Ute. The dancers rest in their stalls while the drummers sing and play. Meanwhile the gifts are sorted into piles of similar items. At both places the committees call for the visiting Indians to line up east of the piles of goods.

Those who have traveled the greatest distances are the first to receive gifts. If Oklahoma Indians attend, as they usually do, they are the first to receive gifts. They are followed by Idaho, Wyoming, and Utah guests. When a man and a woman are together, the woman stands in front of the man. The committeemen give cloth, shawls, Navajo or Chimayo blankets and jewelry to the woman and money or Navajo blankets to the man. There is sometimes enough for two gifts to each family, or even two gifts for each adult in each family. There is an attempt to make all gifts comparable, but of course they never really are. When all gifts have been distributed, the sheets and blankets on which they were placed are collected. The Sun dance chief signals for the dancing to resume as they launch into the last set of the dance.

A somewhat different distribution pattern occurs at Northern Ute, Fort Hall, and Wind River Shoshone. As at the Colorado Ute dances, gifts are collected during the last hour of the dance, but they are not distributed until the last dance has been danced, the chief's final prayer has been given, the sacred water has been drunk, and the dancers have filed out of the lodge. After the dancers have filed out, the visitors are directed into the stall that the dancers have vacated. Those from the greatest distances occupy the stalls along the most northwesterly portion of the corral's arc, and those from lesser distances file in behind them. At the Northern Ute and both of the Shoshone dances in 1966, all the stalls were filled three or four deep with adults. Women line up along the front row and the men line up behind them. Again, women receive yard goods, shawls, blankets, and other items, whereas men usually receive money.

THE FEAST

The traditional feast is sponsored either on the last day of the dance or on the following day. The meal consists of boiled, boneless meat (but not necessarily tongue, as was the practice several decades back), fried bread, corn, fresh fruit, coffee, soda pop, and sometimes candy, and conforms in kind to the feasts which follow peyote meetings, Bear dances, General Council meetings, and other events sponsored by Shoshones, Utes, and other tribes.

The feasts are financed with tribal funds administered by either recreation councils (as at Wind River) or Sun dance committees (as at Northern Ute). Until the 1950s —on all but the Wind River reservation, where the tribe began paying for feasts in the late 1930s—the feasts were contributed by the host families and partially paid for with the modest gate receipts which were charged to whites at all dances. At present the committees usually arranged with local white merchants to deliver the meat already cooked. Bread is fried by Indian women, who also cook the corn. The melons are sliced by Indian men. Indians have kept control over these acts, for they feel that in so doing they are fulfilling an important obligation. All who dance or contribute to the dance are to be repaid for their sacrifices. The feast, following the thirst and fast of the dance, is both a symbolic and an actual recognition of the dance's termination and a return to a new and healthy state.

In 1966, about 900 were served at the Ute Mountain Ute feast, 700 at the Southern Ute feast, 1,400 at the Northern Ute feast, 1,200 at the Wind River Shoshone feast, and 1,200 at the Fort Hall feast. All of these figures are less than the total attendances registered at each dance, for neither all the visitors nor all the members of the host reserve can afford to stay at the dance until the feast is served. The feasts are held either on Monday immediately following the termination of the dance or, as was the case at every dance in 1966, on Tuesday (one day after the dance). Some visitors stayed only Saturday and Sunday—especially if they were employed part-time or full-time. Some locals, especially men, could not attend for the same reasons.

The visitors are always the first to be served, and a special effort is made to heap their plates with large servings of meat, good ears of corn, choice pieces of fried bread and watermelon. Many conversations are struck up, and they often run to discussions of dancers' heroics at the recent dance (or even at earlier dances). Stories are exchanged, kinship is recounted, and the "old Indian way" is lauded. The hosts are happy to serve their Indian "kin" from other reserves, and they look forward to comparable feasting at their visitors' dances. (At Ute Bear dances and Wind River Shoshone Memorial Day celebrations the food is served in paper bags and can be taken home to eat. At the Sun dances people eat together on benches, on the ground, on car hoods, and so forth.)

RECREATION: EXTRACURRICULAR UNIFYING
FEATURES OF THE SUN DANCE

Sun dances are times for pleasure and camaraderie. Each day individuals, in relatively consistent patterns, move on and off the Sun dance grounds, in and out of the Sun dance corral, and shift their attentions from the Sun dance to gambling, social dancing, and other activities which bring personal pleasures. The following reconstruction is a generalized account of most daily routines for spectators at most Sun dances.

5:00 A.M. Adults arise to watch the dancers at the sunrise ceremony. The teen-agers are just going to bed following a night of philandering. The small children stay in bed.

9:00 A.M. Everyone is up, except the teenagers, and everyone has eaten breakfast, which the women have cooked. Adults go to the rivers and cut willows and other greens. They take them back to the dance and offer them to the dancers.

11:00 A.M. Adults may drive to a nearby white town to shop or drink beer. Teen-agers go into town with them and roam the streets.

1:00 P.M. The adults return to the dance grounds, often without the teen-agers. They watch the dancers, sing, perhaps leave to cut more willows along the river banks, and return to offer them to the dancers.

3:00 P.M. Most adults and teenagers are back on the grounds. Large crowds watch the dancers. It is hot, and children and adults walk back and forth to the concession stand for pop.

5:00 P.M. The dancing is over for the afternoon. At the Ute dance everyone convenes around the concession stand to gamble. At the Shoshone reserves they merely convene there to talk, since gambling is proscribed until the termination of the dance.

7:00 P.M. At each camp women cook dinners. Everyone eats. There may be an hour of round dancing (social) at the Northern Ute dance before the evening Sun dancing resumes. Round dancing at the other dances occurs only on the last day.

8:00 P.M. Sun dancing begins, and most people filter over to the dance corral to sing and encourage the dancers. Youngsters move in and out of the corral. Visitors from local towns and members from sponsoring reserves who are not camped at the grounds join the campers in the Sun dance corral.

10:00 P.M. Many Indians move back to their lodges, and some of them drink beer and whiskey. Groups of boys begin following groups of girls around the lodges, in and out of the Sun dance corral, etc. Some adult men and women pair off and cohabit in cars, in lodges, or in the brush (the brush is a favorite among teenagers, who often lose their sleeping bags or coats in these thorny rendezvous).

1:00 A.M. Adults go to bed; youngsters continue to wander.

The gambling, round dancing, trips to town, cutting of willows, offering of gifts to dancers, singing and watching in the corral, evening drinking sessions, and general fraternizing are important elements of each Sun dance. The concession-gambling area of each dance ground is the hub of extracurricular activity. Most of it starts there and spins off to other places.

GAMBLING

At all dances, gambling is conducted around the concession stands. At Ute-sponsored dances, gambling begins on the second night; only poker is proscribed until the dance terminates. But at the Shoshone dances, all gambling is proscribed until the dance terminates (see chapter 7). Nevertheless, crowds collect at the gambling areas of each Sun dance ground each night, for that is where contacts are made for drinking sessions ("having a good time"), where old men and women get together to talk, and where young children collect to drink pop, form packs, and move off to harass the camps.

TABLE 56

GAMBLING ALLOWED DURING OR FOLLOWING THE SUN DANCE, FIVE RESERVATIONS, 1966

Reservation	First Night	Second Night	Third Night	Fourth Night	End of Dance[a]
Southern Ute	−	+	+	+	+
Ute Mountain Ute	−	+	+	+	+
Northern Ute	−	+	+	+	+
Wind River Shoshone[b]	−	−	−	−	+
Fort Hall Shoshone	−	−	−	−	+

a. Only the Northern Utes sponsored a four-day dance in 1966. "End of Dance" was the fourth day for all other groups.
b. Gambling curtailed by thundershower in 1966.

On all reservations, gambling draws huge crowds of participants and kibitzers. On the Ute reserves the activity begins at about five and lasts until eight o'clock each evening (during the dancers' evening rest periods). On the final day of each dance the gambling begins almost immediately when the dance is over and lasts until one or two o'clock in the morning.

Table 57 shows the total number of gambling games played at each dance in 1966. The high average number of participants and spectators per game shows that there are many more bettors and kibitzers than there are people who actually handle the cards and the bones in each monte, poker, and hand-and-stick game. Indeed, probably every person in camp spends part of every night at the gambling area. The Southern and Ute Mountain Ute dances, which have less attendance than the other three, also have fewer games and participants than do the Northern Ute and Fort Hall Shoshone. Southern and Ute Mountain Ute gambling took place on two nights, Northern Ute on three, and Fort Hall Shoshone on one. Gambling at Wind River Shoshone was virtually washed out by torrential summer showers following conclusion of the dance.

Spectators who have made wagers watch the contestants closely. The kibitzers usually identify with the players from their own communities or reservations. The games generally promote fun for everyone, though some people are accused of cheating. By and large the charges are soon forgotten.

Monte and poker are individual games of chance and in these contests it is usually every person against every other. They are also individually waged affairs. In chapter

TABLE 57

GAMBLING ACTIVITY AT SUN DANCES, FIVE RESERVATIONS, SUMMER, 1966

	Tot. Games	Av. Players	Av. Bettors	Av. Kibitzers	Av. Size of Pots[a]
		Monte (Per Game Averages)			
Southern Ute	7	7	15	10	
Ute Mountain Ute	4	8	15	10	
Northern Ute	20	8	20	20	
Wind River Shoshone	0	0	0	0	
Fort Hall Shoshone	7	5	15	15	
		Poker (Per Game Averages)			
Southern Ute	0	0	0	0	
Ute Mountain Ute	0	0	0	0	
Northern Ute	4	5	5	20	
Wind River Shoshone	0	0	0	0	
Fort Hall Shoshone	5	5	5	10	
		Stick-and-Hand Game (Per Game Averages)			
Southern Ute	2	9	25	150	$150
Ute Mountain Ute	2	8	25	50	$200
Northern Ute	8	8	20	200	$150
Wind River Shoshone	1	8	30	150	$150
Fort Hall Shoshone	3	7	30	150	$300

Individuals from all reservations participate in all of these games. Poker is not played until the dance is over. No poker games were seen at Ute Mountain or Southern Ute during 1966 and, because of a torrential shower on the last day of the Wind River dance, only one hand game was played. All other gambling was curtailed.

a. Pot (wager) dollar values often increase from one game to the next, but after three games or so, and especially if one side has lost two times running, pot dollar values decrease.

7 it is pointed out that there is an antagonism between the narrow individual ends and the narrow individual uses of power that accompany card games, and the broad individual ends and the broad uses of power on which the Sun dance is focused. Several factors mitigate but certainly do not obliterate the narrow individual nature of the card games that accompany Sun dances. Let us assess some of these mitigating factors as we describe briefly the gambling games.

At the Northern Ute dance as many as twenty people, crouching or standing, will place bets along with the eight or so players, who sit in a circle on the ground. Usually three or four Northern Utes will play with three or four Shoshones or Colorado Utes. The alignment of players from two or more reservation groups in each game, even though each person is playing against every other person, is common on all reserves. In any game, and they usually last three hours at least, a few changes of personnel are made.

Very few men play two-card monte, because the women, who play the game practically every day of the year on the Ute reservations, have much more expertise then the men. Many more games of monte are played than are games of poker. This may well be influenced by the relegation of women to supportive roles in the Sun dance. In monte games women can demonstrate their individual power and expertise. The preponderance of monte games, too, may well be influenced by the role commonly assumed by women as household budget managers. That men need the financial help of women in order to gamble is apparent at Sun dances. Women help their male kin and affines by giving them parts of their winnings so that the men can continue to play at their own poker games. Women also give money from their winnings to their children, grandchildren, and other kin for pop and candy. Thus the narrow uses of power and the narrow individual ends promoted by monte is accompanied by a broader individualism of sharing with the network of kin.

Women players are generally not averse to the short-shuffle, dealing from the bottom of the deck, or deftly picking up someone else's stakes, and accusations of cheating often begin to fly. Unless the accuser gets some help from several players, bettors, or kibitzers—who are always quick to enter in and frequently offer unsolicited advice—the person who unfairly grabbed the stakes or cheated on the deal will go free. If much fuss is made, the culprit will feign error or will indignantly remark that she will repay or reshuffle but that she is not guilty. This always brings a good laugh from the players, bettors, and spectators.

Poker games, providing an interesting contrast with monte, are much more sedate affairs and are played only by men. Again, men from several reservations join in most games. Except at Northern Ute, no more than ten spectators crowd around the makeshift tables and benches. Usually some person from the host reservation provides the equipment, and a small group of men usually shows up to play, game after game and year after year. Personnel move through these games rather fast, as men lose the five or ten dollars cash they brought with them. When a man's money runs out, he usually sends one of his young kin over to some woman in his household who is known to have money. If the woman who has been solicited has had success in her monte games, she may stake the man to a little more cash.

Of all contests, however, none generates as much excitement, nor seems to be so approved by the collectivity and so consonant with the broad individual and collective ends of the dance, as the hand-and-stick game. It is played by two teams with both men and women on each. They face one another kneeling behind two logs that are separated by about eight feet. The object is for a person on one team to hide a marked and an unmarked set of bones from the other team by sleight-of-hand tricks. Someone on the opposing team guesses which hand or hands the bones are held in. Each time he makes the right selection, he wins the bones for his side. If he guesses wrong, his side loses a stick. When ten sticks are lost by one team, or when one team has all the sticks, the game is over.

The teams are usually composed of eight or nine members. In most instances the host reservation forms one or two teams, which are then challenged by teams composed of members of one or more visiting communities or reservations. For instance, the Uintah–White Rivers from the Northern Ute reservation might play the people from Ute Mountain; Wind River Shoshones might play Colorado Utes from both Ute Mountain and Southern Ute; and Northern and Ute Mountain Utes might combine forces against the Fort Hall Shoshones.

The games are usually played for small stakes. Each player and up to twenty onlookers per side will contribute from one dollar up to perhaps five dollars for each purse. The only firm rule is that each wager be covered. In the late 1950s some purses were as large as 500 dollars, and in the late 1960s the pots averaged 150 dollars, with even larger amounts in the Ute Mountain purses—owing to a greater quantity of available cash—and in the Fort Hall purses. At Fort Hall in 1966 there was a large number of bettors, and three games were played between the same teams on the same night. The losers of the first game bet heavily on the second in hopes of winning their losses back plus a little bit more. When the losers failed a second time, they increased the ante again. That does not happen often. Usually the betting is not very heavy, and the winners, especially if they are the hosts, feel that they should let the losers get even—or close to it. If someone loses twice, the purses get smaller, mainly because the losers are out of money. The players express relief and a considerable amount of pleasure if each side breaks about even. Concern is always expressed for the losers.

The winning team takes the entire purse and divides it among all who have made wagers. At the Ute dances, teams may get locked in combat for two or three days and play as many as five games. When the smoke has cleared and the last bone has been palmed and guessed, the winners may have realized no more than five dollars each.

Each game draws as many as two hundred participants and spectators. The competition is intense, and the air about a game is electric, especially when one side wins several sticks in a row, or one side is near victory. News of the action is passed from spectators at the front to those at the back. The boosters for each side line up behind the team they are supporting. The players for each team are usually pressed into service by those who form the game or make the wagers. Women and men who are known to possess special powers for singing, sleight of hand, or clairvoyance are requested to perform. If a person does not play well, he or she will often drag someone else into the game. Though a player with a bad run of luck may stay in the game, he or she will abstain from guessing and hiding the bones for a while.

The songs each team sings when it has the bones are distinctive, and on tribally mixed teams it is not infrequent that some of the singers will not know the songs that other members of the team are singing. If those people who do the singing are successful in diverting the attention of the opposing team from the manipulation of the sticks, however, no one on the winning side cares whether or not he knew the songs that were used to help accomplish the diversion. Usually a particularly good singer and sleight-of-hand performer—often a respected shaman—guides the attack of the team. When his team wins, the victory is often attributed to his special or supernatural powers.

In sum, gambling is a most important aspect of the extracurricular activities that attend each Sun dance. Monte, which is primarily a woman's game, poker, which is primarily a man's game, and the hand-and-stick game, which draws both sexes together, all serve to draw participants from several reservations into prolonged competition and fraternizing. Although people are drawn together, community, reservation, language, and host-versus-visitor distinctions are stressed in that order. In monte and poker games the narrow individualistic ends that are pursued are mitigated only by sharing of winnings (within the networks). Participants and spectators choose sides and root for their own teams to win. For instance, in choosing a side to root for, or to bet on, a Ute Mountain Ute first and foremost might consider himself to be from Towaoc and align with others from Towaoc, second from Ute Mountain, third a Colorado Ute, fourth a Ute, and fifth a visitor. In the last instance, a Ute Mountain Ute at a Fort Hall Sun dance, if no other options were open, might play with a Wind River Shoshone team against a Fort Hall team. The hand-and-stick games are the highlights of the gambling sessions and stress similarities of, rather than distinctions between, history and language.

ROUND DANCING AND SHOW DANCING

More camaraderie and good times are created by round dancing and show dancing. The former is social and is participated in by most youths and adults. The latter is primarily a performance art and is participated in by only a few adults and children, usually male.

Except at Northern Ute, most of the social dancing takes place in the evening following the end of the dance. At the Northern Ute reservation, social dancing begins on the second evening of a three-day Sun dance and the third evening of a four-day dance (during the dancers' evening rest periods). Five or six men make a large fire and warm up a large drum. The fire often serves to light the dance area near the concession stand and gambling area, although a few bulbs burning from the concessionaire's generator also help illuminate the dance grounds. Often the dance takes place around the fire.

At first few people filter over to the social dance area. Most are gambling or watching the gamblers. Soon, however, several old, middle-aged, and young women begin a "blanket" dance. As the men around the drum sing and beat rhythm, women join into pairs, put a blanket over their shoulders, and march around in a circle to the rhythm of the drum. After five or ten minutes all of the women begin to link their arms and dance sideways in a shuffle-step-shuffle maneuver (the shuffle is merely dragging the trailing foot to catch up to the lead foot). By this time some men, especially teen-agers, have formed on the peripheries. The circle of women expands and moves toward the peripheries, and some women select men to dance with them. The man steps under the woman's blanket and joins in the sideways shuffle.

More and more men move into the area outside the dance circle and, in turn, they are selected to dance. Women are always the aggressors, and the choice of dance partners is strictly up to them. This is a very good time for women to make advances towards more reticent men from their own and other reservations. Ute women have commented that Shoshone and Ute men are "bashful" and go to bed with their clothes on. It is also a fact that teen-age girls generally introduce eleven- and twelve-year-old boys to coitus, and Sun dances are especially good times to carry out the lessons. Whether the reticent behavior of the males has any bearing on the dance protocol one can only guess. Nevertheless, in all social dancing and in the annual Bear dances performed by Utes and attended by some Shoshones each spring, women select men to dance.

Women's dominance in social dancing and in introducing men to coitus, as well as their equality to—if not dominance over—men in initiating courtship may well bear on some of the resistance men have to dancing with women in the Sun dance rituals (see chapter 9).

Round dances like the forty-nine dance, the "blanket," and others are performed at these sessions. An interesting feature of the round dances is that they are said to "get rid of those evil spirits and make the ghosts happy." For instance, at the end of each blanket dance the couple snaps the blanket that has covered them. The intent of this act is to liberate evil spirits, and it is a reworking of a Ghost dance belief that goes back to 1870, when the Utes and Shoshones first danced the Ghost dance. In the blanket dance the supernatural liberates evil spirits, whereas in the hand-and-stick game the supernatural is used to defeat the power of the opposing side. Round dances have their individual social effects as well, for they can lead to some of the couples slipping out for more intimate relations, which does not happen during the hand-and-stick games.

The show dances are performed following the termination of the Sun dance at all reserves. Hosts and visitors, male and female, with proper paraphernalia—feather headdresses, feather arm and hip bustles, porcupine roaches, porcupine quill breast-plates, buckskin leggins and shirts, etc.—perform "turkey" or "war" dances for them-selves and all who care to watch. Dances are performed to precision, even though dancers and singers are in quasi competition with one another. Singers try to sing songs that dancers do not know in order to make them miss a syncopated rhythm. The dances are standardized and performed in all-Indian competitions. The dancers who best follow the singers are acclaimed by all. Those who dance poorly or miss the dance step cues are often eliminated from the dancing. This, too, is a time for a person from one reserve to contact another, or for a bashful young man to be pursued by an interested young girl from his own community or reservation.

The show dancing allows men and women to gain a little prestige through their handsome Indian clothes and dancing skills. The fame of the best dancers spreads throughout the reservations in the Sun dance community and beyond, and show danc-ing not only attends the Sun dances, but is also part of the interreservation basketball tournaments. There are several intra- and interreservation competitions in show danc-ing during each year as well.

OTHER FRATERNIZING

Utes, Shoshones, Paiutes, and others of all ages look forward to sex relations with various partners. Contacts made at the concession, during the gambling sessions, and round dancing sessions, or while watching the show dancing, frequently leads to some men and women coupling off, perhaps having a few drinks, and then retiring some-where together. The interreservation pairing off is especially apparent.

My overall impression is that drinking is most frequent and obvious at Wind River, followed by Northern Ute, Fort Hall, Ute Mountain, and Southern Ute in that order. There is little correlation between the safeguards each reservation dance committee or tribal police force takes to restrict drinking and the amount of alcohol consumed during the duration of the various dances. Southern Ute tribal police normally check each car that enters the dance ground and ask whether anyone has been drinking or whether there is any alcohol in the car. If either is the case, the car and its occupants are turned away. Needless to say, whiskey, beer, and wine are smuggled into the area, and police must then round up those whom they allege to be inebriated.

Neither the Sun dance chiefs, nor the Sun dance ideology, nor the collective Indian ethic, nor tribal laws allow drinking at the dance. The tribal laws, of course, hold for entire reservations including the Sun dance grounds, and the collective Indian ethic is meant to apply to all Shoshones and Utes. Nevertheless, about 10 percent of the Southern Ute tribe's total membership drink to excess (Johnson 1963: 68); many others drink heavily; and practically all drink on occasion. At Southern Ute Sun dances, however, very few people appear to be drunk.

On the other hand, at Northern Ute Sun dances many people drink, though similar precautionary measures are exercised as at Southern Ute and the relative amount of drinking on the two reservations throughout the year is quite comparable. At the first Northern Ute dance in 1966, the tribal police chief—a white who has held the job for about nine years—and his white, mixed-blood, and Indian deputies rounded up and jailed thirty-six alleged drunks. Each was sentenced to a fine of sixty dollars or a thirty-day jail sentence.

More people appeared to be drunk and there seemed to be less police activity in 1966 at Wind River Shoshone than anywhere else.

In these three examples, Northern Ute seems to be the most aberrant: precautions are taken, but there is considerable drinking. Northern Ute, however, also draws more visitors from more reservations than do the other dances. It provides a fine arena for acquaintances to drink so that they can get to know one another better. The "have a good time" intention for drinking, at least at the Sun dances, seems to be important at Northern Ute and perhaps overrides the "escape" function of drinking, which leads to alcoholism.

Verbal fights sometimes erupt when one spouse accuses the other of promiscuity. A near relative or friend may be drawn into the argument and, in turn, may summon the police to settle the dispute. Men dancing in the Sun dance have been known to request police intervention when they learn that their spouses or others in the family are drinking and cohabiting with someone. It is not rare that both spouses are drinking and, perhaps, that each is engaged in an extramarital affair.

Single men between the ages of fifteen and about thirty tend to drink in groups. After a few drinks they are often emboldened to make advances to women, which frequently leads to trouble if they pursue the women into their camps and end up harassing the older people there. No one seems very unhappy when these young men are thrown in jail. When old men and women are pushed into police trucks, however, friends, relatives, and onlookers nearly always protest the action and announce that the alleged violators "were not hurting anybody." This is interesting, for Utes and Shoshones sometimes tell the police that young rowdies *are* hurting people when they are drunk.

If men are placed in a tribal jail, they can either serve their terms or get their kin to bail them out. If they are jailed while in a white town, however, another option is open to them: they can have their fines paid by white ranchers or farmers, whom they then repay in labor rather than in cash. A white deputy on one of the reservations usually requires two weeks' work from each Indian male whose fine he pays or whose bail he posts. Apparently, middle-aged men who have a few children at home are the safest individuals to invest in, for their fines are most often paid. Whites who thus exploit Indians whose lands they have taken, whose status they have denied, and whose behavior they have called immoral appear to believe they are doing the Indians a good turn in the process (see Dorn and Lucas 1966: 74–79).

It is not surprising that the unmarried, under- or unemployed, unskilled, under-educated males between fifteen and thirty are those who cause the most trouble when they drink to "have a good time." It is men in this age group that turn to the Sun dance to redeem themselves, to stop drinking, to transform their personalities, and to acquire some status and self-esteem. Yet drinking can lead Indians directly and rapidly back into the most odious clutches of the system that seems to have been the main force in driving them to drink and to dance the Sun dance in the first place.

PROSPECTS

The sponsorship of rituals on all five reservations provides an arena for people who are disapproved of at home and discriminated against in the white communities around their homes, to enjoy themselves, to gain approval for their own behavior as well as for the behavior of all Indians, and to generate some self-esteem. Courting, dancing, feasting, gift-giving, alternating sharing of trip expenses, some gambling, and even some social drinking (certainly not debauching) serve to promote the Indian collectivity and the individual's place within it.

Economically, Shoshone and Ute prospects for the future are for maintenance or even deterioration of the present situation. The rural satellite economies will probably continue to shrivel as agriculture becomes less and less profitable in the Mountain West states. The slack will probably be taken up by an ever larger welfare system rather than by the creation of viable reservation economies based on Indian control of Indian-owned resources. The gains from the profitable Indian resources will continue to be reaped by white farmers, farm corporations, and food-processing trusts in Idaho, and by national and multinational corporations (oil and mineral especially) operating in Colorado, Utah, and Wyoming.

I do not foresee the death of the Sun dance religion or even its gradual transformation into an establishment religion. The Sun dance will, I suspect, continue to flourish as a redemptive movement. At the time of writing this, in mid-1970, I have no reason to suspect otherwise.

Appendix
Sun Dance Variables And Ratings

I. PRE-DANCE ACTIVITIES	SU	UMU	NU	FHS	WRS
A. *Dance Cycle: Determination of Dates and Announcements*					
1. Determination of dates when dance will be performed each year made partly to accommodate other major Ute and Shoshone dances in the summer cycle and avoid date conflicts	+	+	+	+	+
2. Major dance performed at about the same time each year	+	+	+	+	+
3. Dates for dance announced at Bear dance in the spring (May)	+	+	+	−	−
Dates for dance announced in spring, usually but not always on Memorial Day	−	−	−	+	+
4. Length of dance—three or four days —announced when dates for performing dance are announced	+	+	+	+	+
5. Announcement of dates and length of dance made by Sun dance chief	+	+	+	+	+
B. *Selection of Chief and Committee*					
6. Head chief receives supernatural instructions in dream and then pledges the performance of the dance	+	+	+	+	+
7. Head chief position is quasi-permanent and is occupied by the same person as long as that person is able or desires to maintain the position	−	−	−	+	−
Head chief position is temporary and is determined anew (theoretically if not actually) for each dance	+	+	+	−	+

	SU	UMU	NU	FHS	WRS
8. Head chief is male only	+	+	+	−	+
Head chiefs are male and female (for each dance)	−	−	−	+	−
9. Assistant chief is invited by head chief and must be from another dance sponsoring reservation	−	−	−	+	+
Assistant chief is from same reservation as head chief, and he pledges a dance following super-natural instructions received in a dream	+	+	+	−	−
10. Assistant chief is male only	+	+	+	−	+
Assistant chiefs are male and female (for each dance)	−	−	−	+	−
11. Committee members are selected by head chief	+	+	+	+	+
12. Committee members selected by head chief usually occupy jobs for many consecutive years	+	+	−	+	+
Committee members selected by head chief often vary considerably from dance to dance, as does the head chief	−	−	+	−	−
13. Committee members selected about time the dance is pledged (Bear dance, Memorial Day, etc.)	+	+	+	+	+
14. Committee members include gate keeper, fire tender, waterman, lodge police, camp crier	−	−	−	+	+
Committee members include gate keeper, fire tender, waterman, lodge police	+	+	+	−	−
15. Legal tribal government, through tribally-elected or administration-appointed dance or recreation committees, as a legal right and duty is actively involved in pre-dance arrangements	−	−	+	−	+
Legal tribal government involved in pre-dance arrangements only at the request of dance chief	+	+	−	+	−
C. *Announcements and Invitations to other Reservations*					
16. Formal invitations, usually in letters, are extended by chief to members of other reservation committees encouraging them to attend his dance	+	+	+	+	+

	SU	UMU	NU	FHS	WRS
17. Informal invitations, usually by word of mouth but also by printed flyers, extended by chief, committeemen or other members of the host reservations to members of other reservation committees encouraging them to attend dance. Contacts at Bear dances, peyote meetings, basketball tourneys, etc.	+	+	+	+	+

D. *Song Practice and Song Teams*

	SU	UMU	NU	FHS	WRS
18. Singing practice sessions held throughout winter and spring	+	+	+	+	+
19. Singing practice sessions held at homes of chiefs, committeemen, and other good singers	+	+	+	+	+
20. Singing teams are organized along historic band, reservation community, or factional lines	+	+	+	+	+
21. Singing sessions are led by respected leader or renowned singer who organizes sessions and who takes head seat at drum	+	+	+	+	+
22. Intensive singing practice and the formation of competitive intra-reserve teams about one or two weeks before dance begins	−	−	+	−	+
Intensive singing practice one or two weeks before dance begins, yet intrareserve teams not formalized or noticeably competitive	+	+	−	+	−
23. Final preparation for singing teams is performance at "Baby dance" for evening prior to erection of the Sun dance corral	−	−	−	+	+
Final preparation for singing teams is at Sun dance grounds on the evenings prior to erection of the Sun dance corral, yet not associated with preparatory dance	+	+	+	−	−

E. *Movement to Dance Grounds*

	SU	UMU	NU	FHS	WRS
24. Chief moves to dance grounds, two or three days before erection of center pole	+	+	+	+	+
25. Dancers move to dance grounds any time up to the beginning of the dance (though expected to be there day before commencement)	+	+	+	+	+
26. Local singers move to dance grounds, any time; some commute from their homes and never establish camps	+	+	+	−	−

	SU	UMU	NU	FHS	WRS
Local singers (major ones) move to dance grounds and establish camp the day before the corral is erected	−	−	−	+	+
27. Committee moves to dance grounds two or three days before corral is erected	+	+	−	+	−
Committee moves to dance grounds the day before corral is erected	−	−	+	−	+

F. *Selection and Cutting of Center Pole*

	SU	UMU	NU	FHS	WRS
28. Sun dance chief selects center pole a month or so before dance	+	+	+	+	+
29. A forked willow, cottonwood, or aspen (willow preferred) is sought, usually sought near a river, for center pole	+	+	+	+	+
30. Center pole tree must be alive, and about "a cup of water" should pour out of it when it is cut	+	+	+	+	+
31. Sham battle no longer attends the center pole cutting	+	+	+	+	+
32. Chief uses rifle to shoot center pole just below crotch	−	−	+	−	−
World War II veteran uses rifle to shoot center pole just below crotch	+	+	−	−	−
Center pole is not shot	−	−	−	+	+
33. Chief and all dancers *should* cut down tree with steel axes at about dawn of day corral is erected	+	−	−	−	−
Chief cuts down tree with steel axe at about dawn on day corral is erected	−	+	+	+	+
34. Chief prays at tree when it is still standing and axe is embedded	+	+	+	−	−
Chief prays at tree before axe is embedded	−	−	−	+	+
35. Center pole is stripped of all branches at cutting site (directed by chief)	+	−	−	−	−
Center pole is stripped of all but uppermost branches (directed by chief)	−	+	+	+	+
36. If chief or helper steps over center pole he must retrace his steps	+	+	+	+	+

G. *Selection and Cutting of Lodge Poles and Rafters*

	SU	UMU	NU	FHS	WRS
37. Twelve side poles selected, willows preferred, aspen acceptable	+	+	+	+	+
38. Twelve side rafters selected, pine preferred, willows or aspen acceptable	+	+	+	+	+

	SU	UMU	NU	FHS	WRS
39. Twelve roof (overhead) rafters of pine selected	−	−	+	−	+
Four roof (overhead) rafters of pine selected	−	−	−	+	−
No roof (overhead) rafters selected	+	+	−	−	−
40. Presence, absence, or variation in number of roof rafters explained by dancers (not chief) as caused by availability of trees and their distance from dance grounds; many rafters where trees are numerous and close to dance grounds	−	−	+	+	+
Presence, absence, or variation in number of roof rafters explained by dancers (not chief) as "chief's instruction"	+	+	−	−	−
Poles and rafters are selected and cut by chief, committee members, and helpers	−	−	−	+	−
Poles and rafters are selected and cut by teams, hired and directed by tribal dance committee	−	−	−	−	+
Poles and rafters are selected·and cut by tribal employees from several crews whose service has been especially requested by chief and who are paid regular tribal salaries	+	−	−	−	−
Poles and rafters are selected and cut by tribal construction crews. Service is requested by chief	−	+	+	−	−
41. Poles and rafters cut anytime (1 day to 1 week) before erection of corral	+	+	+	+	−
Poles and rafters cut day before or morning that corral is erected	−	−	−	−	+
42. Chain saw can be used to cut and strip poles and rafters	+	+	+	+	+
43. Blessings are not given to corral poles and rafters	+	+	−	+	−
Chief blesses "east-running roof rafter" or "backbone" but no other pole or rafters	−	−	+	−	+

H. *Movement of Center Pole, Corral Poles, and Rafters*

	SU	UMU	NU	FHS	WRS
44. Center pole can be dragged along ground with mechanical aids and lifted onto truck by a winch	+	+	+	+	+
45. Center pole is "nested" or cushioned by truck	+	+	+	+	+

	SU	UMU	NU	FHS	WRS
46. Corral poles and rafters can be dragged along ground with mechanical aids and lifted onto truck by a winch	+	+	+	+	+
47. Corral poles and rafters are *not* "nested" or cushioned on trucks	+	+	+	+	+
48. At Sun dance grounds after truck is unloaded, center pole, corral poles and rafters are moved to corral site with help of trucks, winches, etc.	+	+	+	+	−
At Sun dance grounds after truck is unloaded, center pole, corral poles and rafters are moved to corral site by being dragged behind a horse	−	−	−	−	+

J. *Ritual Hunt*

49. No ritual hunt prior to construction of corral except for ritualized shooting of center pole before felling	+	+	+	+	+

K. *Parade*

50. Sun dance chief, two committeemen, and one woman don feather headdresses, mount horses and lead truck with center pole to the corral site. Committeeman on truck dons headdress and plays tambourine. Chief, committee and women sing. Other women wait at proposed corral site and make the women's war trill	+	−	−	−	−
No parades are performed	−	+	+	+	+

II. CONSTRUCTION CHANGES THROUGHOUT DANCE, AND MEANING OF SUN DANCE CORRAL

	SU	UMU	NU	FHS	WRS

A. *Name for Sun Dance Corral*

1. "Thirst house," or "Place where one thirsts" is gloss for corral	+	+	+	+	+

B. *Preparation and Erection of Center Pole*

2. First pole erected is center pole	+	+	+	+	−
Last pole erected is center pole	−	−	−	−	+
3. First post hole dug is for center pole	+	+	+	+	+
4. No ritual associated with digging post hole for center pole and nothing put in hole except center pole and dirt from the hole	+	+	+	+	−

	SU	UMU	NU	FHS	WRS
No ritual associated with digging of post hole for center pole. Stick placed in empty hole and left until corral poles are erected and center pole is moved into place	−	−	−	−	+
5. Some of center pole decoration is put on before pole is erected	+	+	+	+	+
6. Center pole decoration varies with chief's dream instructions	+	+	+	+	+
7. Willow bundle or nest is placed in crotch of center pole before pole is erected	+	+	+	+	+
8. Buffalo skin robe is placed over willow bundle in crotch of center pole before pole is erected	+	−	−	−	−
Buffalo skin not used, at least not used in 1966	−	+	+	+	+
9. One scarf tied to each fork of center pole before pole is erected	−	+	+	+	+
Four scarves tied to each fork of center pole before pole is erected	+	−	−	−	−
10. Bark is left on center pole	+	−	+	−	+
Bark is stripped off center pole from ground level up to about five feet above ground (second morning)	−	+	−	+	−
11. Center pole is painted with red, white, and black stripes (varies at No. Ute and Ute Mtn. Ute with chief)	+	+	+	−	−
Center pole painted white or not painted (varies at No. Ute and Ute Mtn. Ute with chief)	−	−	−	+	+
12. Center pole is moved into position by chief and any other man who wishes to help	+	+	+	−	+
Center pole is moved into position by chiefs (male and female) and any other men and women who wish to help	−	−	−	+	−
13. Center pole is moved into place in four separate liftings and thrusts, the first three followed by feints of exhaustion	−	+	+	+	+
Center pole is moved into place in three separate liftings and thrusts, each followed by feints of exhaustion	+	−	−	−	−
14. Four sets of songs and four sets of prayers—one set of each following each lifting of the center pole—are led by chief. Each set is followed by three whistle blasts	−	+	+	+	+

	SU	UMU	NU	FHS	WRS
Three sets of songs and three prayers—one set of each following each lifting of center pole—are led by chief. Each set is followed by whistle blasts	+	−	−	−	−
15. Center pole is nestled between crossed poles as it is lifted (winches and A-frames have been used from time to time)	+	+	+	+	+
16. Center pole is scaled, usually with help of ladder, and a bison head, Eagle, or strip of cloth is attached (item used varies with the chief at No. Ute, Ute Mtn. Ute)	+	+	+	+	+
17. Bison head, Eagle, or strip of cloth is attached just below the crotch of the pole before dance begins	−	−	−	−	+
Bison head, Eagle, or strip of cloth is attached just below the crotch of the pole between sunrise and dance sessions of first day	+	−	−	+	−
Bison head, Eagle, or strip of cloth is attached just below the crotch of the pole whenever chief decides it should be attached. Varies with chiefs	−	+	+	−	−
C. *Preparation and Erection of Corral Posts and Rafters*					
18. Positions for corral posts measured from center post hole by chief	+	+	+	+	+
19. Corral posts (twelve) erected before center pole is erected	−	−	−	−	+
Corral posts (twelve) erected after center pole is erected	+	+	+	+	−
20. Stick placed in center post hole until corral posts are erected, but at no other time	−	−	−	−	+
Stick placed at base of center pole at termination of dance—to ritually "kill" the pole—but at no other time	−	−	−	+	−
Stick not placed in center post hole or at base of pole at any time	+	+	+	−	−
21. All available men are encouraged to dig post holes and erect corral posts	+	+	+	+	+
22. Teams of men dig post holes, but all men under the direction of the chief erect the corral posts	−	+	−	+	−
Erection of corral posts, though ultimately under the direction of the chief, is mostly carried out by hired crews	+	−	+	−	+

	SU	UMU	NU	FHS	WRS
23. Westernmost corral post is lined up with the center post so that both face directly into the rising sun	+	+	+	+	+
24. Side rafters (two) are put in place between the corral posts after the center pole is erected	+	+	+	+	+
25. "East-running rafter" from westernmost corral post ("backbone") to center pole is decorated before it is hoisted into place	−	−	+	+	+
No "east-running rafter" used, but "backbone" is	+	+	−	−	−
26. Pine boughs left on tip of east-running rafter, and eagle feather charm is attached to it	−	−	+	+	+
No east-running rafter and no similar charm located in corral	+	+	−	−	−
27. Pine boughs left on the tips of all roof rafters	−	−	+	+	+
No roof rafters are used	+	+	−	−	−
28. East-running rafter is the first roof rafter to be hoisted into place. This follows erection of corral pole, center pole and side rafters	−	−	+	+	+
No roof rafters are used	+	+	−	−	−
29. Twelve roof rafters, including east-running rafter and rafters running from the other three cardinal directions, are hoisted into place	−	−	+	−	+
Four roof rafters, including east-running rafter and rafters running from the other three cardinal directions, are hoisted into place	−	−	−	+	−
No roof rafters are used	+	+	−	−	−
30. Exterior of corral covered with aspen, poplar, willows and other brush, yet doorway toward the east is left open and free of brush	+	+	+	+	+

D. *Meanings of Center Pole and Corral*

	SU	UMU	NU	FHS	WRS
31. Center pole represents medium through which supernatural power, the life-giving substance, is channeled	+	+	+	+	+
32. Center pole has supernatural power of its own (water in the trunk)	+	+	+	+	+
33. Supernatural power comes from the sun, or god, in the form of the sun's rays	+	+	+	+	+

	SU	UMU	NU	FHS	WRS
34. Sun's rays are "water" or supernatural power that "dry up" the dancer and then "fill" the dancer with "water," i.e., supernatural power	+	+	+	+	+
35. Sun's rays, or power, are channeled through the east-running rafter, the center pole, the willow nest, and the bison head or whatever else is attached to the center pole	−	−	+	+	+
Sun's rays, or power, are channeled through the center pole, the willow nest, and the bison head or whatever else is attached to the center pole. No east-running rafter	+	+	−	−	−
36. Center pole said to represent power. Great variability from person to person, dancer to dancer about symbolism, and most people accept more than one "meaning" for pole (e.g., "God's brain," "crucifix," "Jesus")	+	+	+	+	+
37. Leaves at top of center pole represent the "miracle of life," which comes from the ground and is caused by the "water" (power) that is channeled through the pole	−	−	+	+	+
No leaves at top of center pole, but accept the symbol of the "miracle of life" on poles at other dances	+	+	−	−	−
38. Willow nest in crotch of center pole represents "nest of 'water' (power)," "body of Jesus"	+	+	+	+	+
39. Cloth scarves on center pole are "gifts" to the "old people"	+	+	+	+	+
40. Painted bands on center pole represent "days of dance," "the godhead sans the holy ghost," "sacred three," "three months pole will have water," etc.	+	+	+	+	+
41. General agreement that no individual knows the "complete" meaning of every feature of the Sun dance corral or every ritual act or behavior	+	+	+	+	+
42. Meanings of features in the corral as well as ritual acts can be personal (through dreams), or collective and shared by the group (explained in speeches given by Sun dance chiefs)	+	+	+	+	+

	SU	UMU	NU	FHS	WRS
43. Meanings of corral and of ritual acts and behaviors are additive but not always cumulative, i.e., some personal interpretations of the features of the corral, etc., are learned in dreams, kept as personal property, and die with the bearer	+	+	+	+	+
44. Any meanings of the features of the corral and other ritual acts and behaviors which are advanced by dancers, chiefs or other religious leaders are accepted as religious truths	+	+	+	+	+
45. Corral or "thirst house" is also said to be symbolic of God and God's temple	+	+	+	+	+
46. Corral posts (twelve) are said to represent "twelve apostles of Jesus," "a god's ribs," "twelve days in which each dancer should perform," etc.	+	+	+	+	+
47. Corral posts at cardinal points represent the "sacred directions," "sacred four," "several days of some dances," etc.	+	+	+	+	+
48. North and south corral posts represent "god's ears"	+	+	+	+	+
49. Corral opening, or east entrance, is "god's mouth," "door to god's temple," "door to thirst house"	+	+	+	+	+
50. Boughs on tips of roof rafters represent "life from water" and "god's hair"	−	−	+	+	+
No roof rafters but accept meaning of rafters at other dances	+	+	−	−	−
E. Changes and Additions to Corral as Dance Progresses					
51. Dirt mound (altar) built up around base of center pole	+	+	+	+	+
52. Dirt mound represents "life-giving" soil	+	+	+	+	+
53. Dirt mound constructed on first morning	+	−	+	−	+
Dirt mound constructed on second night	−	−	−	+	−
Dirt mound constructed on second morning	−	+	−	−	−
54. Willows placed upright in dirt mound and replaced by chief as willows wither (depends on chief at Ute Mtn. Ute and No. Ute)	+	+	+	−	−

	SU	UMU	NU	FHS	WRS
Willows tied in bundle and placed on east side of center pole on top of dirt mound	−	−	−	+	−
No willows placed on dirt mound (varies with chiefs at Ute Mtn. and No. Ute)	−	−	−	−	+
55. Stalls made of saplings—aspen, willows, poplars, pine—with leaves, branches, or boughs about five feet above ground, erected for dancers by hosts, friends, relatives, and sponsors	+	+	+	+	+
56. Decorated sheets with Sun dance–quasi Christian symbols or blankets hung between saplings when dancers not dancing	+	+	+	+	+
57. Saplings for stalls stripped up about five feet from ground and usually painted	+	+	+	+	+
58. Preferred color for painting stall saplings of host dancers is white	−	−	−	+	−
Preferred color for painting stall saplings of host dancers is reddish-brown	+	+	+	−	−
Preferred color for painting stall saplings of host dancers is yellow	−	−	−	−	+
59. Visiting dancers can choose the color they wish stalls to be painted	−	+	+	+	+
Chief has all stalls, for hosts and visitors, painted the same color	+	−	−	−	−
60. Paint on stall saplings said to "dry out" *and* "cool" the poles just as it "dries out" and "cools" the dancer. Also controls sap	+	+	+	+	+
61. Stalls erected on first morning following sunrise	+	−	−	−	−
Stalls erected on second morning following sunrise	−	+	+	+	+
62. One dancer per stall	+	+	+	−	+
Two dancers per stall	−	−	−	+	−
63. Dance paths dug or cleared of rocks for dancers at time when stalls are erected	+	+	+	+	+
64. Fence or arbor constructed to separate sacred dance area from singer and spectator area	+	+	+	+	+
65. Fence or arbor constructed following sunrise ceremony on first morning	+	+	−	+	−
Fence or arbor constructed following sunrise ceremony on second morning	−	−	+	−	+

	SU	UMU	NU	FHS	WRS
66. Fence is made of several willows or red birch, which are bent in crescent shapes; each tip is secured in the ground, and three or four pieces make up each side of the fence	+	+	−	−	−
Fence is made of forked sticks topped by stripped saplings	−	−	+	−	−
Fence is made of aspen posts (not forked) and willow rails tied to the posts	−	−	−	+	−
Fence is two logs placed on ground	−	−	−	−	+
67. Sacred pit is dug in northeast corner of dance corral, just east of the the fence that separates the sacred dance area from the spectator area	+	+	+	+	+
68. Sacred pit is used to burn sacred juniper boughs on second and subsequent days of the dance following sunrise ceremonies. Not dug or used on first day	+	+	+	+	+
69. Sacred pit fire is started with embers from sacred dance fire, ashes are disposed of (buried) ritually, and pit is refilled each day	+	+	+	+	+
70. Sacred dance fire is built in front and east of the center pole on the first and each subsequent night of the dance	+	+	+	+	+
71. Sacred dance fire ashes are cleared from in front of the Sun dance pole each morning following the sunrise service. Ashes are ritually buried, and fire is not built again until night	+	+	+	+	+
72. Large drum about four feet across is moved into southeast area of corral each dance session, and circled by benches or chairs	+	+	+	+	+
73. Saplings, willows preferred, are placed in singers' section around the drums, and in spectators' section on last day of dance	+	+	+	−	−
No saplings placed in singer-spectator area	−	−	−	+	+
74. Saplings placed in singer-spectator area represent "life," and willows in particular represent "water" or power itself. Also provide shade for singers	+	+	+	−	−

	SU	UMU	NU	FHS	WRS
Though saplings represent "life" and "water," they are not placed in singer-spectator area	−	−	−	+	+
75. Flag pole erected outside corral adjacent to the south side of the east doorway. (varies with chief at Northern Ute)	−	−	+	−	+
No flag poles erected	+	+	−	+	−

III. DANCERS: THEIR INITIATIONS, INSTRUCTIONS, INTENTIONS, INVITATIONS, AND RELIGIOUS EXPERIENCES

	SU	UMU	NU	FHS	WRS

A. *Initiation and Instructions of Dancers*

	SU	UMU	NU	FHS	WRS
1. If dancer had dream instructions to participate in dance, he must participate lest he wither and die	+	+	+	−	−
Dream instructions less frequent and no mention of death retribution for violation of dream	−	−	−	+	+
2. Young males (usually 14 or 15 years of age) who are initiated into the dance have had recurrent dreams, interpreted by shamans, which instruct them to dance. Sometimes older initiates, men and women, have similar dreams and dream interpretations by shamans (Females can dance at Fort Hall only)	+	+	+	−	−
Dancers may enter dance for first time at any age. A dream interpreted by a shaman is not a prerequisite for participation. A shaman, a parent, another dancer may encourage a man or a woman to dance for his or her own health, or the initiate may enter to dance for an ailing or a bereaved friend or relative	−	−	−	+	+
3. No formal fraternities or sodalities sponsor the dances, nor does a dancer have to belong to a club to perform	+	+	+	+	+
4. Dancers are expected to participate in at least twelve dances, though they should, as a prescription, dance in at least four dances. However, if a dancer cannot dance in as many as four dances or, if he dances more than four but cannot make twelve, he should stop dancing on an even number	+	+	+	+	+

	SU	UMU	NU	FHS	WRS
5. The dancer initiate is counseled not to dance too hard or out of control at the first dance	+	+	+	+	+
6. The dancer initiate is told that each dance gets more difficult and that a dancer must develop his power accordingly	+	+	+	+	+
7. The dancer initiate is counseled that alcohol and dancing do not mix and that a man of bad heart who has been taking alcohol will anger the "power" and, in turn, will be ignominiously "knocked down" in the corral	+	+	+	+	+
8. The dancer initiate is counseled that peyote and dancing do not mix and that only the strongest men get power from both sources	+	+	+	+	+
9. The male dancer initiate is counseled that he must be prudent and wise in post-dance sexual behavior because the accumulation of power earned and invested in the dance makes a person more virile	+	+	+	+	+
10. The dancer initiate is counseled about obligations to Indian kin and friends, especially to close family members and "old folks," told to maintain the integrity of Indian life, and counseled against Anglo ways	+	+	+	+	+
11. The dancer initiate is counseled that he will require considerate thoughtfulness and caution in using the powers that he will acquire through subsequent dances	+	+	+	+	+
12. The dancer initiate is counseled that the bison (on the center pole, or "power" itself) will constantly issue challenges during each dance, and that the dancer should respect but not run away from the challenge. If a dancer is knocked "woozy," he should "fight back"	+	+	+	+	+
13. Dancers are counseled that, though power can be won in each dance, a dancer gets his vision in the twelfth dance	+	+	+	−	−
Dancers are counseled that they can get their visions in the fourth dance	−	−	−	+	+

	SU	UMU	NU	FHS	WRS
14. Vision is usually pursued on last day of dance	+	+	+	+	+
15. Mechanics of vision experience is ritualized as prospective recipient learns that he will be "jolted" by power, lifted into the air, and knocked to the ground. Spirit will then leave body and get vision instruction	+	+	+	+	+
16. If a dancer enters a dance, he must be prepared to dance complete dance. If dancer bolts from the corral and gets away, he will die	+	+	+	+	+
17. Stories told of whites, mixed-bloods, or non-Utes and non-Shoshones who bolted from corral and either were captured and returned, or were later found dead	+	+	+	+	+
18. Dancers cannot eat any food during dance	+	+	+	+	+
19. Dancers cannot drink any water during dance	+	+	+	+	+
20. Dancers should not go into dance inebriated (this rule often broken)	+	+	+	+	+

B. *Intentions and Invitations of Dancers*

	SU	UMU	NU	FHS	WRS
21. Second and subsequent dances are participated in partly because of ritual instructions	+	+	+	+	+
22. Dancers intend to gain supernatural power	+	+	+	+	+
23. Dancers intend to achieve or maintain good health through supernatural means	+	+	+	+	+
24. Dancers intend to direct supernatural power to ailing friends or relatives for whom they dance	+	+	+	+	+
25. Some dancers intend to become shamans, even Sun dance chiefs, depending on dream instructions	+	+	+	+	+
26. Dancers are informally encouraged to attend dances other than those sponsored on their home reserves	+	+	+	+	+
27. Dancers are formally invited by dance chiefs to attend dances at home or away, but ultimate decision to participate is always left to the dancer and, perhaps, to the dancer's dream instructions	+	+	+	+	+

	SU	UMU	NU	FHS	WRS
28. Dancers participate in dances sponsored by dances on distant reserves	+	+	+	+	+
29. A dancer, unless he is an initiate, does not have to tell the Sun dance chief that he is going to participate in the dance	+	+	+	+	+
30. A dancer, a few days before the dance begins, usually informs the Sun dance chief at his home dance of his intention to participate	+	+	+	+	+
31. A visiting dancer may not inform the Sun dance chief of his intention to dance until an hour or so before the dance begins	+	+	+	+	+

C. *Personal Preparation*

	SU	UMU	NU	FHS	WRS
32. Some, but not all, dancers sweat before each dance	+	+	+	+	+
33. Most, but not all, dancers prepare for dance by observing diet of a saltless meat, fried bread, and water for a couple of weeks before the dance begins	+	+	+	+	+
34. Last meal taken with chief in his lodge evening before dance by all dancers present. Individual prayer over saltless meat, fried bread	+	+	+	−	−
Last meal taken any time before going in, not with chief	−	−	−	+	+
35. Last drink taken with chief from pitch-lined basket just before leaving chief's tent, or at back of corral	+	+	+	−	−
Last drink taken anytime. Not ritualized	−	−	−	+	+

IV. DANCER'S DRESS, ITS MEANING AND CHANGES THROUGHOUT DANCE

	SU	UMU	NU	FHS	WRS

A. *Dress (Male)*

	SU	UMU	NU	FHS	WRS
1. Skirts of cotton, satin, velvet, nylon, etc., worn by all men. Majority have fringe along bottom. Hang from waist to ankles	+	+	+	+	+
2. Skirts are usually a single color, though the colors vary from dancer to dancer with blues, greens, reds, and purples dominant	+	+	+	+	+

	SU	UMU	NU	FHS	WRS
3. Each dancer uses several skirts per dance, and skirts are changed twice a day: daylight dance session and night dance session	+	+	+	−	−
Each dancer uses several skirts per dance, and skirts are changed once a day following the sunrise ceremony	−	−	−	+	+
4. Skirts have no prescriptive designs. Choice of decor is up to dancer's whim, dream instructions, the person from whom a skirt is borrowed, or the person who makes the skirt and gives it to the dancer as a gift	+	+	+	+	+
5. Skirts are decorated with embroidery, piping, sequins, beads, ribbon, elk or bear teeth, etc., singly or in various combinations. Some skirts are also undecorated	+	+	+	+	+
6. Skirts are purchased, borrowed, or received as gifts	+	+	+	+	+
7. Common designs on front of skirts are bison, eagle, Jesus, numerals (e.g., "1928"), eagle fan, sun, moon, stars, and geometric patterns	+	+	+	+	+
8. Breechclouts or aprons, usually decorated, are sometimes worn over the skirts. Individual choice	+	+	+	−	−
Breechclouts or aprons, not worn over skirts	−	−	−	+	+
9. Dancers wrap themselves in white sheets when leaving corral and use same sheets to hang between stall saplings protecting them from public view	+	+	+	−	−
Dancers wrap themselves in Pendleton brand woolen blankets and use them in stalls as well	−	−	−	+	+
10. No shoes, moccasins, or other footwear used in sacred dance area	+	+	+	+	+
11. Eagle-bone whistles used by each dancer	+	+	+	+	+
12. Majority of whistles have a white feather attached to the tip	+	−	+	+	+
Majority of whistles do not have feathers attached	−	+	−	−	−
13. Eagle-bone whistle preferred because it "captures" water (power) and soothes the throat	+	+	+	+	+

	SU	UMU	NU	FHS	WRS
14. Whistles are borrowed, purchased, received as gifts. Those borrowed or received from powerful shamans are preferred	+	+	+	+	+
15. Dancers wear pendants or necklaces of beads; satin; cloth with shell designs; ermine skins	+	+	+	+	+
16. Pendants or necklaces changed once or twice a day	+	+	+	+	+
17. Belts, usually 3″ or more wide and preferably beaded, are worn around waist. Usually tied with thong	+	+	+	+	+
18. Belts, usually 3″ or more wide, are sometimes made of tooled leather	+	+	+	+	+
19. Dominant decorations on belts are geometric, flower, and thunderbird designs	+	+	+	+	+
20. Sash often tied around waist with one streamer hanging down side	+	+	+	+	+
21. Beaded bags or hip bustles sometimes worn on hip	+	+	+	+	+
22. Prayer horns not carried or used	+	+	+	+	+

B. *Dress (Female) at Fort Hall Dance Only*

	SU	UMU	NU	FHS	WRS
23. Women wear finest dresses, usually satins, specially prepared for Sun dance	−	−	−	+	+
Women wear everyday calico dresses	+	+	+	−	−
24. Women do not wear shoes	+	+	+	+	+

C. *Changes in Dress and Ornamentation throughout Dance*

	SU	UMU	NU	FHS	WRS
25. White T-shirts worn by some dancers during evening sessions	+	+	+	+	+
26. Sunglasses worn by some dancers during day session and by others day and night	+	+	+	+	+
27. Down feathers attached to tip of fifth finger and allowed to dangle beginning on first day	−	−	+	+	+
Down feathers attached to tip of fifth finger and allowed to dangle beginning on second day	+	+	−	−	−
28. The longer the dance has been in progress (two or more days), the more likely that powerful dancer-shamans will carry special eagle feather or eagle wing or tail fan	+	+	+	+	+

	SU	UMU	NU	FHS	WRS
29. All dancers carry willow wands on last day of dance—chief's discretion	+	−	−	−	−
Some dancers may carry willow wands on last day of dance, but not at chief's discretion	−	+	+	+	+
30. Ermine skins braided in hair or worn around neck beginning on second day. Primarily worn by old men and women	+	+	+	+	+
31. Women (dancers at Fort Hall only) braid hair so that it hangs down front rather than back beginning second day. Decorate with ermine skins or ribbons, beads, elk or bear teeth	+	+	+	+	+
32. No body paints are worn on first day of dance (at Wind River a few Fort Hall boys had lipstick and cheek rouge designs on face)	−	+	+	+	+
Reddish-brown body wash, but no designs on first day	+	−	−	−	−
33. Body paints (without designs) worn by many, but not necessarily all, on second and subsequent days of dance; each day more body paints are worn	+	+	+	+	+
34. Body paints (not for designs) are mixed and distributed by members of Sun dance committee	+	+	+	+	+
35. Body paint (not for design) is reddish-brown	+	+	+	−	−
Body paint (not for design) is white	−	−	−	+	−
Body paint (not for design) is yellow	−	−	−	−	+
36. Women put body paint on face and legs (at Fort Hall)	+	+	+	+	+
37. Paint is said to "dry up" dancer and "cool" him as well	+	+	+	+	+
38. Face and chest painted with designs beginning on second day. Number of dancers with painted designs increase on subsequent day(s)	+	+	+	+	+
39. Face and chest painted with designs on many dancers	−	−	−	+	+
Face and chest painted with designs on few dancers	+	+	+	−	−
40. Red and black striping, circles, and dots are preferred painting designs	−	−	−	+	+

	SU	UMU	NU	FHS	WRS
Red, white, and blue striping is preferred painting design	+	−	−	−	−
No painting design preference	−	+	+	−	−

41. Overall, dress, body paints, ornamentation, and ritual paraphernalia become more elaborate as dance progresses. Within broad limits, each dancer develops own wardrobe and paraphernalia

	SU	UMU	NU	FHS	WRS
	+	+	+	+	+

42. Decorative motifs on dress and body ornamentation can be learned in dreams, borrowed from other dancers, created by friends and kin

	SU	UMU	NU	FHS	WRS
	+	+	+	+	+

V. PERFORMANCE OF THE DANCE

	SU	UMU	NU	FHS	WRS

A. *Commencement of the Dance: Assembly and Parade*

1. Drum is beaten at chief's tent an hour or two after sundown. This is "first call" for dancers to assemble

	SU	UMU	NU	FHS	WRS
	+	+	+	+	+

2. If there is a full moon, the chief will start the dance when the moon is directly overhead

	SU	UMU	NU	FHS	WRS
	+	+	+	+	+

3. Full moon preferred, but no longer prescribed for dance as Sun dance performances are accommodated to performances on other reservations and not to phases of the moon

	SU	UMU	NU	FHS	WRS
	+	+	+	+	+

4. Second and third "calls" are beaten on drum. The third call is the last call for dancers to assemble

	SU	UMU	NU	FHS	WRS
	−	+	+	−	+

Second and third "calls" are not issued; first calls only

	SU	UMU	NU	FHS	WRS
	+	−	−	+	−

5. Dancers assemble at chief's tent due west of the westernmost point of the dance corral

	SU	UMU	NU	FHS	WRS
	−	+	+	−	−

Dancers assemble directly behind the westernmost point of the dance corral

	SU	UMU	NU	FHS	WRS
	+	−	−	+	+

6. All dancers must enter corral at same time during a three-day dance, otherwise they cannot participate

	SU	UMU	NU	FHS	WRS
	+	+	+	−	+

Dancers can enter after opening ceremony and during the first night of a three-day dance

	SU	UMU	NU	FHS	WRS
	−	−	−	+	−

7. Dancers queue up behind chief in single file and march clockwise around corral

	SU	UMU	NU	FHS	WRS
	+	+	+	+	−

	SU	UMU	NU	FHS	WRS
Dancers queue up in two lines, one behind chief and one behind guest chief, and march around corral, one line moving clockwise and the other counterclockwise	−	−	−	−	+
8. Chiefs and dancers blow whistles and circle the corral three times before entering	+	+	+	+	−
Chiefs and dancers blow whistles, each line circling the corral one and one-half times—for a total of three—before entering	−	−	−	−	+
9. Dancers usually enter corral with one or more friend(s) with whom they dance. Get next to one another in commencement line so that they can position themselves side by side in their dance stalls	+	+	+	+	+
10. Chiefs are first persons to enter the empty corral, and they take up their positions directly in front of the backbone, or westernmost point in corral, facing the center pole which is due east	+	+	+	+	+
11. Dancers position themselves on either side of chiefs	+	+	+	+	+
12. If chief is in wrong position, he can correct himself the following morning (get directly in east-west line with center pole)	+	+	+	+	+
13. Dancers shuffle their stall positions after entering the corral, especially women if they are originally located on northeast side which is reserved for men	−	−	−	+	−
Dancers do not shuffle their stall positions in the corral	+	+	+	−	+
14. Gate keeper, the rest of the Sun dance committee, and the drummers follow the dancers into the corral	+	+	+	+	+
15. Spectators immediately follow committee and drummers into the corral. Not restrained, but they stay back from dance area	+	−	−	+	−
Spectators immediately follow committee and drummers into the corral. Restrained by lodge police from crowding into the dance area	−	+	+	−	+

B. *"First Night" Ritual Acts and Observances*	SU	UMU	NU	FHS	WRS
16. Three "opening" songs are sung by the drummers and singers, not by the chief or dancers	−		−	+	−
Four sets of "opening" songs are sung by chief and dancers, each set followed by whistle blasts; chief leads singing	−		+	−	+
No "opening" songs are sung	+		−	−	−
17. Dancers kneel during "opening" songs	−		−	−	+
Dancers do not kneel	+		+	+	−
18. Chief offers first prayer to center pole. Does not include pipe ritual. Precedes dancing	−		+	+	+
Chief offers second prayer to center pole. Includes pipe ritual to cardinal direction. Precedes dancing	+		−	−	−
19. Gate keeper offers first prayer to center pole. Precedes dancing	+		−	−	−
Gate keeper does not offer prayer prior to commencement of dancing	−		+	+	+
20. Gate keeper or crier calls for bedrolls to be passed out to dancers. Dancers' goods are carried in by sponsors and relatives	+		+	+	+
21. Sacred dance fire lighted by fire tender before dancing begins	+		−	−	−
Sacred dance fire lighted by fire tender after dancing begins	−		+	+	+
22. First "dance" song is preceded by a "rest" song and several loud beatings of the drum (four or more beats)	+		+	+	+
23. Chief is first person to commence dancing. Begins with first dance song	−		+	+	+
Chief is usually first person to commence dancing during first dance song	+		−	−	−
24. Chief is not necessarily the first to commence dancing in each dance set following the initial set; anyone can dance	+		+	+	+
25. Dance sets are composed of four songs each	−		+	+	+
Dance sets are one song each	+		−	−	−
26. Dance sets last three to five minutes each	+		+	+	+
27. Dance songs sung at about 180 beats per minute (down to 160 at So. Ute)	+		+	+	+

	SU	UMU	NU	FHS	WRS
28. Rest song interrupts each dance set, one song each	+		+	+	+
29. Rest songs last about one minute each	+		+	+	+
30. Rest songs sung at slower tempo than dance songs—about 120–160 beats per minute (So. Ute had slowest beat)	+		+	+	+
31. Drum beaten loud to signal transition from rest song to dance song	+		+	+	+
32. Dancers need not dance as a prescription; they can rest or merely stand in stall and blow whistle	+		+	+	+
33. Dancers start slowly and do not generally dance all the way up to the center pole	+		+	−	+
Dancers start fast; some women charge the center pole	−		−	+	−
34. Dance steps vary. No two men or women necessarily use the same dance steps	+		+	+	+
35. Dance steps can be changed throughout the dance	+		+	+	+
36. Dance steps learned in dream instructions, borrowed from others, invented by dancers	+		+	+	+
37. Dance steps of women somewhat more similar than those of men, especially on return from pole where they alternate each foot with each beat of the drum in retreat (at Fort Hall only)	+		+	+	+
38. Dancers can bed down for the night whenever they wish, or they can dance all night long if they wish	+		+	+	+
39. Dancers usually bed down at about 1:00 A.M., at which time singers quit singing. Singers sing as long as dancers dance	+		+	+	+
40. "Sunrise ceremony" is last ritual performance of the "First Night"	+		+	+	+
41. Dancers routed out of bed by gate keeper about half hour before sunrise	+		+	+	+
42. Sunrise ceremony conducted by head chief	+		−	−	−
Sunrise ceremony conducted by joint chiefs	−		+	+	+

	SU	UMU	NU	FHS	WRS
43. Dancers line up in four lines behind center pole and blow whistles. Singers sing sunrise song (at Fort Hall men on north and women on south)	+		+	+	+
44. As sun rises, dancers raise arms and then pat bodies with down feathers. Pat in the sun's rays, or power, or water	+		+	+	−
As sun rises, dancers do not raise arms, merely beat time with hands at side holding down feathers	−		−	−	+
45. Sacred dance fire is allowed to burn out and is prepared by fire tender into a circular mound of ashes	+		+	+	+
46. Dancers sit around sacred dance fire ashes, covered with blankets or sheets	+		+	+	+
47. Chief sings four special sunrise songs, each song followed by four whistle blasts	−		+	−	+
Drummers sing four special sunrise songs, each song followed by four whistle blasts	−		−	+	−
Chief sings and leads dancers in six special sunrise songs followed by one, two, three, four, four, four whistle blasts respectively	+		−	−	−
48. Head chief offers prayer following special songs (female at Fort Hall)	+		+	+	+
49. Head chief shamanizes each dancer by brushing him with eagle feather fan and sacred ashes (varies with chief)	+		+	−	−
No special shamanizing of dancer during first sunrise	−		−	+	+
50. Ashes from sacred fire are carried out of corral and buried by fire tender	+		+	+	+
51. Wheelbarrow used to carry ashes	+		−	−	−
Large shovel used to carry ashes	−		−	+	−
Large tarp or skin used to carry ashes	−		+	−	+
52. Spectators allowed throughout entire sunrise ceremony	−		+	+	+
Spectators must leave ceremony when chief sings songs and prays	+		−	−	−
53. Women attend to the dancers' toilets, and dancers have corral to rest, talk, and clean themselves up	+		+	+	+

	SU	UMU	NU	FHS	WRS
54. Dancers can shave with water and shave cream	−		−	+	+
Dancers can dry shave only	+		+	−	−
55. Dancers can use rather wet rags to wash up	−		−	+	+
Dancers can use moist but not dripping wet rags to wash up	+		+	−	−
56. Home dancers can have pictures taken outside corral	−		−	+	+
Home dancers cannot have pictures taken outside corral, but do not stop visiting dancers from having pictures taken	+		+	−	−

C. *"First Day" Ritual Acts and Observances*

	SU	UMU	NU	FHS	WRS
57. First call on drum for day dance session is around 9:30–10:00 A.M.	−		+	+	+
First call on drum for day dance session is around 11:00 A.M.	+		−	−	−
58. "Flag song" is sung by singers at about 10:00 A.M. and is attended by a flag ritual—hoisting of American flag—in front of southeast side of corral entrance. Signals commencement of "key" dance (varies with No. Ute chief)	−		+	−	+
No "Flag song" or flag hoisting in recent years	+		−	+	−
59. Day dancing begins about 10:15 A.M.	−		+	−	+
Day dancing begins about 11:30 A.M. (few singers to kick things off)	+		−	+	−
60. Sun dance committee and spectators roust dancers from their sleep if some are not up and moving by the time the singers assemble	+		+	+	+
61. Male singers sit around drums and female singers sit around male singers in southeast section of Lodge	+		+	+	+
62. Spectators, mostly male, sit in northeast section of corral	+		+	+	+
63. Gate keeper and lodge police keep "doorway" or "water path" to the east open, i.e., no one stands between the center pole and the corral doorway blocking the sun's rays	+		+	+	+
64. One dance song per set	+		−	−	−
Four dance songs per set (sometimes as many as eight at Fort Hall)	−		+	+	+

	SU	UMU	NU	FHS	WRS
65. Dance songs sung at 190–200 beats per minute	+		+	+	+
66. Length of each dance set about 3 minutes	+		−	−	−
Length of each dance set about 20–25 minutes	−		+	−	+
Length of each dance set about 30–40 minutes	−		−	+	−
67. One rest song between each dance set	+		+	+	+
68. Rest songs sung at 160 beats per minute	+		+	+	+
69. Rest songs last about one minute	+		+	+	+
70. Dancers are expected to stay in own dance paths and not cross into those of others	+		+	+	+
71. Dancers who wander out of drum paths may be ridiculed by spectators and redirected by other dancers	+		+	+	+
72. Dancers who drop something while dancing must wait for rest song before they can pick up the fallen object	+		+	+	+
73. Dancers cannot eat or drink and are watched by one another as well as Lodge police	+		+	+	+
74. Stories told informally about how Lodge police chased and captured mixed-bloods, whites, or Indians from other reserves who bolted from the corral	+		+	+	+
75. Some dancers chew "bear root," a bitter plant, to make them salivate during dance	+		+	+	+
76. Dancers can leave corral and go to latrine during rest songs only	+		+	+	+
77. Dancers cover themselves with sheets or blankets when going to and from latrine	+		+	+	+
78. Dancers leave corral singly, in pairs, or in groups of three or more friends when they go to latrine— usually two or more	+		+	+	+
79. Lodge police do not keep a close watch on dancers when they leave corral	+		+	+	+

	SU	UMU	NU	FHS	WRS
80. Exhortations for singers to sing, dancers to dance, importance of seeking power made by committee men and other nondancing shamans	+		+	+	+
81. Shamanizing in corral by Sun dance chiefs for all other dancers, for ailing dancers who request help, and for nondancers who request help	−		−	−	+
Shamanizing in corral by Sun dance chief for all other dancers only, and they all ritually line up behind center pole	+		−	−	−
Shamanizing in corral by Sun dance chiefs only for other dancers who request help	−		−	+	−
No shamanizing on first day	−		+	−	−
82. Day dance session is continuous, not interrupted by midday break	+		−	+	−
Day dance session conducted in two parts separated by a midday break of about one hour	−		+	−	+
83. Day dance terminates at 3:30 P.M. when there were no more singers	−		−	+	−
Day dance terminates at about 5:15 P.M. at chief's instructions	+		+	−	+
84. "Quitting song" is last song of day session	+		−	−	−
"Flag song" and flag ritual (lowering) follows the "quitting song" and is the last song of the day session	−		+	−	+
No special final song	−		−	+	−
D. *"Second Night" Ritual Acts and Observances*					
85. First call on drum to resume dancing is at about 6:30 P.M.	+		+	+	+
86. Night dancing session commences at about 7:30 P.M.	+		+	+	+
87. First song is "evening song." Dancers do not dance	+		+	−	+
First song is not prescribed. Dancers can dance	−		−	+	−
88. Fire built by fire tender after sunset	+		+	+	+
89. Special "fire song" attends building of fire	−		−	+	−
No special "fire song"	+		+	−	+
90. Female chiefs shamanize all dancers during "fire song"	−		−	+	−
No one shamanizes all dancers during "evening" or "fire song"	+		+	−	+

	SU	UMU	NU	FHS	WRS
91. Head chief prays to center pole, spectators doff hats, following group shamanizing	−		−	+	−
No special prayer or fire ritual	+		+	−	+
92. Dance songs are four to a set, followed by a single rest song as during the day session	−		+	+	+
Dance songs are increased to three per set (more than the day session), followed by a single rest song	+		−	−	−
93. Singing and drumming continues throughout the night, though some interruptions occur	+		+	+	+
94. Most dancers bed down between 1:00 A.M. and 3:00 A.M., though some dancing occurs throughout the night	+		+	+	+
95. Singers, male and female, who help out throughout the night session are often seeking special spiritual help in overcoming some ailment or malady. Instructed by chief	+		−	−	−
Special curing intentions of night singers not well developed. Chiefs do not give this counsel to sufferers	−		+	+	+
96. "Sunrise ceremony" preparations begin about one half hour before sunrise as gate keeper and chief roust sleeping dancers	+		+	+	+
97. "Sunrise ceremony" essentially the same as preceding sunrise	+		+	+	+
98. Additions or changes in "sunrise ceremony." Spectators allowed to watch entire "sunrise ceremony"	+		+	+	+
99. Chief gives prayer while sitting around ashes of sacred dance fire; then female dancer is selected to offer prayer to center pole	−		−	+	−
No special prayers by men and women other than chiefs to center pole	+		+	−	+
100. Chief shamanizes singers who have sung through the night and at the sunrise ceremony	+		−	−	−
No special shamanizing of singers or nondancers at sunrise ceremony	−		+	+	+

	SU	UMU	NU	FHS	WRS
101. Chiefs lead singing and run a well planned and well controlled ceremony	+		+	−	+
Chiefs forget songs, bicker over ritual mistakes, rely on singers, drummers, or visiting dancers to sing proper sunrise songs in proper order	−		−	+	−
102. Spectators, dancers, singers—all in attendance—pat themselves while sun is rising and when ceremony is over	+		+	+	+
103. Sacred juniper fire ritual is added to sunrise ceremony. Pit is dug on northeast section of corral and filled with green juniper boughs. Smoky fire is started with embers from sacred dance fire	+		+	+	+
104. If sprig of juniper is dropped by gate keeper while carrying it in for fire, it will not be used	+		+	+	+
105. Dancers called in groups of three to huddle over pit and inhale sacred smoke with sheets or blankets over their heads	+		+	+	+
106. Sacred juniper ashes are buried, and pit is refilled after all have breathed the smoke	+		+	+	+

E. *Interim between Night and Day Sessions*

	SU	UMU	NU	FHS	WRS
107. Corral is modified (see corral and construction)	+		+	+	+
108. Dancers attend to toilets as previously (see dancers' preparation and dress)	+		+	+	+

F. *"Second Day" Ritual Acts and Observances*

	SU	UMU	NU	FHS	WRS
109. First call on drum about 9:30 A.M.; dancers routed from sleep by gate keeper	−		+	+	+
First call on drum about 10:45 A.M.; dancers routed from sleep by gate keeper	+		−	−	−
110. "Flag song" sung at about 10:00 A.M., followed by "morning song" and then by resumption of dancing	−		+	−	+
"Morning song" is only prescribed song, sung at about 11:00 A.M., and it is followed by resumption of dancing	+		−	+	−

	SU	UMU	NU	FHS	WRS
111. Day dance session is continuous until about 5:00–5:30 P.M. No interruptions at midday	+		+	−	+
Day dance session is continuous until about 6:30 P.M. No interruptions at midday (women may make dance longer and more arduous)	−		−	+	−
112. Dance songs sung in sets that last from ten to thirty minutes. Longer dance sets sung when people are being shamanized in corral or when dancers are dancing hard	+		+	+	+
113. Dance songs increase in tempo from morning to afternoon	+		+	+	+.
114. Throughout day dance songs increase from 180 to 200 beats per minute	+		−	−	−
Throughout day dance songs increase from 200 to about 210 beats per minute	−		+	+	+
115. Rest songs not sung at regular intervals	+		+	+	+
116. Rest songs last only thirty seconds to one minute	+		+	+	+
117. Rest songs sung at about 160 beats per minute	+		+	+	+
118. Orations about meaning of Sun dance, exhortations for dancers to dance and singers to sing, made by gate keeper, shamans, males and females, local residents, and Indian guests	+		+	+	+
119. Shamanizing of ailing spectators by Sun dance chiefs. Services requested of particular chiefs by invalids (postponed until third day on four-day dance)	+		+	+	+
120. Shamanizing of themselves by "powerful" dancers	+		+	+	+
121. Shamanizing of dancers suffering from "fever" by Sun dance chiefs or other "powerful" dancers selected by the clients	+		+	+	+
122. Shamanizing of families or parts of nuclear families, often a dancer's. If it is a dancer's family, the dancer is treated for "fever" whereas the rest of the family members are only brushed with a feather wand	−		−	−	+
No family shamanizing	+		+	+	−

	SU	UMU	NU	FHS	WRS
123. Vision seeking by dancers not appropriate on second day. The man or woman who falters is suspected of being incontinent or foolish	+		+	+	+
124. Day dance session concluded with "quitting song." Chief signals intention to quit to gate keeper, who gives information to singers	+		−	+	−
Day dance sessions concluded with "quitting song," followed by "flag song" and lowering of flag. Instructions given by chief to gate keeper, who gives information to singers	−		+	−	+

G. *"Third Night" Ritual Acts and Observances*

	SU	UMU	NU	FHS	WRS
125. Dance session begins about 8:00 P.M. with evening song, ends after sunrise ceremony	+		+	+	−
Dance session begins about 6:30 P.M. with evening song, ends after sunrise ceremony	−		−	−	+
126. Night dance ritual essentially same as previous night rituals	+		+	−	−
Night dance ritual different from previous night rituals because of shamanizing of spectators	−		−	+	+
127. Considerable charging of center pole by dancers. Considerable "hugging" (embracing) of center pole	−		−	+	−
No "hugging" of center pole	+		+	−	+
128. Vision seeking by dancers	−		+	−	−
No vision seeking during night sessions	+		−	+	+
129. Dancers, especially chiefs, selected to shamanize ailing spectators and their families	−		−	+	+
Shamanizing of spectators not done at night	+		+	−	−
130. "Sunrise ceremony" similar to preceding "sunrise ceremonies"	−		−	+	+
"Sunrise ceremony" somewhat different than preceding "sunrise ceremonies"	+		+	−	−
131. Sacred juniper fire not built at third sunrise (last day or fourth day of a four-day dance)	+		+	−	−
Sacred juniper fire built at last sunrise	−		−	+	+

	SU	UMU	NU	FHS	WRS
132. Singers not blessed at last sunrise ceremony	+		+	+	+
133. Chief blesses special person who prepares paint for all dancers on last day	+		−	−	−
Blessing of paint-preparer not part of chief's sunrise ceremony	−		+	+	+

H. *"Last Day" (Third or Fourth) Ritual Acts and Observances*

	SU	UMU	NU	FHS	WRS
134. Dancing begins about 8:30 A.M. with "opening song"	−	−	−	+	−
Dancing begins about 9:30 A.M. with "flag song" and ritual followed by "opening song"	−	+	+	−	+
Dancing begins about 10:00 A.M. with "opening song"	+	−	−	−	−
135. Dance songs four or more per set	−	+	+	+	+
Dance songs one or two per set	+	−	−	−	−
136. Dance sets last 5–20 minutes	+	−	−	−	−
Dance sets last 20–35 minutes	−	+	+	+	+
137. Dance songs played at about 200 beats per minute	+	+	+	+	+
138. Dance songs played up to 220 beats per minute when dancer is seeking vision	+	+	+	+	+
139. Rest songs played at 160 beats per minute and last only one minute	+	+	+	+	+
140. Dance songs are lengthened during vision quests, shamanizing, or family blessings	+	+	+	+	+
141. Singing is stopped for some orations, especially those by Sun dance committeemen and other influential shamans	+	+	+	−	−
Some final day orations follow singing but do not interrupt singing	−	−	−	+	+
142. Some orations, especially exhortations, made while dancers are dancing	+	+	+	+	+
143. War whoops made by spectators when dancer seeks vision	+	+	+	+	+
144. Women wave willows to help dancers receive power	+	+	+	+	+
145. Dancers help fellow dancer in vision quest, stand in stalls and blow whistles	+	+	+	+	+

	SU	UMU	NU	FHS	WRS
146. Shamanizing of invalids by selected chiefs or dancers	+	+	+	+	+
147. Shamanizing of themselves by dancers	+	+	+	+	+
148. Shamanizing of dancers by selected chiefs or other dancers	+	+	+	+	+
149. Shamanizing and blessing of dancers and families or invalids and families by selected chiefs	−	−	−	−	+
Family blessings not performed	+	+	+	+	−
150. Vision recipient is said to be "hit" and knocked down, usually by a jolt of power channeled through the center pole and whatever object is hanging from it (e.g., bison head)	+	+	+	+	+
151. Vision recipient is lifted from ground in a horizontal position so that feet and head are about five feet above ground	+	+	+	+	+
152. Vision recipient lies "stone cold" at base of pole	+	+	+	+	+
153. Vision recipient is moved to stall and covered with sheet, his head closest to the center pole. At this time his spirit leaves and cavorts with the power or an emissary of power	+	+	+	+	+
154. Vision recipient is to lie perfectly still and his body is to be cool for a couple of hours	+	+	+	+	+
155. When recipient gets up, he will dance completely refreshed	+	+	+	+	+
156. "Last Song" is determined by chief and relayed to gate keeper. Time of day that dance is terminated (between 11:30 A.M. and 5:30 P.M.) depends on weather, singing, whether dancers are pursuing visions, and so forth	+	+	+	+	+
157. About one hour before "last song," gifts from donors on sponsoring reservations are collected by Sun dance committee	+	+	+	+	+
158. Each gift and name of donor is announced over loudspeaker	−	−	−	−	+
Gift and donor not announced	+	+	+	+	−

	SU	UMU	NU	FHS	WRS
159. Gifts collected on sheet or buckskin, laid on ground on east side of center pole	+	+	+	+	+
160. Final prayer of dance is made by chief toward center pole and gifts. All dancers stand in stalls	−	+	+	+	+
Final prayer of dance is made by chief over gifts. All dancers stand in stalls	+	−	−	−	−
161. Scarves tacked on center pole by dancers (varies with dance)	+	+	+	−	−
Scarves (except for those at the top of pole) not tacked on by dancers	−	−	−	+	+
162. When dance is over, "old people" take dancers' scarves from center pole	+	+	+	−	−
No dancers' scarves taken from pole	−	−	−	+	+
163. Speeches follow final prayer, given by Sun dance committeemen and/or agency officials	+	−	−	+	−
Speeches do not follow final prayer	−	+	+	−	+
164. Dancers take final blessings for legitimizing of power and preparation to return to secular life from shamans (dancers or nondancers). Dancers "pray" for blessings	+	+	+	+	−
Very few final blessings are taken by dancers	−	−	−	−	+
165. Chief shows Sun dance doll and other ritual objects	+	−	−	−	−
Chief does not show Sun dance doll or other ritual objects	−	+	+	+	+
166. Sacred water brought in by committee	+	+	+	+	+
167. Sacred water blessed by committeeman (gate keeper or water chief)	+	+	+	+	+
168. First drink of sacred water offered to center pole	−	−	−	+	−
First drink of sacred water taken and spat out at base of center pole by man who offers blessing, whereas second drink goes directly to center pole	+	+	+	−	+
169. Dancers receive drinks of sacred water from committeemen. Dancers are hidden behind sheets in stalls	−	+	+	+	+
Dancers receive drinks from visitors who are chosen to circulate the container of sacred water. Dancers are hidden behind sheets in stalls	+	−	−	−	−

	SU	UMU	NU	FHS	WRS
170. Gate keeper fans self and pole	+	+	+	+	+
171. Dancers file out of corral in single line behind chief	+	+	+	+	+
172. Spectators, old people first, allowed to have a drink of sacred water after dancers leave	+	+	+	+	+

Bibliography

Aberle, David F.
  1966 *The peyote religion among the Navaho*. Viking Fund Publications in Anthropology, no. 42.
Aberle, David F., and Stewart, Omer C.
  1957 *Navaho and Ute peyotism: A chronological and distributional study*. University of Colorado Studies, Series in Anthropology, no. 6.
Ablon, Joan
  1964 Relocated American Indians in the San Francisco bay area. *Human Organization* 24: 296–305.
Alfred, B. M.
  n.d.   Demographic description of Ignacio. Mimeo. Boulder, Tri-ethnic Project.
Anonymous
  1911 Indians hold annual dance to cure plague. *Denver Republican*, 3 July.
Armstrong, George W.
  1857 Report of the Commissioner of Indian Affairs (RCIA).
Arny, Wm. F. M.
  1962 RCIA.
  1967 *Indian agent in New Mexico, the journal of special agent W. F. M. Arny 1870*. With introduction and notes by Lawrence R. Murphy. Santa Fe: Stagecoach Press.
Atkins, J. D. C.
  1886–87 RCIA.
Bailey, Paul
  1954 *Walkara, hawk of the mountains*. Los Angeles: Westernlore.
Baran, Paul A.
  1957 *The political economy of growth*. New York: Monthly Review Press.
Bennett, Robert L.
  1961 Building Indian economies with land settlement funds. *Human Organization* 20: 159–63.
Berry, Ray M., and Nybroten, Norman
  1964 Education on the reservation, people, problems, programs and progress. In Nybroten (ed.), pp. 113–38.
Berry, W. H.
  1880–81 RCIA.
Bond, H. F.
  1876 RCIA.
Brimlow, George E.
  1938 *The Bannock Indian war of 1887*. Caldwell: The Caxton Printers, Ltd.
Brophy, William, and Sophie D. Aberle
  1966 *The Indian, America's unfinished business*. Norman: University of Oklahoma Press.
Brown, James S.
  1900 *Life of a pioneer*. Salt Lake City: George Q. Cannon and Sons Co.

Browning, D. M.
  1896 RCIA.
Brunot, Felix R.
  1873 RCIA.
Bureau of Indian Affairs
  1949 *Answers to your questions about American Indians.* Washington: U.S. Government
        Printing Office.
  1955 Ibid.
  1968 Ibid.
Byrnes, T. A.
  1887–89 RCIA.
Chairman, House Committee on Interior and Insular Affairs (CHCIIA)
  1963 *Indian unemployment survey.* Committee Print no. 3, 88th Congress, First Session.
Christiansen, John R.; Clark, James R.; and Sparks, Cynthia
  1966 *Social and economic characteristics of the Indians on the Uintah-Ouray reservation,*
        1965. Brigham Young University, Social Science Bulletin, no. 4.
Church of Jesus Christ of Latter-day Saints
  1848 *Journal history.* 5 September. Salt Lake City.
Clayton, William
  1921 *William Clayton's journal.* Salt Lake City.
Clifton, F.
  1961 Field notes, 31 January 1961. Mimeo. University of Colorado.
Collier, Peter
  1970 The red man's burden. *Ramparts* 8, no. 8: 26–38.
Collins, J. L.
  1857–58 RCIA.
Committee of the National Tuberculosis Association
  1923 *Tuberculosis among the North American Indians.* Washington: U.S. Government
        Printing Office.
Cornish, George A.
  1898 RCIA.
Costo, Rupert, and Henry, Jeanette
  1970 *Textbooks and the American Indian.* American Indian Historical Society. San
        Francisco: Indian Historian Press.
Critchlow, J. J.
  1871–82 RCIA.
Cummings, Alexander
  1866 RCIA.
Davis, Elisha W.
  1883–85 RCIA.
Dale, Harrison C.
  1918 *The Ashley-Smith explorations and the discovery of a central route to the Pacific,*
        1822–1829. Cleveland.
Deloria, Vine Jr.
  1969 *Custer died for your sins: An Indian manifesto.* New York: Macmillan.
Densmore, Frances
  1922 Northern Ute music. *Bureau of American Ethnology Bulletin* 75.
Deseret News, Salt Lake City
  1861 31 August and 25 September.
Dole, William P.
  1861 RCIA.
Dorn, Edward, and Lucas, LeRoy
  1966 *The Shoshoneans.* New York: Morrow.
Doty, James D.
  1862–63 RCIA.

Driver, Harold E., and Kroeber, A. L.
  1932   Quantitative expression of cultural relationships. *University of California Publications in American Archeology and Ethnology* 31: 211–56.
Elkin, Henry
  1940   The Northern Arapaho of Wyoming. *In* Ralph Linton (ed.), *Acculturation in seven American Indian tribes*. New York: Appleton-Century Co. pp. 207–55.
Ellegard, Alvar
  1959   Statistical measurement of linguistic relationship. *Language* 35: 131–57.
Emmitt, Robert
  1954   *The last war trail*. Norman: University of Oklahoma Press.
Euler, Robert C., and Naylor, Harry L.
  1952   Southern Ute rehabilitation planning, a study in self-determination. *Human Organization* 11: 27–32.
Evans, J. N. O.
  1863   RCIA.
Ewing, W. W.
  1904   RCIA.
Farnham, Thomas J.
  1841   *Travels in the great western prairies*. Poughkeepsie.
Ferris, Warren A.
  1940   *Life in the Rocky Mountains, 1830–1835*. Salt Lake City.
Forney, Jacob
  1858–59 RCIA.
Frank, Andre Gunder
  1967   *Capitalism and underdevelopment in Latin America*. New York: Monthly Review Press.
Freeman, Dan A.
  1962   *Four years with the Utes*. Waco, Texas.
Freeman, Major
  1893   RCIA.
Gardner, J. F.
  1884–85 RCIA.
Gilpin, William
  1861   RCIA.
Gottfredson, Peter
  1919   *History of Indian depredations in Utah*. Salt Lake City.
Haas, Theodore H.
  1947   *Ten years of tribal government under I.R.A.* Tribal Relations Pamphlets 1. Chicago: United States Indian Service.
  1957   The legal aspects of Indian affairs from 1887 to 1957. In Simpson and Yinger (eds.), pp. 12–30.
Hall, C. G.
  1904–8 RCIA.
Harmsworth, Harry C., and Nybroten, Norman
  1964   The people and their goals and problems. In Nybroten (ed.), pp. 65–114.
Hatch, F. W.
  1862   RCIA.
Hayt, E. A.
  1879   RCIA.
HCIIA *See* House Committee on Interior and Insular Affairs.
Head, F. H.
  1867   RCIA.
Head, Lafayette
  1861   RCIA.

Heap, Gwinn H.
1957 *Central route to the pacific.* Ed. LeRoy Hafen. Glendale: Clark Publishing. Originally published 1853.

Hebard, Grace R.
1930 *Washakie.* Philadelphia: Arthur H. Clark Co.

Heidenreich, Charles Adrian
1967 A review of the Ghost dance religion of 1889–90 among the North American Indians and comparison of eight societies which accepted or rejected the dance. M.A. thesis, University of Oregon, Eugene.

Hoebel, E. Adamson
1935 The Sun dance of the Hekandika Shoshone. *American Anthropologist* 37: 570–81.

House Committee on Interior and Insular Affairs (HCIIA)
1953 *Investigation of the Bureau of Indian Affairs.* U. S. Congress House Report no. 2503, 82d Congress, Second Session.
1954 *Investigation of the Bureau of Indian Affairs.* U. S. Congress House Report.

Hughes, E. O.
1901 RCIA.

Humphreys, A.
1860 RCIA.

Indian Health Service
1969 1968 Indian vital statistics. Tucson, Arizona: Health programs systems center.

Irish, O. H.
1865a Report, 39 Congress, I Session, House Exec. Doc. I.
1865b RCIA.

Jackson, William H.
1959 *The diaries of William Henry Jackson, frontier photographer, 1866–1874.* Ed. LeRoy Hafen. Glendale, California: Clark Publishing.

Jocknick, Sydney
1913 *Early days on the western slope of Colorado and campfire chats with Otto Mears, the pathfinder, from 1870 to 1883, inclusive.* Denver: Carson-Harper Co.

Johnson, Clark
1963 A study of modern southwestern Indian leadership. Ph.D. diss., University of Colorado, Boulder.

Jones, Daniel N.
1890 *Forty years among the Indians.* Salt Lake City.

Jones, John A.
1955 The Sun dance of the Northern Ute. *Bulletin of the Bureau of American Ethnology* 137, Anthropological Paper 47: 203–64.

Jones, W. A.
1897 RCIA.

Jorgensen, Joseph G.
1964 The ethnohistory and acculturation of the Northern Utes. Ph.D. diss., Indiana University, Bloomington (University Microfilms).
1971a Indians and the metropolis. In J. O. Waddell and O. M. Watson (eds.), *The American Indian in urban society.* Boston: Little, Brown and Co.
1971b On ethics and anthropology. *Current Anthropology* 12.

Klose, Nelson
1964 *A concise study guide to the American frontier.* Lincoln: University of Nebraska Press.

LDS Millennial Star, Liverpool, England
1869 17 July
1870 14, 21 June
1871 13 June, 4 July
1872 11 June

Land Planning Committee of the National Resource Board
  1935   *Indian land tenure, economic status, and population trends.* Part 10 of the Report on Land Planning. Washington: U.S. Government Printing Office.
Lang, Gottfried O.
  1953   *A study in culture contact and culture change: The Whiterocks Utes in transition.* University of Utah Anthropological Papers 15.
Lanternari, Vittorio
  1963   *The religions of the oppressed, a study of modern messianic cults.* New York: Knopf.
Leupp, Francis E.
  1906–9   RCIA.
Linton, Ralph
  1943   Nativistic movements. *American Anthropologist* 45: 230–40.
Littlefield, J. S.
  1871–72   RCIA.
Lowie, Robert H.
  1915   Dances and societies of the plains Shoshones. *American Museum of Natural History Anthropological Papers* 11: 803–35.
  1919   Sun Dance of the Shoshone, Ute and Hidatsa. *American Museum of Natural History Anthropological Papers* 26: 393–410.
  1924   Notes on Shoshonean ethnography. *American Museum of Natural History Anthropological Papers* 20: 185–324.
Mann, Luther J.
  1862–63   RCIA.
  1867   RCIA.
McCunniff, Thomas
  1888   RCIA.
McKewen, William A.
  1886   RCIA.
Meeker, N. C.
  1878–79   RCIA.
Meriam, Lewis and Associates
  1928   *Problems of Indian administration.* Baltimore: Johns Hopkins Press.
Meriwether, D.
  1856   RCIA.
Minnis, J. F.
  1883   RCIA.
Mooney, James
  1892–1893   The Ghost-dance religion and the Sioux outbreak of 1890. *14th Annual Report of the Bureau of Ethnology*, part 2, pp. 641–1136.
Moore, David
  n.d.   *Salmon River Mission journal and record.* Latter-day Saints Historian's Office, Salt Lake City.
Morgan, Dale L.
  1953   Miles Goodyear and the founding of Ogden. *Utah Historical Quarterly*, pp. 195–218, 308–29.
Murphy, Lawrence R.
  1967   Introduction and notes. In W. F. M. Arny, *Indian Agent in New Mexico.* Sante Fe: Stagecoach Press.
Myton, H. P.
  1899–1902   RCIA.
Nader, Ralph
  1968   Lo, the poor Indian. *New Republic*, 30 March, pp. 14–15.
Nelson, Robert
  1963   The churches in Ignacio. Mimeo. Boulder: Tri-ethnic Project.

Nybroten, Norman (ed.)
   1964   *Economy and conditions on the Fort Hall Indian Reservation.* Idaho Bureau of
          Business and Economic Research, Report no. 9. Moscow: University of Idaho.
Nybroten, Norman, and Farmer, Ralph H.
   1964   Credit, finance, and business relationships affecting the Fort Hall Indian Reserva-
          tion. In Nybroten (ed.), pp. 139–78.
Oakes, Daniel C.
   1867–69 RCIA.
O'Dea, Thomas C.
   1957   *The Mormons.* Chicago: University of Chicago Press.
Opler, Marvin K.
   1940   The Southern Utes of Colorado. In Ralph Linton (ed.), *Acculturation of seven
          American Indian tribes.* New York: Appleton-Century, pp. 119–207.
   1941   The integration of the sun dance in Ute religion. *American Anthropologist* 43:
          550–72.
Page, Henry
   1880   RCIA.
Parkhill, Forbes
   1961   *The Last of the Indian wars.* New York: Crowell-Collier.
Peterson, Helen L.
   1957   American Indian political participation. *In* Simpson and Yinger (eds.), pp. 116–26.
Pope, Nathaniel
   1871   RCIA.
Price, John A.
   1968   The migration and adaptation of American Indians in Los Angeles. *Human Organi-
          zation* 27: 168–75.
Public Health Service
   1963–5 *National health survey: Health characteristics by place of residence, United States.*
          Washington: U.S. Government Printing Office.
Randlett, James F.
   1894–97 RCIA.
Rendon, Gabino, Jr.
   1962   Voting behavior in a tri-ethnic community. M.A. thesis. University of Colorado,
          Boulder.
RCIA.
   1852–1936 Report of the Commissioner of Indian Affairs. Washington: U.S. Government
          Printing Office.
Report of Indian Legislation: *see* RCIA.
Rhodes, D. W.
   1867   RCIA.
Russell, S. A.
   1876   RCIA.
Sage, Rufus B.
   1846   *Scenes in the Rocky Mountains.* Philadelphia.
   1956   *Rufus B. Sage, his letters and papers, 1836–1847.* Ed. LeRoy Hafen, Glendale,
          California: Clark Publishing.
Sale, Thomas C. W.
   1864   RCIA.
Salt Lake Herald
   1871   7 May, 12 May, 18 May, 29 May, 14 June.
Schroeder, Albert H.
   1965   A brief history of the Southern Utes. *Southwestern Lore* 30: 53–78.
Scott, General Hugh L.
   1928   *Some memories of a soldier.* New York: The Century Co.

Shimkin, Demitri B.
   1942   Dynamics of recent Wind River Shoshone history. *American Anthropologist* 44: 451–62.
   1947   Wind River Shoshone ethnogeography. *University of California Anthropological Records* 5: 245–88.
   1953   The Wind River Shoshone sun dance. *Bureau of American Ethnology Bulletin* 151, Anthropological Paper no. 41: 397–484.
Simpson, George E., and Yinger, Milton (eds.)
   1957   American Indians and American life. *Annals of American Academy of Political and Social Science* 311.
Smith, Edward P.
   1873   RCIA.
Sonne, Conway B.
   1962   *World of Wakara.* San Antonio: Naylor Co.
Southern Ute Council
   1961   Southern Ute council minutes of 31 August, 1961. Mimeo. Ignacio, Colo.
Spier, Leslie
   1921   *The sun dance of the plains Indians: Its development and diffusion.* American Museum of Natural History. Anthropological papers, 16.
Sprague, Marshall
   1957   *Massacre: The tragedy at White River.* Boston: Little, Brown and Co.
Steiner, Stan
   1968   *The new Indians.* New York: Harper and Row.
Stewart, Omer C.
   1952   Southern Ute adjustment to modern living. In Sol Tax (ed.), *Acculturation in the Americas.* Chicago: University of Chicago Press.
   1960a Shoshone history and social organization. *Proceedings, 33rd International Congress of Americanists,* pp. 134–42. San Jose del Costa Rica.
   1960b Field Notes, recorded at the corral of the Sun dances. Mimeographed. University of Colorado.
   1962   Field Notes, report on Sun dance, Ignacio, 4–9 July 1962. Mimeographed. University of Colorado.
   1966a Tribal distributions in the Great Basin. In d'Azevedo, Warren; Davis, Wilbur; Fowler, Don; and Suttles, Wayne (eds.), *The current status of anthropological research in the Great Basin.* Reno: Desert Research Institute, University of Nevada.
   1966b Ute Indians: before and after white contact. *Utah Historical Quarterly* 34: 38–61.
Swadesh, Frances L.
   1962   The Southern Utes and their neighbors 1877–1926. M.A. thesis, University of Colorado, Boulder.
Thompson, James B.
   1870–75   RCIA.
Tourtellotte, J. E.
   1869–70   RCIA.
Trenholm, Virginia Cole, and Carley, Maurine
   1964   *The Shoshonis, sentinels of the Rockies.* Norman: University of Oklahoma Press.
U.S. Department of Commerce, Bureau of the Census
   1966   *Statistical abstract of the United States* [SAUS] *1966.* Washington, U.S. Government Printing Office.
   1967   *Statistical abstract of the United States 1967.* Ibid.
   1967   *County and city data book 1967* (CCBD). Ibid.
U.S. Department of Health, Education and Welfare, Public Health Service
   1963   *Illness among Indians 1962.* Washington, U.S. Government Printing Office.
United States President's National Advisory Commission on Rural Poverty (USPNACRP)
   1967   *The people left behind.* Washington, U.S. Government Printing Office.

Utah State Historical Society
   1854   *Military records division, Nauvoo Legion or Mormon Militia.* Salt Lake City.
Ute Bulletin, published by Ute Indian Tribe, Fort Duchesne
   1962   June, September, October, November, December.
   1963   January–December
   1964   January–May
   1969   28 March, 3 May.
Ute Commission
   1881   RCIA.
Ute Indian Tribe
   1948   Annual report of the Uintah and Ouray tribal business committee. Mimeographed.
           Fort Duchesne.
   1949   Annual report of the Uintah and Ouray tribal business committee. Minutes of the
           General Council. Ibid.
   1954   Three year report to the Commissioner of Indian Affairs, Bureau of Indian Affairs,
           U.S. Department of Interior. Ibid.
   1956   Ten year development program. Ibid.
   1958   Annual report of long range development program. Ibid.
   1959   Annual report of long range development program. Ibid.
Valentine, Robert G.
   1911–12   RCIA.
Voget, Fred W.
   1953   Current trends in the Wind River Shoshone sun dance. *Bureau of American Ethnology*
           151, Anthropological Paper no. 42, pp. 485–500.
Waddell, O. M.
   1904   RCIA.
Walker, Francis A.
   1872   RCIA.
Wallace, Anthony F. C.
   1956   Revitalization movements. *American Anthropologist* 58: 254–81.
Waugh, Robert
   1890–94   RCIA.
Whiteley, Simeon
   1863   RCIA.
Wind River Agency, Department of the Interior, Bureau of Indian Affairs, Branch of Land
           Operations
   1965   *Wind River agency annual narrative report: Pictorial highlights.* Billings, Montana.
Witherspoon, Younger T.
   1961   Cultural influences on Ute learning. Ph.D. diss. University of Utah, Salt Lake City.
Worsley, Peter
   1957   *The trumpet shall sound: A study of "cargo" cults in Melanesia.* London: McGibbon
           and Kee.
Wright, Coulsen, and Wright, Geneva
   1948   Indian-white relations in the Uintah Basin. *Utah Humanities Review* 2: 319–46.
Young, Brigham
   1956   RCIA.
Young, Robert W. (comp.)
   1961   *Navaho year book. Report No. 8, 1951–1961, a decade of progress.* Navaho Agency:
           Window Rock.

Index

For specific materials relating to the Sun dance ritual, the reader should consult the Appendix.